World History and National Identity in China

Nationalism is pervasive in China today. Yet nationalism is not entrenched in China's intellectual tradition. Over the course of the twentieth century, the combined forces of cultural, social, and political transformations nourished its development, but resistance to it has persisted. Xin Fan examines the ways in which historians working on the world beyond China from within China have attempted to construct narratives that challenge nationalist readings of the Chinese past and the influence that these historians have had on the formation of Chinese identity. He traces the ways in which generations of historians, from the late Qing through the Republican period, through the Mao period to the relative moment of "opening" in the 1980s, have attempted to break cross-cultural boundaries in writing an alternative to the national narrative.

Xin Fan is Associate Professor of History at the State University of New York at Fredonia.

T0345469

World History and National Identity in China

The Twentieth Century

Xin Fan

State University of New York at Fredonia

CAMBRIDGE
UNIVERSITY PRESS

Shaftesbury Road, Cambridge CB2 8EA, United Kingdom

One Liberty Plaza, 20th Floor, New York, NY 10006, USA

477 Williamstown Road, Port Melbourne, VIC 3207, Australia

314–321, 3rd Floor, Plot 3, Splendor Forum, Jasola District Centre, New Delhi – 110025, India

103 Penang Road, #05–06/07, Visioncrest Commercial, Singapore 238467

Cambridge University Press is part of Cambridge University Press & Assessment, a department of the University of Cambridge.

We share the University's mission to contribute to society through the pursuit of education, learning and research at the highest international levels of excellence.

www.cambridge.org
Information on this title: www.cambridge.org/9781108829502

DOI: 10.1017/9781108903653

First published 2021
First paperback edition 2022

A catalogue record for this publication is available from the British Library

Library of Congress Cataloging-in-Publication data
Names: Fan, Xin, 1977– author.
Title: World history and national identity in China : the twentieth century / Xin Fan, State University of New York at Fredonia.
Description: Cambridge, United Kingdom ; New York, NY : Cambridge University Press, 2021. | Includes bibliographical references and index.
Identifiers: LCCN 2020034426 (print) | LCCN 2020034427 (ebook) | ISBN 9781108842600 (hardback) | ISBN 9781108829502 (ebook)
Subjects: LCSH: Nationalism – China. | World history.
Classification: LCC JC311 .F25 2021 (print) | LCC JC311 (ebook) | DDC 951.0072–dc23
LC record available at https://lccn.loc.gov/2020034426
LC ebook record available at https://lccn.loc.gov/2020034427

ISBN   978-1-108-84260-0   Hardback
ISBN   978-1-108-82950-2   Paperback

To Yan and Eric

Contents

Figures and Tables

Figures

Tables

Preface and Acknowledgments

Nationalism is pervasive in China today. Yet nationalism is not entrenched in China's intellectual tradition. Over the course of the twentieth century, the combined forces of cultural, social, and political transformations nourished its development, but resistance to it has persisted. In this book, I tell the important and neglected story of some critics of narrow nationalism and detail their influence on the formation of Chinese identity.

These critics are world historians with various social and political upbringings, from gentry scholars in the late Qing era, academic professionals in the Republican period, and thought workers in the early People's Republic, to specialized experts in the post-Mao era. In this book, drawing on published materials, university archives, and party reports, I focus on a small group of those historians, who study the ancient non-Chinese world, a topic that seems irrelevant to modern China. This choice reflects their attempts to break cross-cultural boundaries in writing an alternative history to the national narrative. They are Zhou Weihan (or Xueqiao, 1865/1870–1910), Lei Haizong (1902–1962), Tong Shuye (1908–1968), and Lin Zhichun (1910–2007). Through a century-long effort, they established the subdiscipline of ancient world history as a professional field of scholarly studies. To place this process within a wider historical context, I also include some discussion on Chen Hengzhe (1890–1976), He Bingsong (1890–1946), Gu Jiegang (1893–1980), and Wu Mi (1894–1978), who are important figures in Chinese intellectual history but not necessarily "ancient world historians" according to today's standards.

The historians focused on in this book have dealt with a wide range of significant topics in historical teaching and research, from the heated debates on key concepts such as "classical antiquity" and the "Asiatic mode of production" to the nuanced discussions on historical methodology such as "evidential learning" and "historical materialism," as well as professional reflections on the role of ancient and world histories in school curricula. Despite their diverging interests, most of them share a consensus that centers on a single belief, that is, the common nature of humanity. Armed with this belief, they have firmly and continuously insisted on treating China as an organic part of the world. Yet, at the beginning of the twenty-first century, world history as a discipline has effectively become foreign history in China, and the discourse of a common humanity has been trumped academically by one of cultural difference.

In this book, I trace three stages of the development of world history into an academic field of teaching and research over the course of the entire twentieth century: the rise of amateur world-historical writing in late Qing era, the inclusion of world history as a mandatory teaching component in the school curricula in the Republic, and the establishment of world history as a research field from the early People's Republic to the 1980s. Throughout this process, the historians in focus constantly negotiated the relationship between national identification and global outlook in their teachings and research. By examining this process, I show how the separation of world history from national history came about as an unintended consequence of the state's massive social engineering projects.

The tensions between state control and intellectual resistances are a central theme at play. In the early Republican period, a generation of historians insisted on professional standards in historical studies and believed in the noble dream of pursuing objectivity after the introduction of a modern higher education system. Yet history became overtly politicized during the war with Japan, when a group of historians decided to adopt history as an ideological tool to rescue the falling nation. The communist takeover, to some extent, furthered the politicization of historical studies. The government borrowed ideas from the Soviet Union and established social institutions such as the Teaching and Research Unit System to force the intellectual community into submission. The external pressure antagonized Chinese intellectuals. Unable to openly reject state ideology, historians resorted to the assertion of Chinese exceptionalism, implying that Marxism as a foreign ideology was not suitable for the study of Chinese history. Thus, the intricacy of academic politics gave rise to the belief in the uniqueness of Chinese civilization and undermined the consensus of a common humanity. After Mao's death, a series of influential academic debates further paved the way for the rise of academic nationalism in China today. In a review of these critical moments in the development of world history as a professional discipline, I attempt to demonstrate how nationalist history was born out of a reaction to state imposition via cultural exceptionalism.

Chinese studies of world history have left a significant legacy in intellectual history. In this book, I identify the complicated relationship between world history and nationalist history projects and attempt to tell stories about both, yet with a focus on the former. World history can be nationalist, as scholars have already identified in the world-historical writing in China today, but it does not have to be this way as I contend in the book. In examining the cases centered on these world historians in China, I argue that a belief in the common nature of humanity can still serve as an antidote to the rise of academic nationalism in the twenty-first century.

A minor portion of Chapter 2 was published in *Berliner China-Hefte* (*Chinese History and Society*) in 2013. A part of the Conclusion appears in my coedited volume, *Receptions of Greek and Roman Antiquity in East Asia* (2018) as well as a minor portion of Chapter 1 in *The Routledge Companion to World History and Literature* (2018). All these sections have gone through significant changes when they reappear in this book.

Writing this book has been an intellectual journey. The idea was vaguely conceived of when I was a graduate student in China. From Europe to the United States, I gradually developed it into a book. I was fortunate enough to receive a substantial amount of help in the course of my work. Without this, I could not have completed the book. My home institution, the State University of New York at Fredonia, offered me academic leave to allow me to focus on writing. My colleagues in the Department of History have always encouraged me to pursue this project and given me the warmest moral support. In Germany, the VolkswagenStiftung granted me a research fellowship and the Centre for Modern East Asian Studies at Göttingen University graciously hosted my residency. In China, the International Center for Studies of Chinese Civilization at Fudan University supported me with a summer scholarship and sponsored me to organize a workshop on case studies and history.

As a historian, I was especially lucky to receive generous financial support and attentive assistance at various libraries and research centers in China, Germany, and the United States. Many critical materials for this book came from the East Asian collection at Indiana University where Wen-ling Liu always works very hard to fulfill researchers' needs. The Harvard-Yenching Library offered me a grant during the early stages of this project, and during the visit to the library its staff members helped me locate some important materials. Nancy Hearst at the Fairbank Center for Chinese Studies further enlightened me on a few leads on contemporary issues in China. At Freie Universität Berlin, the China librarian Tao Jian has built an impressive collection on Chinese intellectual history. I acquired valuable materials at the University Service Centre in Hong Kong and also the Global Resources Center at the George

Washington University, where Qi Gao, Jin Xiao, and other staff members offered a great deal of help. At the Northeast Normal University Archive, I was able to access some crucial materials thanks to my colleagues and mentors. In Shanghai, Chen Yun graciously hosted me during my visit to the Shanghai Cishu Chubanshe Library, a hidden gem for modern Chinese historical studies. The China librarian Ding Ye at Georgetown University helped me further in seeking leads on several sources. In the summer of 2019, the Library of Congress offered me a fellowship. With the help of Qi Qiu and Yuwu Song I was able to further revise the manuscript at the Asian Division Reading Room of this world-leading library.

I also owe an enormous debt to my mentors and colleagues. Yang Gongle, Lynn Struve, and Klaus Mühlhahn introduced me to the professional study of history and have guided me throughout my career. At Fredonia, Dave Kinkela read the entire manuscript and offered me useful suggestions from a non-China specialist's perspective. Dominic Sachsenmaier at Göttingen University hosted my residency as a visiting scholar and further introduced me to a group of global historians. In Changchun, Cheng Shuwei offered endless hospitality during my field research, and Qu Xiaofan and Wu Yuhong also provided me with enormous support. Likewise, Li Jianming, Liao Xuesheng, Liu Jiahe, Ge Zhaoguang, He Ziquan (1911–2011), Wang Dunshu, Q. Edward Wang, Yang Juping, Zhao Yifeng, and Zhu Huan all spent hours talking with me about their experiences of studying history in China, and my conversations with them laid the foundations for this book.

For me, writing is not a solitary enterprise either. Shadi Bartsch, Jingjing Chang, Roger Des Forge, Hajo Frölich, Ronald Gary, Han Xiaorong, Fabio Lanza, Joseph Lawson, Niall Michelsen, Bénédicte Miyamoto, Augustin Normand, Don Price, Amanda Shuman, John David Smith, Kristin Stapleton, Marie Strauss, John Staples, Heather Streets-Salter, and Jacky Swansinger read various parts of the manuscript, and I am very grateful for their constant and constructive feedback. Cynthia Col and Matthew Fennessy offered help with extensive editing. In Europe, Fritz-Heiner Mutschler has graciously provided me with the photos back from his days at the Institute for the History of Ancient Civilizations (IHAC). I also thank Zhou Weihan's great-grandchildren, especially Luyen and Sumin, for granting me the copyright for use of their father, the great music composer, Chou Wen-chung's image for this book.

In North America, Western Europe, and East Asia, I also received various kinds of help from the following individuals: Emily Andrew, Antoon De Baets, Bao Maohong, Stefan Berger, Kerry Brown, Huaiyu Chen, Ruma Chopra, Jenny Huangfu Day, Chunmei Du, Steve Fabian,

Han Ce, Tze-ki Hon, Ian Johnson, Cho-yun Hsu, Robert Graham, Xiaofei Kang, Rebecca Karl, Michael Lackner, Mechthild Leutner, Ning Liu, Xiaoyuan Liu, Zhao Ma, Pat Manning, Adam McKeown (1966–2017), Niu Dayong, Christopher Reed, Ivan Sablin, Michael Schimmelpfennig, Axel Schneider, Emily Straus, Sun Jianing, Luo Zhou, Zou Zhenhuan, and Zuo Ya. They either answered my questions or helped me with locating crucial leads on research. Without them, this would be a very different book. In addition, I would like to thank the anonymous reviewers for their constructive suggestions as well as the individuals who have offered all kinds of help in this process yet for various reasons whose names are not mentioned here. Of course, it is my greatest honor to work with Lucy Rhymer and Emily Sharp from Cambridge University Press. Their endless assistance eventually allowed this book to happen.

Last, but certainly not least, I am eternally grateful for the unwavering support of my loved ones. Both my parents-in-law Zhang Yujie and He Zhiqiang and my parents Chen Shuhua and Fan Songli have traveled from China to offer help to my family and me whenever and wherever it is needed. I am deeply indebted to them for their attentive care and unreserved enthusiasm, and I hope this book makes them proud. My grandfather Fan Jipu taught history in Changchun for more than four decades and my father has always considered himself a historian, so I guess I get this from both of them. While writing this book, I observed my son Eric growing and acquiring an inquisitive mind. Chinese parents rarely say this to their children, but, in concluding this book, I want to tell him, "Son, you are the best thing that ever happened to me!" My wife He Yan is not only the unequivocal cheerleader of this project but also my lifelong intellectual companion. With her strong support and encouragement, I freed myself from teaching duties for two periods of research leave, which was critical for me to finalize this project. Many ideas in this book also came from our everyday conversations. In China, Europe, and America, together we pursue history, knowledge, and truth. Without her, this book would have been impossible. I thus dedicate it to her.

Introduction: Control and Resistance
The Social Production of World History under the Influence of Radical Politics

On November 7, 1955, at a faculty meeting of the Department of History at Southwest Teacher's College, Sun Peiliang, chairperson of the department, suddenly stood up and shouted, "I, as chair of the department, order Wang Xingyun out!" Wu Mi, director of a newly minted academic structure, the teaching and research unit of ancient world history (*jiaoyanshi*), immediately followed: "I, as director of the *jiaoyanshi*, order Wang Xingyun out!" Two weeks later, the secretary of the *jiaoyanshi* Sun Furu, asked if Wu Mi had something else to say in closing another faculty meeting. The latter replied, "I just want to kill Wang Xingyun."[1]

Wu Mi is a familiar name to many people in China today, remembered by some as the "founding father of China's comparative literature study."[2] As an early-generation Chinese student to the United States, in the late 1910s and early 1920s, he studied with Irving Babbitt (1865–1933), the famous scholar of comparative literature in the West. As a public intellectual, he was a leading voice in the *Critical Review* (named after the journal *Xueheng*) group who spoke of the ills of modernity and openly defended the traditional values in the iconoclastic New Culture Movement.[3] As an administrator, he directed the School of National Studies at Tsinghua University and chaired the departments of Foreign Languages at both Tsinghua University and Southwest

---

[1] Wang Xingyun, "Wo suo liaojie de Wu Mi jiaoshou" [The Professor Wu Mi that I know], *Nanfang zhoumo* [Southern Weekly], September 30, 2009; for more information about Wu Mi, see *Biographic Dictionary of Republican China* (hereafter *BDRC*), ed. Howard L. Boorman and Richard C. Howard (New York: Columbia University Press, 1967), 3:442b–444.

[2] In the late 1990s, Zhang Zige's memoir on Wu Mi became a bestseller in China. Its popularity registered a revived interest in Wu Mi studies. Zhang Zige, *Xinxiang leijiu ji Wu Mi* [Commemorating Wu Mi with the heart as incense and tears as wine] (Guangzhou: Guangzhou chubanshe, 1997).

[3] Yiqun Zhou, "Greek Antiquity, Chinese Modernity, and the Changing World Order," in *Chinese Visions of World Order: Tianxia, Culture, and World Politics*, ed. Ban Wang (Durham, NC and London: Duke University Press, 2017), 118–120; Jinyu Liu, "Translating and Rewriting Western Classics in China (1920s–1930s): The Case of the *Xueheng* Journal," in *Receptions of Greek and Roman Antiquity in East Asia*, eds. Almut-Barbara Renger and Xin Fan (Boston: Brill, 2018), 91–111.

Associated University in the 1930s and 1940s, the most prestigious schools in China. As a scholar, he befriended great names such as Chen Yinke (1890–1969) and educated people such as Qian Zhongshu (1910–1998); but who is Wang Xingyun?

Wang Xingyun (1930–) was an obscure teaching assistant in the *jiaoyanshi* when the incident took place.[4] A twenty-five-year-old, he had just graduated from the postgraduate program at Northeast Normal University in Changchun (an important site for socialist education and world history in the early People's Republic) and spent less than half a year at this new post. What did he do in such a short period of time to so infuriate Wu Mi?

The answer to this question touches on several themes in this book: the establishment of world history as a professional academic field of teaching and research; the specialization of world-historical studies according to the Soviet model; and the emergence of China's world historians as newcomers to the field of historical studies as well as their conflicts with other scholars. A careful examination of this rancorous exchange will allow us to understand the social and political conditions that in a subtle way shaped the trajectory of the development of world history as a field of knowledge production.

The incident took place under a higher education system where individual rights were assumed to be subjected to collective interests. As China cut off its Western ties and joined the socialist camp in the early Cold War, English language had become a less useful subject. So the communist state terminated the English programs at many institutions of higher learning including the one at Southwest Teacher's College. This change directly affected individuals like Wu Mi. As a professor of English literature, he lost his home department. Transferred to the Department of History against his own will, he was assigned to teach an introductory level course on ancient world history (*shijie shanggu shi*). This arbitrary decision became the source of conflict.

In the early People's Republic, the new communist government overhauled China's higher education system following the Soviet model. This change profoundly affected the discipline of history. Despite its original goal of ideological control, professionalization and specialization shaped its development. For the first time, world history (*shijie shi*) grew into a clearly defined and largely independent field of teaching and research, achieving an equal status to national history within the reformed

---

[4] *Zhujiao* (teaching assistant) is the lowest level of academic staff at Chinese universities and colleges. Technically, teaching assistants must be supervised by senior faculty members when offering courses and cannot teach independently.

academic infrastructure. Both Chinese and world histories were now divided into three *jiaoyanshi* (literally translated as the units of teaching and research): ancient, medieval, and modern. In the early 1950s, Wu Mi was officially listed as director of ancient world history *jiaoyanshi*; he became one of the first generation of professional "ancient world historians" in China.

Ancient world history was not an easy subject to teach. As the first period in the tripartite structure of world history, it mimicked its Soviet counterpart, and the theoretical foundations of this periodization were heavily influenced by state ideology. Its coverage was artificially and arbitrarily dated from the birth of human civilization to the rise of "feudalism." (As the following chapters show, this is a very controversial term when applied to China.) To build this new field overnight, the state forced many scholars to change their research fields and assigned them to world history. Lei Haizong, Tong Shuye, and Lin Zhichun, three protagonists of the book, were among the scholars affected by this development. The state also launched a national project to nurture a new generation of young world historians in the early years of the People's Republic. As such, many of China's "ancient world historians" were not only unprepared to read primary sources in ancient languages, including Greek, Latin, Egyptian hieroglyphs and Mesopotamian cuneiform but also not satisfied with their new teaching role. For his part, Wu Mi was a literature scholar who took enormous pride in his established scholarly prestige. He was unwilling to submit to the state ideology and to follow the Soviet model of ancient world history, nor did he care to switch to a new teaching and research field that required learning ancient languages from scratch. Knowing that he was not a good fit to teach such a course, he repeatedly asked the school to relieve him from his teaching duties. In spite of his persistence, the vice president of the school declined his request and asked him to continue teaching the subject.[5]

The intrusive collective workspace magnified minor tensions among individuals, especially between the "new" world historians and the "old" scholarly authorities. As a variation of the *danwei* system (a state-supervised social network for work often translated as "work unit") in the higher education system, the new *jiaoyanshi* system placed individual teachers within a workspace where they had to both mutually supervise and collectively criticize each other. Teaching, then, became collective enterprise of which the entire *jiaoyanshi* shared responsibility. This new

---

[5] Chen Zhongdan, "Beisong zhujiao de jianggao: Wu Mi jiao 'shijie gudaishi'" [Reciting teaching assistants' lecture notes: Wu Mi teaches "Ancient World History"]. *Nanfang zhoumo* (Guangzhou, China), July 15, 2009.

idea of "mutual responsibility" of teaching contradicts the cherished idea of intellectual autonomy that evolved during the Republican period. At the time of this incident, young students at the school, who were full of revolutionary fervor, demanded an ideologically driven course, and Wu Mi was poorly prepared to provide it. His teaching was badly reviewed.

To add to Wu Mi's frustration, his young colleagues, Sun Furu and Wang Xingyun, thought that it was their responsibility to "assist" the older instructor. As they had been educated at Northeast Normal University, a new-type socialist university, they were more accustomed to collective discussion and mutual criticism. For these younger colleagues, this would have been the norm in their new work unit.[6] At faculty meetings they openly criticized Wu Mi and other senior colleagues for deviating from the Marxist doctrine in their teaching. These criticisms were serious accusations within the context of a tightening of party-state controls, so the school leaders could not just simply ignore them. They asked these young scholars to "assist" Wu Mi to improve his teaching. They revised Wu's lecture notes before class, and the latter had to recite these notes while teaching. Whereas the young scholars considered this a normal practice, Wu Mi took it as a personal insult. After all, he was a well-established scholarly authority who had achieved fame at least three decades earlier and it was unacceptable for him to be criticized in front of people by youngsters whom he considered, no matter how competent in reciting Soviet communist doctrine, to barely know how to conduct real research.

Wu Mi's frustration and humiliation also had something to do with generational politics in Chinese academia in the 1950s. In his seminal work on this subject, Pierre Bourdieu metaphorically defines the generational conflicts within the field of cultural production between a younger generation and an older generation of scholars as "conflicts between father and son." According to Bourdieu, the key issue concerns who controls the authority in the process of knowledge production. In his work, he elucidates that the conflict between younger and older scholars shows an interesting dynamic, as the younger generation tends to collaborate with external forces to challenge the authority of their old masters.[7]

---

[6] Because such discussions were a regular part of school activities at Northeast Normal University, Wang Xingyun claimed that his conflict with Wu Mi would never have happened there. Wang, "Wo suo liaojie de Wu Mi jiaoshou."

[7] Pierre Bourdieu, "The Field of Cultural Production, or: The Economic World Reversed," *Poetics* 12, no. 4 (1983): 311–356. Recent research in Chinese history also confirms the existence of such generational conflicts. See Huaiyin Li, *Reinventing Modern China: Imagination and Authenticity in Chinese Historical Writing* (Honolulu: University of Hawai'i Press, 2013), 21.

In this story, Wu Mi fulfilled all the criteria of "an old-generation scholar" in the early People's Republic: he had studied in the United States, the leading "imperialist country"; he had openly opposed the New Culture Movement, one that allegedly gave birth to the Chinese Communist movement (according to party propaganda);[8] and he refused to change under the new regime and to give up what he had learned from the "imperial country" and the "feudal tradition" in order to embrace "new" world-historical knowledge from the Soviet Union. In contrast, Wang Xingyun and his colleague Sun Furu were representatives of the new-generation scholars: they had graduated from the center of socialist world history education; they were versed in Stalinist Marxist theory and Soviet historiography; and they believed in communist ideals. (Wang Xingyun belonged to the Youth League of the Chinese Communist Party, an official organization that prepared youth for party membership.) In their eyes, Wu Mi was more like a symbol of the outdated and even reactionary intelligentsia; by criticizing Wu, they were eager to embrace a new system of knowledge production of their own.

Aside from ideological differences, many old-generation scholars feared the impact of this generational shift – "What if junior scholars all over China turned into people like this!"[9] When Wang Xingyun reflected on the incident more than fifty years later, he told a story of a generational conflict, saying "According to Mr. Wu's view of history and the ideological system at that time, [he] would inevitably collide with any teaching assistants and lecturers who were educated after Liberation (i.e., after the founding of the People's Republic in 1949)."[10] Archival sources confirm this view. In a report to the Central Committee of the Chinese Communist Party (CCP), the party branch at the newly founded Chinese Academy of Sciences, the highest level of national research organization, estimated that the tension between the young generation and the "old scientists" ubiquitously existed in all its affiliation institutions.[11] The conflicts took place not only at the college in the

---

[8] Tse-tsung Chow, *The May 4th Movement: Intellectual Revolution in Modern China* (Cambridge, MA: Harvard University Press, 1960), 347–355.

[9] Wu Mi, *Wu Mi riji xubian* [The continued collection of Wu Mi's diaries] (Beijing: Sanlian chubanshe, 2006), 2: 228.

[10] Wang, "Wo suo liaojie de Wu Mi jiaoshou."

[11] "Zhongguo kexueyuan guanyu muqian kexueyuan gongzuo de jiben qingkuang he jinhou gongzuo renwu gei zhongyang de baogao" [The report to the Central Committee by the party branch of the Chinese Academy of Sciences regarding its state of affairs as well as its future tasks], in *Zhonggong zhongyang wenjian xuanji* [The selected documents by the Central Committee of the CCP] (October 1949 to May 1966) (hereafter *ZZWX*) (Beijing: Renmin chubanshe, 2013), 15:378.

provincial town Chongqing but also at the major research centers in Beijing and other cities.[12]

Certainly, few people would dare to directly challenge the Communist Party in the highly ideological pressure of the early 1950s. Yet the significance of this story lies in the fact that the intellectuals as a community often found subtle ways to circumvent the influence of state control. Halfhearted submission is one way, and appropriating the existing social structure to marginalize the external influence in the name of academic professionalism is another. Both led to some unintended consequences that affected the development of world history.

Let us first examine the halfhearted submission to ideology. In the summer of 1955, the year the incident took place, Sun Peiliang, the chairperson, had a conversation with Wu. Sun frankly told the latter that what the government, students, and the school wanted now were people like Sun Furu who "just read two or three Chinese-translated Soviet textbooks and references." He also commented that the standard to judge the quality of scholars was highly politicized. Scholars of the older generation like Wang Guowei (1877–1927), Liang Qichao (1873–1929), and Chen Yinke would not have been treated well in such a context. He said, "If one follows Marxism-Leninism, then one is a good teacher, even without a great knowledge background." The only solution suggested by Sun Peiliang was to come to terms with Marxist-Leninist ideology.[13] A few weeks later, Sun further advised Wu Mi on how to succeed in teaching world history in the new environment. This time he made his point even more clear:

[When you teach, you] must not speak of anything unrelated to the topic at the beginning of the lecture. Every sentence must be taken from translated Soviet sources, and [you] must cite more from the sentences in Marx's, Engels's, Lenin's, and Stalin's classical works, and point out from which chapter and which section those sentences are taken, then all students will be impressed and submit to you. After several weeks, everything will be easy. Also, with regard to picking words and sentences, [you] must follow today's students' habits and standards. For example, you should not say "rex" but rather "military leader" though it is a very long [term in Chinese]. Also, try to avoid those European-style long sentences.[14]

Many scholars like Wu regarded teaching world history merely as a political obligation; there was a lack of a genuine scholarly interest in

---

[12] In Chinese historical studies, this generational conflict became more outspoken during the "historiographical revolution" when a new generation of revolutionary radicals started to take over control of the field from older-generation professional historians after the Great Leap Forward (starting in 1958). Li, *Reinventing Modern China*, 132–133; 166–169.

[13] Wu, *Wu Mi riji xubian*, 2:228.   [14] Wu, *Wu Mi riji xubian*, 2:257.

the subject among historians. The same was true for Gu Cheng (1934–2003), as another example, a scholar who was once assigned to study American history and was later famous for his meticulous works on Ming history in the 1990s. Like them, scholars at that time were forced to study world history; it was not based on personal choice. This explains why so many scholars eventually chose to leave the field. Even Lin Zhichun, "the founding father of ancient world history," constantly complained about being assigned to study world history against his will and wanted to return to the study of Chinese history.

Resistance in the name of academic professionalism was another way. Despite the penetrating influence of the party-state, old-generation scholars still occupied the leadership positions in academic institutions and claimed their right to interpret the nature of scholarly research. In the incident described at the opening of this Introduction, school leaders such as the vice president and the chair of the department were both senior scholars and on Wu's side. The vice president assigned Wu to be the instructor of the course on ancient world history and designated Sun Furu and Wang Xingyun as his teaching assistants. He mandated an agenda to let Wu "teach the youngsters a lesson," and it was the chairperson who first spoke out when Wang Xingyun criticized Wu at the faculty meeting on November 7.[15] In hindsight, generational politics had the upper hand against external political pressure at least in this case. The young scholars suffered the most. As Wang Xingyun bitterly related in 2009, after the incident he did not receive any promotions in the department and remained a teaching assistant for the subsequent twenty-two years. He insinuated that the department and school leaders considered him a troublemaker and that this was a punishment for his attempt to challenge their authority.

This story between Wu Mi and Wang Xingyun is just one of many conflicts that were caused by state control and intellectual resistance in the emergence of the new research field of world history. As I will document in this book, the dynamic between control and resistance is an important key to understanding the development of the world-historical studies. It not only affected the lives of individual historians like Wang Xingyun, whose career was damaged by his attempts to challenge academic authorities, it also led to the unintended rise of academic nationalism and the simultaneous marginalization of the discipline of world history. This social and political dimension is a crucial factor in shaping the tension between national and world histories in China; and,

---

[15] Wu, *Wu Mi riji xubian*, 2:258.

in a subtle way, it was also a factor in the formation of twentieth-century Chinese identity.

When it comes to the study of the formation of twentieth-century Chinese identity, the focus of scholarly inquiries is often on the rise of nationalism. Some scholars argue that modern nationalism is a reflection of the primordial cultural belief, while others believe that it is more or less an imaginary project that political elites exploit to mobilize a wide spectrum of the population. In either case, it is a narrative of the triumph of national preoccupation over other views of the world through the lens of the recent past.[16] Within this interpretative framework, the story of the "modern" history of the Chinese "nation" often grasps historians' central attention.[17] In this book, I tell the other side of the story. Its perspective features how scholars formed world history as a scholarly discipline of inquiry with which to provide consistent critiques of and alternatives to the national narratives of history over the course of the entire twentieth century.

World history in China is a product of the global entanglement. Yet scholars in the past tended to dismiss its scholarly value. The exemplar case is Dorothea Martin's *The Making of a Sino-Marxist World View* (1990). In the first monograph in English on world history in China, she surveys the Chinese study of world history and underscores the political nature of world-historical studies in the early years of the People's Republic. In overlooking the early development of world history during the late Qing and the Republican periods, Martin, like many others, asserted that the Chinese study of world history was a project sponsored by the communist state. Thus, it is a "handmaiden of political ideology."[18]

This view has been gradually abandoned in recent scholarship.[19] The rapid rise of China's economy and political influence makes people

---

[16] To date, the best scholarship on this topic remains Prasenjit Duara's *Rescuing History from the Nation: Questioning Narratives of Modern China* (Chicago: University of Chicago Press, 1995).

[17] For the best work on the invention of modern Chinese history as a scholarly discipline, see Li, *Reinventing Modern China*. Li argues that the writing of modern Chinese history in China is dominated by the tension between the two conflicting frameworks of interpretation: the modernization narrative and the revolution narrative. As part of the general discipline of historical studies in China, world history has recently been influenced by the above-mentioned tension. Yet, as I will demonstrate in this book, the long-term temporal scale and the massive spatial coverage in world-historical studies allow world historians in China to test alternative interpretative frameworks to these two in their own works.

[18] Dorothea Martin, *The Making of a Sino-Marxist World View: Perceptions and Interpretations of World History in the People's Republic of China* (Armonk, NY: M. E. Sharpe, 1990), 15.

[19] To name just a few examples, Q. Edward Wang, "Encountering the World: China and Its Other(s) in Historical Narratives, 1949–89," *Journal of World History* 14, no. 3 (2003):

wonder about its future global strategies. Political scientists and policy advisors, especially international relations specialists, in China and abroad have developed a renewed interest in China's historical views of its own position in the world. In analyzing Chinese worldviews, they write either about how Chinese political thinkers should internalize world affairs and adopt ancient Chinese history as a way to make sense of the future (as represented by Yan Xuetong's analogy of the Spring and Autumn period in Chinese history with the future of the world) or about how the Chinese traditional cosmology would contribute to a new arrangement of a global order alternative to the one centered on Europe and America (as shown in Zhao Tingyang's famous discussion on the concept of "Tianxia").[20]

Shying away from these utilitarian views of historiography, historians have returned to a more nuanced view of the dynamics of historical writing under an oppressive regime. This is a theme that both Q. Edward Wang and Luo Xu have explored in their articles on world-historical writing in the People's Republic. Despite their informative work, one still wonders about the relationship between Marxist ideology and nationalism in China, two central themes in the history of twentieth-century China. As Nicola Spakowski has shown in her 2009 survey "National Aspirations on a Global Stage," recent developments in the field signal that nationalism is already dominating the writing of global history in contemporary China.[21] Yet the process of how nationalism replaced other competing visions of the world in China remains unclear to the reader. This is not necessarily a deficiency in the existing scholarship, as most of these journal articles have laid the foundations for future research. To build on these, a more comprehensive overview of the development beyond the People's Republic is needed.

World history in China becomes an even more meaningful topic if we recognize the growing criticism of the Eurocentric bias in national historiography. Prasenjit Duara critically examines the rise of national history in twentieth-century China in *Rescuing History from the Nation* (1995). The

---

327–358; Luo Xu, "Reconstructing World History in the People's Republic of China since the 1980s," *Journal of World History* 18, no. 3 (2007): 325–350.

[20] Yan Xuetong, *Ancient Chinese Thought, Modern Chinese Power*, ed. Daniel A. Bell and Sun Zhe, trans. Edmund Ryden (Princeton: Princeton University Press, 2011); Zhao Tingyang, *Tianxia tixi: Shijie zhidu zhexue daolun* [The Tianxia system: An introduction to the Philosophy of World Institution] (Beijing: Renmin daxue chubanshe, 2011); Dingxin Zhao, *The Confucian-Legalist State: A New Theory of Chinese History* (Oxford: Oxford University Press, 2015). For more recent discussions, see Wang, *Chinese Visions of World Order*.

[21] Nicola Spakowski, "National Aspirations on a Global Stage: Concepts of World/Global History in Contemporary China," *Journal of Global History*, 4, no. 3 (2009): 475–495.

Enlightenment project in Europe has shaped a linear, evolutionary view of time wherein each country's level of development is measured by how far it has progressed toward becoming a nation-state. Duara argues that this European understanding of history has deeply influenced the writing of history in China and eventually silenced various alternative modes of historical writing, one of which is world history. Duara's theoretical contribution is particularly significant, but he needs more solid case studies to historically ground his point.

Be that as it may, Duara's critique of national history is part of a global trend that rethinks the agency of the non-Western world in the modern system of knowledge production, which is professed in Martin's assumption of Chinese world historians merely as the "handmaidens" of the political ideology. Theoretically speaking, an increasing number of scholars have now recognized the value of non-Western world-historical writing. For instance, in *Provincializing Europe* (2007) Dipesh Charkarbarty argues for the decentralization of European historiographical narratives in a postcolonial setting; and in *The Theft of History* (2007) Jack Goody discloses how the marginalization of non-Western history became the very foundation of Eurocentrism. Speaking about the global relevance of the Chinese study of world history, Dominic Sachsenmaier in his *Global Perspectives on Global History* (2011) compares the development of world-historical studies in China to its German and American counterparts. By doing so, he presents a positive view of the past achievements of world-historical studies in China. His more recent work, *Global Entanglements of a Man Who Never Travel* (2018), further documents the overlooked globally entangled views among Chinese intellectuals even prior to the intensified contact between China and the wider world in the nineteenth century.

To build on the existing scholarship, this book is an appreciation of the agency of non-Western world historians in writing history based on the lived experiences of some of the most significant Chinese world historians. This perspective is little known to people outside of China due to the scarcity of English-language literature on the subject. These individuals include Zhou Weihan (or Xueqiao), an early world-historical writer who has been largely neglected by professional historiography; Lei Haizong, the most influential world historian in Republican China; Tong Shuye, one of the earliest Marxist world historians who started the debate on the periodization of world history in the 1950s; and Lin Zhichun, allegedly the "founding father" of ancient world-historical studies in China. Loosely regarded as world historians, these authors have framed the study of China's past more or less within a world-historical context. The stories of their aspirations, struggles, and setbacks as they sought to connect ancient foreign worlds to twentieth-century China underscore the political, social, and personal tensions that accompanied and influenced the formation of the modern discipline of world history in China.

In this book, I survey the development of the entire discipline of world history. For both historiographical and practical considerations, I place a special focus on the subdiscipline of ancient world history. Speaking about historiography, one needs to stress the significant influence of ancient history on the formation of modern Chinese identities. Most works on world history in China, exemplified in Martin's pioneering study, pay an out-of-proportion amount of attention to the writing of "modern world history" and have neglected the significant debates that took place in "ancient world history." This makes some sense in the scholarly context as the discourse of modernity once occupied a central place in the Eurocentric narratives of world history. However, in analyzing the past scholarship of ancient world history in China, I point out in this book that Chinese world historians, as a scholarship community, were never fully satisfied with the discourse of modernity as a framework for world history. Their resistance, protests, and even rebellion against the discipline of world history in the West are only fully manifested in particular writings about the ancient world in which the discourse of Eurocentric modernity loses its magical power of hegemony.

Studying ancient world history in China has recently become possible. History is, after all, about people, and it is historians' mission to write human-centered stories. To achieve such a goal, it is essential to utilize various materials such as diaries, autobiographies, correspondences, and, most of all, archival sources. This is especially challenging for the study of the period of the early People's Republic, a crucial time for the development of world-historical studies in China as a scholarly field, as personnel archives remain mostly closed to researchers. By a stroke of luck, I have been able to access, for the first time, some valuable personnel archival materials on Lin Zhichun, the "founding father" of ancient world history in China. Along with other documents such as declassified municipal archives and secret party reports, we are able to establish a more nuanced understanding of the fate of Chinese historiography under a totalizing regime. That is, with all the radical agendas, the socialist state by and large failed to completely control Chinese historians. Despite all the attempts, historians, including some Marxist world historians, still cherished the value of academic professionalism. These archival sources document the tension between state intervention and intellectual resistance as a profound theme in modern Chinese intellectual history.

Despite its emphasis on the role of the 1950s in shaping the development of world history in China, I distinguish this book from other works on Chinese intellectual history and historiography in its long-term approach. I contend that the writing and rewriting of world history in China today have to be understood through the continuity and contingency of certain dynamics that developed over the course of the entire twentieth century. Among them is the tension between state intervention and the pursuit of intellectual autonomy. These dynamics affected individual lives, as well as the intellectual and political writing of world history in China. Isolating individuals from the long-term development would sometimes lead to misunderstandings and misjudgment about the nature of their works. Just to name one example, one of the protagonists of the book, Lin Zhichun, is often labeled a "red professor" in post-Mao China. Indeed, many liberal thinkers insinuate that his collaboration with the communist state may jeopardize his scholarly integrity. His conflict with the chair of the department in the early 1950s has been disclosed in the declassified archives (for more details, see Chapter 3). Despite his political ideology, Lin shared the goal of the pursuit of objective knowledge in historical research with the generation of scholars who grew up in the Republican period. Moreover, his research methods in world history were deeply rooted in the Chinese tradition of classical studies (*Jingxue*).

Similarly, Lei Haizong today is often remembered as a liberal thinker who was brave enough to challenge communist authority during the political campaigns in the 1950s. Yet a careful examination of his political writings in the 1940s uncovers his close connection with the cultural fascist movement in wartime China. Digging even further, I pinpoint the origin of Lei's conservative worldview to his experience of studying in the United States where his disillusionment with global politics and his concerns over China's future planted the seeds for his later conservative thought. Thus, this attempt to employ a long-term view will allow us to tell a very different story of the Chinese intellectual history of the twentieth century.

The book has five chapters, an introduction, and a conclusion. In the chapters, I document and analyze the gradually narrowing scope of world-historical studies in China and the simultaneous rise of nationalism among Chinese academics.

Prior to the late nineteenth century, Chinese scholar-officials studied ancient Chinese history to make sense of contemporary affairs. Thus, rather than situating themselves in global space when they traveled outside China, they attempted to situate the world within China's historical time.

In Chapter 1, I contend that world-historical writing emerged in China in the early twentieth century after the rise of print capitalism as an attempt to address concerns about global space. Specifically, the question of how to make sense of China's decline in the global order motivated scholarly interest. In this effort, the temporal dimension of ancient history remained relevant. For instance, in *An Outline of Western History*, Zhou Weihan juxtaposes the histories of foreign countries with Chinese chronologies. Zhou's book is possibly the first Chinese-language work on ancient world history written by a Chinese scholar. In it, he stresses the value of ancient history and dismisses notions of fundamental differences among cultures in modern identities. As he repeatedly asserts, "Peoples throughout China and the West are alike – their intellects are the same." Zhou's absence of a cultural nationalist view is especially striking compared to the views expressed in later nationalist works published in China by the end of the twentieth century.

World-historical writing in the early twentieth century took place within regional networks of gentry scholars, publishers, and governmental bureaucrats. The academic, financial, and educational motivations of participants in these networks intermingled. The professionalization of historical studies during the Republican period transformed how Chinese historians understood their work. As the century progressed, the works of old gentry scholars like Zhou were quickly forgotten.

With this transformation, a new generation of academic professionals emerged. These new professional historians criticized the centrality of ancient historical time in Chinese historical studies. In contrast, they embraced objectivity as a goal of historical practice and regarded intellectual autonomy as integral to the discipline. With the shift in focus of historical studies, in the 1920s, some new academic professionals carved out a niche for themselves by developing world history into a specific teaching field. By the early 1930s, world historians such as Lei Haizong dedicated themselves to placing China's past and future within a world-historical context. In Chapter 2, I contend that the pursuit of intellectual autonomy was, however, interrupted by the war with Japan. At this moment of crisis, world historians exemplified by Lei Haizong became increasingly nationalistic. These historians glorified the unique nature of Chinese culture to promote national identity at a moment of crisis. As a result, a binary opposition between China and the world gradually emerged in Chinese historiography.

In the early People's Republic, the socialist state sought total control of history as a field of knowledge production. The state introduced Soviet concepts of Marxist historiography, established a standard curriculum, and put a new academic infrastructure into place that was characterized by a teaching and research unit system. This development, I contend, placed the world-historical discipline in a difficult position and shaped the key dynamic for the later rise of nationalism among Chinese historians. In Chapter 3, I analyze the paradox facing world historians Lin Zhichun and

Tong Shuye as they tried to negotiate this emerging and complex academic, political environment. On the one hand, as up-and-coming professionals eager to develop their careers, they were inclined to collaborate with the state; on the other hand, as academics, they still cherished the ideal of intellectual autonomy. Their experiences with the regime formed a sharp contrast to those who were less willing to be coerced by the regime, such as Lei Haizong and Wu Mi. The latter found themselves constantly facing the distrust, surveillance, and oppression of the totalizing state.

The increasing pressure of state control had a subtle effect on the position of world history within the general discipline of history. World historians remained a vulnerable minority among the community of historians. In Chapter 4, I examine why many historians chose to dismiss the universalism espoused by China's world historians as a "forced analogy." For many historians, this universalism was an unwelcome ideological Marxist intrusion into historical studies; moreover, world historians who were working closely with the state were not considered serious scholars. Owing to such attitudes, many historians neglected the significant developments that took place in world-historical studies of the time. Among these, as the chapter contends, were various attempts by world historians to place China within a world-historical narrative that is based on a non-Eurocentric schema. The debates between Lin Zhichun and Tong Shuye on the Asiatic mode of production are indicative of this alternative perspective. These developments planted the seeds for the future development of the field.

World history like most academic disciplines stagnated during the Cultural Revolution. However, Chapter 5 argues that, with Mao's death, world-historical studies witnessed a new wave of professionalization within the Marxist ideological framework. Following the liberalization of historical studies in the late 1980s, this ideological framework collapsed – even historians who were famous for their ideological correctness like Lin Zhichun abandoned it. In a series of influential debates, these historians searched for alternative paths to global modernity to replace the Eurocentric schema in Marxist historiography. Through this process, these former Marxist historians became increasingly nationalistic, which, as I explain in Chapter 5, filled an ideological vacuum in post-Mao China.

Finally, in the Conclusion, I summarize the emergence of nationalism among Chinese world historians in the late twentieth century. However, it makes a case for the significance of the work of decades of Chinese scholarship in world history and reaffirms Chinese scholarship's contributions to contemporary historical debates. I conclude that the most important legacy of this scholarship is its profound and multifaceted critique of Eurocentrism and its vigorous pursuit of alternative visions of world history. I also criticize the gender imbalance in the field as, still today, most "renowned" scholars in world-historical studies in China continue to be male scholars. The lack of a prominent voice from female scholars is still a challenge that the field has to confront in the twenty-first century. Thus, the Chinese study of world history is an important contribution to global historiography, nationalism studies, and the intellectual history of twentieth-century China. It is a mixed legacy likely to shape how we understand China's place in the world for the foreseeable future.

1 The Confucian Legacy
World-Historical Writing at the Turn of the Twentieth Century

In 1878, Naser al-Din Shah (1831–1896), the Persian king, was visiting Europe for the second time. Having enjoyed a glamorous first visit a few years earlier, he was invited to a British Royal Navy fleet review. Reading British news reports on the visit, Guo Songtao (1818–1891) felt uneasy. As one of the first generation of Chinese ambassadors to the West, Guo had resided in London for a little more than two years and gained a vague sense of solidarity with countries in the colonial and semicolonial world.[1] The news reports he had come across appeared to brush aside the significance of the visit – the West called countries with good political and cultural systems "civilized," he noted in his diary. Like Turkey and Persia, China was not placed among "civilized" countries but rather considered "half-civilized." What did this mean? Guo continued to reflect on this: To be "half-civilized" was akin to being "half-barbarian," and "barbarian" was the status China had ascribed to its neighboring peoples, the Yi and Di, in ancient times. Since the Han dynasty, China's culture had been in gradual decline, while Europe's was on the rise. Now the West treated China the same way in which ancient China had treated its barbarians. Alas, few scholar-officials actually knew about this, lamented Guo.[2]

Guo did not write diaries just for self-reflection. The newly formed Chinese foreign policy apparatus, the Zongli Yamen, required that Chinese diplomats who visited the West kept diaries as a way to gather information about the outside world.[3] In this case, Guo wanted to explain to his readers China's decline. As most of the readership would be the

---

[1] For recent work on Guo Songtao's visit to the West, see Jenny Huangfu Day, *Qing Travelers to the Far West: Diplomacy and the Information Order* (Cambridge: Cambridge University Press, 2018), especially chapter 4.

[2] Guo Songtao, *Guo Songtao riji* [The dairies of Guo Songtao] (Changsha: Hunan renmin chubanshe, 1980), 439. Similarly, in Meiji Japan, the thinker Fukuzawa Yukichi also wrote extensively on the subject and called the divide between "civilized," "half-civilized," and "barbarian" peoples a "common view" of the world. Fukuzawa Yukichi, *Bunmeiron no gairyaku* [An outline of a theory of civilization] (Tokyo, Meiji 8 [1875]), 1:21a–22a.

[3] Day, *Qing Travelers to the Far West*, 133–134.

educated elite, he resorted to what they were most familiar with – Confucian ideas, especially the cosmological-moral concept of *dao*. Guo believed that the *dao* was the ultimate principle of human society and civility. He explained that possessing the *dao* was the reason that China was able to overawe the barbarians (who lacked the *dao*) in the Three Dynasties. China had lost the *dao* during the Qin–Han transition, and thus lost its advantage over the barbarians. During the nineteenth century, as China was dealing with the West, it seemed that the West, with the *dao*, had been attacking China, which was without the *dao*. As a result, China's situation had become extremely perilous.[4]

Guo Songtao's reflection is illuminating, as it underscores the role of neo-Confucianism in shaping world-historical consciousness among Chinese scholar-officials in late Qing society. Prior to the Opium War (1839–1842), the Manchu Qing court, as scholars point out, monopolized information from the frontier regions. Thus, Han scholar-officials were unable to obtain access to information so as to establish a panoramic view of the globalized world. This situation slowly changed. Some scholar-officials in Guo's generation had come to the realization that the outside world was a unified entity.[5] Yet, less familiar with globally circulated concepts such as the nation, progress, and imperialism, they were still struggling with China's place within the wider world and insisted on applying neo-Confucian concepts and classical references to the world beyond China.[6] Their attempt to "internalize" the world laid the foundations for world-historical studies. For better or worse, world-historical writing in China since its incipience has maintained some distinctive, indigenous characteristics.

In this book about world history in China, I discuss the origins of world-historical studies in this opening chapter and argue that the late Qing era was a critical moment. During this period, a dynamic exchange of various intellectual streams took place in China. From the transformation of the indigenous intellectual tradition to the spread of exogenous "Western learning," the combined forces gave rise to a new genre in Chinese historiography, world-historical writings. I not only stress the continuity in Chinese historiography in this so-called modern transformation but also acknowledge the external sources of knowledge that came not just from Meiji Japan, Western Europe, and North America but also from non-Western countries such

---

[4] Guo, *Guo Songtao riji*, 548.

[5] Mo Matthew Mosca, *From Frontier Policy to Foreign Policy: The Question of India and the Transformation of Geopolitics in Qing China* (Stanford: Stanford University Press, 2013), 3, 13.

[6] For additional evidence, see Day, *Qing Travelers to the Far West*, 205–208.

as the Philippines, Turkey, and India.[7] By probing into the panoramic world of thought at the turn of the century, it is possible to uncover the path through which world-historical writings gradually emerged. Early world-historical writers, on the one hand, wrote in a language familiar to their neo-Confucian audiences, using concepts such as the *dao* and adopting formats of traditional historiography; on the other hand, they embraced a global view with an attempt to rethink Chinese identity both within world space and through historical time. Of the many fascinating works of the time, I have chosen to focus on Zhou Weihan's *An Outline of Western History*. This lesser-known text is significant because it may well be the first Chinese-language book on ancient world history written by a Chinese scholar. To place its production and circulation within the context of the rise of print capitalism across the regional network of the Yangzi Delta area at the opening of the twentieth century, we have discovered a group of Changzhou-based gentry scholars who embraced global progress and scientific knowledge without abandoning Confucian identity. Thanks to their belief in humanism, they developed a view of the world that transcended cultural difference and formed a holistic understanding of world history. In order to examine this process, let us first take a brief look at the "world-historical" elements in Chinese historiography prior to the late Qing.

History provides an important resource for people to make sense of the world in which they live. Along with other major civilizations, China has an extraordinarily rich tradition of history writing. Over the course of more than two millennia, Chinese historians have produced a great number of historical works in various historiographical formats.[8] To name just a few, official dynastic histories (*zhengshi*), general histories (*tongshi*), alternative histories (*bieshi*), chronicles (*biannian*), historical commentaries (*shiping*), historical narratives (*jishi benmo*), and case studies (*xue'an*) were all common historiographical genres that historians in China adopted to record history. In doing so, contemporaneous Chinese created, preserved, and

---

[7] The rise of the histories of falling nations was an example of this. See Rebecca Karl, *Staging the World: Chinese Nationalism at the Turn of the Twentieth Century* (Durham, NC: Duke University Press, 2002); Mosca, *From Frontier Policy to Foreign Policy*.
[8] The Chinese term *shixue* (historiography) first appeared in AD 319 during the Five Dynasties and Ten Kingdoms period. However, the actual writing of history began much earlier. Jin Yufu, *Zhongguo shixueshi* [History of Chinese historiography] (Shanghai: Shangwu yinshu guan, 1957), 218. Recent scholarship points to the connection between Chinese historiography and early historical documents such as *Zuozhuan* and *Guoyu*. See David Schaberg, *A Patterned Past: Form and Thought in Early Chinese Historiography* (Cambridge, MA: Harvard University Asia Center, 2001).

constantly reconfigured the image of the past to serve the needs of particular times.

The study of China in antiquity, especially the era of the Three Dynasties (or *sandai* in Chinese), was essential in shaping Chinese intellectuals' perceptions of the world and political consciousness prior to the twentieth century; to some extent, this continues even today.[9] The Three Dynasties refers to the purported initial era of Chinese history, including the legendary Xia, the Shang (from roughly the sixteenth to the eleventh century BC), and the Zhou (from the eleventh to the third century BC). It was during this early time, many scholars believe, that certain essential characteristics of Chinese civilization, such as Confucianism, Legalism, and Daoism, emerged.[10] Beginning in the Han dynasty (206 BC to AD 220), Chinese Confucian scholars invested a great deal of effort in studying this period. By preserving, elaborating on, or inventing ancient texts, major portions of which were believed to have been created during the Three Dynasties, they created "a literary double of the actual world," wherein "a text-based kingship that originated in the absence of a true king, paralleled the real world as a critique, and ultimately became the basis of legislation when a true sage ruled once again, that is, with the rise of the Han dynasty."[11] In other words, the writing of the ancient past was not merely an intellectual practice; it was also a way for Confucian scholars to participate in contemporaneous politics.[12]

The perception of the ancient past continuously exerted its influence along with the evolution of Confucian thought. In the subsequent millennium after its invention, the rise of neo-Confucianism was one of its many major changes. However, the political nature of interpreting the past remained an essential component of Chinese intellectuals' conception of history. Neo-Confucianism (also called the school of "Song learning") was primarily based on a synthesis of Confucianism, Buddhism, and Daoism, three schools that had coexisted and flourished in traditional China. Song scholars such as Zhu Xi (1130–1200) and the Cheng brothers (Cheng Yi, 1033–1107, and Cheng Hao, 1032–1085) transformed

---

[9] For instance, under the state sponsorship the famous Xia–Shang–Zhou Chronology Project mobilized more than 200 scholars from 1996 to 2000 to investigate the early development of Chinese society during the Three Dynasties. See Li Xueqin, "The Xia-Shang-Zhou Chronology Project: Methodology and Results," *Journal of East Asian Archaeology* 4, no. 1 (2002): 321–333.

[10] For example, Benjamin Schwartz, *The World of Thought in Ancient China* (Cambridge, MA: Harvard University Press, 1989).

[11] Mark Edward Lewis, *Writing and Authority in Early China* (Albany: State University of New York Press, 1999), 7.

[12] Lewis, *Writing and Authority in Early China*, 7, 363; for a recent survey of scholarship on the issue, see Vincent S. Leung, *The Politics of the Past in Early China* (Cambridge: Cambridge University Press, 2019), 3–17.

Confucian doctrines in some philosophical respects. They argued that certain ontological entities, such as *xin* (mind), *li* (principles or reason), and *qi* (gas or energy flow), played an essential role in the formation of the physical and moral world. They not only clung to "the doctrines on human morality, human nature, and the cosmos developed from that foundation" but also participated in the "social activities that linked adherents of these views together and allowed them to put their ideas into practice."[13] From the early Ming to the late Qing era, this neo-Confucian thinking remained highly influential in Chinese society.

Taking a synthetic approach to understanding the world, neo-Confucians emphasized the value of the ancient past. They adopted the concept of the *dao* as a universal principle in politics and, revolving around this, developed a cyclical view of the past.[14] An imagining of the Three Dynasties as a golden age was the historiographical foundation of this conception of history. Instead of periodization by dynasties, they divided historical time into three long eras. First was antiquity, when the early sage-kings of the Three Dynasties put the *dao* into practice in governance and propagated correct learning. Second was the period when the Way was lost during the eras of Han through Tang. It was neither practiced in government nor understood by scholars. Song-period neo-Confucian scholars argued that their contemporary age was the third stage. Although not yet practiced in governance, Song Confucian scholars' efforts had made the *dao* manifest once again.[15] Neo-Confucianism remained influential among Chinese intellectuals in late imperial China as well as in Vietnam, Korea, and Japan. Although the Manchu conquest temporarily repressed neo-Confucian thinking and drove scholars to focus more on textual criticism in their research, there was a particularly reinvigorated interest in neo-Confucian ideas among Chinese scholar-officials after the Taiping Rebellion (1850–1864).[16]

Once proud of being a central power in East Asia, late Qing scholar-officials witnessed China's abrupt decline by the late nineteenth century. Western powers "opened up" the Middle Kingdom through a series of military conflicts and diplomatic arrangements and gradually placed the country within a system that was dominated by global capitalism, colonialism, and imperialism. Knowledge is power. Western imperialists worked with ethnographers, Orientalists, as well as historians to promote the discourse of civilization to ideologically justify their atrocious

---

[13] Peter Bol, *Neo-Confucianism in History* (Cambridge, MA: Harvard University Press, 2010), 78.

[14] For the origins of the term, see Leung, *The Politics of the Past in Early China*, 82–87.

[15] Bol, *Neo-Confucianism in History*, 101–102.

[16] This is evidenced in Guo Songtao's reference to the *dao* introduced earlier in this chapter.

behaviors. They divided the world according to the civilized, half-civilized, and non-civilized and refused to treat those "non-civilized" or "half-civilized" peoples on equal footings within international society. Chinese scholar-officials such as Guo Songtao were stunned by the realization that the West now despised China and considered it a land of barbarism. It therefore became an urgent intellectual challenge to make sense of China's decline in the globalized world.

Some blamed China's decline on its isolation from and ignorance of the outside world. Chinese isolationism may well be an overgeneralized argument, as even the most well-known cases – such as the one in which the Qianlong Emperor (r. 1735–1796) boasted about China's self-sufficiency in his letters to the British king George III – need careful reexamination.[17] China was never fully isolated in world history. From the early phases of Chinese civilization, there was clear evidence that China was already in constant contact with other parts of the world, including but not limited to Inner Eurasia, South Asia, Mesopotamia, and the Mediterranean.[18] Chinese historians also knew about the geography and histories of foreign lands. They wrote about these subjects in sections on border regions, foreign lands, and foreigners in most of the standard histories and in some local gazetteers. Yet their narratives were, by and large, fragmented and even atomized.[19] Confucianism was not necessarily the primary cause of the lack of synthesis, either. In terms of the Qing dynasty, for instance, the Manchu court's regulation of the information flow from border areas blocked Confucian scholar-officials from receiving sufficient information about the outside world.[20] As

---

[17] For instance, Joanna Waley-Cohen challenges the assumption that Qianlong was not interested in foreign technology and held strong opinions of Chinese isolationism. Instead, she argued for internal reasons that pressured Qianlong to make such a performance. Waley-Cohen, "China and Western Technology in the Late 18th Century," *American Historical Review* 98, no. 5 (1993): 1525–1544.

[18] For a comprehensive history of China's interaction with the wider world, see, for instance, Joanna Waley-Cohen, *The Sextants of Beijing: Global Currents in Chinese History* (New York: W. W. Norton, 1999). For recent work on China's interactions with South Asia, Central Eurasia, and Southeast Asia, see a very select list: Tansen Sen, *India, China and the World: A Connected History* (London: Rowman & Littlefield, 2017); Peter Perdue, *China Marches West: The Qing Conquest of Central Eurasia* (Cambridge, MA: Belknap Press, 2010); Bin Yang, *Between Winds and Clouds: The Making of Yunnan (Second Century BCE to Twentieth Century CE)* (New York: Columbia University Press, 2008); Erica Fox Brindley, *Ancient China and the Yue: Perceptions and Identities on the Southern Frontier, c. 400 BCE–50 CE* (Cambridge: Cambridge University Press, 2015).

[19] For the lack of synthesis in traditional Chinese writings on India, see Mosca, *From Frontier Policy to Foreign Policy*, esp. chapter 1.

[20] Merchants, sailors, and sojourners often brought back knowledge about the outside world to the country. Yet the critical issue was how to propagate that knowledge into the information networks that were accessible to political elites and scholar-officials. Mosca, *From Frontier Policy to Foreign Policy*, 3, 15.

a result, prior to the nineteenth century, little effort was made by historians in China to devote *primary* attention to synthesizing historical events beyond the scope of traditionally Chinese-controlled areas.

The control of information on the borderlands and foreign countries among scholar-officials was gradually lifted in the wake of the Opium War. As an increasing number of Qing diplomats traveled the world, their travelogues became available to the public, which provided more information for the educated elite to rethink China's position in the world. From learning about geography, some pioneers started to study world history and to investigate the roots of this country's decline through the lens of world history.[21]

The process started with translation work.[22] Buddhist monks, Muslim advisors, and Jesuit missionaries had already introduced non-Chinese knowledge about history, geography, religion, and philosophy into the Middle Kingdom prior to the nineteenth century.[23] After the Opium War, Protestant missionaries were increasingly becoming the leading force of this cultural exchange. In order to contextualize Christian theology, Protestant missionaries such as Robert Morrison (1782–1834) and William Milne (1785–1822) first started to translate some world-historical texts and published them in Southeast Asia. These translations gradually reached the elites in coastal China. These missionaries often collaborated with Chinese scholars. For example, in 1838, in Singapore, the American missionary E. C. Bridgman (1801–1861) published the first book about American history written in Chinese, *Meilige heshengguo zhilue* (*Brief Geographical History of the United States of America*). Several revised versions of this book soon appeared in Hong Kong, Canton, and Shanghai.[24] Later in the century, W. A. P. Martin (known as Ding Weiliang in Chinese, 1827–1916) was hired by the Chinese government and translated a series of books introducing foreign histories, ranging from ancient Greece and Rome to discussions of contemporary international legal systems. Meanwhile, the early Jesuit translations of the

---

[21] This global space as a unified entity shall be distinguished from the fragmented and even "atomized" frontier regions, each of which the Qing state chose to individually and separately deal with. Mosca, *From Frontier Policy to Foreign Policy*, 10–11.

[22] Day, *Qing Travelers to the Far West*.

[23] Historian Ge Zhaoguang offered an excellent essay-long summary on this in a keynote delivered at a conference on "Conceptions of the World in Twentieth-Century Chinese Historiography" that I organized at the University of Göttingen on October 26, 2017. Ge Zhaoguang, "The Evolution of a World Consciousness in Traditional Chinese Historiography," *Global Intellectual History* (2020), https://doi.org/10.1080/23801883 .2020.1738651 (accessed June 1, 2020).

[24] Michael Lazich, "Placing China in Its 'Proper Rank among the Nations': The Society for the Diffusion of Useful Knowledge in China and the First Systematic Account of the United States in Chinese." *Journal of World History* 22, no. 3 (2011): 540.

European texts were still in circulation and maintained a steady influence on later world-historical writing all the way to the late nineteenth and early twentieth centuries. By the end of the nineteenth century, these missionary works had laid the groundwork for the rise of world-historical studies in China. In contrast to Confucian scholars' emphasis on temporality, these sources outline a landscape of world space for the educated elite. The challenge remained how to relate ancient history from the West, such as the period of Greek and Roman antiquity, to the Chinese.[25]

In addition to missionary translations, some Chinese intellectuals and scholar-officials had also translated world history–related knowledge into Chinese. Among these projects, the most famous – and probably also the most influential – was Wei Yuan's *Haiguo tuzhi* (*Illustrated Treaties on the Maritime Kingdoms*) (1794–1857). This project was part of Chinese scholar-officials' response to the First Opium War. Based on existing missionary sources and some new Chinese translations, this project eventually produced 100 volumes of gazettes on world geography. Divided by regions and countries as well as by thematic topics, a lot of its content touches on the issue of world history. A synthesized view of world geography started to emerge among scholar-officials.[26]

The demand for world-historical knowledge continued to grow. At the end of the nineteenth century, China acquired another major source for world history – Japan. After 1895, increasing numbers of Japanese works appeared in China, many of which still had a majority of their content written in classical Chinese. Thanks to this linguistic affinity, the Japanese works on world history became a major source for the future development of world-historical studies in China, especially regarding history textbooks.[27] Out of many translated works from Japan, for instance, the twenty-volume *The Record of World History* (*Wanguo shiji*) compiled and published by the Japanese scholar Okamoto Kansuke (1839–1904, *Gangben Jianfu* in Chinese pronunciation) was in wide circulation and heavily influenced early Chinese works on world history.[28] Late Qing Chinese writers often copied and pasted Japanese sources in producing their own world history texts, as Wang Tao (1828–1897) did in his well-known book on French history. Until the early twentieth century, the scholar-official Wang Shunan (1851–1936) still followed Okamoto's translations of people and place names in his book *Xila chunqiu* (*Annals*

[25] Mosca, *From Frontier Policy to Foreign Policy*, 215–216.

[26] Mosca, *From Frontier Policy to Foreign Policy*, 272; Day, *Qing Travelers to the Far West*, 15.

[27] Douglas Reynolds, *China, 1898–1912: The Xinzheng Revolution and Japan* (Cambridge, MA: Council on East Asian Studies, Harvard University, 1993), 112–121.

[28] Okamoto Kansuke (Gangben Jiangfu), *Wanguo shiji* [The record of world history] (n.p.: Huaguo tang, 1900).

of Greece).[29] More importantly, these Japanese works introduced crucial concepts, such as the nation, civilization, and progress, as well as their makeshift Chinese translations that would frame later Chinese works on world history. As one can see, influenced by Meiji intellectuals such as Fukuzawa Yukichi and Katō Hiroyuki (1836–1916), the public intellectual and journalist Liang Qichao promoted concepts such as civilization and progress at the turn of the century, and in China history textbook writers such as Liu Yizheng and Xia Zengyou had already accepted a progressive view of history.[30] As such, multiple streams of knowledge flow nurtured a flourishing publishing market in world history in late Qing China. Between 1822 and 1900, an estimated total of eighty-nine translations of Western history books alone had appeared in the Chinese language.[31]

The rise of world history in the late nineteenth century not only reflects the dynamics of China's intellectual movement but also took place in a changing social and political environment. A nationwide educational system was not established in the nineteenth century. The system in place was largely decentralized and community-based, and its curricula were heavily focused on the Confucian Classics. The continued decline of China's position in international politics forced some scholar-officials to realize that China's educational system might need a fundamental change. In the wake of the Boxer Uprising, the Chinese public openly debated education in newly established newspapers and journals. Some of these were entirely devoted to education, such as *Jiaoyu shijie* (*Educational World*) and *Jiaoyu zazhi* (*Educational Review*). A demand to establish a national curriculum for popular education emerged out of these debates.[32]

Despite the fact that the nationwide change took place slowly, in some local areas, especially the treaty ports, new school curricula started to replace outdated ones. The new curricula included components on the sciences, technology, and foreign languages and histories. As a process,

[29] Wang Shunan, "Preface," in *Xila chunqiu* [Annals of Greece] in *Taolu congke* [Taolu serial] (Series No. 24) (Lanzhou; 1905).

[30] Prasenjit Duara, "The Discourse of Civilization and Pan-Asianism," *Journal of World History* 12, no. 1 (2001): 109; Peter Zarrow, *Educating China: Knowledge, Society, and Textbooks in a Modernizing World, 1902–1937* (Cambridge: Cambridge University Press, 2015), 23–24; on Zhou Weihan, see the discussion later in this chapter.

[31] Zou Zhenhuan, *Xifang chuanjiaoshi yu wan-Qing Xishi dongjian: yi 1815 zhi 1900 xifang lishi yizhu de chuanbo yu yingxiang wei zhongxin* [Western missionaries and the eastward spread of Western histories: Focusing on the spread and influence of translated Western histories from 1815 to 1900] (Shanghai: Shanghai guji chubanshe, 2007), 312.

[32] Paul John Bailey, *Reform the People: Changing Attitudes towards Popular Education in Early Twentieth-Century China* (Vancouver: University of British Columbia Press, 1990), 64–65, 83; Zarrow, *Educating China*, 11–12.

foreign history and geography courses first appeared in government-sponsored secondary school curricula in the late nineteenth century. An increasing number of new-style schools, many of which were founded by Western missionaries, began to include foreign history courses as part of the curriculum. In Shanghai, for instance, courses such as "Greek History," "Roman History," and "Probing the Origins of Ancient History" (*Gushi tanyuan*) were listed in some local school catalogs.[33]

The following New Policies reforms furthered this development. From 1902 to 1904, the Qing government called for a national discussion on educational reforms and eventually approved a new set of education standards often known as the "Gui-Mao School System." (The system was designed primarily in 1903 – the year of Gui-Mao in the traditional Chinese calendar.) The system consisted of twenty-two regulations. It reduced the study load for the Confucian Classics, though the latter still occupied a significant part of the curricula. World history (known as "foreign history") was included as a required course in the newly established national curricula for middle school students.[34] Since then, at least on paper, the teaching of world history has remained an important component of China's secondary and higher education systems (despite some ups and downs such as in the radical years of the Cultural Revolution).[35] The inclusion of world history in the new education system boosted a demand for world history textbooks. The previous world history–related books could not satisfy the educational need for world history textbooks, as most of them were either translations or of poor quality. Thus, Chinese world history writers at the turn of the twentieth century targeted this niche in the book market.

At the same time, one has to be careful to evaluate the impact of the state initiative. Indeed, under the Gui-Mao system, the Board of Education was created in 1904 to supervise educational affairs at the state level. This would have been a new state apparatus. Yet state regulations in many cases merely registered popular enthusiasm. In China's education reform, the local gentry elite by and large took the lead.[36]

[33] Chen Dezheng, "Wan-Qing waiguo lishi kecheng yu jiaokeshu lunshu" [A comprehensive survey of foreign history curricula and textbooks in late Qing]. *Lishi jiaoxue* [History pedagogy], 549, no. 8 (2008): 97.

[34] Chen, "Waiguo lishi kecheng," 98; Robert J. Culp, *Articulating Citizenship: Civic Education and Student Politics in Southern China, 1921–1940* (Cambridge, MA: Harvard University Asia Center, 2007), 29.

[35] Please refer to the chart found in Zhang Tianming and Zhou Shengming, "20 shiji shangbanqi woguo zhongxue shijieshi jiaoyu de zongti tedian ji xianshi qishi" [The general features and real inspiration of our country's world-historical education in middle schools in the early half of the twentieth century]. *Nei Menggu shifan daxue xuebao* [Journal of Inner Mongolia Normal University (Education science edition)] 32, no. 2 (2010): 96–97.

[36] Bailey, *Reform the People*, 98.

During the last decade of the dynasty, they established thousands of educational venues to promote popular education. These included lecture halls, newspaper reading rooms, half-day schools, and literacy schools as well as vocational schools. For one category alone, by 1909, 941 half-day schools had been established in China with a student body reaching 24,699.[37] While a rising percentage of the Chinese population had access to literacy, the demand for knowledge of world history became even greater.

The rise of world history, to a certain degree, was a response to the rising demand for educational reform and the associated emergence of a popular readership. In contrast to earlier world-historical works that were more or less supplementary to the introduction of world geography knowledge, world-historical writers were now seriously discussing temporal dimensions within world space. This gave birth to some very interesting experiments through which Chinese gentry scholars strove to place China within both historical time and world space.[38]

The rise of world history in China also has to be understood in the context of the transformation of scholarly networks. Intellectuals rarely work alone; owing to the nature of their work, they often need to communicate with each another. Through this process, they form various organizations such as scholarly societies and academic professions. In early modern societies in Europe and North America, the "Republic of Letters" offered a cultural, social, and political network. Intellectuals relied on it to interact with each other, exchange opinions, form groups, and disseminate knowledge. In China, similar intellectual networks also existed over the course of the same period, though often heavily based on a shared local identity. During the twentieth century, a key change took place in the structure of these intellectual networks, that is, these intellectual networks began to move away from regional affiliations toward associations that were based more on shared ideas and ideologies or professional practices.[39] At the turn of the twentieth century, various intellectual groups competed for influence over

---

[37] Bailey, *Reform the People*, 98–122, esp. 104.

[38] Scholars have been writing about Chinese intellectuals' engagement with the spatial dimension. Examples include Tang Xiaobing's stimulating discussion on Liang Qichao as well as Rebecca Karl's works on some less-known Shanghai writers. Their works are a tremendous help in understanding how elite intellectuals and popular writers imagined China's position in the contemporary world that was dominated by global colonialism and imperialism. Xiaobing Tang, *Global Space and the Nationalist Discourse of Modernity: The Historical Thinking of Liang Qichao* (Stanford: Stanford University Press, 1996); Karl, *Staging the World*.

[39] Zhang Qing, "Hu Shi pai xuerenqun yu xiandai Zhongguo ziyou zhuyi" [The Hu Shi group of intellectuals and the trend of liberalism in modern China], *Shilin* [Historical Review] no. 1 (1998): 36–49; Xiaoqun Xu, *Chinese Professionals and the Republican State:*

Chinese politics and society, and they played a significant role in the rise of world history in China.

Among scholars with a growing interest in world-historical knowledge, there has been much research on the reformist group headed by Kang Youwei (1858–1927), who hailed from the south. This neo-Confucian scholar used to teach in Guangzhou where a number of his students would later emerge to become his associates in the 1898 reform. Coming from a special lineage of the Chinese classical tradition, Kang was able to critically examine and creatively reinterpret the Confucian Classics to support his reform agenda. He argued for three stages of social development: "decay and chaos" (*juluan*), "rising peace" (*shengping*), and "universal peace" (*datong*), and he believed that the realization of the final stage should be based on a continuous and gradual human effort.[40] As universal peace could only be achieved in a globalized world, there was no reason for his followers to reject new ideas from other countries. In order to better understand this "world," the reformist group turned to history.[41] Still working within the realms of Confucianism, they developed an alternative to the Western view of nationalism (national autonomy and ethnocentrism) and grasped human affairs as a world-historical synthesis.[42] This group included Kang's outstanding disciple and famous public intellectual Liang Qichao. Like his teacher, Liang also wrote on ancient Greece and published various essays between 1898 and 1903. He believed that ancient Greece was the foundation of Western civilization. Without studying it, one could not fully understand "European superiority and the Chinese deficiency" in contemporary times.[43]

Scholars from the north tended to be more conservative in their political stance, perhaps partially due to their proximity to the capital and their governmental affiliations.[44] Yet some of these scholar-officials were also actively promoting knowledge about world history, and they were doing so through government-sponsored programs. For instance, Wu Rulun

The Rise of Professional Associations in Shanghai, 1912–1937 (Cambridge: Cambridge University Press, 2001).

[40] Hao Chang, *Chinese Intellectuals in Crisis: Search for Order and Meaning (1890–1911)* (Berkley: University of California Press, 1987), 50–54.

[41] Wang Yue, "Jindai Zhongguo de zhishi fenzi, weishenme xihuan taolun Xila Luoma" [Why did intellectuals in modern China like discussing ancient Greece and Rome], *Pengpai xinwen* (The Paper), www.thepaper.cn/baidu.jsp?contid=1313047 (accessed January 7, 2018).

[42] Wang Hui, "From Empire to State: Kang Youwei, Confucian Universalism, and Unity," in *Chinese Visions of World Order*, ed. Wang, 56.

[43] Zhou, "Greek Antiquity, Chinese Modernity, and the Changing World Order," 109.

[44] There has been limited scholarship on these scholars. I am especially grateful to Don Price who allowed me to read his unpublished conference papers on Wang Shunan, an overlooked but important figure in the history of world-historical writing in China.

(aka Zhifu, 1840–1903), who hailed from Tongcheng where the Tongcheng School of literature had flourished, was one of the forerunners of China's educational reform. He was closely associated with prominent Han mandarins such as Zeng Guofan and Li Hongzhang, who rose to power after the Taiping Rebellion. Open to new ideas of education, Wu established several academies in the Hebei area such as the famous Lianchi Academy and Jizhou Academy. At these schools, he hired teachers to promote "new" knowledge.[45] One of his protégés was Wang Shunan (1852–1936). Wang published several books on world history in the early years of the twentieth century. Their subjects ranged from the histories of modern Europe and Russia to the history and philosophy of ancient Greece.[46] The Northern group was part of the confluence of intellectual streams contributing to the rise of world-historical studies, though often overlooked by scholars today.

Like these two groups, scholars from the Yangzi Delta area, especially the Changzhou region, also contributed to the rise of world history in China. Changzhou was a provincial town located on the south bank of the Yangzi River, now overshadowed by neighboring cities like Shanghai, Suzhou, and Nanjing. In the past, it had long been a major site of intellectual activity and where the Changzhou School originated.[47] This school of thought, also called the New Text School in contrast to the Old Text School, was an important branch of the hermeneutical tradition of Confucian Classical Studies. Over the course of the entire nineteenth century, Changzhou took pride in the quality of its intellectual life and the high standard of its local education. As a result, Changzhou had produced the second largest group of *jinshi* degree holders in Jiangsu, after Suzhou, during the Ming–Qing period.[48] At the same time, Changzhou also boasted a fine artistic and cultural milieu. During the Qing dynasty alone, 158 painters came from this region, many of whom were from the Yun family. The patriarch Yun Shouping (1633–1690) was regarded as the founder of the Changzhou School of Painting. The family produced more than fifty painters in later generations, including dozens of female painters. Aside from art and culture, Changzhou witnessed the rise

---

[45] Wang Shunan, *Taolu laoren suinian lu* [Yearly record of the old man under the Tao Hut], in *Jindai shiliao biji congkan* [Series on modern historical materials collections: Miscellaneous notes] (Beijing: Zhonghua shuju, 2007), 25.

[46] For a discussion on Wang Shunan's works on Western history, see Don Price, "A Foreign Affairs Expert's View of Western History: Wang Shu-Nan 王樹枏," paper prepared for delivery at the Twentieth-Ninth International Congress of Orientalists, Paris, July 16–22, 1973. (Unpublished paper.)

[47] Benjamin Elman, *Classicism, Politics, and Kinship: The Ch'ang-chou School of New Text Confucianism in Late Imperial China* (Berkeley: University of California Press, 1990).

[48] Elman, *Classicism, Politics, and Kinship*, 96.

of medical practice in the late Qing period, especially practice centered in Menghe County. In 1880, Empress Dowager Cixi summoned Menghe physician Ma Peizhi (1820–1905) for a diagnosis. During his nine-month sojourn in Beijing, he cured many high officials of complex diseases. The Menghe physicians thereafter achieved national fame. Later, Ma's discipline, Deng Xingbo (1862–?), was also called by the Qing regent Zaifeng to visit Beijing to provide a diagnosis; and the heirs of Menghe's practitioners became key players in creating the institutional framework for contemporary Chinese medicine.[49]

As Changzhou scholars, painters, and doctors rose to national fame, they quickly gained a cultural and political sensitivity. They became the first to feel the impact of China's decline and were keen to learn about the outside world. Shortly after the Qing's defeat in the First Sino-Japanese War, Zhang Heling (1867–1908) and Tu Ji (1856–1921) returned to Changzhou and started to promote Western knowledge.

Originally from Changzhou, both Zhang and Tu succeeded in the imperial exams in 1892, the same year as the famous education reformer Cai Yuanpei (1868–1940) and the calligrapher Yun Yujia (1857–1919). Zhang achieved second place in the second level of the palace exam in this crowded talent pool. In the winter of 1901, he became the chief instructor of the Imperial University of Peking. One of the earliest new-style schools in China, after 1912 it was known as Peking University or Beijing University (colloquially known as "Beida"). As a scholar, Zhang was famous for his classical-style prose and poetry, and some considered him to have been a leading scholar of a literature-style group during this time in China.[50] Tu followed a different direction on the scholarly path. After the exam, he worked in several governmental posts primarily in charge of national survey projects in Manchuria. After the 1911 Revolution, he focused on the history of "Chinese frontiers" and published a fifty-volume history of Mongolia. His scholarship would have a great impact on later historian Lü Simian (1884–1957), another Changzhou native. As painting and calligraphy were often considered an integrated artistic practice in China, Yun Yujia was considered to be continuing the development of this tradition. After the 1911 Revolution, Yun Yujia moved to Shanghai and interacted with Wang Xun and Wu

---

[49] Dong Honggen, Zhai Huaiqiang, and Wang Yanping, "Menghe yipai de xueshu puxi ji yongyao guilü chutan" [A preliminary study of the intellectual genealogy of the Menghe School of Medicine and the common principles of their medical practice], *Guoji Zhongyi Zhongyao zazhi* [International Journal of Chinese Medicine] 34, no. 6 (June 2012): 481; the most comprehensive study of Menghe physicians is Volker Scheid's *Currents of Tradition in Chinese Medicine, 1626–2006* (Seattle: Eastland Press, 2007).

[50] Timothy Weston, *The Power of Position: Beijing University, Intellectuals, and Chinese Political Culture, 1898–1929* (Berkeley: University of California Press, 2004), 50.

Changshuo (1844–1927), some of the most famous painters of the twentieth century.[51]

As various lineages, networks, and traditions were being reshuffled in the late Qing period, Zhou Weihan (aka Zhou Xueqiao), an obscure Changzhou native, was surprisingly at the center of all these connections.[52]

Zhou Weihan was born in the Changzhou area in 1870 (see Figure 1).[53] His family ran a local business. Though they were well off, Zhou's father was probably not well educated.[54] Weihan was a particularly bright child. At the age of fifteen, he was determined to devote his life to transmitting the learnings of Confucius. Yet he only achieved mediocre success as a scholar when he grew up. He passed the local exam and was registered as a tributary scholar (*lin gongsheng*). This title would have allowed him to have the opportunity to sit the metropolitan exam, but he never excelled in the advanced levels of the imperial examination and thus did not go on to earn recognition as a scholar among later generations.[55]

Compared to his undistinguished scholarly life, Zhou's accomplishments in medical practice were more impressive.[56] We are not sure whether Menghe physicians had any influence on Zhou, but he practiced

---

[51] Zhou Rongjia and Ding Jie, *Tianxia mingshi you buluo: Changzhou renwu yu wenhua qunti* [The prestigious have their own community: Changzhou people and their cultural community] (Hong Kong: Sanlian shudian, 2013), 20–21.

[52] The best research on Zhou Weihan so far is Ye Zhou, "Rongzhu zhongwai: Zhou Weihan yu *Yixue bao*" [Bridging China and the West: Zhou Weihan and the *Yixue bao* (Journal of medical sciences)], *Difang wenhua yanjiu* [Studies on local cultures] 34, no. 4 (2018): 93–101. As for local gazette sources, see, for example, Chen Jilong, "Changzhou jindai bufen lishi renwu minglu zhi er" [A partial list of people in the modern history of Changzhou: Part II], in *Changzhou wenshi ziliao dijiu ji* [Historical and literary sources for Changzhou], Vol. 9 (Changzhou: Changzhou wenshi ziliao weiyuanhui, 1989), 223. In my private correspondences with Wen-chung Chou, Professor Chou refers to his grandfather as "Chou Xue-Qiao" instead of Weihan. This can also be founded in Wen-chung Chou's biography. Peter M. Chang, *Chou Wen-Chung: The Life and Work of a Contemporary Chinese-Born American Composer* (Lanham, MD: The Scarecrow Press, 2006), esp. 12.

[53] Most sources suggest 1870, including the information from Zhou's grandson Wen-chung Chou's personal website: https://chouwenchung.org/about/biography/ (accessed July 5, 2019); see also Chang, *Chou Wen-Chung*, 12. However, based on family genealogies, Ye contends that Zhou was born in 1864 instead. Ye Zhou, "Rongzhu zhongwai," 93. Some sources refer him as "Xueqiao." In this book, for the purpose of consistency only, I use "Weihan."

[54] Ye Zhou, "Rongzhu zhongwai," 93–94.

[55] According to Zhou's grandson, he refused to attend the palace exam as he became disappointed at the Manchu government. Yet evidence seems to be thin to support this opinion. See Chang, *Chou Wen-Chung*, 12, and my private correspondences with Chou.

[56] Yao Yanli, "Qingmo yijia Zhou Xueqiao yishi huodong jiqi Zhong-Xi yi huitong tantao" [An investigation of the late Qing medical specialist Zhou Xueqiao's medical activities and his attempt to integrate Chinese and Western medicine], *Zhongyi wenxian zazhi* [Journal for documentation of Chinese medicine], no. 2 (2011): 46.

Figure 1 Zhou Weihan (aka Xueqiao). Photo Source: *Xishi gangmu*, cover page.

in Suzhou for "many years."[57] At the turn of the twentieth century, he moved to Shanghai where he started to promote Western medicine. In 1904, he participated in a movement centered on reforming traditional Chinese medicine with Western science.[58] He organized the Chinese Medical Association and also became one of the chief editors for the *Journal of Medicine* (*Yixue bao*), a periodical issued by the association.[59] Later, he left Shanghai for a northern sojourn. He was invited to serve as

---

[57] Ye believes that Zhou resided in Suzhou in the 1890s. Ye Zhou, "Rongzhu zhongwai," 94.

[58] Ye Zhou, "Rongzhu zhongwai," 97–98; concerning Zhou Weihan's contribution to Chinese medicine, see also Yao Yanli, "Qingmo yijia Zhou Xueqiao yishi huodong jiqi Zhong-Xi yi huitong tantao," 46–48.

[59] *Yixuebao*, a biweekly, was the first Chinese-language journal of medicine. From the first issue in 1904 to its last issue in 1910, some 154 issues were published in total. The journal was in circulation in six provinces as well as in Hong Kong and Japan. Chen, "Changzhou jindai bufen lishi renwu minglu zhi er," 223.

provost at Shangxi Medical College in Datong.[60] He then accepted a teaching position at the Academy of Medicine (Yixue tang) in the capital from early 1909 to early 1910, a newly established national institution for medical education.[61] After that, he returned to Shanghai but passed away in the same year. Thanks to his pioneering works in promoting Western medicine, scholars today praise him as "one of the representative figures of the movement to combine Western and traditional Chinese medicine in the late Qing," calling him "the first one in modern methods to introduce Western medicine."[62]

In contrast to his work in medicine, Zhou's contribution to world-historical studies has long been overlooked. As I argue in this chapter, he was a forerunner in spreading knowledge of the world. In this, his connections to the matrix of intellectual networks played a crucial role. For one, Zhou was a longtime friend of Zhang Heling. After Zhang's return to Changzhou in 1896, they cofounded the Jingshi xueshe (the learned society to order the world). The group purchased recent publications on Western learning and attracted a group of local young scholars to embrace the new ideas emerging in world scholarship.[63]

By the late nineteenth century, the introduction of foreign technology, including Western-style print technology, invigorated trans-local elite networks and gave rise to a national book market. Local and trans-local publications such as the *Jingbao* (*Peking Gazette*, ca. 1730s–1912) and *Shenbao* (*Shanghai News*, 1872–1949) contributed to the rise of a public sphere where the court, foreigners, and the Chinese public negotiated their respective interests during the last decade of the century.[64] As for newspapers, the increase in publication and circulation was

---

[60] Chang, *Chou Wen-Chung*, 13.

[61] His friend Yun Yuding recorded the dates that Zhou Weihan started his work and that he announced his resignation to students in diaries. Yun Yuding, *Yun Yuding Chengzhai riji* [Yun Yuding Chenzhai dairies] (Hangzhou: Zhejiang guji chubanshe, 2004), 2:426 and 485 (February 19, 1909 and April 15, 1910); as for information regarding the Academy of Medicine, see Lu Caixia, "Qingmo Jing Jin yongyi wenti chutan" [A preliminary study of the problem of the "crooked doctors" in the Beijing and Tianjin areas in the late Qing dynasty], *Zhongguo shehui lishi pinglun* [The Chinese review of social history] 8, no. 3 (July 2007): 140.

[62] Ye Zhou, "Rongzhu zhongwai," 93. "Zhou Xueqiao shishi" [Zhou Xueqiao's obituary], *Zhongxi yixue bao* [Journal of Chinese and Western medicine] no. 8 (1910): 4; Ni Bo, Mu Weiming, and Zhang Zhiqiang (eds), *Jiangsu chuban dashiji, 77 BC to 1948* [Chronicle of major events in Jiangsu publishing, 77 BC to 1948] (Nanjing: Jiangsu renmin chubanshe, 1996), 194.

[63] Xie Yinchang, "Yancang nianshi" [Yearly history of Yancang], in *Jindai renwu nianpu jikan* [Collected series on the nianpu of modern figures] (Beijing: Guojia tushuguan chubanshe, 2012), 390; Ye Zhou, "Zhongzhu zhongwai," 95.

[64] Barbara Mittler, *A Newspaper for China? Power, Identity, and Change in Shanghai's News Media, 1872–1912* (Cambridge, MA: Harvard University Press, 2004), 39.

unprecedented in Chinese history. Overall, the number of newspapers increased from 100 in the late 1890s to 700–800 by 1911, including those that were short-lived.[65] The circulation of information through the new print media brought Chinese intellectuals into a more closely tied regional and cross-regional network of information flow.

Zhou Weihan and Zhang Heling, following the trend of the times, founded the Jingshi wenshe (the literary society to order the world) in Shanghai, with perhaps some financial support from Lu Ding (1873–1930), another offshoot of a prominent Changzhou family. Lu would later study in Japan and become known as Prince Itō Hirobumi's favorite student, and he was father to the socialite Lu Xiaoman (1903–1965) whose romantic affair with the poet Xu Zhimo (1897–1931) has become a household story in China.[66] The organization soon grew into an influential publishing house, along with the most famous ones such as the World Book Store (*Shijie shuju*) and the Commercial Press. Compared to other publishers, the Jingshi wenshe was more famous as a result of its forty-volume comprehensive collection on political essays, governmental archives, and historical documents from the years leading to the 1911 Revolution, the *Minguo jingshi wenbian* (*Collected Essays on Statecraft from the Republic of China*), published in 1914. The Jingshi wenshe was also a forerunner in introducing Western knowledge. Rooted in the open-mindedness and diversity of the Changzhou tradition, the organization published pioneering works including translations of novels and Western literature as well as, such as in Zhou's own case, on world history.[67] In 1900, for instance, it published the first Chinese translation of the French author Jules Verne's science fiction *Around the World in Eighty Days* by Xue Shaohui (1866–1911), in collaboration with her husband Chen Shoupeng (1855–?). It was for this publication that Xue was later

---

[65] Joan Judge, *Print and Politics: "Shibao" and the Culture of Reform in Late Qing China* (Stanford: Stanford University Press, 1996), 21. In the Shanghai area, thirty-two new newspapers and thirty-four new magazines appeared between 1895 and 1897. Christopher Reed, *Gutenberg in Shanghai: Chinese Print Capitalism, 1876–1937* (Vancouver: UBC Press, 2004), 103–104.

[66] Ye Zhou, "Rongzhu zhongwai," 96. In light of the scarcity of primary sources on the publishing house, I still have some reservations about whether or not we can pinpoint Zhou Weihan and Zhang Heling as its cofounders. Ye Zhou's speculation is primarily based on Zheng Yimei's later recollection. However, Zheng was something of a "paparazzi" type of figure in the Shanghai publishing cycle, though most of his stories are actually creditable. Be that as it may, the evidence is not thin – especially if one argues that Zhou was one of its active members and was well connected to the publishing circles in Shanghai.

[67] According to Wen-chung Chou, his grandfather also published a number of Lin Shu's translations of Western literary books. The latter is known as a pioneer in modern Chinese literature. Chang, *Chou Wen-Chung*, 13.

accredited as arguably being "the first female translator in modern Chinese history."[68]

Through his connections with the publishing circle, Zhou Weihan published his own work, *An Outline of Western History*. To a certain degree, this book was a product of Changzhou's proud intellectual tradition. Several pieces of evidence seem to support this assertion, as we can see in Figure 2. First is Zhou's connection to a group of prominent scholars who originated in the Changzhou intellectual tradition, the New Text School in the Classical Studies tradition. These scholars embraced a critical reading of classic texts and were more open to new ideas. From Wei Yuan and Gong Zizhen (1792–1841) to Kang Youwei and Tan Sitong (1865–1898), thinkers of this school embraced the idea of *jingshi* ("statecraft," or literally "ordering the world") and maintained a more open view of the world than other contemporary Confucian scholars. Zhou was not a celebrated scholar in this school, to be sure, but Zhang Heling, Zhou's friend and cofounder of the Jingshi xueshe, served as the tangible link and provided the preface for Zhou's book. Zhang was a noted scholar of the Changzhou School, and people of the time often compared his works to those of Gong Zizhen, the prominent figure in the Next Text School.

Second, Zhou collaborated with Changzhou scholars in writing the book. Trained in Chinese classics, Zhou was not yet able to access foreign-language learning. In the process of writing his book, he primarily relied on Chinese-language sources, including Chinese-language works, Chinese translations of Western-language works, and Japanese works that were written in classical Chinese. This was not enough. For some non-Chinese sources, he turned to the help of Feng Dansheng (sobriquet Xiaopeng), who was again a Changzhou native. We do not know much about Feng, but he was the uncle of the famous linguist Zhao Yuanren (1892–1982) and belonged to an influential lineage in the Changzhou area. Feng's grandfather Guangshi (sobriquet Zhongzi) once served as governor of Shanxi province.[69]

Third, Zhou Weihan, to a certain degree, followed the trajectory of the Menghe physicians in his professional career. While he worked in Beijing, he practiced medicine among high officials. Just as in his study of world history, he was open to new ideas from Western medicine, and he had also

---

[68] Luo Lie, "Nü fanyijia Xue Shaohui yu *Bashi ri huanyou ji zhong nüxing xingxiang de chonggou*" [Woman translator Xue Shaohui and the image of woman in *Around the World in Eighty Days*], *Waiguo yuyan wenxue (jikan)* [Foreign languages and literature (quarterly)] 98, no. 4 (2008): 262.

[69] Zhao Yuanren, *Zhao Yuanren zaonian zizhuan* [Yuen Ren Chao's autobiography: First 30 years, 1892–1921] (Taipei: Zhuanji wenxue chubanshe, 1984), 49; as for Zhao Yuanren's biographical information, see *BDRC*, 1:148a–152b.

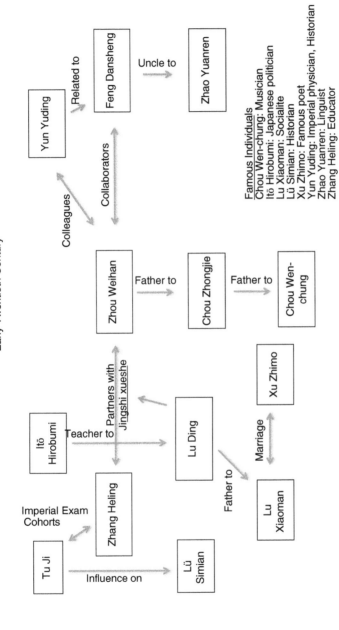

Changzhou Network
Early Twentieth Century

Yun Yuding — Related to → Feng Dansheng — Uncle to → Zhao Yuanren

Colleagues — Collaborators (Zhou Weihan / Feng Dansheng)

Zhou Weihan — Father to → Chou Zhongjie — Father to → Chou Wen-chung

Itō Hirobumi — Teacher to → Partners with Jingshi xueshe

Lu Ding — Father to → Lu Xiaoman

Lu Ding — Partners with → Xu Zhimo

Lu Xiaoman — Marriage — Xu Zhimo

Imperial Exam Cohorts — Zhang Heling

Tu Ji — Influence on → Lü Simian

Famous Individuals
Chou Wen-chung: Musician
Itō Hirobumi: Japanese politician
Lu Xiaoman: Socialite
Lü Simian: Historian
Xu Zhimo: Famous poet
Yun Yuding: Imperial physician, Historian
Zhao Yuanren: Linguist
Zhang Heling: Educator

Figure 2 Mapping the Changzhou intellectual network

published a series of short essays introducing Western science. In those essays, he talked about chemistry, physics, and medical science. He discussed such things as how to calculate horsepower and what equipment one should purchase to study chemistry and provided a medical explanation for human body hair.[70] This interaction between medicine and history reflects the dynamics of the increasing knowledge exchanges between China and the wider world before the era of professionalization. Zhou, like other open-minded intellectuals at the opening of the twentieth century, was among the pioneers who introduced new ideas to the existing framework of knowledge in China. He was a friend of Yun Yuding (1862–1917), another offspring of the famous Yun household, and Zhou's collaborator Feng Dansheng was a relative of Yun's as well. After his success in the civil exam three years prior to Zhang Heling and Yun Yujia, Yun worked in the Bureau of Imperial History and was in charge of editing the *Veritable Records of Qing* (*Qing shilu*). Like Zhou, Yun was also famous for his medical skills. Before meeting Zhou in 1909, Yun had already read Zhou's works and praised him for introducing many historical events that remained unknown to Chinese scholars in 1906.[71]

With the rise of print capitalism, the Jingshi wenshe embraced market strategies and vigorously promoted its publications. The production of *An Outline of Western History*, for instance, reflected a change in print technology. The first edition was printed using lithography, a relatively old-style printing technology. The second edition was printed using the latest technology and included five pages of illustrations produced by means of engraved copperplates imported from Japan.[72] At the same time, Chinese publishing business owners became increasingly outspoken about protecting their profits. Owing to its increasing popularity, *An Outline of Western History* became a target for piracy. The Jingshi wenshe drew on the close connection between provincial governors and the local gentry elite and lobbied the local government to protect their business interests. This seemed to work. On September 19, 1901, the intendant of the Suzhou-Songjiang-Taicang circuit Yuan Shuxun (1847–1915) issued an order to prohibit any attempts at piracy. He warned, "If there are any attempts to reprint *An Outline of Western History* or any other books that were published by the Jingshi wenshe,

[70] Zhou Weihan, "Da wen" [Answers to questions], *Gezhi xinbao* [Inquiry news], no. 7 (1898): 12–14.
[71] Yun Yuding, *Yun Yuding Chengzhai riji*, 1:319 (June 17, 1906); on the relationship between Yun and Feng, *Yun Yuding Chenzhai riji* (May 11, 1908).
[72] William Rowe, *China's Last Empire: The Great Qing* (Cambridge, MA: Harvard University Press, 2009), 257. The publication of *Xishi gangmu* also reflected a change in print technology in Shanghai. Reed, *Gutenberg in Shanghai*.

[the governor] will allow the latter's petition and will punish [those pirating] as strictly as possible, in order to reward the publishing and writing [business] and block any greedy and treacherous behavior." At the opening of the century, the pursuit of profit had become an important goal in the print industry in the Shanghai area.[73]

With the support of the intellectual network and a sales-driven publisher, *An Outline of Western History* was well received by the Shanghai book trade. Important local organizations such as the Society for the Diffusion of Christian and General Knowledge (first founded in 1884 and reorganized in 1887), the Society for the Diffusion of Useful Knowledge, Nanyang College, and various translation bureaus in Shanghai all collected copies. Beyond the Yangzi Delta network, a Hunan edition of this book also is still extant. The book seems to have circulated even more widely, as both Harvard and Stanford libraries hold copies of it today. Thus, in examining the production of *An Outline of Western History*, this study uncovers a cross-regional community of scholars, intellectuals, and businessmen who have often been neglected in previous studies and yet played important roles in introducing world-historical knowledge to China. Their shared Changzhou origin suggests continuity, however subtle, between intellectual movements in Qing China and early interest in world-historical learning.

Be that as it may, *An Outline of Western History* was a book of its own times. Turning to the content of the book, professional historians today would consider it a flawed work. Like many early world history writers in China at that time, Zhou Weihan did not have the qualifications that professional historians would consider essential, such as the ability to read primary sources in their original languages, access to a state-of-the-art library and archival collections, and background in world-historical training. Yet, as a careful reading of this book will show, despite their flaws, early world-historical writings in China provide us with a fascinating window through which we can examine how early world history writers developed a worldview that allowed them to overcome cultural differences. This worldview, however vulnerable and fragile, laid the

[73] Missionary publishing groups had urged local officials to protect intellectual property rights a few years early, and a large number of Chinese publishers started to do so in 1902–1903. Fei-Hsien Wang, *Pirates and Publishers: A Social History of Copyright in Modern China* (Princeton: Princeton University Press, 2019), 121–125. To be sure, profit had been a major incentive for printers in several regions in China, including the Lower Yangzi, since the late Ming era. In contrast to modern capitalism, however, publishers in late imperial China had an ambivalent view of profit. Reed, *Gutenberg in Shanghai*, 177. Regarding the absence of the concept of intellectual property rights in traditional Confucian values, see William Alford, *To Steal a Book Is an Elegant Offense: Intellectual Property Law in Chinese Civilization* (Stanford: Stanford University Press, 1995).

foundation for world-historical development, leading to the incipience of global identity.

To prove this point, let us take a closer look at *An Outline of Western History*. While avoiding summarizing the entire work, we will hereby selectively focus on how the author negotiated the spatial divide between the East and the West, the temporal difference between the ancient and the modern, and the place of Confucianism in the future world by referring to the lessons of history.

An Outline of Western History was an ambitious project, for the scale of his world-historical inquiry was unprecedented. Yet the nature of the work has to be understood in the context of late Qing intellectual movements. To a certain degree, Zhou's work was a continuation of the *jingshi* (statecraft) historiography after Wei Yuan, who invented a tradition in which Chinese scholars pieced together all the extant sources on foreign geography and formulated a coherent and holistic understanding of the geopolitics of the world.[74] Like Wei, Zhou attempted to exhaust the existing Chinese-language sources on world history. His reference list (see the chapter appendix) is indicative of the level of accumulation of world-historical knowledge in China at the turn of the twentieth century. Zhou wanted to fill 120 volumes (*juan*).[75] Of the first thirty-five volumes that were actually published, he divided them into two parts. The first part comprises twenty volumes and covers history from the beginning of human civilization to AD 1. The second part has fifteen volumes and covers history from AD 1 to AD 1500.

How did Zhou document historical events on such a huge scale? He adopted a *biannian* chronology that was rooted in the Chinese historiographical tradition. The twentieth century witnessed a process in which Chinese historians submitted to a Western-centered world-historical chronology that was based on Christian calendar years. This was not a small change. For instance, the twenty-sixth year of King Zheng of Qin (commonly known the First Emperor) originally appeared in traditional Chinese historiography. Rather than referring to this date, nowadays Chinese school students are asked to memorize 221 BC as the founding year of unified Chinese "feudal society." In this Eurocentric world-historical narrative, reference to BC or AD has little significance for Chinese history, and placing China's past within this Eurocentric temporal schema, as shown in the later chapters, would create enormous confusion and stimulate much resistance among Chinese historians.

---

[74] Mosca, *From Frontier Policy to Foreign Policy*, 272.

[75] In citations from *Xishi gangmu*, I keep the original Chinese "juan" instead of "volume" to avoid the confusion with "ce," which means a bound volume in the Western sense. I choose not to cite page numbers, either, as some of them are illegible in the original text.

An Outline of Western History was written before this Eurocentric transition. Prior to the total embracing of the Christian calendar, Chinese *biannian* writers as well as Protestant missionaries often used the outline-and-detail format (*gangmu ti*) to chronicle world-historical events. For instance, Young John Allen (known as "Lin Lezhi" in Chinese, 1836–1907) and his Chinese collaborator Yan Liangxun translated *The Book of the Dates*, a universal chronology of world history that charted the beginnings of history up to 1862 as *Siyi biannian* (*Chronicle of Foreigners*).[76] They placed historical events in world history according to the ancient Chinese chronicle the *Bamboo Annals* (*Zhushu jinian*).[77] Like them, Zhou divided historical events into categories organized under each year by cultural regions. This included major ancient civilizations such as Egypt, Babylonia, India, Persia, Greece, and Rome as well as Japan. (Zhou's use of "Western" is rather liberal.) For instance, on pages 13b and 14a of *juan* 7, large characters 三十三年 are used to state the thirty-third year of the reign of King Hui of Zhou. Below this, the corresponding year 六百六十四年 (664 BC) of the Western calendar is inserted with smaller characters. After that, historical events that took place in that year are recorded with larger characters: the battle between Rome and Alba Longa. A new line explains this event in greater detail. After narrating the event, Zhou also inserts his comments by adopting the name "Waishi shi" (author of foreign history), just as Sima Qian (145 [or 135]–86 BC) had used the sobriquet "Taishi gong" (grand historian) in the *Records of the Grand Historian* (*Shiji*). These notes are embedded within the main text in small-sized characters.[78]

Unlike the *jingshi* historiography that put emphasis on world geography, Zhou stressed the significance of the temporal dimension in reconciling the alleged cultural differences between the East and the West. Many historians have written about the strong anti-foreign sentiments among the Chinese educated elite in late Qing China, especially through

[76] Zou, *Xifang chuanjiaoshi yu wan-Qing Xishi dongjian*, 367–368. Although I could not locate *The Book of the Dates* attributed to Henry Bohn, I did find an anonymously edited book published in England in 1866 titled *The Book of Dates; Or, Treasury of Universal Reference: Comprising a Summary of the Principal Events in All Ages, From the Earliest Records to the Present Time, With Index of Events* (London: Charles Griffin and Company, 1866).

[77] The *Zhushu jinian* was arguably compiled in the state of Wei during the Warring States period (fifth century to 221 BC). The book's name comes from a later date. It was formerly known as the *Jizhongshu* [Book from the tomb in Jixian], because around AD 281 some grave robbers found these texts by accident. Zhou acknowledged that there was also a forgery issue concerning the *Zhushu jinian*, but he was not interested in getting involved in the debate regarding when the book was written. Zhou, *Xishi gangmu*, juan 3: 2.

[78] The practice did not end with Zhou, either. In the early years of the twentieth century, scholars followed similar formats in their works on world history, such as Wang Shunan's *Xila chunqiu* (The chronicle of Greece).

the idea of segregating China from foreigners (*Yi Xia zhi fen*). Yet not all Chinese intellectuals held such a view, and Zhou is an outstanding example. In his work, he wrote repeatedly, "There is no China or West among people, for their intellects are the same."[79] He returned to the neo-Confucian concept of a common nature (*xing*) of humanity that transcended cultural differences. For him, such nature includes ten basic features: sexual desire, caring for youth, respecting elders, selfishness, contentiousness, seeking repute, attraction to beauty, competitiveness, fear of disasters, and pursuit of comfort.[80] Interesting enough, this neo-Confucian belief in the common nature of humanity echoes nineteenth-century Christian missionaries' views. In his letter to his wife in 1836, for instance, E. C. Bridgman, an American missionary and the first person to translate American history into Chinese, wrote that, despite the different circumstances causing some awkward misunderstandings between Chinese and Westerners, "Truth is one, human nature is one" and "Man has a common origin."[81]

In embracing this common humanity, Zhou joined a group of early world-historical writers such as Kang Youwei, Liang Qichao, and Zhang Taiyan (1868–1936), who argued for the relevance of the past while facing the rapid changes in late Qing society. Rooted in the Confucian tradition, they had more or less a view of historical synthesis. To them, cultural tradition was a holistic whole and, in order to get to its essence, one must grasp its root – classical antiquity. Zhou wrote a book covering ancient history only. To justify this, he stated that the scholarly tradition was key to understanding the success of Western learning in his own day. "Without the ancients," he asked, "how could modern learning be possible?" This does not mean that everything from the past was perfect, to be sure. A selective view of knowledge from the past is needed; as Zhou suggested, "discard the dross and select the essence."[82]

The key connection between the ancient past and modern society was the concept of *gongli* (universal principles), as the neo-Confucian scholar Zhang Heling explained in the preface. Zhang believed that *gongli* are universal truths beyond any temporal or spatial confines. There is no real difference between the "way of ordering chaos" (*zhi luan zhi dao*) in the past and the present. However, it is not easy for people to apprehend *gongli*. In a society where *gongli* is not yet understood, people's minds are dominated by their pursuit of power and profit. They place their private

[79] Zhou mentions this multiple times in juan 3, 4, and 7 of the *Xishi gangmu*.
[80] Zhou, *Xishi gangmu*, juan 3.
[81] Eliza J. Gillett Bridgman (ed.), *The Pioneer of American Missions in China: The Life and Labors of Elijah Coleman Bridgman* (New York: Anson D. F. Randolph, 1864), 109.
[82] Zhou, *Xishi gangmu*, juan 3:1.

views (*sijian*) over public principles (*gongli*). Since people's ability to comprehend *gongli* has always been limited, as time has gone by, they continue to add layers of *sijian* over *gongli*. Thus, in order to get to know real *gongli*, one has to go back to the earliest stages of human history when so many layers of *sijian* did not obscure the truth. This, Zhang argued, was the benefit of studying ancient world history.[83]

In Meiji Japan, a similar concept of "universal truths" offered an opportunity for the educated elites to promote political changes while maintaining a distinctive Japanese identity. Similar to what neo-Confucian scholars argued at the time, some Japanese scholars agreed that "[Certain] great universal truths had been discovered outside Japan." These truths were "universally applicable." Therefore, by borrowing them from outside Japan, they believed that they would "enhance rather than degrade Japanese culture."[84] Zhou never went to Japan. Yet, as well connected in the late Qing intellectual network as he was, Japanese works on world history apparently had an impact on him, especially regarding the question of historical progress.

If universal principles or truths apply to different cultures, how did scholars of the time make sense of Europe's rise and China's decline in recent decades? As Guo Songtao had done a few decades earlier, Zhou was also searching for the answer to this question. Based on a religious-like pride in Chinese culture, Zhou was frustrated with how "[Westerners] bully and despise us, calling us half-civilized barbarians, or they pity us as sick men, going to all extremes." Yet he disagreed with "petty scholar-officials and straight-laced Confucians" who "pursue Western studies to verify [Chinese] classical canons and ridicule [the West] for stealing [China's ancient knowledge], saying that there is nothing in the present-day West that was not [already there] in China's past." For him, the intention of those people was "to lead those with a narrow knowledge of Confucianism to think that the trend of our age is to return to the ancients";[85] such a simple return was not the way for the future.

In recognition of change, Zhou diverged from earlier Confucian scholar-officials in his view of classical antiquity. Through a world-historical reflection, Zhou historicized the nature of the Chinese Three Dynasties, finding that previous scholars had exaggerated the level of Chinese social sophistication in classical antiquity. In ancient times, lands under government control were limited and communication was difficult. This restricted what China could achieve. Placing Three

[83] Zhang Heling, *Xishi gangmu*, "Preface."
[84] Mark Ravina, *To Stand with the Nations of the World: Japan's Meiji Restoration in World History* (Oxford: Oxford University Press, 2017), 11.
[85] Zhou, *Xishi gangmu*, juan 4.

Dynasties China within a world-historical context, he observed that ancient Egypt might have been more advanced than Shang China. Many contemporaneous achievements in the rest of the world were more "advanced" than those in China, such as the trade activities conducted by the Phoenicians, the Long Walls in Athens (Μακρὰ Τείχη),[86] gun emplacements in Syracuse, and chariots in Egypt. China might have been more advanced in some areas, but the rest of the world might have been ahead in others. There was no way to argue that one was stealing from another.[87] Both China and the West shared the common legacy of humanity.

To return to the question – but why did the West leave China behind today? – Zhou argued that it was because there was a more dynamic exchange of ideas among European intellectuals than among Chinese ones. He offered this critical view: "Learning in Europe is dynamic, precise, reasoned, and collaborative." Countries communicated with and improved by learning from each other. So "during the last one hundred years [European] scholarship has risen vigorously daily and has become more dominant." By contrast, "we stick to the old and are not good at change."[88] This changing relationship between China and the West, again, had little to do with the nature of their civilizations. Instead, it was a historical development.

This concept of development shaped Zhou's view of the human past; he held a progressive view of history. In the section on the origin of human civilization, Zhou concluded that there are four material foundations of human society: dwellings (*juchu*), clothing (*yifu*), tools (*qiyong*), and music (*yinyue*); each of those foundations advanced as human society progressed. The evolution of human political and social systems follows similar progressive rules. He wrote that human political systems had developed from barbarian to civilized in seven progressive stages – successively evolving from hunting to nomadism, agriculture, fixed settlement, urbanism, chieftaincy, and kingdoms. China had entered the stage of urban society very early – in the age of Tang and Yu, legendary rulers at the beginning of Chinese history – but this did not make China an exceptional case. Believing that universal principles are manifest in world history, Zhou speculated that, prior to the urbanism stage, China must have experienced other earlier stages of development.[89] Zhou's view on progress seems to echo that of Meiji thinkers in Japan, especially

---

[86] During the classical era, the Athenians built the Long Walls to protect the connection between the city and the harbor. Apparently, Zhou was impressed by this architectural achievement.
[87] Zhou, *Xishi gangmu*, juan 4.   [88] Zhou, *Xishi gangmu*, juan 4.
[89] Zhou, *Xishi gangmu*, juan 2.

Fukuzawa Yukichi's stages of human progress, from barbarian hunting societies, half-civilized agricultural communities, to civilized industrial societies.[90] Writing nearly three decades after Fukuzawa Yukichi, Zhou developed a more sophisticated analysis with reference to cases in world history.

Related to Zhou's belief in progress was his critical view of the role of religion in world history. He did not believe in the existence of gods or the supernatural, although he acknowledged that there was a unitary goal behind all religions that was to encourage people to follow virtue.[91] He examined the origins of humanity and argued that, in the beginning, there were no writing systems – let alone systematic thought. Lacking knowledge, human beings imagined gods or ghosts to explain things that they were not able to understand and would assume that spirits were the cause when people were unable to understand the logic of certain events. In the section "On the Origins of Ghosts and Gods," Zhou launched a full-fledged attack on religions and superstitions. He asked rhetorically whether the rise and fall in the belief in ghosts and gods had been "inverse in relation to people's wisdom." The more stupid people are, the more popular are arguments for the existence of ghosts and gods; the wiser people are, the less interest there is in talk of ghosts and gods.[92]

Like the Enlightenment thinkers in Europe, Zhou stressed the distinction between religions and superstitions, and he blamed China's backwardness on its people's infatuation with superstitious ideas. On this issue, Zhou was at the cutting edge of scholarly trends, for, exactly at this moment, famous public intellectuals such as Liang Qichao had just started to separate superstitions from religions. Influenced by Japanese Meiji scholars, this intellectual movement would redefine the understanding of religion for the entire twentieth century in China.[93] To Zhou, this argument was derived from world-historical comparisons. He criticized the worship of ghosts, gods, and animals in both Egypt and China. Using the worship of domestic animals in Egypt as an example, he considered animal worship to be an extreme example of bad and backward customs. The case in Egypt reminded him of China. China and Egypt shared the same level of stupidity regarding

---

[90] Fukuzawa, *Bunmeiron no gairyaku*, 1:22a–23b.   [91] Zhou, *Xishi gangmu*, juan 3.

[92] Zhou, *Xishi gangmu*, juan 2; Zhang Shunan, a scholar-official who wrote on the history of ancient Greece, also held a similar view in his works. Zhang Shunan, *Xila chunqiu*, juan 1; "Helakelidi" [Heraclitus], *Xila xuean* [Intellectual History of Greece] (Taolun kecong 21, 1905), juan 1.

[93] Rebecca Nedostrup, *Superstitious Regimes: Religion and Politics of Chinese Modernity* (Cambridge, MA: Harvard University Asia Center, 2009), 8, 18–21; Vincent Goossaert, "1898: The Beginning of the End for Chinese Religion?" *Journal of Asian Studies* 65, no. 2 (2006): 320.

superstitions. As he put it, "Although China considered [its ancestors] to be the gods and its civilization ancient, if we trace back its bad customs of worship, though they have not been as awful as Egypt's, we should not think ourselves superior for being half as bad."[94] There were many superstitious traditions in China in Zhou's day, and these contributed to the country's backwardness.[95] Zhou embraced science and rejected the existence of the soul. "The soul in a human being is like the relationship between fire and smoke," he wrote. "Sometimes when fire burns itself out, smoke will last for a while; but as time goes by, it too will eventually disappear."[96] For Zhou, ghosts, gods, fairies, and buddhas were all manmade illusions.

Science and progress did not contradict Zhou's strong belief in Confucianism, and on this issue he diverged from Meiji thinkers who had chosen to abandon Confucianism and embrace Western civilization. This distinction reflects a common feature shared by early scholars of world history in China: on the one hand, they were eager to learn from the outside world; on the other hand, most of them still adhered to aspects of their cultural identity in a moral and metaphysical sense. In Zhou's view, Confucianism was a moral belief system superior to any other in the world. To prove this point, he compared Confucianism with religious belief systems including Christianity, Buddhism, and Islam and predicted that Confucianism would be the only one to unify the world in the future.[97]

Zhou initially had a relatively pessimistic view of the status of Confucianism in his contemporary world. He calculated that Christianity was the most popular religion of the time, influencing more than 80–90 percent of the people in all the major continents. Islam and Buddhism came next. The influence of Confucianism, on the other hand, was limited to China. He estimated that, "Although the population of China is allegedly 400 million, women who do not study constitute half of them, and those registered as scholars are only one or two percent of the whole population."[98] Thus he believed that it was a mistake to consider all Chinese as Confucian. Still, this did not affect his belief in that way of thinking.

Zhou believed in Confucianism because of its humanistic value. As an ideal system, Confucianism had three basic layers, as he explained. The

---

[94] Zhou, *Xishi gangmu*, juan 9.   [95] Zhou, *Xishi gangmu*, juan 3.
[96] Zhou, *Xishi gangmu*, juan 3.
[97] Zhou was influenced by Kang Youwei's view of Confucianism. However, he also could rightfully claim originality for his own thoughts; he had been studying Confucianism since the age of fifteen and had already written a book titled *Kongmen bianyuan lu* (Record in defense of Confucius and his school). Perhaps, Zhou was reluctant to cite Kang Youwei because the latter was censored by the Qing government after the failure of the 1898 reform.
[98] Zhou, *Xishi gangmu*, juan 9.

first layer is what he called "words for myriads of generations" (*wanshi zhi yan*). Those were the universal principles and the essence of Confucian philosophy. The second layer is "words in temporal context" (*yinshi zhi yan*). That is to say, these words were subject to the historical conditions when Confucius uttered them. For instance, Westerners convinced of the despotic nature of the Confucian tradition, often ridiculed this statement from the *Analects*: "The people may be made to follow, but may not be made to know."[99] Zhou protested. He contended that these Westerners failed to understand that ancient Chinese people during Confucius' time were not yet enlightened; the idea from the sentence was merely applicable to a specific moment in history. The third layer is "words for accomplishment" (*youwei er yan*). In order to achieve his political agenda, Confucius had to meet with political leaders and persuade them. Under such circumstances, what Confucius said had a specific function. Like the critics of Song learning in the Ming and Qing periods, Zhou Weihan blamed Zhu Xi and his followers for the decline of Confucianism in China. According to him, Song scholars treated Confucius' disciples unfairly since they were looking only for those "words for myriads of generations." They failed to contextualize the meanings in the Confucian canon.

Zhou further elaborated on a comparison of Confucianism with other world religions. He argued that each religion or system of ideals has its own strength. He implied that it would be unwise to compare Confucianism on every single point with other religions. For instance, if people stress the idea of "what you do not wish upon yourself, extend not to others,"[100] then this is the strength of Christianity; if people emphasize the idea of "to learn without flagging, to instruct others tirelessly,"[101] then this is the strength of Buddhism. People had to compare belief systems as organic wholes. Zhou contended that the fundamental reason why Confucianism was superior to other religions was that Confucianism was a belief system grounded in humanity. By contrast, Buddhism, Christianity, and Islam were not satisfied with the human world: they claimed godliness. Because of his disbelief in supernatural existence, he predicted that Confucianism would be the ideal system to unify the world in the future.[102]

In retrospect, the publication of *An Outline of Western History* represents a moment of change in the history of Chinese intellectual culture at the

---

[99] "Taibo," in *Lunyu* [*The Analects*], chapter 8, passage 9.
[100] "Wei Linggong," in *Lunyu*, chapter 15, passage 23.
[101] "Shu er," in *Lunyu*, chapter 7, passage 2.
[102] Zhou, *Xishi gangmu*, juan 9. Zhou also believed that the trend of thought in the world was progressive and that supernaturalism had become outdated.

opening of the twentieth century – the rise of world-historical consciousness. This dynamic engagement with both historical time and world space in historical studies would continue to develop over the course of the twentieth century. Eventually world history became an independent academic discipline in China.

In examining this early work written by a Chinese scholar focusing exclusively on ancient world history, we can identify an interesting perspective in early world-historical works in China. It appears that early world-historical writers cared about the question of cultural relations between China and the rest of the world, and they held a belief in a common humanity through a revisionist view of Confucianism. Even after changing from a writer of history to a promoter of medical science, Zhou Weihan did not give up his belief in the common nature of humanity. Citing his experiences in medical practice, he stated, "The way I treat [patients is like this]: for all my equipment such as thermometers and stethoscopes, I adopt the Western way; as for the prescription, [I] use the Chinese way. If there are developments such that the effect of the Chinese prescription is not fast enough, then [I] add Western medicine."[103] It seems that Zhou held a similar view in writing a world history that transcends the cultural differences between the East and the West.

Moving to the perspective of historiography, one may well say that *An Outline of Western History* was a book for its time. While Zhou Weihan was promoting the view of a common humanity, he could not escape the dark side of the global circulation of ideas in the late nineteenth and early twentieth centuries. As a medical practitioner who was interested in the Western sciences, Zhou Weihan was particularly vulnerable to some so-called scientific theories, especially racism. In the book, he discusses racial issues and divides humanity into five races according to the color of their skin, namely "yellow, white, black, brown, and red." He blindly dismisses the role of the "black," "brown," and "red" races in civilizational achievements.[104] Like other popular writers (the most famous one being Yan Fu), he then predicts the

---

[103] Chen, "Changzhou jindai bufen lishi renwu minglu zhi er," 223.

[104] Zhou, *Xishi gangmu*, juan 2; It is noticeable that Yan Fu, the influential translator during the time, did not include the "red" race in his classification. Zhou's classification was more in line with Japanese author Okamoto Kansuke, though the latter used the purple and cupreous in contrast to his "red" and "brown." Frank Dikötter, *The Discourse of Race in Modern China* (Hong Kong: Hong Kong University Press, 1992), 67; Okamoto Kansuke [Gangben Jianfu], *Wanguo zongshuo* [Complete survey of myriad countries] in *Dunhuai tang yangwu congchao* [Various collected works on Western learning in Dunhuai Hall], ed. Zhang Shusheng (Hefei: 1884), juan 1.

future of the world really concerned a competition between the "white" and "yellow" races.[105] The latter included the "Chinese" and the "Siberians," which contained subcategories such as Han, Tibetans, Mongols, and Manchus. Yet Zhou was a half-hearted racist at most. Instead of stressing ethnic differences, he claimed that the ancient Chinese practice of eliminating differences through an interethnic marriage policy (*heqin*) was a success story. In predicting future conflicts between the "yellow" and "white" races, he lamented that this policy had fell into disuse in China during the past 300 years under the Manchu dynasty.[106] Zhou's promotion of ethnic togetherness would resonate with many in his day. Such views would make him a less attractive figure in the coming debates between the revolutionaries and the constitutionalists, such as those that featured confrontations between Liang Qichao and Wang Jingwei a few years later.[107] After the populace embraced race as the foundation for the future Chinese nation and revolutionary radicals rallied "to expel the Tatar barbarians (i.e., Manchu)," Zhou's mild view became increasingly irrelevant. Yet his book was relevant in its day. After the initial publication of its first part on ancient world history, within two years the book had been reprinted three times and become widely popular in China.[108]

Another factor to account for the fleeting popularity of the book is the question of what makes "good history." Prior to the establishment of modern universities in China, scholars who worked on world history did not have enough resources to conduct professional research, as do today's historians. They did not have training in foreign languages, nor did they have access to comprehensive libraries. Sometimes they had to base their study of world history on philosophical presumptions. Zhou Weihan's conception of progress alongside his reinterpretation of Confucianism exemplifies this. In all aspects, their works were rather like a "philosophical history," a term introduced by Patrick Manning to describe early Western works on world history. Early Western world history texts share the same problems as contemporaneous works of world history in China: lacking modern libraries, their authors "relied more heavily on philosophical presumption than on historical documentation."[109]

Like Western historical philosophers before the twentieth century, early Chinese writers on world history had many shortcomings when

[105] Dikötter, *The Discourse of Race in Modern China*, 67–71.
[106] Zhou, *Xishi gangmu*, juan 4.   [107] Dikötter, 87, 107, 113–115.
[108] Li, *Xifang shixue zai Zhongguo de chuanbo*, 133.
[109] Patrick Manning, *Navigating World History: Historians Create a Global Past* (New York: Palgrave Macmillan, 2003), 18.

judged by today's professional historiographical standards. Yet they also addressed some foundational issues in the history of the world.[110] Most conspicuous is Zhou Weihan's attempt to embrace the belief in a common humanity in overcoming the differences between the East and the West. Study of *An Outline of Western History* shows that the evolution of Confucianism did not necessarily lead to a Sino-centric view of the world, at least in this early attempt to write world history. The combined forces of "traditional" influence and "foreign" ideas might have shaped a new sense of global consciousness in late Qing China. As I will show in later chapters, this development contrasts strikingly with the rise of academic nationalism in China's world-historical writing today.

How, then, did this early pursuit of a common humanity give away to a blind belief in cultural or ethnic centrism as embodied in nationalism? In order to answer this question, we need to examine the development of world history in China over the course of the twentieth century.

---

[110] Manning, *Navigating World History*, 18. In the case of China, in his preliminary survey of Wang Shunan's works on world history, Don Price also has argued that, despite Wang's conservative views on reform and revolution, "[He] transcended traditional Sinocentric parochialism and emerged with a far clearer perception of his own Confucian commitments." Price, "A Foreign Affairs Expert's View of Western History," 10.

Appendix

Table 1 *Reference list:* An Outline of Western History

<table>
<tr><th rowspan="2">References in
Chinese</th><th rowspan="2">References in
Japanese</th><th colspan="3">References in An Outline of Western History 西史綱目</th></tr>
<tr><th>References from translated Western sources</th><th>References from
non-translated
Japanese sources</th><th>References from
non-translated
Western sources</th></tr>
<tr>
<td>瀛寰志略 by 徐繼畬
海國圖志 by 魏源
四國日記 by 薛福成
使俄草 by 王之春
俄遊彙編 by 繆佑孫
西國天學源流 by 王韜
西學原始考 by 王韜
法國志略 by 王韜
重學淺說 by 黃遵憲
日本國志 by 黃遵憲
采風記 by 宋育人
西學通考 by 江標
各國統系考
各國交涉源流考</td>
<td>萬國史記
十五戰記
經國美談
萬國通商史
東洋史要
歐羅巴通史 (西洋史綱)
印度蠶食戰史
世界商業史</td>
<td>新舊約   二約釋義叢書
萬國通鑑 萬國通史
四裔編年表 古史探原
格致彙編 職方外紀
坤輿外紀 博物新編
動物學新編 古教匯參

希臘志略 羅馬志略
歐洲志略 八大帝王傳
三十一國志要 萬國輿圖
俄羅遊記 西學考略
大英國志 各國交涉公法論
幾何原本 談天
法人遊探記 民約論
萬法精理 政治學
天演論   猶太地志</td>
<td>萬國史要
日耳曼史略
萬國通史攬要</td>
<td>猶太列王傳
以色列列王傳
希臘古史</td>
</tr>
</table>

2 The Cultural Destiny
Nationalism and World History in Republican China

War is a crime against culture; but war is not unavoidable. Historical study has proved to be an effective way to expose the lies of militant statesmen who have distorted history and manipulated people. Chen Hengzhe, the first female professor in China, expressed this sentiment in a textbook for high school students in the 1920s.[1] In the wake of World War I, growing doubts about Western modernity emerged across the world. Chinese intellectuals shared these concerns.[2] Some held fast to their belief in modern ideals – however defined. Others contended that Western modernity should be held responsible for the destruction of the war and the downfall of the civilization. In reference to this debate, Chen wrote that it is wrong to blame everything on the West. She reminded readers that freedom and democracy still held true value for contemporaneous Chinese society. Yet she admitted that the situation in China was not rosy; the postwar world order remained one haunted by imperial and colonial conflicts.

In concluding her popular textbook, Chen pointed out that Asian countries faced three possible paths to the future: to embrace modernity and militarize like Western countries, to refuse modernization and end up being enslaved by the West, or to seek an alternative path to development.[3] She rejected the first two choices. With respect to the first choice, she did not want to witness China as a fallen nation devoured by imperialism. With respect to the second choice, she took issue with total Westernization. Taking Japan as an example, she argued that Japan had uncritically embraced Western imperialism in order to gain the capacity to militarize and defeat Russia and win the respect of White nations. To her, Japan was the enemy of China. At the time, many

---

[1] For Chen Hengzhe's biography, see *BDRC*, 1:151a.
[2] Jerome Grieder, *Hu Shih and the Chinese Renaissance: Liberalism in the Chinese Revolution, 1917–1937* (Cambridge, MA: Harvard University Press, 1970), 129–151; Chunmei Du, "Gu Hongming as a Cultural Amphibian: A Confucian Universalist Critique of Modern Western Civilization," *Journal of World History* 22, no. 4 (2011): 715–746.
[3] Chen Hengzhe [Sophia H. Chen], *Xiyang shi* [History of Western Countries] (Shanghai: Shangwu yinshuguan, 1926), 313.

Chinese intellectuals held strong negative opinions about Japan. Many believed that Japan had been secretly planning to transform China into its colony. Chen's view of Japan was perhaps tainted by such bias. In addition, she felt that total Westernization would eliminate the individual identity of the country – that Westernization was another crime that Western powers forced upon Asian nations. Chen thus urged China to seek the third path – one that transcended the dichotomy between being colonized and becoming imperialistic.[4]

In reviewing the history of "Western countries," Chen identified two dominant cultural forces that were at play and also in contradiction with each.[5] First, imperialism was a force that brought disorder to the world. It emerged in Europe after the "great discovery of geography" and colonial competition.[6] She observed that, with the rise of nationalism in the nineteenth century, imperialism took a new form (she called this "New Imperialism" or "National Imperialism"), and competition among imperial powers became even more fierce and cruel. As a result, China as a non-Western country became "a victim of global imperialism."

The second force was "internationalism" (guoji guannian). For Chen, this was the good one. She explained, "The goal of internationalism is to seek mutual understanding among humanity and to draw on the cultures of different countries as one common legacy." Internationalism was an important tool by which to bring perpetual peace to the world.[7] To be sure, Chen did not invent the term. China's young republic had already embraced the ideal of international cooperation since its incipience. In a public statement issued several days after the founding of the Republic (January 5, 1912), the Chinese government announced China's goodwill in joining the international community and promoting world peace.[8] A decade later, Chen still believed that history education was the best way to promote internationalism among China's youth. To her, having knowledgeable human communities could reduce the chance of conflicts and misunderstanding while increasing communication and cultivating sympathy.[9]

As discussed in Chapter 1, gentry scholars who were connected through regional networks played a significant role in producing, promoting, and disseminating world-historical knowledge at the turn of the twentieth century. These individuals had received a Confucian

---

[4] Chen, *Xiyang shi*, 314.   [5] Chen, *Xiyang shi*, 323.   [6] Chen, *Xiyang shi*, 141.
[7] Chen, *Xiyang shi*, 324.
[8] Guoqi Xu, *China and the Great War: China's Pursuit of a New National Identity and Internationalism* (Cambridge: Cambridge University Press, 2005), 60–61.
[9] Chen, *Xiyang shi*, 1–4; Chen Hengzhe, "Lishi jiaoxue yu renlei qiantu" [History education and the future of humanity], *Chenbao qi zhounian jinian zengkan* [Supplement in celebration of *Chenbao*'s seventh anniversary], no. 7 (1925): 198.

education, participated in imperial exams, and aspired to serve as government officials. Confucian influence did not preclude the development of a belief in common humanity among these groups. This belief is a crucial foundation for world-historical studies.

During the Republican years, the professionalization process took place in urban China. A new generation of academic professionals became the leading voices of China's historical studies. Compared to the earlier world-historical writers in the late Qing period, these scholars often had opportunities to study abroad and had received professional training. In this chapter, I select three individuals who greatly contributed to the development of world history during this period: Chen Hengzhe, He Bingsong, and Lei Haizong. All three had studied in the United States, received a professional education in history, and returned to China to teach at elite institutions. Yet these shared experiences did not necessarily lead to a homogeneous voice in their individual writing about world history.

To a certain degree, Chen's works register the liberal roots of world-historical teaching and research in the early Republican period. In the 1920s, Chen was well connected to the liberal circle and was active in various areas as an educator, a writer, a professor, and a novelist. As a historian, her textbooks had been widely adopted by high schools all over China. Her influence was far-reaching. Years later, when Zhou Enlai, the communist leader who was eight years younger, visited Chen Hengzhe's family in wartime Chongqing (1943), he greeted the latter with humble gratitude, saying, "Professor Chen, I am your student. I have listened to your lectures and read your books."[10] The liberal consensus of world history, however, did not continue to dominate the field. He Bingsong and Lei Haizong both held views that were more conservative than Chen's. Their continuous rise in the later years marked a conservative turn in this newly emerged field.

If Chen believed the dominant conflict in world history was one between imperialism and internationalism, He Bingsong replaced internationalism with nationalism. For him, the central question became how to ensure the survival of the Chinese nation in the 1930s. By the 1940s – when China was engaging in a life-or-death struggle with Japan – Lei Haizong had become even more radical in his view of history. He rejected national history because of its Eurocentrism. At the same time, he embraced cultural conservatism and endorsed the concentration of

---

[10] *Ren Hongjun Chen Hengzhe jiashu* [Family correspondences by Ren Hongjun and Chen Hengzhe], ed. Qiangjiu minjian jiashu xiangmu weiyuanhui [Committee on the project to preserve private correspondences] (Beijing: shangwu yinshuguan, 2007), 111.

power by the Nationalist Party leadership. Communist propagandists called this power grab "cultural fascism" – perhaps rightly so. In contrast to Chen's strong opposition to war, Lei now celebrated war as the moment that marked the rejuvenation of Chinese culture. Along with this change, world history in China became increasingly nationalist.

Before diving into these intellectual aspects, let us first take a brief overview of how the professionalization process transformed the discipline of history and laid the foundations for world-historical teaching and research in the early Republican period. If we want to understand the formation of divergent views on cultural issues among historians in the later years, it is essential to grasp first the social and political dimension.

The early Republican period was a time of rapid change in China's education system. Western-style colleges and universities superseded old-style Confucian academies, and courses on science and modern languages began to dominate the new national curriculum.[11] This new system increasingly flourished in academic disciplines and was ingrained in modern institutions of scholarship and higher learning, that is, colleges and universities – including public ones such as Peking University and private ones such as Tsinghua University. Government-sponsored research institutes and privately funded scholarly societies, among others, also joined colleges and universities as institutions of scholarship and higher learning.

With the shift in educational focus, new, urban professional intellectuals (most of whom were university professors) supplanted the social role of scholar-officials, as we have seen in the example of the Changzhou group described in Chapter 1.[12] These individuals were active in academic institutions, education, publishing circles, and the government sector. Major urban centers like Shanghai and Beijing emerged as centers of professional historical scholarship. By the late 1920s, this included the first superstars in the field.[13]

The Republican-era professionalization of historical studies created and consolidated academic leadership (or academic authority) within the field by reshuffling the power structure in China's academic system. It also transformed the old regional intellectual networks such as the Changzhou group into associations based on shared ideas and ideologies.

[11] Wen-hsin Yeh, *The Alienated Academy: Culture and Politics in Republican China, 1919–1937* (Cambridge, MA: Harvard University Press, 1990), 3.
[12] Tze-ki Hon and Robert Culp, "Introduction," in *The Politics of Historical Production in Late Qing and Republican China*, ed. Robert Culp and Tze-ki Hon (Leiden: Brill, 2007), 5.
[13] For an overview of the rise of professional organizations in Shanghai during this period, see Xiaoqun Xu, *Chinese Professionals and the Republican State: The Rise of Professional Associations in Shanghai 1912–1937* (Cambridge: Cambridge University Press, 2001).

The liberal group was particularly vocal in the decade leading to the New Culture Movement.[14] Chen Hengzhe and her husband Ren Hongjun both belonged to this circle, and their friend Hu Shi was often perceived as an opinion leader for the group. As a group of academic professionals heavily influenced by American empiricism, their goal was to pursue "pure scholarship," with the aspiration of establishing an "academic society" (*xueshu shehui*) in China.[15]

For many scholars, the ideal "academic society" was significant because it helped to solve the identity crisis that arose after the abolition of the imperial examination system in 1905. For many centuries, Chinese students studied the Confucian Classics diligently with expectations that it would lead to success in the examinations. This, in turn, would provide opportunities to serve their country and obtain glory for their families. Confronted with the mission to redefine the meaning of scholarly life, many intellectuals were confused about the future. In 1918, the suicide of Liang Ji (1858–1918; father of the famous scholar Liang Shuming, 1893–1988) had already deeply disturbed the scholarly community in Beijing; indeed, his death contributed to questions related to scholarly identity in the postimperial age.[16] In 1927, the mysterious suicide of Wang Guowei (1877–1927), a renowned scholar of the Chinese classics, further provoked nationwide discussions among scholarly groups. Gu Jiegang (1893–1980), a student of Hu Shi and a rising star among new academic professionals, bemoaned that it was a lack of institutional support for Wang's scholarly research that eventually killed Wang. The gentry class was gone, and, to replace it, China needed a new system that could provide consistent and stable incomes for academic professionals, free of political influence.[17]

From the 1910s to the 1920s, the professionalized academic system continued to grow. Many believed that this was the future. They

[14] For example, Hu Shi embraced cosmopolitanism while studying in the United States. Grieder, *Hu Shih and the Chinese Renaissance*, 57–61. So did Chen Hengzhe, but Chen believed that her cosmopolitan view was rooted in her family tradition. Though her neighbors often made derogatory comments about outlanders, her family never did. Chen Hengzhe [Chen Nan-hua], *Chen Hengzhe zaonian zizhuan* [Autobiography of a Chinese young girl], trans. Feng Jin (Hefei: Anhui jiaoyu chubanshe, 2006), 25; Zhang Qing, "Hu Shi pai xuerenqun yu xiandai Zhongguo ziyouzhuyi de quxiang" [The Hu Shi group of intellectuals and the trend of liberalism in modern China], *Shilin* [Historical Review], no. 1 (1998): 36–38.

[15] See Wang Fansen, "'Zhuyi Chongbai' yu jindai Zhongguo xueshu shehui de mingyun: yi Chen yinke wei li" [The "blind belief in isms" and the fate of modern Chinese academic society: Chen Yinke as an example], in *Zhongguo jindai sixiang yu xueshu de xipu*, 463–88.

[16] Guy Alitto, *The Last Confucian: Liang Shu-ming and the Chinese Dilemma of Modernity* (Berkeley: University of California Press, 1986), 64–69.

[17] Gu Jiegang, "Dao Wang Jing'an xiansheng" [Mourning for Mr. Wang Jing'an], *Wenxue zhoubao* [Literature weekly], no. 5 (1929): 5.

embraced the identity of "scholar" as academic professionals, believing that as a "new" scholar one had to apply "scientific" methods of study.[18] The scientific method was an incremental, value-free process of specialized research, through which individuals were making steady and accumulative discoveries simply based on direct evidence, regardless of their social applications and consequences. To maintain ultimate scholarly value, scholars must restrain from overstretching arguments or getting involved in politics.[19] At the same time, these academic professionals also believed that specialized research was integrated with a comprehensive system of knowledge. According to Gu, scholarly research also required a balanced development of all subjects; without this, the overall field could not advance. This interdependence was almost like the difference between urban and rural lives. In contrast to the relatively autonomous nature of a countryman, urbanites had to rely on a system of support to fulfill the basic needs of life. Scholarly research required a similar network.[20] Because of this thinking, scholars should speak for each other on behalf of the profession and consolidate the scholarly community – the "academic society" – against external influences.[21]

Yet this idealized "academic society" was not a value-free place. The institutionalization of historical studies came at the price of state regulation and standardization. The revolution in 1911 overthrew the old imperial system, but it failed to establish a strong and centralized new government. The early Republican period witnessed a weak presence of the state in China's intellectual life. After the consolidation of power within the Nationalist Party in the late 1920s, the fledgling Nanjing government tried to establish a stronger influence over China's new higher education system. Regulations required schools to apply for accreditation from the Republican government before enrolling new students. Governmental mandates prescribed "sets of financial, academic, and organizational criteria with which the various types of academic institutions were to be evaluated in their application for accreditation." The Nationalist government's presence in intellectual life was still minimal compared to the later Communist era, to be sure. Yet, in rare but extreme instances, the government could

---

[18] Gu Jiegang, "*Gushibian zixu*" [Introduction] in Gu Jiegang (ed.), *Gu shi bian* [Debates on Ancient History] (Shanghai: Shanghai guji chubanshe, 1982), 109–110.

[19] Gu, "*Gushibian zixu*," 98. Hu Shi shared a similar idea. See Grieder, *Hu Shih and the Chinese Renaissance*, 180–216.

[20] Gu, "*Gushibian zixu*," 99–100.

[21] Gu Jiegang, "1926 nian shikanci" [Dedication to the first issue of 1926], *Beijing daxue yanjiusuo guoxuemen zhoukan* [Division of national studies at the graduate school of Peking University weekly] (1937 reprint): 9, originally printed on January 1, 1926.

exercise arbitrary power over institutions, such as to relocate and reorganize them.[22]

As a general trend, governmentally imposed standardization focused on secondary education. As for history education, the Nationalist government introduced a series of national history teaching curricula. The Ministry of Education's 1929 national middle school history curriculum is perhaps the most representative of these; it became the foundation for later revisions. It assigned history education the task of instilling in a new generation of Chinese citizens a national spirit in the wake of the consolidation under the Nanjing government.[23]

Aside from state intervention, China's new academic profession comprised a small circle during the entire Republican period. With a limited academic market and resources, a select group of individuals emerged as the leaders of a few self-identified groups that attracted followers through creating master–disciple patronage. They became academic authorities, who were well respected in society and were able to mobilize vast resources to develop their fields by nurturing successive generations of scholars. Aspiring younger scholars had to struggle to find patronage in this highly imbalanced academic world. The complex relationship between "academic authorities" and "aspiring young scholars" would develop into a source of conflict in later years when the communist government attempted to take total control of the system in the early 1950s.

As for a discipline that embraced worldwide history, its development was a product of the increased level of specialization in historical teaching and research. The establishment of new subfields such as world history (often in the name of "foreign history" [*waiguo shi*] or "Western history" [*xiyang shi*]) dramatically expanded the scope of historical knowledge among China's educated classes. In world history, the sweeping processes of professionalization evidenced three transformations in the related teaching and research during the Republican period: the introduction and translation of recent world-historical scholarship from the West, the inclusion of world history in secondary curricula, and the emergence of

---

[22] Culp, *Articulating Citizenship*, 38. As for the case of the Ministry of Education's order to disband Labor University in Shanghai and the university's petitions, see *Zhonghua minguo shi dang'an ziliao huibian* [A collection of archival documents on the Republic of China] (hereafter *ZMSDZH*), 5:pt. 1., no. 24, 189–198, and Yeh, *The Alienated Academy*, 172–173.

[23] "Zanxing kecheng biaozhun" [Provisional curriculum standards], in *Zhongxiaoxue kecheng zanxing biaozhun* [Temporary standards for middle and primary school], ed. Jiaoyubu zhongxiaoxue kecheng biaozhun qicao weiyuan hui [Ministry of education committee on drafting elementary and high school curricula] (Shanghai: Qingyun tushu gongsi, 1930), 2:25–26. Also, Shi Guirong, "1929 *nian zhongxue lishi zanxing kecheng biaozhun yanjiu*" [A study of the temporary standard for the middle school history curriculum in 1929] (Master's thesis, Yangzhou University, 2007), 14.

a flourishing textbook market for world history, despite the fact that world history remained primarily a teaching field.

The first effect indicates the level of cultural exchange in the writing of history. Scholars have already praised Republican China's openness to international society.[24] A sizable number of the graduates of some of the most elite schools in China such as Tsinghua University (formerly known as "Tsinghua College"), as seen in Figure 3, went abroad and continued to study. Returning to China, they had greatly contributed to China's modernization efforts. So it was for historical studies. During this period, a great number of Chinese intellectuals either studied abroad or stayed acutely abreast of the development of foreign academic scholarship. Some estimate that, by 1931, 39.8 percent of faculty members at Chinese universities had studied abroad.[25] Not only did they return to China with the knowledge they had learned in the West but they also recognized the importance of the translation of foreign works on history for scholarly work. Take He Bingsong as an example. As a well-regarded historian, the bulk of his work was on translation. He often collaborated with others and translated popular works on European history and historiography in the West. His translations ranged from James Harvey Robinson's *The New History* and James T. Shotwell's *An Introduction to the History of History* to Henry Johnson's *Teaching History in Elementary and Secondary Schools*. Drawing on a selected translation of James Harvey Robinson's *An Introduction to the History of Western Europe*, Robinson and Charles A. Beard's *Outline of European History*, and Charles Seignobos's *La Méthode historique appliquée aux sciences sociales*, he also edited history textbooks for use in middle school, high school, and college classrooms. As many others joined the translation efforts, Chinese historians became well acquainted with the very latest academic works on history in the West.[26]

The second impact was the integration of world history into the national education curriculum. Non-Chinese history was already part of the national curricula in the late Qing era, as discussed in Chapter 1. During the Republican period, world history in its various forms (often known as "foreign history") remained a key component of history

[24] William Kirby, "The Internationalization of China: Foreign Relations at Home and Abroad in the Republican Era," *The China Quarterly*, no. 150 (1997): 433–458.

[25] Wang Qisheng, *Zhongguo liuxuesheng de lishi guiji, 1872–1949* [The historical pattern of Chinese students who have studied abroad, 1872–1949] (Wuhan: Hubei jiaoyu chubanshe, 1992), 270–271.

[26] Li Xiaoqian, *Xifang shixue zai Zhongguo de chuanbo, 1882–1949* [The spread of Western historiography in China, 1882–1949] (Shanghai: Huadong shifan daxue chubanshe, 2007), 4. On Robinson's influence on Chinese historians, see Li, *Reinventing Modern China*, 58–59.

Figure 3 Returned students' conference at Tsinghua College, ca. 1918–1919. Photo: Sidney D. Gamble photographs, 244A_1370, David M. Rubenstein Rare Book & Manuscript Library, Duke University

education in the secondary education system. Under such a system, a middle school student needed to spend a significant amount of time studying world history related subjects.[27] For instance, the national curriculum issued by the Ministry of Education in 1913 regulated that students take four years to complete high school. In the first and second years, they were required to earn four credit hours in total on Chinese history – including the ancient, medieval, and modern periods. In the third year, they took two credit hours on the history of East Asia (*dongya geguo shi*) and the history of Western countries (*xiyang shi*) in total, with an additional two credit hours on the history of Western countries in the fourth.[28] In other words, they needed to spend an equal

[27] Culp, *Articulating Citizenship*, 37.
[28] "Jiaoyubu gongbu zhongxue kecheng biaozhun ling" [The decree issued by the Ministry of Education concerning the standards of high school curriculum] (August 19, 1913), in *ZMSDZH*, 3:pt.9, 284.

amount of time on studying Chinese and non-Chinese history.[29] This forms a sharp contrast to Western curricula in history. During this same period, Western curricula barely covered non-European and non-American cultures.

The significant role of world history in the secondary education system gave rise to a flourishing textbook market.[30] This is the third major impact in the development of world history. The national book market that had emerged in Ming–Qing China flourished in the Republican period. Economic concerns interacted with the production of knowledge, giving rise to fierce competition among publishers.[31] This was particularly the case in the textbook market.[32] After the introduction of the national curriculum, publishers recognized the opportunities and challenges inherent in the fledgling national textbook market. Private publishing houses were especially eager to invest in editing and publishing world history textbooks.[33] An incomplete survey suggests that at least sixty-two world history survey texts appeared in the Republican period.[34] Chen Hengzhe's textbook on high school–level European history was among the most popular. The editing and writing of new world history textbooks drove the development of the study of world history in China.

In summary, the timely introduction and translation of Western world-historical literature, the inclusion of world history into the secondary education system, and the flourishing textbook market contributed to the development of world history as a teaching field. The curricula of Chinese universities and colleges reflected this growing interest in teaching world history. By the 1930s, some elite institutions offered as many foreign history courses as their American counterparts, or even more.[35]

---

[29] "Xuezhi xitong tu bing shuoming" [Annotated chart on the system of education] (1932), in *ZMSDZH*, 5:pt.1, no.24, 15.

[30] On the rise of textbook market during the Republican period, see Zarrow, *Educating China*, esp. chapter 1.

[31] Reed, *Gutenberg in Shanghai*, esp. chapter 5, 203–256; Culp, *Articulating Citizenship*, 43–47.

[32] Ling Shiao, "Printing, Reading, and Revolution: Kaiming Press and the Cultural Transformation of Republican China" (PhD thesis, Brown University, 2009), 33–34, 234–235.

[33] Robert Culp, "'Weak and Small Peoples' in a 'Europeanizing World': World History Textbooks and Chinese Intellectuals' Perspectives on Global Modernity," in *The Politics of Historical Production in Late Qing and Republican China*, ed. Hon and Culp, 216–217.

[34] Zhou Mingsheng, "Minguo shiqi zhongxue de shijieshi jiaoyu de tedian ji qishi" [The special characteristics and inspiration of secondary-school world history pedagogy in the Republican period], *Zhongguo jiaoyu xuekan* [Journal of the Chinese Society of Education], no. 9 (September 2009): 62.

[35] According to Lei Haizong's survey, the main problem with the history curriculum in Chinese higher education was the overly heavy course loads. In his view, Chinese college students studied not "too little" but "too much" world history. For instance, the Department of History at Yenching University offered eleven courses in world history,

Yet, despite the progress in teaching world history, world-historical research was still largely underdeveloped in Chinese academia as elsewhere in the world.

Three factors caused the underdevelopment of world-historical research in Republican China. The first was that Chinese intellectuals lacked access to basic language training. This was particularly glaring vis-à-vis American and European scholars, who devoted years to learning the foreign languages of the subjects of their study – especially ancient languages such as Greek, Latin, and Sanskrit. Chinese historians, in contrast, had little opportunity to acquire these linguistic skills.[36] In relation to this, the second factor was concerned with the availability of translated non-Chinese language primary sources. Chen Hengzhe, for instance, once complained about this issue in a public talk at Peking University.[37]

The third factor was that most scholars in the field lacked an active research agenda. If we merely look at numbers, the inclusion of non-Chinese subjects in history teaching in the Republican period is impressive. At least one-third of university history professors taught courses that could be considered as "world history," a far higher percentage than in the West. Few of these scholars, however, made substantive research contributions to the field. Famous world historians of the time such as Liu Chonghong (1897–1990) and Kong Fanyu (1894–1959) left no research works at all. Scholars who were later regarded as world historians after the founding of the People's Republic, such as Zhou Yiliang (1913–2001), Jiang Mengyin (1907–1988), Wu Yujin (1913–1993), and Lin Zhichun, published little on world history during this period. Lei Haizong, a well-respected forerunner in world-historical studies in this period, addressed this lack of enthusiasm in research among world history teachers. Writing satirically, Lei observed that the complexity of "Chinese history is already enough to confuse our studies, and there is nothing left [for scholars] in China to go beyond our ability and try to study Western history."[38] In the age of academic professionalization, world history was unable to gain gravity and respect in Chinese academia for its lack of original research. After all, world history remained primarily a teaching field.

more than any elite American university of the time. While no American university offered instruction in Chinese history, Chinese universities offered far more extensive curricula than their American counterparts. Lei Haizong, "Duiyu daxue lishi kecheng de yidian yijian" [One suggestion on the college history curriculum] *Duli pinglun* [Independent review], no. 224 (October 25, 1936): 7.

[36] Shang, "Jindai Zhongguo daxue shixue jiaoshou qunxiang," 103–104.

[37] "Chen Hengzhe xiansheng yanshuo ci" [Speech by M. Chen Hengzhe], *Beijing daxue rikan* [The daily journal of Beijing University], September 18 (1920): 2.

[38] Lei, "Duiyu daxue lishi kecheng de yidian yijian," 11.

This was not a Chinese problem, however. Only a few scholars of world history in the early twentieth century obtained academic credentials and positions in institutions of higher education, and most works produced in this period have substantive shortcomings, particularly as early world historians wrote "on their own, or in disciplines outside history, and often for a general audience." At the same time, it would be a mistake to disregard their contributions. As Patrick Manning cogently argues, "[Understanding] their efforts, their insights, and their failures is a prerequisite to the work of future generations in developing original and appropriate concepts and generalizations for understanding world history."[39] In China, the greatest contribution of world historians in the Republican period to the general field of historical studies was to open up debates on the place of China in a world-historical context. This has been an extremely complex topic in Chinese historiography, to be sure, as almost all the leading historians in China during the time had something to offer on this. In this chapter, I select three world historians (loosely defined), Chen Hengzhe, He Bingsong, and Lei Haizong, and examine how their experiences of teaching and writing about world history affected their view on China. I put a special emphasis on Lei, for he was the crucial link in the formation of world history as a scholarly discipline and the rise of academic nationalism in wartime China.

As stated at the opening of this chapter, as a liberal intellectual, Chen Hengzhe regarded imperialism and internationalism as a pair of contradicting cultural forces that would determine the future of the world. Within this dynamic, she identified nationalism as a significant and less predictable variable. Nationalism could be dangerous. World history had entered into the stage of "National Imperialism" by the nineteenth century. Aside from the scramble for raw materials, she believed that nationalism was the other driving factor that intensified colonial competition among the Western imperial powers.[40] At the same time, nationalism could serve as a positive force, too, if each individual took pride in their own country's contribution to world culture and strove for it.[41] By and large, however, Chen regarded nationalism as an antidemocratic force.[42] As a cultural cosmopolite, she was at best lukewarm about it. Her discussion on nationalism was overall concise and limited.

Chen's coeval, He Bingsong, was another well-known world historian in the 1920s.[43] Like Chen, he had studied in the United States and

[39] Manning, *Navigating World History*, 52.   [40] Chen, *Xiyang shi*, 304.
[41] Chen, *Xiyang shi*, 324.   [42] Chen, *Xiyang shi*, 315–316.
[43] He's biographical information is cited from Fang Xinliang, "He Bingson nianpu" [He Bingsong chronicle], in *He Bingsong wenji* [Collected papers by He Bingsong], ed. Liu Yinsheng and Fang Xinliang (Beijing: Shangwu yinshuguan, 1997): 4:661–864.

obtained an MA degree from Princeton University in 1916. He returned to China a few years earlier than Chen. At first, he worked in his home province, Zhejiang, and then started teaching Western history at Peking University in 1917. In the coming years, he served in various capacities from university professor, high school principle, textbook writer, translator, and publishing editor to university chancellor until his sudden death in 1946.

While both had taught Western history at Peking University, He had a more favorable view of nationalism than Chen did. In contrast to Chen's view that internationalism and imperialism were the two leading cultural forces in world history, He substituted internationalism with nationalism. He explained the relationship between the two in a 1926 essay. In this, he first defined imperialism as "a strategy to expand territory with a goal to take over its products, monopolize its commerce, and invest in developing its natural resources." He then moved on to nationalism, describing it as a principle by which "one or multiple nationalities can claim sovereignty within their territory, not allowing any foreign powers to unjustly interfere with their domestic politics and to insult their honor," which was much in line with the anticolonial nationalism promoted by the Nationalist state.[44]

Imperialism and nationalism shared common features. As He contended, both contain elements concerned with territory, people, and sovereignty. Imperialism was a drive for aggressive expansion, and nationalism was a weapon for passive resistance. The two were thus in constant conflict. Western powers achieved imperial control through military conquests, economic coercions, and cultural invasions. In contrast, countries in the colonial world defended their sovereignty through military, economic, and cultural resistances. In the wake of World War I, He was cheered by the rise of global anticolonial movements in Ireland, Egypt, and India as well as the achievements in Poland, Czechoslovakia, and Turkey, asserting that the nationalist movement would eventually overcome imperialism and bring great harmony to the world (*Datong*).[45] As China was continuously struggling within the colonial world, He believed that the history of nationalist movements in the West would serve China as a roadmap to its struggle for national sovereignty.[46]

---

[44] He Bingsong, "Diguo zhuyi yu guojia zhuyi" [Imperialism and nationalism], in *He Bingsong wenji*, 2:198.

[45] He Bingsong, 202. For a global historical study on these anticolonial movements, see Erez Manela, *The Wilsonian Moment: Self-Determination and the International Origins of Anticolonial Nationalism* (Oxford: Oxford University Press, 2007).

[46] He Bingsong, "Xiandai xiyang guojia zhuyi yundong shilue" [A concise history of the nationalist movements of modern Western countries] in *He Bingsong wenji*, 2: 204–220. The original piece was published in 1926.

The different perspectives on nationalism drove a wedge between liberalism and conservatism among Chinese intellectuals in the 1920s.[47] By the 1930s, cultural conservatism steadily gathered strength. This movement further spurred nationalist sentiments among world historians. As a female scholar, Chen Hengzhe already faced pressures to balance family life and a career in the 1920s. After teaching for one year at Peking University, she became pregnant and decided to quit her position as a professor to focus on writing. She became more involved with cultural affairs. Along with the most renowned Chinese intellectuals such as Cai Yuanpei, Hu Shi, and Ding Wenjiang, she represented China and attended the prestigious Institute of Pacific Relations conferences in 1927, 1929, 1931, and 1933.[48] She also wrote extensively on cultural issues ranging from secondary education and women's rights to American culture in China as a public intellectual. Her interest gradually moved away from professional teaching and research on world history.

By contrast, He Bingsong, as a male scholar, continued to shine in his professional career. He accepted senior editorial positions at the Commercial Press and took on leadership roles at various higher education institutions. As Japan tightened its grip on China, He also became increasingly outspoken about public affairs. On January 18, 1932, the Japanese army launched attacks on the Chinese territory in Shanghai, and the Nationalist army fought back. On January 29, the Japanese air force bombed the headquarters of the Commercial Press and set its warehouse on fire. Several days later, the Japanese army again bombed the Oriental Library and the translation bureau. These attacks caused the loss of 16 million items in total, as estimated by He Bingsong. Among them included thousands of valuable rare books and print copies. It was an atrocity against culture, and the entire nation was shocked. For the rest of the 1930s, China was constantly living in fear of total foreign invasions, and He like many other Chinese intellectuals became increasingly concerned about the survival of the Chinese nation.

---

[47] This was a general divide among Chinese scholars rather than merely world historians. Edmund Fung, "Nationalism and Modernity: The Politics of Cultural Conservatism in Republican China," *Modern Asian Studies* 43, no. 3 (2009): 780.

[48] Chen Hengzhe also served as the editor of the conference volume *Symposium on Chinese Culture*, which was based on the papers from the 1929 conference. Sophia H. Chen Zen, ed., *Symposium on Chinese Culture: Prep. for the 4th Biennial Conference of the Institute of Pacific Relations, Hangchow, Oct. 21 to Nov. 4, 1931* (Shanghai: Institute of Pacific Relations, 1931). For a recent Chinese translation, see Chen Hengzhe, ed., *Zhongguo wenhua lun ji: 1930 niandai Zhongguo zhishi fenzi dui Zhongguo wenhua de renshi yu xiangxiang* [Symposium on Chinese culture: the understanding and imagination of Chinese culture among Chinese intellectuals in the 1930s], trans. Wang Xianming and Gao Jimei (Fuzhou: Fujian jiaoyu chubanshe, 2009).

For these scholars, Chinese culture was the Chinese nation. On January 10, 1935, ten professors issued a public statement, entitled "Declaration on Reconstructing a China-centered Culture" (*Zhongguo benwei de wenhua jianshe xuanyan*). As an active voice in the group, He signed the document and arduously endorsed its agenda in the following public debates. In this short document, these professors stated that China as a country has lost its system of politics, organization of society, and substance and form of thought. As such, the Chinese people were no longer Chinese. They bemoaned that "China had disappeared from the modern world." To save the falling nation, they called for collective action to reconstruct a China-centered (*benwei*) culture. Only by doing so could China survive as a nation and contribute to the world in its unique way.[49]

The statement was no scholarly work. One could even argue that it was part of the Nationalist Party's efforts to take direct control over cultural affairs. Many individuals who were signatories to the statement were members of the Association of Cultural Reconstruction, a group with close ties to the conservative wing of the Nationalist Party. On March 25, 1934, the association was established in Shanghai. More than 200 people attended the meeting, and Chen Lifu (1900–2001), the head of the CC Clique, was elected its president.[50] In the following year, He became the next president of the association, a sign of his intimate connection to or at least active collaboration with the right-wing element of the party.

This public statement immediately provoked protests from the liberals. Hu Shi, a leading voice among Chinese liberals and He's former colleague at Peking University, leveled an incisive critique. He called the statement an echo of "Chinese essence and Western utility," the failed formula that late Qing reformers adopted to save the falling dynasty. It was already outdated.[51] More importantly, Hu pointed out four flaws in the group's attempts to engineer culture. In dissecting the concept of culture, he pointed out that, first, culture was a passive existence, and thus it needed no artificial protection by the state. Second, culture evolved, and it was natural that one culture lost certain elements when it encountered another. Third, in this complex dynamic, one could find no "scientific"

---

[49] "Zhonggguo benwei de wenhua jianshe xuanyuan," in *Zhongguo benwei wenhua jianshe taolun ji* [The collection on the discussions on the China-centered culture] (Taipei: Pamier shudian, 1980), 9–15.

[50] Fang Xinliang, "He Bingsong nianpu," 735; for more on the CC Clique, see Maggie Clinton, *Revolutionary Nativism: Fascism and Culture in China, 1925–1937* (Durham, NC: Duke University Press, 2017), esp. 30–35.

[51] Hu Shi, "Shiping suowei 'Zhongguo benwei wenhua de jianshe'" [A preliminary review of the so-called "reconstruction of China-centered culture"], *Dagong bao* [Ta Kung Pao] (Tianjin), March 31, 1935, B.

standards by which to facilitate a wholescale change of a culture. Lastly, Hu questioned the concept of *Zhongguo benwei*, which I translate as "China-centered." He argued that this *benwei* was the habitual existence of Chinese people. Thus, as long as the people existed, there was no need to worry about the loss of this *benwei* culture.[52]

Hu's critique touched on the significant question of the limits of state power. As a student who was trained in the American liberal tradition, he was naturally suspicious of any attempts by the state to control cultural affairs. It was his instinct as a liberal to protect the autonomous realm of thought from external impositions. Through his knowledge of world history, He, in a response, was able to make sense of the other grave concern that was the driving force behind the rise of conservatism in China, one that emerged out of colonial anxiety and the world-historical context. To He and many others, the question was, what if the "Chinese people" that Hu Shi talked about no longer existed? Just take a look at what happened to the peoples in India, Africa, and Vietnam, He wrote.[53] Liberals were making many beautiful promises, but a country like China still needed a strong and centralized state to ensure its sheer survival in a world that was dominated by colonial aggressions and imperial expansions.

The discussion on the question of China-centered culture developed into a national debate prior to the full-scale war with Japan. After its original release in early 1935, the editor of the *Cultural Reconstruct Monthly*, the official outlet of the Association of Cultural Reconstruction, had collected works comprising more than a million characters on this topic by August 1936, and senior leaders from the Nationalist Party such as Chen Lifu and Dai Jitao (1891–1949) showed their support for the ten professors.[54] He Bingsong had played a significant role in this debate. In his case, his knowledge about world history had served as a powerful reference in this national dialogue about the preservation of Chinese culture and the reconstruction of national identity.

As Chen Hengzhe and He Bingsong gradually veered away from teaching world history in the 1930s, Lei Haizong stayed on in his position as professor while maintaining public engagements. Lei did not directly participate in the earlier debates on Chinese culture. Yet his knowledge about ancient history allowed him to contribute to the ongoing discussions on nationalism, Chinese culture, and world history in a unique way.

---

[52] Hu Shi, "Shiping suowei 'Zhongguo benwei wenhua de jianshe'," B and D.

[53] He Bingsong, "Lun Zhongguo benwei wenhua jianshe da Hu Shi xiansheng," *Zhongguo benwei wenhua jianshe taolunji*, 252.

[54] Fan Zhongyun, "Bianzhe xuyan," *Zhongguo benwei wenhua jianshe taolunji*, 3. For Dai's role in ideological education, see Zarrow, *Educating China*, 36.

Twelve years younger than Chen and He, Lei Haizong gradually emerged as the leading voice of the next generation of world historians in Republican China from the 1930s to the 1940s.[55] In contrast to the previous one, Lei's generation had gathered some momentum in research. On the one hand, they identified and criticized the Eurocentric pitfalls in the existing scholarship on world history in the West. On the other hand, as they became even more concerned with the fate of Chinese culture in the ongoing war with Japan, they abandoned the liberal view of and the empirical approach to historical studies. Instead, they increasingly embraced a culturally conservative position in historical studies. This approach raised concerns among professional historians as well as communist propagandists; it also placed the newly emerged field of world history in a dilemma between academics and politics.

As a professor, Lei Haizong' career followed a typical trajectory in the Republican period – he studied in the United States and returned to teach at elite universities in China; yet he had an unusual family upbringing.[56] Lei Haizong's father Lei Mingxia (Lei Ming-hsia) served as a reverend in Yongqing, Hebei, a county between Beijing and Tianjin that celebrates its long Christian tradition. When Lei Haizong was eleven years old (1913), his father was ordained by the British missionary Charles Perry Scott (1847–1927), the first bishop in North China. Mingxia remained a capable worker in the local church.[57] In accordance, the church provided free primary and secondary education for his children.[58] Excelling in his studies, Lei Haizong earned a Boxer Indemnity Scholarship in 1922 to study in the United States. At the University of Chicago, he studied with James Westfall Thompson (1869–1941), who was an established scholar of medieval and early modern Europe and later served as

---

[55] Xu Guansan, *Xinshixue jiushi nian* [New historiography of the last ninety years] (Hong Kong: Chinese University Press, 1986). There is a growing interest in Lei Haizong in English-language scholarship today. Michael Godley introduced the tension between politics and history in Lei's works in the late 1980s. Godley, "Politics from History: Lei Haizong and the Zhanguo Ce Clique," *Papers on Far Eastern History* 40 (September 1989): 95–122. Prasenjit Duara also briefly mentions Lei in his discussion of modern Chinese historiography. Duara, *Rescuing History from the Nation*, 40–42. The Cambridge University Press is publishing the English translation of Lei Haizong's essay collection, and my introduction to the volume provides an overview of Lei's life and work for English-language audiences. Lei Haizong, *Chinese Culture and the Chinese Military*, trans. George Fleming (Cambridge: Cambridge University Press, 2020).

[56] For the most authoritative biographical information on Lei, see *BDRC*, 2:283–285.

[57] G. F. S. Gray, *Anglicans in China: A History of the Zhonghua Shenggong Hui* (Chung Hua Sheng Kung Huei) (The Episcopal China Mission History Project), 37, http://anglican history.org/asia/china/cpscott/07.html.

[58] Zhang Jingfu, "Wo de huiyi" [My memories], in *Zhongguo de bing* [China's military] (Beijing: Zhonghua shuju, 2005), 194–195.

president of the American Historical Association in 1941. Perhaps influenced by his advisor's early interest in French history, Lei wrote a PhD thesis on "The Political Ideas of Turgot," a progressive thinker and statesmen in eighteen-century France (1727–1781).[59] On receipt of his doctorate in 1927, Lei returned to China, taking up a teaching position at National Central University in Nanjing, a school officially sponsored by the Nationalist Party. After several years' work in Nanjing, he moved to Wuhan University in 1931 and taught there for a short period until 1932.[60] In 1932, Lei joined the History Department at his alma mater, Tsinghua University. From there, he eventually served as chair of the History Department in the 1940s, and even served as acting dean at the faculty of Arts and Letters in the academic year 1946–1947.

As a pioneer in world-historical teaching, Lei escaped the professional boundaries between "foreign" and "national" histories and taught extensively from ancient and medieval world histories to the general surveys of Chinese history. In research, he also published on many diverse topics, including early Chinese history, Western classical antiquity, European medieval history, early modern European history, the history of Christianity in China, Chinese historiography, the history of nomadic peoples, terminology and periodization in Chinese and world history, Buddhism, medieval European philosophy, and international politics.

Despite Lei Haizong's relative lack of subject or period specialization judged by today's professional standards, his attention to concepts and periodization in history reflects his professional consciousness in a way far more sophisticated than earlier world historians such as He Bingsong and Chen Hengzhe. His works, as I contend in this chapter, predate some postmodern and postcolonial critiques of Eurocentrism and national history in Western historiography that would emerge much later in the twentieth century.

Let us first start with Lei's take on basic concepts in world history. In an important essay that he published in 1936, he analyzed *shijie shi* (world history), *xiyang shi* (history of the West or the Occident), and *waiguo shi*

---

[59] Lei Haizong (Barnabas Hai-Tsung Lei), "The Political Ideas of Turgot" (Ph.D. diss., University of Chicago, 1927). Also, Wang Dunshu, "Qianyan: Lei Haizong de shengping, zhixue tedian he benjuan shuoming" [Preface: Master Lei Haizong's life, unique contributions to scholarship as well as notes on this volume], in *Bolun shixue ji* [A collection of Lei Haizong's historiographical works], ed. Wang Dunshu (Beijing: Zhonghua shuju, 2002), 1. For a recent essay contextualizing Lei Haizong's academic training in Chicago, see Yang Zhao, "Lei Haizong de boshi lunwen yu Zhijiage daxue de xiyang shi xueshu chuantong" [Lei Haizong's PhD thesis and the academic tradition on the studies of Western history at the University of Chicago], *Jiangsu shifan daxue xuebao (zhexue shehui kexue ban)* [Journal of Jiangsu Normal University (Philosophy and social sciences edition)], no. 3 (2018): 10–15, 116.

[60] Zhang Jingfu, "Wo de huiyi," 194.

(history of foreign countries), three prototypes of world history in China.[61] In a Chinese context, Lei wrote that, in most cases, *shijie shi* was regarded as *waiguo shi*. He accepted this equation for the sake of convenience, while he found that *xiyang shi* was problematic for its ambiguity about time and space. Was *xiyang shi* all about what happened in Europe? He questioned, if this was the case, why it did not include much about the Ottoman Empire, part of whose territory was located in the continent? Similarly, what about the Islamic empire or ancient Egypt, both of which had no less influence on Europe as well?[62]

With those questions in mind, Lei further dissected *xiyang* (the West or Occident, or literally Western Ocean), arguing that it usually possessed three layers of meaning. The first narrow spatial meaning included territory west of Poland (excluding Eastern Europe) to North America. The second layer referred to general cultural meaning, referring not only to medieval and modern European cultures but also to Greco-Roman (i.e., Western Classical) culture. The third layer, broadly defined, covered ancient civilizations from Egypt, Babylonia, Greece, Rome, and Islam to today's Western Europe.[63] From this list, he observed that, although the meaning of *xiyang* was extremely broad, it always excluded China and India. At the same time, he pointed out that, even within *xiyang*, things were not homogeneous, either. Westerners presumed that Greek and Roman civilizations were similar if not identical. He countered that it was rather arbitrary to place those two civilizations in the same category as the core of Western civilization. For one, they were geographically separated.[64]

In relation to *xiyang*, Lei also found *dongfang* (the East or the Orient, or literally Eastern Ocean) problematic. He observed that, although the term *xiyang* covered a great scope of time and space, it did not include peoples that flourished before the rise of Greek civilization. Lei felt that Westerners were reluctant to use *xiyang* to cover those peoples, so they created the term *dongfang* (the Orient). The word basically covered the rest of the non-Western world. The boundary between *xiyang* and *dongfang* was often ambiguous or fluid. For instance, as the center of Greek civilization was located on the same longitude as that of Egyptian

---

[61] Lei Haizong, "Duandai wenti yu Zhongguo shi de fenqi" [The question of dividing history and the problems of periodization in Chinese history], *Qinghua daxue shehui kexue* (Social sciences at Tshinghua University) 2 (October 1936 to July 1937): 1–34.
[62] Lei, "Duandai wenti yu Zhongguo shi de fenqi," 7.
[63] Lei, "Duandai wenti yu Zhongguo shi de fenqi," 8.
[64] Lei, "Duandai wenti yu Zhongguo shi de fenqi," 9–10. English-language scholarship echoes Lei Haizong's concerns about the ambiguity of the term "West." See Martin Lewis and Kären Wigen, *The Myth of Continents: A Critique of Metageography* (Berkeley: University of California Press, 1997).

civilization, why did people call Greece the "Occident" and Egypt the "Orient"? By the same token, as the Islamic civilization extended its influence into Spain during its peak, why was it still called "*dongfang*"? Lei pointed out that it was confusing to use the East/West dichotomy as a framework for world history, implying that a Eurocentric cultural bias existed within these spatial concepts *xiyang* and *dongfang*.[65]

From space to time, Lei criticized Eurocentric bias embedded in the periodization of world history. He deemed problematic the concepts "classical ages" (*gudai*) and "antiquity" (*shanggu*), owing to the Western origins of the division of history into ancient, medieval, and modern. Western scholars assumed classical antiquity was a global concept that transcended spatial differences. Yet a quick review of the history of classical studies in the West would reveal that the "classical age" initially referred to ancient Greece and Rome in Europe during the Renaissance. Since European scholars of the time had little knowledge about cultures beyond their own continent, they could not have intended this term to be used as a global reference. Thus, Western scholars had to keep stretching the original point of the "classical age" while archaeological discoveries about ancient civilizations prior to European ones continued to grow. The term eventually encompassed at least 4,000 years![66]

These confusing aspects of *xiyang*, *dongyang*, and *shanggu* were, however, to a certain degree, just symptoms. For Lei, the root cause of these problems was the uncritical acceptance of the problematical paradigm of "national history" in historical teaching and research. In the Chinese linguistic context, one often conceptualizes "national history" as the history possessed by a nation. For example, *Zhongguo shi* literally means "China's history," *Yingguo shi* "Britain's history," and *Ouzhou shi* "Europe's history." Lei understood this to be wrong, for one should not assume "a given place naturally owns its history." "Places do have histories," as he furthermore explained, but these histories "belong to geology and natural geography, which has nothing to do with [human] history *per se*." As people constantly changed even within the same space, the history of the space was not the same history as that of the people.[67] As such, Lei stressed the interplay between time, space, and peoples; he also criticized national history for its simplistic handling of changes in the past.

Aside from rethinking historical concepts, Lei was also an unequivocal critic of the Eurocentrism embedded in the works of Western scholars,

---

[65] Lei, "Duandai wenti yu Zhongguo shi de fenqi," 4.

[66] Lei, "Duandai wenti yu Zhongguo shi de fenqi," 3. Lei Haizong was not alone on this. Several Chinese historians had cast doubts on the division of ancient, medieval, and modern in Chinese historiography. Zarrow, *Educating China*, 155.

[67] Lei, "Duandai wenti yu Zhongguo shi de fenqi," 6.

who often treated "Western history" as "world history." He took *The Outline of History* by H. G. Wells as an example. As the book was a bestseller in post–World War I Europe and America, the Commercial Press anticipated its market value in China and put together an all-star team to translate it into Chinese. It enlisted five scholars as translators, with another ten as editors. Liang Sicheng (1901–1972), an architectural historian educated in the United States, served as the lead translator; his father, the prominent historian Liang Qichao, helped to promote the book. He Bingsong was also listed as chief editor. Lei, however, spoke against the currents.[68] He noted in a review of Wells's original work that, of the total forty chapters, thirteen focused on the world before civilization, fifteen focused on the West, and one focused on the Aryan people. This left Wells to cram the history of the rest of the world's peoples, including Assyrians, Egyptians, Indians, Chinese, Jews, Islamists, Mongols, and Japanese, into the eleven remaining chapters. This was clear evidence of a Eurocentric bias.[69]

Seeing all sorts of problems related to Eurocentrism in the existing scholarship of world history, Lei called for an alternative. It was time to abandon national history and to replace its tripartite periodization of "ancient," "medieval," and "modern."[70] Lei proposed a history based on cultures, for he believed that culture embodied a unique identity that derived from the ancient past and had yet to unfold within its own temporal and spatial schema. At the same time, only through a world-historical gaze could one grasp the morphology of change in cultures. He divided the world into seven cultures/civilizations: Egyptian, Babylonian, Indian, Chinese, Greco-Roman, Islamic, and Western European.[71] All these cultures shared five equivalent stages of world-historical development: the Feudal Age (which, as he calculated, lasted about 600 years); the Age of Aristocratic States (300 years); the Imperial Age (250 years); the Great Unification Age (300 years); and, finally, the Age of Political Collapse and Cultural Destruction (indeterminate length).[72]

Cultures were like living organisms that flourished and perished. While trying to grasp the rhythm of change, Lei moved away from the belief in a common humanity and stressed the uniqueness of Chinese culture. The

---

[68] Lei Haizong, "Review, *The Outline of History* by H. G. Wells," *Shixue* [Historiography], no. 1 (1930): 233–34. This review was a reprint based of a 1928 version published in *Shishi xinbao* [New newspapers on recent events], March 4, 1928. It appeared first in English.

[69] Lei, "Review," 237–238.

[70] Lei, *Bolun shixue ji,* 139, Lei Haizong, "Lishi de xingtai yu lizheng" [Historical Morphology and Its Examples], in *Bolun shixue ji,* 243. See also, Duara, *Rescuing History from the Nation,* 40.

[71] Lei, *Bolun shixue ji,* 243.   [72] Lei, *Bolun shixue ji,* 243.

Table 2 *Lei Haizong's double life cycles of Chinese culture*

Periodization	China Cycle I	China Cycle II	Lei's Interpretations
Feudal Age	Shang and Western Zhou (1300–771 BC)	Southern and Northern dynasties, Sui, Tang, and Five Dynasties to the Spread of Buddhism (AD 383– 960)	Religious Age
Age of Aristocratic States	Spring and Autumn Age (770–473 BC)	Song dynasty (AD 960–1279)	Philosophical Age
Imperial Age	Warring States Age (473–221 BC)	Yuan and Ming (AD 1279–1528)	Partisanization and Decline of Philosophical Age
Great Unification Age	Qin to Western Han and Eastern Han (221 BC to AD 88)	Late Ming and High Qing (AD 1528– 1839)	Downfall of Philosophical and Academic Age
Age of Political Collapse and Cultural Destruction	Eastern Han to Eastern Jin (AD 89–383 AD)	From the Fall of the Qing (1839 to present)	Cultural Disintegration Age

other six cultures all had one life cycle, he observed, and the Chinese civilization was the only one that had experienced the cycle twice: the first was what he called "Classical China" (Shang dynasty through Eastern Jin) through AD 383; the second he called "Synthesized China" (Eastern Jin through Qing dynasty).[73] One followed the other, exhibiting the five stages of a cultural cycle (see Table 2).

Lei's structure, on the one hand, seems to be rooted in the indigenous intellectual tradition, especially the view of neo-Confucian scholars on historical ruptures. As mentioned in Chapter 1, they argued, as exemplified by Guo Songtao, that the *dao* was lost in China during the Qin–Han transition. On the other hand, it registers the extraneous influence and recalls German scholar Oswald Spengler's work.[74] In his controversial *Der Untergang des Abendlandes* (*The Decline of the West* [or, the Occident]) published between 1918 and 1922, the then high school teacher imagined

---

[73] Lei, *Bolun shixue ji*, 256; Duara, *Rescuing History from the Nation*, 41.
[74] Xu, *Xinshixue jiushi nian*, 59–74. For a discussion on Oswald Spengler and the discourse of civilization, see Duara, "The Discourse of Civilization and Pan-Asianism": 99–130, esp. 100–105.

culture as a superorganism and divided its lifespan into five stages. Drawing from his observations from world history, he predicted the inevitable downfall of Western civilization. Tapping into the anxiety in Europe after World War I, the book quickly became a bestseller in his native land, spawning an English translation. Like other major works in the West, it took no time for someone to introduce Spengler into China.[75] Lei knew about Spengler's work, especially the latter's formula to place culture at the center of world-historical narratives and as an alternative to national concerns. Yet their conceptions of culture were different – Spengler was pessimistic; he held that a distinction marked civilization and culture. Civilization marked a culture's destined stage of demise; as he famously stated, "Civilization is the inevitable destiny of a Culture."[76] In contrast, Lei was more optimistic. He rejected the distinction between culture and civilization, despite his tendency to prefer culture (wenhua) to civilization (wenming) in most of his works. He recognized human agency, holding special hope for Chinese culture.[77] He compared China with other ancient cultures such as Egypt, Babylonia, and Rome, asserting that Chinese culture was unique in world history for it had undergone two progressive life cycles in the past.[78] Thus, he called for Chinese people to get ready for the coming of the third life cycle of Chinese culture in the time of war.[79] Like He Bingsong and the Cultural Reconstruction group, Lei Haizong believed that it was historians' duty to offer historical insight in order to engineer the cultural change in society.

[75] Li Xiaoqian, *Xifang shixue zai Zhongguo de chuanbo, 1882–1949* [The introduction and spread of Western historiography in China, 1882–1949] (Shanghai: Huadong shifan daxue chubanshe, 2007), 241–251 covers the early translation, introduction of, and reception to Spengler in China. The earliest introduction was by Wang Guangqi (1892–1936), a Chinese doctoral student and journalist writing for *Shen Bao*, an influential newspaper based in Shanghai. The report appeared on August 4, 1921 in *Yazhou xueshu zazhi* [Asian journal of academics], no. 1 (December 1921): 2, cited in Li, *Xifang shixue zai Zhongguo de chuanbo*, 245.

[76] Spengler, *Decline of the West*, 31. Duara, "The Discourse of Civilization and Pan-Asianism," 102.

[77] Paul Costello, *World Historians and Their Goals: Twentieth-Century Answers to Modernism* (DeKalb: Northern Illinois University Press, 1993), 68.

[78] Lei, "Duandai yu zhongguoshi de fenqi," 157.

[79] Lei, *Bolun shixue ji*, 157–58. Moving away from Europe, Lei, like many Republican Chinese intellectuals such as Liang Shuming and Zhang Junmai, felt the urge to compare China with India. Without a professional background on India, Lei fumbled with cultural stereotypes. He acknowledged that Indian culture predates Chinese history; but, he argued, because India remained constantly under foreign control after the reign of Ashoka (304–232 BC), it did not experience a second cultural cycle. As a result, India failed to develop an organized political system. This lack of historical consciousness, he maintained, made it impossible for scholars to even evaluate India's religious and philosophical achievements.

If Chinese culture was so impressive, why was China in a deep crisis in the contemporary world? Lei offered some historical analysis. According to him, China prior to the Qin era had a flourishing culture rooted in its militia tradition. Every individual was mobilized, and the state was powerful. However, this tradition was lost during the Qin–Han transition. The lack of militarism became a systematic flaw in the second life cycle of Chinese culture. In order to revive China, Chinese people had to revive the tradition of militarism while concentrating power in the hands of a strong leadership.[80] Lei's promotion of militarism formed such a strong contrast to Chen Hengzhe's anti-war stance in the 1920s. It marked a sharp transition among world historians in China from the pursuit of liberal ideals to the promotion of power politics entering into the 1930s.

In terms of historical methodology, Lei's cultural approach, however, stood him in good stead in the emerging field of Chinese world history. For one, he was among the first professional historians to attempt to link the ancient world and modern China through defining concepts and discussing periodization, thereby advancing world-historical research in China. Some historians admired his grand views of historical synthesis. His contemporary, Jin Yufu (1887–1962), an expert on Chinese historiography as well as Manchu history, praised Lei's ability to offer "a concise general history and an alternative genre of historical writing" after reviewing his seven-volume lecture notes.[81] His student Ping-ti Ho, a famous historian of economic history and president of the Association for Asian Studies in 1975, held dear to Lei's "macroscopic" view in historical analysis.[82]

Many of his contemporaries, however, remained skeptical of the lack of specialization in Lei's world-historical approach. The respected Chen Yinke once ridiculed Lei before students at Tsinghua University. Chen spoke loudly in front of Lei that he could not understand how one could teach the general history of ancient China (*Zhongguo shanggu shi*), a topic so broad and general, in one course. It clearly was meant to be an insult, for this was a course that Lei taught regularly. Lei chose not to respond.[83] Later, in Kunming, Wu Han (1909–1969), a rising young scholar who later became a major Marxist historian and the deputy major of Beijing, also satirized Lei's cultural-morphologist approach to historical studies.[84]

[80] Lei, "Wubing de wenhua," 102.
[81] Jin Yufu, *Jingwushi riji* [Diaries in the Jingwu Room] (Shenyang: Liaoshen shushe, 1993), 151: 6886.
[82] Xin Fan, "The Anger of Ping-Ti Ho: The Chinese Nationalism of a Double Exile," *Storia Della Storiografia* (History of Historiography) 69, no. 1 (2016): 147–160.
[83] He, *Dushi yueshi bashinian*, 115.   [84] He, *Dushi yueshi bashinian*, 116.

Others offered more direct criticism, among them the outspoken critic Zhao Lisheng (1917–2007), who had studied at Tsinghua University in the 1930s. Zhao particularly derided Lei's teaching style, recalling the following:

[He] probably thought that in teaching general history, if you go into anything very deeply, students don't understand, so [he] "bullshitted" like performing stand-up comedy. Sixty years later, I still clearly remember that in the first class the teacher [Lei] opened his lecture by reciting, "The chaotic universe was like a chicken egg, wherein Pangu was born.[85] [That was] eighteen thousand years ago." If it were a lecture in mythology, it would have been all right. But this was about the general history of China! From ancient times to today, where [can one find] such teaching about the general history of China?! In no way could [I] really understand this.[86]

Zhao's remarks remind us of the tensions that existed between various conceptions of history in the Republican period. In a sense, the rise of world history represented by Lei's cultural morphology was a direct critique of mainstream historical research by relying on evidential learning or textual criticism.

As mentioned, "evidential learning" from the Chinese term *kaoju* or *kaozheng* includes the study of book editions and philology. The former includes examining the authenticity of editions or the content of ancient books. The latter focuses on retracing the original meaning of certain words in ancient documents.[87] The method emerged in the early Qing dynasty.[88] By the Republican period, evidential research existed as the dominant paradigm in historical studies.

World history as an alternative approach to historical inquiries challenges the dominance of evidential learning. Since evidential scholarship was centered on certain ancient texts and the reconstruction of the interrelations among those texts, it tended to result in a narrow view of history.[89] Jiang Tingfu (1895–1965), Lei's mentor and chair of the

---

[85] Early Chinese mythology presents Pangu as the creator of the world.

[86] Zhao Lisheng, *Lijintang zixu* [Self-account in the Lijin Hall] (Shanghai: Shanghai guji chubanshe, 1999), 35. Both Zhao Lisheng and Wu Han became Marxist historians. Their political views likely influenced their opinions of Lei.

[87] Hu Shi, "Hu Shi koushu zizhuan" [An oral autobiography of Hu Shi], in *Hu Shi wenji* [Hu Shi's selected writings], ed. Ouyang Zhesheng, Vol. 1 (Beijing: Beijing daxue chubanshe, 1998), 290.

[88] Benjamin Elman, *From Philosophy to Philology: Intellectual and Social Aspects of Change in Late Imperial China* (Los Angeles: UCLA Asian Pacific Monologue Series, 2001), 59–60.

[89] Lin Tongji, "Disanqi de Zhongguo xueshu sichao: xin jieduan de zhanwang" [The intellectual trend of the third period: Prospects for a new stage], *Zhanguo Ce* [Strategies of the Warring States], no. 14 (1940): 2–16..

History Department at Tsinghua University in the late 1920s and early 1930s, for instance, observed that some scholars of evidential learning were incapable of understanding the full sweep of Chinese history.[90] This was problematical, for without a holistic view of the field "[each] single individual more or less had to repeat rather than continue to develop his predecessors' research" and "time was wasted" in nonproductive, redundant labor.[91] He once asked Yang Shuda (1885–1956), a reputed historian of the Han dynasty, to offer a general course on that era, but, as a specialist on the key texts on the history of the Han dynasties (*History of Han* and the *History of the Later Han*),[92] Yang was unable to critically interpret ancient documents and generalize about major political, social, and economic movements during those four centuries. This led Jiang to the view that evidential learning had grown obsolete. In response, he sought to cultivate a new generation of scholars who could argue, "where China originated, into what areas it developed, and where it eventually settled down."[93] Lei Haizong belonged to this new generation of scholars.

Lei never hid his contempt for evidential learning. In an essay published in 1940, he launched a full-fledged attack on the methodology.[94] He asserted that this approach failed to address the most critical issue in shaping historical consciousness, the interaction between subjectivity and the zeitgeist (the spirit of the age). He connected evidential learning to experimentalism (i.e., the empiricism espoused by liberal scholars such as Hu Shi and Gu Jiegang), noting that

For many years, Chinese academia has consciously or unconsciously accepted the influence of experimentalism, looking upon many questions too mechanically, too simplistically.[95] Take historiography as an example: not even to mention those who believe that tedious text criticism or piling up facts is history, even scholars who know that one must seek truth aside from facts often believe that if [one] has collected enough historical facts, then the truth will naturally become visible. In actuality, I am afraid that it's not at all like this.[96]

[90] As for Jiang's biography, see *BDRC*, 1:354b–358b; Li, *Reinventing Modern China*, 44–52.
[91] Jiang Tingfu, *Jiang Tingfu huiyilu* [Memoir of Jiang Tingfu], trans. Xie Zhonglian (Taipei: Zhuanji wenxue chubanshe, 1979), 124.
[92] The Han dynasty, the second Chinese imperial dynasty, is often divided into two periods: the Western Han (206 BC–AD 9) and the Eastern Han (or Later Han, AD 25–220). The Ban family compiled the *Book of the Han*, mostly credited to Ban Gu (AD 32–92), at the beginning of the Later Han dynasty. Fan Ye (AD 398–445) then compiled the *Book of the Later Han* in the fifth century. Scholars consider these histories as part of the official history tradition in China.
[93] Jiang, *Jiang Tingfu huiyilu*, 124.
[94] Lei Haizong, "Lishi jingjuexing de shixian" [The temporality of historical sensitivity], in *Bolun shixue ji*, 213–216.
[95] Scholars have also translated this as "pragmatism," which is linguistically closer to *shijian zhuyi* in Chinese. Chinese scholars tend to use the terms interchangeably, however.
[96] Lei, "Lishi jingjuexing de shixian," 213.

If historical studies are not about fact seeking, how can one acquire historical knowledge? Lei held that the process of historical conception involved the implantation of a zeitgeist into one's consciousness. This process contained both active and passive elements. The active element required one to achieve a complete awareness of the contemporaneous knowledge, aspirations, ideas, and beliefs in order to arrive at historical insights. The degree of conflict in each epoch served as a precondition for those few who possessed historical acumen, which was the passive element. In other words, subjectivity was a product of the zeitgeist. Zeitgeist has different levels of intensity at different times, depending on the amount of tension in society. One could acquire historical sensitivity by actively observing the contemporary world, though individuals have no choice about the historical era into which they are born. The more tension an epoch produced, the more dynamic the zeitgeist would be and the better chance that few individuals would attain deep historical discernment, with which they would understand past events. In ordinary, placid times, people were utterly incapable of clearly understanding any major events in the past.[97]

If historical consciousness resulted from the interaction between one's subjectivity and the zeitgeist, textual criticism was irrelevant. After all, it was merely a method for compartmentalized research. On this basis, Lei brushed away Chinese scholarship after the Qin and Han eras as a period defined by a lack of dynamics and one low in zeitgeist, asserting, "There were only a few small adjustments but never really significant innovations in Chinese society during the past two thousand years."[98] In contrast, Lei underscored the significance of his own age. He maintained that his generation existed amid dramatic tensions, which spurred the development of historical understanding. He thus urged his compatriots to devote themselves to understanding the past macroscopically. The tedious and detailed study of texts could wait for the reestablishment of order. Connecting individual consciousness to the zeitgeist, Lei became an example of a tide in historical studies in Republican China that called for political activism in historical research.

The controversies over methodologies in historical research point to the intricate tension between historians as the political situation became increasingly depressing in the 1930s. Although autonomy was still a much-appreciated idea, intellectuals, especially ones that were connected to the Nationalist Party regime, became increasingly outspoken about scholars' "social responsibilities." Jiang Tingfu wrote about the

---

[97] Lei, "Lishi jingjuexing de shixian," 213.   [98] Lei, "Lishi jingjuexing de shixian," 213.

relationship between the intelligentsia and politics in 1933 while chairing the Department of History at Tsinghua University.[99] Comparing his views to those held by Gu in the 1920s, one can perceive some subtle changes. In line with Gu, Jiang was conscious of the question of scholarly identity. He defined the "intellectual class" as a group of people that used their knowledge to make a living; in other words, they regarded pursuing or disseminating knowledge as a career. He also agreed that intellectuals should distance themselves from politics, especially "the militaries" (i.e., the warlords). Different from Gu, Jiang stressed that intellectuals had "social responsibilities." As the Chinese state remained vulnerable due to China's lack of social organizations, intellectuals should embrace the "modern identity" as socialized and organized beings supporting the Nationalist government.[100] As Jiang explained in a later essay, China's politics was so disorganized that the only viable way leading to China's modernization was an enlightened party dictatorship.[101] Although liberal scholars like Hu Shi opposed this idea, Jiang's view gained influence among his followers – including Lei Haizong. Embracing social responsibility, these intellectuals gradually gave up their pursuit of intellectual autonomy as the ultimate goal of academic life.

The sense of national crisis worsened after 1937, the de facto beginning of the "War of Resistance." As Japan's occupation extended across North China, universities and colleges relocated inland from Beijing and Tianjin. Officials reorganized Tsinghua University, Peking University, and Nankai University into the Southwest Associated University in Kunming.[102] This retreat remained a painful memory for many Chinese intellectuals.[103] As Lei's student Ping-ti Ho later recalled, at the peak of the Japanese invasion, "all of us were constantly haunted by the presence of the spearhead of the Japanese Kwantung Army merely 200 kilometers

[99] Jiang obtained his PhD degree in history at Columbia University. As a historian, his textbook on modern Chinese history is considered to be a masterpiece and continues to be referenced by historians today. As an administrator, he supervised the reform of Tsinghua University's Department of History, leading the Tsinghua administration to recruit scholars like Lei Haizong. After 1935, Jiang became very active in politics and closely connected to the leadership of the Nationalist Party, which, after 1949, led him all the way to a position as the Republic of China's (Taiwan) ambassador to the United Nations and the United States successively.

[100] Jiang Tingfu, "Zhishi jieji yu zhengzhi" [The intellectual class and politics], Duli pinglun 51 (1933): 15–19.

[101] Jiang Tingfu, "Lun zhuanzhi bing da Hu Shizhi xiansheng" [On dictatorship and in reply to Mr. Hu Shizhi (Hu Shi)], Duli pinglu 83 (1933): 2–6.

[102] Refugees from Beijing and Tianjin founded this university after the Japanese invasion in the late 1930s.

[103] Qian Zhongshu, Weicheng [Fortress besieged] (Beijing: Renmin wenxue chubanshe, 1991). The novel vividly describes the journey of a group of Chinese professors moving to an inland city.

from Peiping [Beijing]."[104] The traumatic experience of the war led Chinese historical circles to recognize an unprecedented national crisis.[105] Lei took a sharp turn in his thought, which manifested in his interaction with a group of conservative intellectuals.

This group was often referred to as the "Zhanguo Ce clique." These scholars, including Lei, were deeply concerned with how to preserve the Chinese nation within a threatening world order. They applied ancient Chinese history to make sense of the world order and saw a historical parallel between World War II and the Warring States period ("Zhanguo" in Chinese; 475–221 BC) in ancient Chinese history. This period was a critical moment of transition in Chinese history during which it moved from the Spring and Autumn period when feudal-like, ritualistic politics dominated Chinese political scenes and entered into an era when massive wars of destruction eliminated weak regional kingdoms leading to the unification of China under the brutal Qin military regime. "Zhanguo Ce" (often translated as "Stratagems of the Warring States") refers to the collection of rhetorical prose writings by scholars, strategists, and political advisors who were active in the Warring States period. For the sake of convenience, I refer to these scholars in this chapter as "Zhanguo scholars."

The key figures in this group included Lin Tongji (BA University of Michigan, MA and PhD University of California, 1906–1980), who was a political scientist; Chen Quan (MA Oberlin College, PhD University of Kiel, 1905–1969), who was a playwright and literary critic; and Lei Haizong.[106] These professors had all earned foreign doctoral degrees and gained positions at prominent Chinese universities. Among them, the political scientist Lin Tongji was the most active; he organized many group events.[107] Chen Quan admired German philosophy and literature and was more active in philosophical and literary debates. Lei's work offered a historiographical foundation for the ideas shared by the group. The group began with the short-lived journal *Zhanguo Ce* that was published biweekly from April 1940 to July 1941. From December 1941 to

---

[104] He Bingdi [Ping-ti Ho], *Dushi yueshi bashinian* [Eighty years of studying history and experiencing the world] (Guilin: Guangxi shifan daxue chubanshe, 2005), 150.

[105] For instance, Gu Jiegang became more nationalist. See Xin Fan, "Gu Jiegang and the Creation of Chinese Historical Geography," *The Chinese Historical Review* 17, no. 2 (2010): 193–218.

[106] Wen Rumin and Ding Xiaoping, "'Zhanguo ce pai' de wenhua fansi yu chongjian gouxiang," [The proposal for cultural reflection and reconfiguration from the Zhanguo Ce clique], in *Shidai zhi bo: Zhanguo ce pai wenhua lunzhu jiyao* [Tide of the times: A selection of the main cultural works from the Zhanguo ce Clique] (Beijing: Zhongguo guangbo dianshi chubanshe, 1995), 2.

[107] Lin Tongji and Lei Haizong had a close relationship. Both graduated from Chongde high school in Beijing and attended Tsinghua University. They then pursued doctoral degrees in the United States.

July 1942, the group continued to organize the "Zhanguo Supplement" in the *Dagong bao* (Ta Kung Pao; orginally known as *L'Impartial*), an influential paper in the wartime Nationalist capital of Chongqing. Its authors included an array of famous scholars and writers from He Lin (1902–1992) to Shen Congwen (1902–1988).[108]

Despite their diverse profiles, this group was particularly interested in adopting culture as a basic unit to understand the world and taking history as a guide to make sense of contemporary politics. The synthesis of time, space, and peoples was central to Lei Haizong's conception of history. It also formed the historiographical foundation for Zhanguo thought.[109] In their works, they emphasized the link between cultural reconstruction and national power, the necessity of war, the will to power, and hero worship. The obsession with these ideas would eventually bring the nation-state back to the central stage of wartime cultural polemics.[110]

Lin Tongji was a leading voice in this group, and his view on war represents the conservative nature of this group's thought. Writing in the high time of the war (1940), Lin accepted war as reality, arguing that it manifested in the three trends of international politics. First, war had become the center of life and endowed the era with its own gravity. The original Warring States era in China had been shaped by war, which had become "the standard for all the major activities in society." Beliefs, enterprises, and social reforms all became auxiliaries to the goal of war.[111] Second, Lin predicted that, as in the ancient Warring States era, the current war would become total. As a result, democracy must submit to the goal and purpose of war. Lin implied that a brutal and despotic leader like Shang Yang (395–338 BC) could better attain wartime victory than a group of specialists sitting around a table and following a democratic process of debate. Shang Yang, as a minister in the Qin era, introduced radical reforms in military and governmental centralization. These laid a foundation that allowed the Qin dynasty to unify China in 221 BC. For Zhanguo scholars, Shang Yang represented the legalist tradition that preferred law to moral values as the foundation for a political system. Third, war in the twentieth century would go beyond mere victory to total annihilation of the defeated – which had happened in China from the Spring and Autumn to the Warring States period. Desolation would

---

[108] Godley, "Politics from History," 95. A total of only seventeen scholars published in both journals.

[109] Lei, "Duandai wenti yu Zhongguoshi de fenqi," 136.

[110] Edmund Fung, *The Intellectual Foundations of Chinese Modernity: Cultural and Political Thought in the Republican Era* (Cambridge: Cambridge University Press, 2010), 126.

[111] Lin Tongji, "Zhanguo shidai de chongyan" [A repetition of the Warring States period], in *ZXZZH*, 3: series 3, 104.

ultimately result in the creation of a world empire – just as the Qin dynasty had done by the end of the Warring States period in China.[112]

The gloomy prospects in world politics encouraged a turn from a world-historical focus to a China-centered one. If countries would not coexist peacefully, then how was it possible to make sure your nation survived this disorderly world? This became an urgent concern. Having a strong military was the key. Yet China had lost its own militaristic tradition, according to Lei. To revive it, Zhanguo scholars again referenced the historical analogy between the contemporary world and ancient China, when the first emperor centralized power and established a powerful and totalitarian regime. As the gloomy assessment of world politics called for a revival of Chinese militarism, these scholars believed that strong leadership in this chaotic age was the only way to ensure the survival of the Chinese culture. As an educator, Lei Haizong thus proposed that China should work military education into its curricula.[113] In his view, this could be achieved only through the stable and absolute leadership of Chiang Kai-shek (1887–1975).

Zhanguo scholars discarded moral values and adopted a purely utilitarian view of international politics. World War II was another "Zhanguo period," Lei wrote in an op-ed. He went on to claim that history lessons told that the diplomacy of the time must be "merciless in its method and relentless in its purpose," warning, "[If one were] living in the Warring States and following the diplomacy in the Spring and Autumn period, then the minor consequence would be to lose one's sovereignty and the major consequence would be the downfall of the nation." Referring to the Qin unification after China's Warring States period, Lei predicted that the future of the current Zhanguo period for all nations "will be the unification of the entire cultural zone: India, China, Greece, and Rome all followed the same principle." He continued, "Today's major powers in Euro-America, I am afraid, cannot skip this fate in history, and the most merciless and relentless country will usually be the one that achieves final success."[114] This strong utilitarianism and the support of Chiang Kai-shek drew further barbs from their contemporaries and students alike.

The political situation in the early 1940s was extremely delicate. After the first round of fighting, Japan took control of the major industrial zones before shifting its focus to the Pacific. This offered a little time for the various political forces in China to reshuffle. The Nationalist government

---

[112] Lin, "Zhanguo shidai de chongyan," 105.
[113] Lei Haizong, "Jianguo: zaiwang de disanzhou wenhua" [Founding the nation: the third period (of Chinese culture) in sight], in ZXZZH, 3: series 3, 189.
[114] Lei Haizong, "Waijiao: Chunqiu yu zhanguo" ["Diplomacy": Spring and Autumn (period) and "Warring States" (period)], in ZXZZH, 3: series 3, 183.

retreated to Chongqing, attempting to consolidate its power there. Facing an exhausted nation torn apart by the atrocious war, Nationalist leaders hoped to boost popular support through propaganda. In early 1941, the Ministry of Propaganda launched a national cultural campaign. It aimed at strengthening the nation with the power of culture by spreading nationalism and promoting China-centered (*benwei*) culture.[115] In a campaign to reconstruct the nation with a revival of traditional Chinese ethics and culture, the government called for tighter control of historical, civic, and geographical education.[116]

At the same time, the CCP survived the Long March and settled in Yan'an with ambitions to gain a larger sphere of influence in national politics. Agreeing to join the Second United Front, they accepted the leadership of the Nationalist government and presented themselves to the nation as a "democratic force." Following the guidelines of the Sixth Congress of the Communist International Movement, the CCP started to promote the Sino-Japanese War of Resistance as part of the global anti-fascist movement.[117] A fierce ideological battle emerged in Yan'an in the early 1940s. This infighting allowed Mao Zedong to tighten the reins on literature and political thought within the Communist movement. Yet in the Nationalist-controlled area, the CCP relied on democratic rhetoric to maintain an independent status while in nominal cooperation with the Nationalists.[118] The CCP thus sent a team of propagandists to the war capital, Chongqing. These party propagandists, journalists by name, had a mission to foil Nationalist attempts to consolidate power and to seek wider support among various democratic alliances in wartime China. They sought to demonstrate that the CCP remained an important demo-cratic force in the resistance movement. The Zhanguo scholars' cries for a strong centralized government and their antidemocratic stance were potentially harmful to this goal. This prompted the CCP propaganda machine to orchestrate waves of attacks on those scholars. Party

---

[115] Chiang Kai-shek also took a personal interest in this. On May 1, 1942, he sent a telegram to the minister of education Chen Lifu. In it, he attached a policy paper titled "Dangqian zhi wenhua zhengce yu xuanchuan" [The current policy of culture and propaganda] and endorsed several proposed ideas in the document. *ZMSDZH*, 5:pt.2, [no.22], 12, 15.

[116] Wai-keung Chan, "Contending Memories of the Nation: History Education in Wartime China, 1937–1945," in *The Politics of Historical Production in Late Qing and Republican China*, ed. Tze-ki Hon and Robert Culp (Leiden: Brill, 2007), 173–174.

[117] Jin Chongji, *Yi ben shu de lishi: Hu Qiaomu, Hu Sheng tan Zhongguo Gongchandang de qishinian* [The history of a book: Hu Qiaomu and Husheng on *Seventy Years of the Chinese Communist Party*] (Beijing: Zhongyang wenxian chubanshe, 2014), 86.

[118] Yang Kuisong, *"Zhongjian didai" de geming: Zhongguo gemin de celue zai guoji beijing xia de yanbian* [Revolution in the "middle zone": evolution of the Chinese revolution strategy in the international context] (Taiyuan: Shanxi renmin chubanshe, 2010).

intellectuals claimed that the Zhanguo scholars supported violent and aggressive domestic and international politics and labeled them "cultural fascists."

Hanfu's article in 1942 summarizes this position. As a Marxist scholar and CCP propagandist, Hanfu was an alias for Zhang Hanfu (1905–1972), editor-in-chief in CCP's *Xinhua Daily* in Chongqing and later one of the "most important diplomats" in the early People's Republic.[119] He disparaged Zhanguo scholars' cyclic view of history, arguing that history is a progressive movement in which human society increasingly moves forward. Although there might be some minor setbacks in its development, history never repeats itself. In accordance with this view, he accused Zhanguo scholars of having drawn only superficial analogies between the Warring States period and the contemporary world, thereby neglecting a fundamental difference: the role of justice. In contrast to annexation as the sole purpose of war in the feudal period, the participants in World War II included semi-colonial China pursuing liberation, liberal capitalist nations such as the United Kingdom and the United States fighting fascist aggression, and socialist states such as the Soviet Union seeking to defend their motherlands. This great alliance featured a democratic coalition opposing the injustices of fascism.[120] Hanfu maintained that Zhanguo scholars were anti-democratic and that their goal was to consolidate the Nationalist government, centralize the military, manipulate the economy, forge a national religion, and control the will of the people.[121] He praised democracy. The CCP saw no conflict in respecting individuals while developing national power, he insisted. As such, democracy was an appropriate and necessary stage as China transformed from a feudal society into a developing capitalist society. It was an efficient tool with which a government could mobilize power.[122] An overemphasis on autocratic power would be harmful to China, as well as to all the anti-fascist nations and peoples. He also praised the role of moral values in history. He wrote that justice played a fundamental role in wartime, offering a foundation for coalitions among the nations. Denial of the significance of justice in modern warfare could only help enemies. Therefore, combining the above arguments, Hanfu concluded that the Zhanguo Ce group by nature was fascist.

---

[119] As for Zhang's biography, see *BDCC* 1:27a–30.

[120] Hanfu [pseud.], "'Zhanguo' pai de Faxisi zhuyi shizhi" [The true Fascist nature of the "Zhanguo" clique], In *ZXZZH* 3: series 3, 1. During the war, the CCP promised to give up anti-capitalist goals in order to form a United Front with the Nationalist party. As for Hu's biography, see *BDCC*, 1: 381a–383.

[121] Hanfu, 2.   [122] Hanfu, 3.

Hanfu's article offers but one example of CCP criticism of Zhanguo scholars. Active CCP propagandists and intellectuals, including Hu Sheng (1918–2000), deputy-director of CCP's Propaganda Department in the People's Republic, also wrote extensively on the group.[123] Newspapers and journals in Chongqing and Yan'an printed these articles and circulated them widely.[124] Even left-leaning students at Southwest Associated University, such as He Zhaowu (1921–), criticized the lack of humanism in Zhanguo scholars' writing.[125] After 1949, an association with the Zhanguo group marred the political files of former participants; many continued to be attacked in political campaigns in the following decades.

In 1947, shortly after the war, Lei Haizong wrote, "Idealization and reality are the two conditions in one's life. Some pay more attention to reality, and other more to ideals. These two types of people are actually living in two different worlds. Currently, political interest is profound; this makes the distinction between the two worlds appear especially clear."[126]

Indeed, the troubled state of development in world-historical studies in Republican China was torn between idealization and reality. On the one hand, the growth of world-historical studies was partly the result of the professionalization of historical studies during the time. These early world historians were academic professionals who shared the ideal of seeking pure knowledge as a career in the "academic society." They were frank about the shortcomings of their own field, just as Chen Hengzhe had been in her Peking University talk; they were also critical of the Eurocentric slant in the existing paradigm of historical studies in the West, as Lei Haizong had been in his review of H. G. Wells's world history. On the other hand, as analyzed by Jiang Tingfu, these scholars also had an enormous sense of social responsibility. During a time of national crisis and personal suffering, they were not hesitant about embracing political activism as a way to reconstruct national solidarity in the dispirited nation. This sense of social responsibility, however, warped their view of history.

Despite such a flaw, world-historical studies in the Republican period remain significant. They are a great source for studying how Chinese

---

[123] Hu Sheng, "Lun fan lixing zhuyi de niliu" [On the counter-trend of anti-rationalism] and "Shi shengren haishi pianzi: Lun weixinlun zai shiji shenghuo zhong de biaoxian" [Are they saints or swindlers? On the implications of idealism in daily life], in *ZXZZH*, 3: series 3, 21–34.

[124] Editorial, "'Minzu wenxue' yu Faxisi miulun [National literature and the fallacy of Fascism], in *ZXZZH*, Vol. 3, series 3, 40–41. This article appeared in *Jiefang ribao* [Liberation daily] on August 8, 1944.

[125] He, *Shangxue ji*, 65.   [126] Lei, *Bolun shixue ji*, 265.

historians conceptualized the relationship between China and the world. With He Bingsong as a transitional figure, the contrast between Chen Hengzhe's liberal cosmopolitanism and Lei's cultural conservatism is revealing. Both assumed universal impulses, although divergently constructed. Chen rejected war and Lei embraced it; Chen promoted internationalism and Lei stressed the uniqueness of the Chinese culture. Be that as it may, Chen, Lei, and He Bingsong as forerunners of world-historical studies all attempted to situate China's past, present, and future within a world-historical context in their scholarly works. They realized the value of non-Chinese history; they cared about what was being taught and understood as well as the value of carrying out research in world history. In promoting world-historical knowledge, they became teachers, translators, textbook editors, public intellectuals, and professional historians.

From Chen Hengzhe and He Bingsong to Lei Haizong, one can observe the gradual rise of cultural nationalism in the Republican period. A strong concern of the survival of the Chinese nation signaled a major change in world-historical writing from the late Qing era. Conceptions of history turned away from a holistic view based on a common humanity and back toward a special focus on China. Chinese conservatives were often nationalist, if not vice versa.[127] The study of world history thereby grew less inclusive and more nationalistic.

Scholars have observed that 1937 was a noticeable landmark in Lei Haizong's study of history: prior to then, he often spoke of the weakness of Chinese culture; thereafter, he energetically underscored Chinese cultural hopes.[128] In the midst of war (1942), Lei argued that, although Chinese culture faced a moment of darkness, hope remained. Through a world-historical gaze he predicted that, as the only culture that had two cycles in world history, Chinese culture would eventually be rejuvenated. He proclaimed:

Chinese culture's second cycle is indeed a miracle in human history. But now it comes to its end. Its future is to end the old pattern, and create a new world so as to realize a third cycle of Chinese culture. Why past cultures must destroy themselves, we do not know. Why only China was able to survive, we do not know either ... If we draw an exaggerated similitude, we can say that cultures are like flowers. All other cultures are like grassy [i.e. annual] flowers. After these flowers flourish, they die; China is like woody [i.e. perennial] flowers. They open this year; next year they will open again. If we plant it [China] well, it will sustain its life forever.[129]

[127] Fung, "Nationalism and Modernity," 788.
[128] Godley, "Politics from History," 100.   [129] Lei, "Lishi de xingtai yu lizheng," 257

To be sure, this was more a political manifesto than a purely scholarly theory. Nevertheless, it struck a powerful chord in his students and general readers who desperately sought to save the nation.[130] To many of them, Lei's cultural thesis was like a light in a dark moment of history.[131] Lei's transition was personal, but it also registered a dramatic change in Chinese historiography. Now, during the war, political activism returned to historical studies. In this regard, Lei's introduction and flirtation with "cultural history" would become a significant but flawed foundation for the future development of world history.

---

[130] He, *Dushi yueshi bashinian*, 119–120.
[131] As his student, historian Ping-ti Ho fondly remembered Lei; see Fan, "The Anger of Ping-Ti Ho," 153.

3   Becoming the "World"

World Historians in the Early People's Republic

In July 1955, the historian Lin Zhichun submitted a report to the Department of History at Northeast Normal University in Changchun. In the middle of two political campaigns (the Anti-Hu Feng Campaign and the Cleansing Anti-Revolutionaries Campaign), Lin kept a humble tone and offered self-effacing criticism. Yet, despite the rhetoric, the document discloses the tension between Lin and Zou Youheng (1912–), the director of the *jiaoyanshi* and chair of the department.

In this as well as several other reports, Lin complained about the bureaucratization of the department. In the *jiaoyanshi* of ancient and medieval world history, a small research area, there were already two directors (one for ancient history and the other for medieval) and one secretary. The department planned to add more group leaders and group secretaries. Lin commented, "There are more leaders than the led" in the department. His criticism was directed at Zou Youheng, a fellow world historian who received a PhD in Western History from the Imperial University of Tokyo in 1939. Lin complained that, after assuming leadership, Zou stopped showing interest in participating in research and switched to teaching Asian history. To Lin, this became "one more bureaucrat, one less practitioner."[1] He also complained in private that if a chair could choose to teach his own subject of interest, then he himself would leave ancient (world) history and return to studying Chinese history.

Lin was under pressure during the campaigns. Today the archives still keep letters from informants reporting Lin's past behavior prior to the People's Republic, and Zou's review of Lin's file was indeed not all positive. As director of the *jiaoyanshi*, Zou left a mixed review of Lin's performance. Conventionally, he starts by praising Lin's dedicated work ethic in directing graduate studies. He then switches to a sharp criticism of other aspects of Lin's life. He remarks that Lin had a lopsided view in

[1] Lin Zhichun, "Shuocuo le he zuocuo le naxie?" [What did I do wrong and say wrong], July 12, 1955, Lin Zhichun Personnel Archives, Northeast Normal University Archives, Changchun, Jilin, China. (Original page numbers are not available.)

his thinking, dismissing principles and policies in the workplace. Bourgeois thought had a strong hold on him, as he often neglected orders from the *jiaoyanshi*. Moreover, Lin lost touch with reality and mechanically cited Marxist classics; and, in terms of interpersonal behaviors, Lin also had a short temper, lacked principles, and exuded bourgeois snobbishness.[2]

The tension between Zou and Lin underscores the complicated academic politics that surrounded the formation of world-historical studies in the 1950s, especially the conflicting pull between party control and intellectual autonomy. Lin was lucky, as he was not greatly affected by the later political campaigns. He Shanzhou (1910–2008), chair of the Chinese Literature Department at the same university, on the contrary, was labeled a rightist during the Anti-Rightist Campaign, due to his disagreement with the party secretary over a new hiring.[3]

Lin Zhichun is a key figure in the development of world history in China. Today he is regarded as "the founding father of ancient world history" in the country. This is not only because he was involved with the Ancient World History Seminar in Changchun in the early 1950s that educated an entire generation of specialists in ancient world history but also because he actively participated in debates and directed research projects that defined the theoretical framework for the development of the field for nearly half a century. Despite his significant role, people are often ambivalent about Lin's leftist position and his collaboration with the government. Once an anonymous interviewee, an old professor who used to be Lin's friend, complained to the author of this book, saying, "During the Cultural Revolution, all of us (intellectuals) went down to the countryside." "Not him." He became a little emotional: "Lin is a red professor!" "You know. Later, he came to Beijing to visit me," the old professor continued, "I refused to let him into my house!" "Red professor" is certainly a derogatory reference in this conversation. Like this old professor, many assumed that Lin submitted to communist ideology and betrayed his academic integrity in exchange for personal benefits.

Yet the archival sources offer a more nuanced picture of Lin's position in the early 1950s. Various personnel reports to the state show that Lin admired "old" universities such as Peking University and Tsinghua University. He wrote that, although the "new" universities founded by the CCP during the Civil War were bigger in size and had more young

---

[2] Lin Zhichun, "Ziwo jianding" [Self-evaluation], June 1955 (?), Lin Zhichun Archives. (Original page numbers are not available.)

[3] As for the tension between political cadres and professional leaders, see Ning Wang, *Banished to the Great Northern Wilderness: Political Exile and Re-education in Mao's China* (Vancouver and Toronto: UBC Press, 2017).

scholars and experienced party cadres, there were fewer specialists and scholars, and he admitted his goal used to be "to separate academics from politics."[4] This pursuit of objectivity echoes views held by Hu Shi and Gu Jiegang back in the early Republican years.

The archival sources also confirm that Lin was obsessed with scholarship. After the communist takeover, he was contacted about relocating from Shanghai to Changchun. His immediate concern was whether there would be enough time for scholarship in the new work environment.[5] During the Korean War, air raid alerts often rang at night in Changchun, thanks to this city's adjacency to the North Korean border. Lin would try everything to make up for missed time. He wanted to practice Russian with Russian specialists, but they needed to go to the bomb shelters. Lin, who was dedicated to his studies, refused to go with them. He covered his windows with thick curtains and continued his work in his apartment, despite the sirens.[6]

By the early 1950s, changes to China's political fortunes – the rise of the CCP, the global Cold War, and the Korean conflict – recast the political balance within the academy. Many world historians, for example, were left-leaning scholars, and some of them were even radical Marxists, who supported the rise of the CCP. Others did not and paid dearly for their opposition. However, even a "red professor" was still a professor, who shared the aspiration of defending intellectual autonomy in a tightening political environment. Between increasing state control and resisting intellectual autonomy, China's new world historians struggled with their own identity, and such a tension affected their views of world history, however subtly. This is a legacy that is often misunderstood but one that profoundly shaped the formation of world history in China for years to come.

The early 1950s were a critical moment in the rise of the tension between state control and intellectual resistance in Chinese intellectual history. A significant development was the party-state's attempt to fully control the production of historical knowledge within the needs of radical politics.

The party was unapologetically outspoken about this goal. In 1958, in the context of the Great Leap Forward and amid a state of confusion among the educated classes, Chen Boda (1904–1989), who was Mao's trusted secretary and commonly regarded as his "interpreter," gave a talk at Peking University. The minutes of his talk were later published in

---

[4] Lin, "Ziwo jianding."

[5] Lin Zhichun, "Sixiang jiancha baogao" [Report on thought examination], July 7, 1952, Lin Zhichun Archives, 3.

[6] Lin, "Sixiang jiancha baogao," 5.

Hongqi (*Red Flag*), the flagship journal of the party's propaganda machine.[7] At this venue, which had been the center of China's intellectual productivity for the past half a century, Chen brought up the issue of academic authority. He said, "Quite a few intellectuals like talking about something called 'academic authority' and are afraid of losing it." "Do Communists acknowledge authority?" he asked. Yes, authority is needed indeed. Chen followed with a comparison: "[It is just like] when you are on a boat, you must respect the helmsman; when you are on a train, you must respect the conductor." The problem was who controlled the authority. Chen continued that there were the authorities that represented the people's interests and will, and thus truth and progress, and there were also "outdated authorities" and "false authorities." For those who used to be the authorities at certain times in the past, rather than feeling satisfied, they should continue to make progress. Society was moving forward, and they would be social dropouts if they refused to change. The party would expose these false authorities. Yet it would give outdated authorities a chance to reform as long as they were willing to become "little pupils" again and learn from the masses. Who, then, represented the ultimate authority in China? Chen blatantly pointed to Mao, for Mao was always learning from the masses.[8]

Chen and Mao shared similar ideological interests, and both had a negative view of Chinese intellectuals. Through Chen's talk, the radicals in the party were sending a threatening message to the intellectuals across China that now was the time to accept Mao's leadership and submit to the regime. Chen's talk was immediately echoed by another Maoist theorist, Ai Siqi (1910–1966) in the same journal, which certainly raises questions regarding whether the two events were orchestrated by Mao's followers or even by Mao himself.[9] A philosopher by name, Ai further explains the issue concerning the source of truth by pointing out generational differences. According to him, there was a tendency among "older intellectuals" to refuse to acknowledge the role played by the masses in creating new knowledge. The fundamental problem was that the old intellectuals (many of whom were well-known professors) privileged "book knowledge" over "knowledge produced by the people."[10] The Maoists in the 1950s rejected academic objectivism, and eliminating the distinction

---

[7] The Great Leap Forward was a radical economic and social campaign engineered by Mao Zedong and his partisans to speed up the process of industrialization and collectivization. As for Chen's biography, see *BDCC*, 1:122–125.

[8] Chen Boda, "Zai Mao Zedong tongzhi de qizhi xia" [Under the flag of Comrade Mao Zedong], *Hongqi* [Red flag], no. 4 (July 16, 1958): 11–12.

[9] As for Ai's biography, see *BDCC*, 1:1a–3.

[10] Ai Siqi, "Nali zhao genju?" [Where to find the basis?], *Hongqi* [Red flag], no. 4 (July 16, 1958): 13.

between "political" and "academic" knowledge was high on their agenda. In doing so, they were determined to control the production of knowledge. Renowned intellectuals who held authoritative positions in academia naturally became their targets.[11]

In recent years, scholars have gradually reached a consensus that the communist state in the 1950s was a high modernist state. High modernism, according to James Scott's definition, refers to "self-confidence about scientific and technological progress, the expansion of production, the growing satisfaction of human needs, the mastery of nature (including human nature), and, above all, the rational design of social order commensurate with the scientific understanding of natural laws."[12] The bold attempt of the state to control the right to produce knowledge can be seen as "state simplification," large-scale social engineering by which a homogeneous state is created. This simplification process is an administrative ordering of nature and society based on a blind belief in high modernist ideology (in the case of China, it is Mao's version of Marxism-Leninism). It usually takes place in an authoritarian regime where civil society is largely incapacitated by the state apparatus.[13]

Yet the state apparatus can never fully control everything. The CCP's influence in intellectual circles – especially in the field of history – had been slight prior to 1949.[14] During this period, the CCP's influence over ideological issues remained mainly in rural Soviet bases and so-called liberated areas. The party never achieved strong control over members of the intellectual community, most of whom lived and worked in major urban centers. Strategically, CCP intellectuals chose to form a coalition, in the name of democracy, with liberal intellectuals such as Zhang Bojun (1895–1969) and Liang Shuming; many of these intellectuals held sympathetic views of the Chinese communist revolution during the Sino-Japanese War period.[15] In the major urban centers, left-leaning historians who were approved of by the party started in the lower tiers of China's academic world and generally had less academic power.[16] When the party

[11] For a detailed discussion concerning Mao's view of authority, see John Starr, *Continuing the Revolution: The Political Thought of Mao* (Princeton: Princeton University Press, 1979), 72–96.

[12] James C. Scott, *Seeing Like a State: How Certain Schemes to Improve the Human Condition Have Failed* (New Haven, CT: Yale University Press, 1999), 4.

[13] Scott, *Seeing Like a State*, 4–5.

[14] Dominic Sachsenmaier, *Global Perspectives on Global History: Theories and Approaches in a Connected World* (Cambridge: Cambridge University Press, 2011), 187.

[15] Edmund S. Fung, *In Search of Chinese Democracy: Civil Opposition in Nationalist China, 1929–1949* (Cambridge: Cambridge University Press, 2000), 233, 244.

[16] He Ziquan, *Aiguo yi shusheng: Bashiwu zishu* [A scholar who loves his country: An autobiography at the age of eighty-five] (Shanghai: Huadong shifan daxue chubanshe, 1997), 54.

came to power and sent its members to seize positions at universities, there was strong resentment. For instance, on the eve of the communists' national victory, the party attempted to arrange to place Jian Bozan (1898–1968), a leftist historian, at Yenching University in Beijing, but the History Department refused to accept him.[17] It was a new mission for the CCP to seek full control of the field of historical studies in the early years of the PRC.

To achieve this goal, the communist state tirelessly tested new ideas from psychological punishment to disciplinary control. First, the party-state tried to reshape the "soul" of Chinese historians ideologically through a series of political campaigns.[18] These campaigns had deep roots in the Yan'an era. In principle, they followed the same format established in the Rectification Campaigns from 1942 to 1944, which were based on the idea of collectivization and used two essential procedures: Individuals were first organized into study groups and urged to conduct a close collective examination of Maoist documents within their group, and then, after study, they had to present themselves for self-criticism within the group. Afterward, the group would vote on whether the individual had met the expectations in the campaigns.[19] A huge challenge of such group study was that party branches usually did not disclose any clear goals at the initial stage of the campaign, and yet they expected a certain percentage of participants to fail. For instance, during the Three-Antis Campaign the party ordered that 2 percent of college teachers should not pass the campaign along with 13 percent who should go through a "repeated process of critical examination" prior to passing.[20] Therefore, individuals had to try very hard to figure out what the party expected of them. Sometimes it would take several rounds for an

---

[17] Zhang Chuanxi, *Jian Bozan zhuan* [Biography of Jian Bozan] (Beijing: Beijing daxue chubanshe, 1998), 242.

[18] Scholars have been aware of the role played by political campaigns in the early People's Republic's state-building project. For instance, Julia Strauss, "Morality, Coercion and State Building by Campaign in the Early PRC: Regime Consolidation and After, 1949–1956," *The China Quarterly* 188, no. 1 (2006): 896; Aminda M. Smith, *Thought Reform and China's Dangerous Classes: Reeducation, Resistance, and the People* (Lanham, MD: Rowman & Littlefield, 2012).

[19] Leaders in the early People's Republic gained insight into how to run political movements both from earlier Soviet experiences and from experiences under the Nationalist regime, such as the New Life Movement in the 1930s. Strauss, "Morality, Coercion and State Building," 897–898.

[20] "Zhonggong zhongyang guanyu zai gaodeng xuexiao zhong jinxing pipan zichan jieji sixiang yundong he zhunbei jinxing qingli 'zhongceng' gongzuo de zhishi" [Directive on conducting the campaign of criticizing bourgeois thought and preparing to cleanse 'mid-level' [workers] among higher-education schools by the Central Committee of the CCP], in *ZZWX*, 8:304.

individual to pass the collective criticism sessions, and the huge psychological pressure on participants even drove some crazy.

Second, the party-state attempted to control intellectuals by restructuring the higher education system. This process started with reforming the decentralized structure of "old" Chinese universities and colleges. The key was collectivization in the name of professionalization and specialization.

The Nationalist government had been relatively weak and adopted a loose approach in dealing with the higher education system in China. It did not have a clear agenda or a master plan for the system. As a result, schools managed to maintain a relatively high level of autonomy. This condition had both positive and negative effects on the development of China's higher education system. It created an atmosphere of liberalism and individualism among China's educated class, wherein Chinese intellectuals were relatively free to debate certain academic issues. This led to the flourishing of historical studies. At the same time, as scholars argue, this system led to "an over-concentration of resources on subjects such as literature, law, and political science" and "an insufficient commitment of resources to science, technology, and other professional subjects."[21] Because of the imbalance in higher education, an increasing number of college graduates majoring in the social sciences and humanities were unable to find jobs after graduation. Identifying the problem, the CCP regarded strong liberal-democratic ideas among intellectuals as harmful for building up a new socialist state. In both theory and practice, they preferred unity or even homogeneity of thought centered on historical materialism in the field of historical research and education, as they considered this an important component in the development and assertion of national strength and social justice.

Party ideologues believed that the old system, due to its lack of organization, allowed college teachers to hold too much power over students. Cheng Fangwu (1897–1984), who was an influential reformer of the higher education system in the 1950s and a party intellectual, believed that the problem with old-style universities and colleges was the absence of any organization. Individual teachers had direct contact only with the chairperson as opposed to a collective leadership and had too much control over teaching. They gave lectures depending on their personal understanding of the assigned courses and their individual interests. They refused to take others' suggestions, as seen in the conflict between Wu Mi and Wang Xingyun. At the same time, old-style college teachers took no responsibility for the outcome of students' studies. According to Cheng,

[21] Yeh, *The Alienated Academy*, 172.

the system was unable to guarantee the ideological and scientific quality of the content of courses.[22] Like him, many CCP ideologues considered the decentralized system a considerable barrier to implementing the party's higher education policy. They believed that the system was in need of urgent restructuring.[23] The rationale was clear: Through collectivizing college education, the CCP would assert state control over ideological issues.

From June to August 1952, the CCP government initiated a nationwide program to restructure China's higher education system through professionalization and specialization. Its main goals were to (1) focus on nurturing talents for industrial construction; (2) develop specialized faculties and schools; (3) adjust and strengthen comprehensive universities; (4) gradually establish correspondence schools and night colleges; and (5) prepare institutional foundations for educating students from peasant and worker families.[24] The government therefore increased investment in technological and engineering schools and created new types of specialized colleges and universities. It added specialized institutions, closed down private schools, and restructured the curricula of comprehensive colleges and universities. During the process, the government closed down thirty universities and colleges, including the prestigious St. John's University and Yenching University, relocating their faculties to other schools.[25] After the changes, the new system included three types of institutions: comprehensive universities, which combined the humanities, social sciences, and natural science faculties; polytechnics, with several applied science faculties in a single institution; and specialized colleges, which focused on a single faculty.[26]

With the redistribution of resources in the higher education system, the new government also integrated college professors into the socialist work

[22] Cheng Fangwu, "Zhongguo Renmin daxue de jiaoyanshi gongzuo" [The work of the unit of teaching and research at Chinese Renmin University], *Renmin jiaoyu* [People's education], no. 4 (1951): 11. Yu Piao and Li Hongcheng, *Cheng Fangwu zhuan* [A biography of Cheng Fangwu] (Beijing: Dangdai Zhongguo chubanshe, 1997), 469.

[23] For instance, Franz Schurmann, *Ideology and Organization in Communist China* (Berkeley: University of California Press, 1968), 213.

[24] *Jianguo yilai zhongyao wenxian xuanbian* [Select collection of important sources since the founding of the People's Republic of China] (Beijing: Zhongyang wenxian chubanshe, 1992), 3:346. The original document was released as a *People's Daily* editorial on September 24, 1952.

[25] For instance, all eighteen private universities and colleges in East China were closed. "Huadong qu gaoxiao yuanxi tiaozheng gongzuo shengli wancheng" [The victorious completion of the restructuring of the higher education units in East China], *Wenhui bao* [Wenhui Daily], October 30, 1952.

[26] Suzanne Pepper, *Radicalism and Education Reform in Twentieth-Century China: The Search for an Ideal Development Model* (Cambridge: Cambridge University Press, 2000), 175.

unit system (the *danwei* system).[27] In the Republican period, except for the main administrative staff assigned by the government at national universities, college teaching positions were based on an appointment system. Professors moved from one institution to another at various times. According to the government's surveys, only around a quarter of history professors remained at the same university for more than five years.[28] College professors thus were considered "free-floating workers" (*ziyou zhiye zhe*) rather than organized workers.[29] During restructuring in the early 1950s, the government established party branches in the university system, thus creating a dualism in Chinese higher education where the party branches took over the real leadership. The newly inserted party cadres often held a negative view of college professors.[30] The government also claimed the right to implement extensive personnel shifts in the higher education system, relocating college professors whenever and wherever it saw fit. For instance, it redefined the status of Tsinghua University from a comprehensive university to one specializing in applied sciences and relocated the humanities and social sciences faculties to other schools. As part of this process, Lei Haizong of Tsinghua University was transferred to Nankai University in Tianjin, along with his friend Zheng Tianting (1899–1981) from Peking University, due to their relationship with the Nationalist government.[31] As such, relocation became a way to exile "questionable" intellectuals from the political center, Beijing.

As historians were gradually integrated into the socialist work life, the introduction of the *jiaoyanshi* system came to most directly affect historical studies.[32] This new system became an effective control mechanism

[27] David Bray, *Social Space and Governance in Urban China: The Danwei System from Origins to Reform* (Stanford: Stanford University Press, 2005).

[28] Shang, "Jindai Zhongguo daxue shixue jiaoshou qunxiang," 96.

[29] *Jianguo yilai zhongyao wenxian xuanbian*, 3:347; the term *ziyou zhiye zhe* often refers to a wide range of professionals from doctors, lawyers, and accountants to journalists, engineers, and professors in the Nationalist governments' official documents after 1929. Xu, *Chinese Professionals and the Republican State*, 2.

[30] For a general introduction to the role of party cadres in China's higher education system in the early People's Republic period, see Lee Zhu, "Communist Cadres on the Higher Education Front, 1955–1962," *Twentieth-Century China* 34, no. 1 (2008): 73–95; in parallel, the party also inserted a substantial number of party members often known as "transferred cadres" into the secondary education system. Eddy U, *Disorganizing China: Counter-Bureaucracy and the Decline of Socialism* (Stanford: Stanford University Press, 2007), 43.

[31] Huang Kewu [Max K. W. Huang], "Jiang Jieshi yu He Lin" [Chiang Kai-shek and He Lin], *Zhongyang yanjiuyuan jindaishi yanjiusuo jikan* [Bulletin of the Institute of Modern History, Academia Sinica] 67, no. 3 (2010), 49.

[32] Cheng, "Zhongguo Renmin daxue de jiaoyanshi gongzuo," 11–12; Zhang Aohui and Song Binyu, "Cheng Fangwu nianpu" [Annalistic biography of Cheng Fangwu], *Dongbei shifan daxue xuebao (zhexue shehui kexue ban)* [Journal of Northeast Normal University

that deeply intruded on the everyday lives of Chinese intellectuals. A product of "learning from the Soviet Union," the Chinese *jiaoyanshi* system closely followed the Soviet model (*Kafedra* in Russian). According to Chinese educators like Cheng Fangwu, it entailed a strong specialization within higher education.[33] At the same time, the establishment of the *jiaoyanshi* system can also be seen as a more intense continuation of Republican-period professionalization and specialization. The key character of this *jiaoyanshi* system was its concentration of power and resources in specialized fields for both teaching and research. Initially, the units "served essentially as the basic units for collective course preparation, teacher training, and mutual supervision."[34] The tasks of a *jiaoyanshi* included (1) preparing assignments for workers in the unit (lectures, class discussions, exercises, labs, tutoring, internship, etc.) and maintaining the quality of teaching; (2) understanding pedagogical work (to edit syllabi, plans for class discussions, plans for labs, exercise questions, selected answers, etc.); (3) editing textbooks (lecture notes, references, charts, etc.); (4) conducting scientific research; (5) coordinating with enterprises and governmental organizations; (6) improving ideological training among teachers; and (7) training postgraduate students. Teaching and research units usually consisted of professors, associate professors, teaching assistants, and postgraduate students. Each was a semi-autonomous entity in the academic structure headed by a director, who was usually a senior scholar, and one or two deputy directors. Despite the collective nature of the *jiaoyanshi*, the director had direct power to interfere with their group members' teaching and research.[35]

The essential element of the new *jiaoyanshi* system was the commitment to collectivization and specialization in teaching and research. It required intensive collective work from each individual member, and its goal was to integrate all the teachers into this system.[36] With regard to teaching, each member of the unit had to constantly participate in the collective preparation process (*jiti beike*). According to this process, each individual first needed to prepare lecture notes and then the work unit had

(Edition on philosophy and social sciences)] (1986) 1, 89. Pepper, *Radicalism and Education Reform in Twentieth-Century China*, 174–175.

[33] *Sulian zonghe daxue xi zhuanye shezhi yilanbiao* [The chart of the overview of the departments and concentrations at the comprehensive universities in the Soviet Union], Shanghai Municipal Archives (hereafter SMA), A26-2-115.

[34] Pepper, *Radicalism and Education Reform in Twentieth-Century China*, 175.

[35] Cheng, "Zhongguo Renmin daxue de jiaoyanshi gongzuo," 12.

[36] *Ben xuenian jiaoxue gaige gongzuo jihua shixing cao'an* [The tentative schedule for this school year's pedagogy reform], SMA, A26-2-154.1: 48.

to meet to discuss these notes before each class.[37] Group members were required to observe each other's teaching and, after class, each member would offer suggestions and critiques to others.[38] The *jiaoyanshi* also organized activities such as mid-semester teaching reviews to supervise teaching.[39] Along with collectivizing teaching, the *jiaoyanshi* system also transformed research at Chinese universities. Because of the collective nature of the *jiaoyanshi* system, scholars developed more collective projects and teamwork beginning in the 1950s, and collectively edited textbooks and reference works dominated these efforts.

Transforming teaching and research into a collective practice, the *jiaoyanshi* system was an important tool for the state to implement its ideological agenda through administrative orders. Scholars argue that the introduction of the work unit system weakened the existing civil society and increased the power of the state. This was certainly the case for the *jiaoyanshi* system.[40] As the low end of the work unit, the *jiaoyanshi* was responsible for the execution of the directives from its higher level, the Office of Academic Affairs. As part of the administrative leadership, this office constantly inspected its function and reviewed its work. In the second semester of the academic year of 1952, for instance, it planned to have from two to three in-depth inspections (April and June) on each *jiaoyanshi* at East China Normal University in Shanghai.[41]

The *jiaoyanshi* was not only an extension of the party supervision. It was also an important channel for promoting Marxist education. At Northeast Normal University, Cheng Fangwu created four special teaching and research units at the university: the history of the Chinese revolution, the basics of Marxism-Leninism, Political Economy, and Dialectic Materialism and Historical Materialism. He assigned senior administrative university staff members, some of whom were experienced party cadres, to take over the leadership of each unit. He personally served as

---

[37] The Ministry of Higher Education issued a teaching plan for every specialty, as well as a course outline for every course in the system of China's higher education. Lee Zhu, "Communist Cadres on the Higher Education Front," *Twentieth-Century China* 34, no. 1 (2008): 89; Pepper, *Radicalism and Education Reform in Twentieth-Century China*, 229.

[38] He, *Aiguo yi shusheng*, 261. Collective teaching was also a common practice at Chinese universities in the 1950s. For example, Zhao Lisheng discusses the tradition of collective teaching at Shandong University in the early 1950s. Zhao Lisheng, "Wo de chubu jiantao" [My preliminary self-examination], *Wenshizhe*, no. 4 (1952): 31 (or 373).

[39] For example, the same practice was also adopted at Southwest Teachers College where Wu Mi taught. Chen, "Beisong zhujiao de jianggao."

[40] Michael Dutton, *Policing Chinese Politics: A History* (Durham, NC: Duke University Press, 2005), 165–166.

[41] *Huadong shifan daxue 1952 niandu di'er xueqi gongzuo jihua gangyao (cao'an)* [The work schedule for the second semester of the academic year of 1952 at East China Normal University (draft)], SMA, A26-2-154.1: 12.

director of the unit for Dialectic Materialism and Historical Materialism.[42] This inclusion of political ideology became a model for China's higher education.

The important function of the *jiaoyanshi* system as a tool of ideological control was particularly evident during political campaigns. He Ziquan (1911–2011), who then was teaching at Beijing Normal University, recalls that political campaigns took place almost every year in the 1950s. During those campaigns, his *jiaoyanshi* would constantly receive directives from the party branch. Accordingly, he and his colleagues had to modify their lecture notes repeatedly. As a result, his lecture notes piled up very high on a table because he had to revise them so many times.[43] Despite its cumbersome demands, the new *jiaoyanshi* system became a main avenue for the Chinese state to pass on its orders and instructions to intellectual circles, more directly and effectively than ever before.

The introduction of the *jiaoyanshi* system also increased the level of specialization in the field of historical studies. After the establishment of the new system, more specialized teaching and research units were created. In world history, teaching and research were now divided into three *jiaoyanshi*: ancient and medieval world history, modern world history, and contemporary world history. A similar division was implemented for Chinese history teaching and research.[44]

One of the major challenges in creating the new subfields in historical teaching and research in the early 1950s was the shortage of professional historians.[45] In order to compensate for the shortage, the CCP state assigned historians to the newly established fields, in some cases, against the individual's own will. In 1953, for example, Wu Mi was transferred to the Department of History and served as director of the Ancient World History and Medieval World History *jiaoyanshi* at Southwest Teachers College in Chongqing, after the Department of English was disbanded under the policy of "leaning to one side."[46] Others would share a similar experience. Lei Haizong was assigned to the Ancient World History *jiaoyanshi* at Nankai University. Lin Zhichun, a leftist-leaning young

---

[42] Zhang and Song, "Cheng Fangwu nianpu," 89.   [43] He, *Aiguo yi shusheng*, 261.

[44] In most cases, ancient world history and ancient medieval history were combined into one *jiaoyanshi*.

[45] Martin, *The Making of a Sino-Marxist World View*, 25.

[46] "Leaning to one side" was a policy that the CCP adopted in the early 1950s, which emphasized China's solidarity with the socialist camp in the Cold War context and its ties with the Soviet Union. However, the relationship between China and the Soviet Union deteriorated in the late 1950s, leading to growing tension between these two countries in the 1960s. Consequently, the policy was soon abandoned in China. There are a good number of recent publications in the People's Republic addressing this issue. For the case in ancient world history, see Chen, "Beisong zhujiao de jianggao."

historian of ancient China in Shanghai, was relocated to Changchun, where he later would emerge to become one of China's leading world historians. Tong Shuye, a rising young historian of ancient China, would find a new position in Qingdao at Shandong University and prepare to switch his research field to world history. For the first generation of "professional" world historians in China, most of them were assigned to the field of world history even though they did not have a strong professional background in either language training or content knowledge. In the context of the increasing specialization and professionalization in historical studies, the new generation of world historians started out from an awkward position.

The forced specialization process also reduced historians' choices in the subjects of their studies. The new *jiaoyanshi* system came with the expectation of obedience – that one needed to focus one's research on the field to which one was assigned. It was social responsibility instead of personal interest that determined the courses one had to teach and the specialty one needed to command. This was in stark contrast to the freedom of choice over teaching subjects and research fields enjoyed by college professors in the Republican period. For instance, Lei Haizong often switched his teaching and research interests between Chinese and world history. After being transferred to the ancient world history *jiaoyanshi*, however, Lei dramatically decreased the number of publications he wrote on Chinese history and correspondingly increased his output of publications on ancient world history. In the early 1950s, Lei wrote increasingly like a professional world historian and talked about nothing outside his assigned research field. By the same token, Lin Zhichun, though loyal to the party-state, had grudgingly complained about his wanting to switch back to ancient Chinese history during his conflict with the departmental bureaucracy.

Professionalization and specialization did not reduce the conflicts between the state and intellectuals. Academia became a more contested space where the communist state attempted to achieve dominant control, while intellectuals struggled to maintain a certain level of intellectual autonomy. This tension constitutes a major theme in the intellectual history of twentieth-century China and had a deep impact on the development of world history.

In his study of authoritarian high modernist regimes, James Scott concludes that there are three factors contributing to the fermentation of resistance against a totalizing state control.[47] The first is "the existence

---

[47] Scott, *Seeing Like a State*, 101–102.

and belief in a private sphere of activity in which the state and its agencies may not legitimately interfere"; the second is the private sector in a liberal political economy; and the third and by far most important barrier limiting thoroughgoing high modernist schemes has been the existence of working, representative institutions through which a resistant society could make its influence felt. In the case of 1950s China, after the establishment of the work unit system and the elimination of private property rights, the first two conditions for resistance ceased to exist. Resistance mainly took place through the channel of old power structures that were imbedded in the existing working institutions.

Despite these changes, world history in China evolved in interesting ways during the early PRC period. Scholars today generally regard the 1950s as the beginning of the professional study of world history in China. To some extent, this is a legitimate argument, since the establishment of world history teaching and research units in China's higher education system in the 1950s had a great impact on the development of this field.

For curricula, world history had already become an important component in the teaching of history at the secondary school level by the early People's Republic. In the early 1950s, junior and senior high school students were required to take four semesters of world history courses in total. From 1953 to 1956, this increased to six semesters. This trend of increasing world history in the secondary education system was reversed in the 1960s, with the radicalization of party ideology. Beginning in 1961, world history was taken out of junior high school curricula. In 1964, the proportion of world history courses further decreased. Students were only required to take two semesters of history (world history and Chinese history combined) over the entire five years of secondary school education. After the Cultural Revolution broke out, as schools devolved into chaos or in some cases closed down altogether, the high number of world history courses became almost impossible to sustain.[48] At the same time, the early 1950s also provided the opportunity for historians to reconceptualize the teaching of world history in China.

To implement the change, an increasing number of scholars pursued teaching and research in world history as their professional career, although the first generation of professional world historians of this period still faced enormous difficulties in their studies, as they lacked both basic training. For ancient world history, only a handful of individual scholars

---

[48] Chen Qineng, "Zong lun: Chengjiu, buzu yu zhanwang" [Achievement, problems, and prospect], in *Jianguo yilai shijieshi yanjiu gaishu* [A survey of the study of world history after the founding of the People's Republic] (Beijing: Shehui kexue wenxian chubanshe, 1991), 5.

commanded ancient languages such as Greek, Latin, Egyptian hieroglyphs, and Mesopotamian cuneiforms, and they lacked a supporting
infrastructure of libraries and archaeological collections for research. In
order to meet professional standards, Chinese world historians considered it an urgent task to introduce the scholarship of world history
from abroad. Those who studied in North America and Europe during
the Republican period provided the intellectual work to introduce international scholarship on world history to China. The victory of the communist revolution interrupted this vibrant trend of exchanges between
China and the West. Yet it did not stop its international exchanges with
other socialist countries. From 1950 to 1978, the Chinese government
sent 12,775 students abroad, and a small number of them studied world
history and cultures. Under the policy of "leaning to one side," a majority
of them (8,414) went to the Soviet Union.[49] Along with other venues of
exchanges, including academic visits and special training programs,
Chinese scholars produced a large number of translations of texts on
ancient world history from the Soviet Union, some of which later became
standard textbooks for scholars in the field (see Table 3).

Aside from textbooks, scholars also translated the latest Soviet scholarly
research on ancient world history. From 1959 to 1960, the first two volumes
of *The General History of the World* (*Shijie tongshi*) edited by the Soviet
Academy of Sciences in Chinese translation appeared.[50] Soviet professional
journals on ancient history such as *Vestnik Drevnej Istorii* (*Gushi tongbao*
[Journal of ancient history]) were introduced into China. Owing to this
journal's influence on this field in the Soviet Union, many articles in the
journal were translated into Chinese.[51] Based on those translation activities,
the editorial committee of *Historical Research* (*Lishi yanjiu*) launched a new
bimonthly entitled *The Series of Historiographical Translations* (*Shixue yicong*)
for translated academic articles primarily from Soviet sources. Several articles published in this journal were taken from *Gushi tongbao*.[52]

The translation of Soviet academic works on ancient world history was
not only extensive in scope but also timely. For instance, a debate on the

---

[49] *Sanshinian quanguo jiaoyu tongji ziliao, 1949–1978* [The statistics of national education
during the past thirty years, 1949–1978] (Zhonghua renmin gongheguo jiaoyubu, 1979),
collected in *Zhonggong zhongyao lishi wenxian ziliao huibian* [The collection of important
historical documents of the CCP], vol. 30 (Los Angeles: Zhongwen chubanwu fuwu
zhongxin, 2010), 98–99.

[50] *Liu Jiahe and Liao Xuesheng, eds, Shijie gudai wenmingshi yanjiu daolun* [An introduction to
the study of the history of ancient civilizations] (Beijing: Gaodeng jiaoyu chubanshe,
2001), 201.

[51] This journal, founded in 1937, was considered the most authoritative forum for academic
discussion in the field of ancient history and thus was collected at several libraries in
China. Liu and Liao, *Shijie gudai wenming shi yanjiu daolun*, 212.

[52] Liu and Liao, *Shijie gudai wenming shi yanjiu daolun*, 18.

Table 3 *Chinese translation of Soviet ancient world history textbooks in the early 1950s*

Title	Russian Author	Chinese Translator	Publication Info.
Gudai shijie shi 世界古代史 [Ancient world history][53]	Aleksandr Vasil'evich Mishulin Ch. 米舒林	Wang Yijin 王易今	Beijing: Zhongguo qingnian chubanshe, 1954
Gudai shijie shi 古代世界史 [Ancient world history][54]	Ch.B. H. Diyakefu 狄雅可夫, H. M. Nikeersiji 尼柯爾斯基, et al.	Lin Zhichun 林志純 [pseud. Rizhi 日知]	Beijing: Zhongyang renmin zhengfu gaodeng jiaoyu jiaocai bianshen chu, 1954
Gudai Dongfang shi 古代東方史 [History of the ancient Orient][55]	V. I. Adviev Ru. В.И Авдиев Ch. Afujifu 阿夫基耶夫	Wang Yizhu 王以鑄	Beijing: Sanlian shudian, 1956
Gu Xila shi 古希臘史 [Ancient Greek history][56]	V. S. Sergeev Ru. Владимир Сергеевич Сергеев Ch. Saiergeyefu 塞爾格葉夫	Mou Lingzhu 繆靈珠	Beijing: Gaodeng jiaoyue chubanshe, 1955
Gudai Luoma shi 古代羅馬史 [Ancient Roman history][57]	Sergei Ivanovich Kovalev Ch. Kewaluefu 柯瓦略夫	Wang Yizhu 王以鑄	Beijing: Sanlian shudian, 1957

[53] This was a history textbook written for high school students in the Soviet Union. The textbook was adopted at some Chinese universities. Wang, "Wo suo liaojie de Wu Mi jiaoshou."

[54] This was a history textbook for history majors at teachers colleges and universities in the Soviet Union. Liu and Liao, *Shijie gudai wenmingshi yanjiu daolun*, 17. The original Russian names of the authors are missing.

[55] The first edition of this book was published in 1948 and was awarded a first-level Stalin Prize. The Chinese translation was based on the 1953 edition. V. I. Avdiev, "Gudai Dongfang shi xulun" [Preface to the history of the ancient Orient], trans. Rizhi [pseud., Lin Zhichun], *Lishi jiaoxue* [History pedagogy], no. 6 (1954): 6.

[56] In 1934, the Communist Party of the Soviet Union (CPSU) passed a resolution to strengthen the development of Marxist historiography. Vladimir Sergeyevich Sergeyev's *The Outline of Ancient Greek History* was published in the same year. In 1939, the expanded edition was published. The book was the first Soviet Marxist textbook on ancient Greek history and was widely adopted as a textbook in the Soviet system of higher education. Liu and Liao, *Shijie gudai wenming shi yanjiu daolun*, 211.

[57] This was originally published in 1948. Professional translators, rather than historians, translated these books. For example, Wang Yizhu (1925–) was a professional translator who had studied at Peking University but did not receive a degree. He worked in the National Translation Bureau from 1950 to 1953; he was then transferred to *Renmin chubanshe* [People's publishing house] to serve as editor. Wang Yizhu, "Fanyi shi mafan, feixin dan ting youyiyi de shi" [Translation is a troublesome, mentally taxing, but quite meaningful thing], *Nanfang dushi bao* [Southern metropolitan daily], May 9, 2007.

collapse of Roman slavery took place among Soviet scholars in *Vestnik Drevnej Istorii* from 1953 to 1956. Two years later, most of the relevant articles had been translated into Chinese, and they were soon collected into a book and published in 1958.[58] Therefore, the globalization of historical studies took another dimension during the time in China. Although Chinese scholars had less access to the latest scholarship from Europe and the United States than they had had in the Republican era, they were not completely isolated from the outside world. In general, translated Russian works maintained a fairly high quality. Russian historians had a long tradition of classical antiquity and Oriental studies, and some of them still produced some fine scholarship after the Russian Revolution.[59] At the same time, Chinese translators considered the translation of Russian sources a mandatory political assignment and maintained a high standard in their work.[60] As a result, some translations became classics in modern Chinese intellectual history, and some early-translated Soviet books remain important sources for studying ancient world history in China today, most notably *Ancient Roman History* and *Ancient Oriental History* translated by Wang Yizhu in the 1950s. Furthermore, some scholars were even able to obtain a few recent English-language publications on their research topics, though Western scholarship was heavily repressed in China during this time. For instance, the archaeologist Xia Nai (1910–1985) was able to follow some of the latest Western work on world history and archaeology while working at the Chinese Academy of Sciences in the 1950s.

Along with translating textbooks and using secondary Soviet research, scholars started to work on translating primary sources on ancient world history into Chinese. Classic works in Western antiquity like those written by Herodotus and Thucydides were translated into Chinese during this period.[61] Scholars also conducted collective projects to translate primary sources to assist teaching, one of which was a series entitled *Collected Sources for World History: Series I* (*Shijieshi ziliao congkan chuji*) translated and edited by historians Yang Renpian (1903–1973), Geng Danru, Liu Qige, and Zhang Zhilian beginning in the 1950s. Yang Renpian, an Oxford educated historian, was chief editor for the first several books in

[58] *Luoma nuli zhanyou zhi bengkui wenti yiwen ji* [Collection of translated essays on the issue of the collapse of the Roman slavery system], ed. and trans. the editorial branch of *Lishi yanjiu* (Beijing: Kexue chubanshe, 1958).
[59] With regard to the survey of Soviet scholarship on ancient history, see Hugh Graham, "The Significant Role of the Study of Ancient History in the Soviet Union," *The Classical World* 61, no. 3 (1967): 92.
[60] Wang, "Fanyi shi mafan, feixin dan ting youyiyi de shi."
[61] Herodotus was translated by Wang Yizhu. Thucydides was translated by Xie Defeng in the 1950s, and the first edition was published in 1960.

this series prior to August 1957 before he was labeled a rightist in the Anti-Rightist Campaign. An ambitious project, this series was originally designed to include thirty to forty volumes, and a portion of its content was related to ancient world history. For the content, Chinese historians paid special attention to non-European sources of ancient world history, which offers a striking contrast to the primary interest in Greek and Roman classical antiquity in the study of ancient history in Europe and North America.[62] For instance, the volume on ancient Egypt and ancient Mesopotamia (*Gudai Aiji yu gudai Lianghe liuyu*), edited by Lin Zhichun (aka. Rizhi) published in 1962, includes some basic non-European sources such as the *Admonitions of Ipuwer* (*Yipuwei chenci*) and the *Code of Hammurabi* (*Hanmolabi fadian*).[63] However, most of those translation projects were not finished due to increasing political pressure in China in the late 1950s and the 1960s.

Based on these translated sources, world historians in China began to pursue their own research agendas. College textbook writing was one of the most productive of those agendas in the 1950s. In 1949, a leftist historian, Zhou Gucheng (1898–1996), published a three-volume world history, *A General History of the World* (*Shijie tongshi*), in Shanghai, which was credited with being the first general history of the world written by a Chinese scholar.[64] It became a popular textbook for teaching world history in the early 1950s, partially thanks to his leftist background. As Mao Zedong's long-time friend since the early 1920s, Zhou Gucheng published a general history of China in 1939. The Nationalist government barred him from teaching Chinese history for his left-leaning views. In the early 1940s, Zhou began to teach world history at Fudan University. He soon realized that there was a lack of high-quality world history textbooks in China written by Chinese scholars. So he started to write a general history of the world and the first three volumes were published in 1949.[65]

[62] During the same period, most world-historical works in the West remained Eurocentric, such as was the case in West Germany. Sachsenmaier, *Global Perspectives on Global History*, 119–122.

[63] This was a product of the ancient world history seminar. Students and instructors of this seminar together translated some primary sources on ancient world history, which were later collected into two publications: this one and *Shijie gudai shi shiliao xuanji* (in two volumes) [Selection of sources in ancient world history], coedited by the Departments of History at Beijing Normal University and Northeast Normal University. This second volume was published in 1958. Liu and Liao, *Shijie gudai wenming shi yanjiu daolun*, 78.

[64] Jiang Yihua and Jiang Fen, preface to the new edition of Zhou Gucheng, *Shijie tongshi* [A general history of the world], new ed. (Shijiazhuang: Hebei jiaoyu chubanshe, 2000), 9.

[65] Zhou Gucheng, "Wo shi zenyang yanjiu shijie shi de" [How I studied world history], in *Zhou Gucheng shixue lunwen xuanji* [A selective collection of Zhou Gucheng's essays on historiography] (Beijing: Renmin chubanshe, 1982), 110–111.

In this book, Zhou criticized Eurocentrism, as did many Chinese intellectuals including Lei Haizong in the Republican period. According to Zhou, the overconcentration on classical antiquity in the West in world history textbooks written by Euro-American scholars was an indicator of this regional bias. In order to correct this problem, he instead adopted six cultural zones to record world-historical events: Egypt, Babylonia, Persia, India, China, and Mexico. Unlike works on world history in China that often exclude the discussion of China, Zhou included Chinese history in his textbook. Despite the fact that this book heavily relied on English-language sources, it was considered to be the greatest achievement of world history textbook writing in the period 1949–1952. It was reprinted in both 1950 and 1958.[66]

In the early 1950s, under the policy of "leaning to one side," the People's Republic encouraged scholars to translate and adopt Soviet textbooks as well as to continue publishing textbooks written prior to the revolution.[67] In 1952, Lin Zhichun translated three sections of a Soviet textbook on world history, and the Ministry of Education distributed it to Chinese universities. The complete translation was published in Chinese in the spring of 1954. Based on that translation, Lin Zhichun and Shi Yamin edited the textbook *Ancient World History* (*Gudai shijie shi*) and published it in 1958. By working on projects ranging from translating Soviet works to editing their own textbooks, Chinese ancient world historians gradually developed their scholarly knowledge and skills in the early 1950s.

The late 1950s and early 1960s were a transitional period in world-historical studies in China. As Mao Zedong and other party leaders gradually moved away from the Soviet model, they attempted to expedite the social and economic transformation in China through mass political movements. During the climax of this effort, the Great Leap Forward of 1958–1962, Chinese historians were under pressure from political radicalism, and some of them gave up on their professional standards to engage in a "revolution in historiography" (*Shixue geming*). This event marked a radical change in the study of modern Chinese history, as the revolutionary narrative finally dominated Chinese historiography.[68] It also had subtle impact on world-historical studies, for it was the time when amateurism temporally replaced academic professionalism and

---

[66] Martin, *The Making of a Sino-Marxist World View*, 22. Sachsenmaier, *Global Perspectives on Global History*, 187.

[67] Along with Zhou Gucheng's textbook, the textbook *Waiguo jindai shigang* (*Outline of Modern Foreign History*) by Lin Judai was reprinted in both 1950 and 1951. Sachsenmaier, *Global Perspectives on Global History*, 187.

[68] Li, *Reinventing Modern China*, 132–169.

dominated world-historical studies. In the name of an "education revolu-tion" (*Wenhua geming*), for instance, history professors and students at Northeast Normal University went down to the countryside and estab-lished dozens of "temporary universities" for the peasants within just a few months.[69] Some amateur research teams also put together booklets and essay collections on world-historical studies, though these works were often of poor quality and written in an ideologically charged tone. They were quickly abandoned by later historians.

At the same time, the study of world history continued to develop. In the context of the "historiographical revolution," some world historians were also engaged in an attempt to edit their own textbook series and to supersede Soviet influence. The publication of the textbook series *A General History of the World* (*Shijie tongshi*) came right after the Great Leap Forward in 1962, and it represents the highest achievement of these government-initiated projects.[70] Edited by Zhou Yiliang and Wu Yujin, this textbook series followed the Stalinist five stages of world history, dividing human development into primitive (communal) society, slavery, feudalism, capitalism, and socialism (ultimately communism). In the volume on ancient world history, the authors claim that the convergent theme across the history of the ancient world was the rise and fall of slave society.[71] The series was flawed in several aspects. First, it was heavily charged with Marxist teleology and portrayed ancient world history as largely a story of class struggle between slaves and slave owners. Shying away from nuanced historical analysis, it offered footnotes to the state ideology.[72] World history in this regard became the handmaiden of political ideology.[73] Second, this textbook separated China from the rest of the world and did not include any discussion of Chinese history in its content. This textbook became a model for Chinese world history education. As such, the separation of China from world history had a negative impact on the Chinese study of world history. Despite these shortcomings, its editors devoted a great deal of the content of the book series to non-European regions, which included not only Egypt,

[69] More research needs to be done on the Education Revolution of 1958. However, to the best of my knowledge, the archives on these activities were already removed from the university archives. I came across some of these materials once in my field research. They were in the hands of private collectors. However, I doubt that these materials will resurface any time soon.

[70] Luo Xu, "Reconstructing World History in the People's Republic of China since the 1980s," *Journal of World History* 18, no. 3 (2007): 326.

[71] Qi Sihe, "Daoyan" [Preface], in *Shijie tongshi: Shanggu bufen* [A general history of the world: Part on antiquity], ed. Qi Sihe (Beijing: Renmin chubanshe, 1973), 1.

[72] Qi Sihe, "Daoyan,"5.

[73] See the conference collection, Jonathan Unger, ed., *Using the Past to Serve the Present: Historiography and Politics in Contemporary China* (Armonk, NY: M. E. Sharpe, 1993).

Mesopotamia, and India but also Japan, Vietnam, and Korea. To some extent, this textbook series can be regarded as an early Chinese attempt to challenge Eurocentrism in world history.

In sum, the 1950s witnessed a rapid development in world-historical studies in China. This included the translation and introduction of Soviet sources (textbooks and academic works) and primary sources from non-European contexts. Basing their work on these two developments, Chinese scholars began to formulate their own view of the ancient world by editing textbooks on this subject. All of these activities contributed to the rise of scholarly research on the subject, which eventually led to the establishment of the World History Institute, the first national research institute for world history in the early 1960s.

Prior to the People's Republic, there was a lack of national research organizations for world history in China. World historians, or rather world history teachers, were scattered in their own academic departments, and they did not actively interact with each another. After the revolution, the Chinese Communist state established a government-affiliated think tank and research institution, the Chinese Academy of Sciences (CAS) in 1949. In 1959, the Research Unit of World History was organized under the Department of Philosophy and Social Sciences. A few years later, this unit was gradually expanded into a research group. Growing out of it, the World History Institute was established in 1964. It became China's first national organization for world-historical research. As a government think tank, its early agenda was heavily devoted to political revolutions in Asia, Africa, and Latin America. Be that as it may, as the Institute would be playing a leading role in the development of the field in the post-Mao era, its foundation remained a significant development in world history in China.

Yet history does not merely take place on paper. While appreciating the positive development of the field, the 1950s remains a painful memory for the collective community of Chinese historians. Facing the intrusion of the totalizing state, individuals were making different choices. The fate of three individuals – Lei Haizong, Tong Shuye, and Lin Zhichun – represents a profound transformation in Chinese historiography during the early 1950s.

Before the revolution, Lei Haizong was already an established scholar. Tong Shuye and Lin Zhichun were lesser-known figures in the same field. However, their stories converged in the creation of a field of world history out of the existing order of Chinese historiography and in the various roles each played in the establishment and development of this field. Their mixed feelings of fear, conviction, and opportunity encapsulated the mindset of Chinese intellectuals during the early 1950s.

The CCP's attempts to achieve stricter control over the higher education system had created a strong tension between intellectuals and CCP members even before 1949. He Ziquan, who had a strong attachment to several Nationalist-affiliated scholars such as Tao Xisheng (1899–1988) and Fu Sinian, has analyzed that tension. He has argued that intellectuals who came from the "old society" and received a Euro-American liberal, democratic education, had worldviews that differed from those of CCP cadres – especially regarding the issue of democracy. These old intellectuals were more individualistic and believed in a liberal democracy that would allow them to follow their own free will. By contrast, most party members were more collectivistic and accepted Mao's idea of a New Democracy in which the party would play the role of the Western bourgeoisie or even of a democratic dictatorship, a seeming oxymoron in which the party would speak for the masses.[74] He felt that the only way for old intellectuals to survive in the new system was to completely submit to party rule and give up the pursuit of liberal democracy.[75] Thanks to this decision, he survived various political campaigns and ideological battles.

Those such as Lei Haizong who did not yield to the party leadership generally suffered. Lei had already had conflicts with leftist intellectuals in the 1940s, who criticized Lei as a reactionary scholar due to his sympathy with the Nationalist consolidation of power, his negative view of the Soviet Union, his affiliation as a Nationalist Party member, and his involvement with the Zhanguo Ce clique. Yet, strangely enough, Lei had chosen to stay on the mainland in 1949, even though Chiang Kai-shek had invited him to Taiwan.[76] Owing to his previous connections with the Nationalist Party, Lei had considerable distrust of the new government. In September 1949, he was forced to resign from the chair position in the Department of History at Tsinghua University. Soon he was placed under "supervision" for a year, during which he was asked to stay in his residence and could not move freely.[77] In 1951, he was assigned to a land reform investigation team in a rural area of Northwestern China. This team included several other "questionable" intellectuals, including He Lin and Wu Jingchao (1901–1968) both of whom had ties with the

---

[74] Mao Zedong, *Lun renmin minzhu zhuanzheng* [On the people's democratic dictatorship] (Beijing: Renmin chubanshe, 1949).

[75] He, *Aiguo yi shusheng*, 227.

[76] There is no clear explanation for why Lei chose to stay. Perhaps his daughter, who seemed to have been pro-CCP, influenced his decision. A similar case is He Lin, a philosopher with a strong attachment to the Nationalist Party who also chose to stay on the mainland. Huang, "Jiang Jieshi yu He Lin," 19–20. For a recent discussion on this issue, see Zong Liang, "1949 nian qianhou de Lei Haizong" [Lei Haizong before and after 1949], *Zhonghua dushu bao* [Chinese Reader's Weekly (Beijing)], July 10, 2013."

[77] Zong Liang, "1949 nian qianhou de Lei Haizong."

Nationalist government. It was apparently a government-orchestrated project, with a plan to transform these "questionable intellectuals" by offering them the opportunity to witness revolutionary reform in China's countryside.[78] Back from this mission, Lei announced in an essay that he had abandoned his past scholarship, which he admitted he had learned from Western imperialist countries, and that he had decided to study the new knowledge of the people and revolutionary cadres. This essay became an example of how the Chinese Communist Party was successfully transforming old intellectuals and was widely circulated in China.[79]

In the following years, Lei distanced himself from politics and acted like a specialist in ancient world history. If he had to, he was willing to contribute one or two short essays that would be acceptable to the party ideology. For instance, in 1951, Lei published an article criticizing Catholicism as a tool used by imperialist powers to invade China. Considering his religious background, it, again, signaled his willingness to collaborate with the government.[80] Mainly, however, he kept silent. After being transferred from Beijing to Tianjin in 1952, he retained his professorship and worked as director of the world history *jiaoyanshi* at Nankai University. His lectures were well received by students and colleagues alike. He remained a respected figure among his colleagues and his fellow historians; in spite of this, the university did not treat him well economically. In 1956, Lei was only classified as a Level IV professor, which was relatively low in the academic hierarchy that ranged from Level VI to Level I. By contrast, some scholars, with fewer achievements but better political connections than Lei, had received better classifications.[81]

The situation in China dramatically deteriorated during the Anti-Rightist Campaign in 1957, as affected by the global politics. In 1956, two political events deeply shook the communist world: the anti-Soviet political protests in Poland and Hungary and the resulting military interventions in these countries by the Soviet Union. Some Chinese leaders felt that China was facing similar dangers from within and thus must critically examine the imported Soviet system. In 1957, Mao Zedong and his followers initiated the Hundred Flowers Campaign, which invited public criticism of the party.

---

[78] "Zhonggong zhongyang guanyu dongyuan minzhu renshi canjia huo canguan tugai de zhishi" [The directives on mobilizing democratic public figures to participate in or observe land reforms by the Central Committee of the CCP], in *ZZWX*, 3:401.

[79] Wu Jingchao, Yang Renpian, Lei Haizong et al., *Tudi gaige yu sixiang gaizao* [Land reform and thought transformation] (Beijing: Guangming ribao chubanshe, 1951), 19–29.

[80] Lei Haizong, "Zhongguo jindaishi shang de Tianzhujiao yu Fandigang" [Christianity and the Vatican in modern Chinese history], in *Bolun shixue ji*, 312–325.

[81] Shu Shicheng, "Xinji bu gongping de ying chongxin ping" [On the need to re-evaluate the unfair payment scale]. *Huadong shifan daxue xiaokan* [Magazine of East China Normal University], June 21, 1957.

As criticism increased, the top leaders in China, however, realized that it potentially endangered the party's power. In response, Mao dramatically changed his stance and launched the Anti-Rightist Campaign, which aimed to stamp out and punish what he considered to be too much criticism from intellectuals.[82] Unfortunately, Lei became a victim in this transition.

Lei's tragedy started with some careless comments. In April 1957, in the context of the Hundred Flowers Campaign, the party's leading newspaper, the *People's Daily*, invited him to a panel discussion on the state of social sciences in China. During the event, he offered a scathing critique of the current state of world-historical studies in China. The problem was the lack of primary and secondary sources. Only using Soviet sources was far from enough. As a matter of fact, as he asserted, except for a few new ideas from Lenin and Stalin, Marxism remained at the same level as it had been in 1895 (which was the year Engels died). He took *The Origin of the Family, Private Property and the State*, a classical canon for Marxist world historians, as an example and explained that, when Engels published this text in 1884, *The Athenian Constitution* had not yet been discovered. (It took place in Egypt in 1890.) Without citing new materials, some of Engels's arguments in that text were less than reliable. Lei continued and made his point even more clear that, since Marx and Engels's works were written sixty-two years ago and based on Greco-Roman historical sources, some of their arguments could not be applied to ancient Chinese history.[83]

Lei did not mean to be bold, claiming that what he discussed was just an academic issue. Yet, for party intellectuals, it was about politics. The panel discussion was soon released in the newspaper on April 21–22. To people's surprise, the *People's Daily* violated the Hundred Flowers policy that encouraged intellectuals to speak out freely and published an editorial after Lei Haizong's talk. It stated that the newspaper did not agree with Lei and asked readers to continue to discuss it.[84] Lei sensed that the

---

[82] Shen Zhihua, "Cong Bo-Xiong shijian dao fanyoupai yundong" [From the Poland-Hungary Incident to the Anti-rightist Campaign], in *Wushinian wujieji* [To commemorate after no commemoration in fifty years], ed. Zhang Yihe (Hong Kong: Thinker, 2007), 15–124. Roderick MacFarquhar, *The Origins of the Cultural Revolution* (New York: Columbia University Press, 1974); Frederick Teiwes, *Politics and Purges in China: Rectification and the Decline of Party Norms, 1950–1965*, 2nd ed. (Armonk, NY: M. E. Sharpe, 1993), esp. chapters 6 and 7. Compared to MacFarquhar and Teiwes, Shen's recent research emphasizes global factors that contributed to the transformation of Mao's thinking, as well as that of other CCP leaders during these two campaigns.

[83] *People's Daily*, April 23, 1957, 24. As discussed in the Chapter 2, Lei objected to using European terms to study Chinese history.

[84] This was an unusual case. Up to this moment, the main policy of the CCP was still to encourage intellectuals to speak out. This case sheds light on different voices within the CCP. Current research indicates that Mao Zedong was very disappointed and angry at Deng Tuo, the chief editor of the *People's Daily*, due to the latter's lukewarm attitude toward the Hundred Flowers Campaign. Timothy Cheek, *Propaganda and Culture in*

editorial was a sign of danger. On the same day the minutes were released (April 28, 1957), Lei wrote to the *People's Daily*, saying that it had distorted his meaning. He urged the newspaper to publish the original version of his talk. His letter was published on April 28, 1957. In it, Lei stated that he had no intention of looking down on Lenin's or Stalin's revolutionary achievements and that his main purpose in that speech was to criticize the current state of the lack of access to recently published sources in the field of social sciences, which was purely an academic issue and by no means political.

Lei Haizong's talk touched on the sensitive issue of the relationship between politics and academics in the early 1950s. As discussed in Chapter 2, Chinese scholars developed a strong sense of autonomy in the Republican period, and this shaped their professional identity. As the state media pressed the boundaries between academics and politics, scholars in Beijing and Tianjin rallied around Lei and showed support. After the editorial on April 22, secret reports indicate that the party was worried; a long list of scholars supported Lei, including Luo Changpei (1899–1958) and You Guo'en (1899–1978) from Peking University; Zhang Xianglin (1908–1968) from Tianjin University; and Yang Zhijiu (1915–2002), Li Helin (1904–1988), Xing Gongwan (1914–2004), and Zheng Tianting (1899–1981) from Nankai University. Some were in the humanities and social sciences but others were even from the faculties of the natural sciences and engineering.[85] About two weeks later, the historian Yang Zhijiu's letter supporting Lei appeared in the same newspaper on May 7, 1957. As Lei's colleague at Nankai, he regarded this as the *People's Daily*'s mistake, which was contrary to revolutionary principles. The case had become a sign of the increasing tension between the party and the intelligentsia.

Perhaps because of the wide support in intellectual circles, Lei Haizong lost sight of the imminent danger. On June 8, 1957, the *People's Daily* published an editorial "What is this for?" in which the party propaganda organ openly referred to some criticism during the Hundred Flower movement as a "class struggle." This signaled the beginning of the Anti-Rightist Campaign.[86] Two days later (on June 10), Lei gave a public

---

Mao's China: Deng Tuo and the Intelligentsia (Oxford: Clarendon Press, 1997), 175; Shen, "Cong Bo-Xiong shijian dao fanyoupai yundong," 72–74; MacFarquhar, *The Origins of the Cultural Revolution*, 193–194; Teiwes, *Politics and Purges in China*, 195.

[85] *Neibu cankao* [Internal reference], April 28, 1957. *Neibu cankao* are important media sources for the history of the early People's Republic. Considered secret or sensitive information, only high-level CCP cadres had official access to the reference. Published by the Xinhua Agency, *neibu cankao* included articles written by Xinhua Agency reporters from all over China. Sometimes they also included readers' letters.

[86] Teiwes, *Politics and Purges in China*, 217.

lecture in Tianjin. Another secret report captured the gist of his talk, in which Lei openly challenged the state of world-historical studies in China. In line with his earlier critique of the Eurocentric nature of Western world history in the Republican period, Lei refused to accept Marxist historiography for its teleological framework. Specifically, speaking now as an ancient world historian, he did not believe that slavery was a common stage in world history – an essential view in Marxist history of the ancient world. He rephrased his points in the 1930s and argued that the West and East followed distinct paths of development. Thus, the classical picture of slavery represented in Greece and Rome did not exist in China.[87] Lei challenged the cultural determinism of Spengler's work in the 1930s. In the same way, he called for recognition of human agency and refused to accept the economic determinism of Marxist ideology. Furthermore, he challenged the idea that state apparatus had emerged by the end of the primitive society stage, another important thesis in Marxist historiography. Sticking to academic professionalism, he made fun of those who stressed the relationship between ancient history and contemporary politics, saying that he did not understand why people got emotional when they talked about bronze or iron artifacts (i.e., the debate over the nature of ancient Chinese society). It was well known among historians that Guo Moruo (1892–1978), the leftist historian and director of the CAS, got very upset when discussing the nature of early Chinese society with another veteran Marxist historian Hou Wailu (1903–1987). Lei insinuated that such Marxist historians became sentimental when discussing ancient Chinese society. He joked in a cheerful mood, "This probably was a psychological symptom that demanded medical attention."[88]

For senior CCP cadres who had access to this report, Lei's critique was humiliating; but the even more disturbing message was the favorable response expressed by young audiences. Despite its "obvious counter-revolutionary" nature, students seemed to have quite enjoyed it. After the talk, some talked to each other as they stepped out of the lecture hall, saying things like "The past interpretation of the origins of the state was too simplistic. He [Lei Haizong] gave a wonderful talk!"; "Today it would have been better if those dogmatists had been asked to listen to this talk. If they had heard it, they would have felt very

---

[87] Most Western scholars today argue that Athenian slavery was a special case in world history. See M. I. Finley, *Economy and Society in Ancient Greece* (New York: Penguin, 1983). I discuss this in greater detail in Chapter 4.

[88] *Neibu cankao*, June 10, 1957. Hou Wailu, *Ren de zhuiqiu* [The tenacious pursuit] (Beijing: Shanlian shudian, 1985), 139; Wang Weijiang, "Wushi niandai lishi xuejia de mingyun" [The fate of historians in the fifties], *Yan-Huang chunqiu* [Yan-Huang chronicle], no. 6 (2009): 40–41.

uncomfortable."[89] Secret agents nervously reported these random comments to the party.

The shifting line between politics and academics confused Lei Haizong and many other intellectuals. After allowing a relatively short period of freedom, the CCP began to tighten the net in June 1957. The campaign followed. It was said that Kang Sheng (1896–1975), head of the PRC security and intelligence apparatus at various points, urged the Tianjin government to denounce Lei Haizong as a rightist in 1957 – even though the municipal government was reluctant to do so.[90] It is hard to assess the reliability of this anecdote, but clearly officials had been suspicious of Lei Haizong even before the Anti-Rightist Campaign.[91] For instance, on February 26, 1957, *Neibu cankao* had already referred to Lei Haizong as a consistently anti-Soviet and anti-Marxism professor. Anyway, after being labeled a "rightist," he was subsequently treated as an enemy or potential enemy. He was prevented from teaching, and the value of all his past scholarship was discredited by the official historiography. He was no longer a respected master, and many people vehemently scolded him.[92] In particular, there was the example of Jian Bozan, who was once rejected by the Department of History at Yenching University and now chaired the Department of History at Peking University. Now considered the leading Marxist historian, Jian called Lei a typical class enemy who used history as a weapon to topple the Chinese communist regime.[93]

Placing Lei in the context of broader trends in Chinese politics, one can reconstruct the basic storyline of how Lei Haizong, a self-restrained scholar working on ancient world history and seemingly detached from the world of politics, then joined the "Five Biggest Rightists" in the field of history along with Huang Xianfan (1899–1982), Xiang Da (1900–1966), Wang Zhongmin (1903–1975), and Chen Mengjia (1911–1966). There were both theoretical and practical reasons for this change. In theory, Lei's perception of history diametrically contradicted Marxist

---

[89] Hou, *Ren de zhuiqiu*, 40–41.

[90] Feng Chengbai, "Shixue dashi Lei Haizong xiansheng 1957 nian mengnan shimo" [A note on how the great historian Lei Haizong met with disaster in 1957], *Lishi jiaoxue* [History pedagogy] 471, no. 3 (2003): 13.

[91] Scholars have been debating the rationality of the Anti-Rightist Campaign. Teiwes underscores the "selective and surgical" nature of the campaign as was planned out by the top party leadership. Yet recent scholarship has begun to shift the focus to the local level and argues that this process could be "arbitrary, irrational, and even preposterous." Teiwes, *Politics and Purges in China*, 26; Ning Wang, *Banished to the Great Northern Wilderness*, 30.

[92] Sun Dingguo, "Jielu Lei Haizong fan Makesizhuyi de zhongzhong edu shoufa" [Exposing Lei Haizong's various pernicious anti-Marxist methods], *Lishi yanjiu* [Historical research], no. *11* (1957): 28–30.

[93] Jian Bozan, "Lishi kexue zhanxian shang liangtiao luxian de douzheng" [The struggle between two lines in the battlefront of historical science], *Renmin ribao*, July 15, 1958.

teleology. Influenced by Enlightenment ideals, Marxist historians in the Soviet Union followed a linear and evolutionary view of time outlined by Joseph Stalin (1878–1953) They claimed that world history had five common stages that evolved from primitive society, slave society, feudal society, capitalist society, to a communist utopia. Locating society in this teleological agenda was critical for Marxists in their efforts to reform the world, as each stage of development required a proper strategy for class struggle. Lei disagreed with this teleological thinking; back in the 1930s, he already had understood the application of such European concepts to Chinese history as Eurocentric.

In daily life, Lei was also resentful that he was unable to express his opinions. The CCP state was even worse than the Nationalist one. Lei later explained his reticence when the party encouraged nonparty intellectuals to express their criticism during the Hundred Flowers Campaign. He said that, in the old times (before the People's Republic), intellectuals did not care about freedom of expression since they did not have the power to participate in politics. If they had problems, they at least had the right to protest. Intellectuals now all kept silent; or they spoke in order to court certain people, which was the equivalent of saying nothing.[94] In light of the attempts at thought control and the pursuit of free expression, the clash between the party-state and scholars like Lei Haizong seemed inevitable.

Yet not all intellectuals suffered as Lei did. For those who were willing to collaborate with the party-state, the 1950s opened up opportunities for personal success, as the new state actively nurtured a group of new intellectuals who were willing to embrace Marxist ideology as a guide for their studies in history. Tong Shuye and Lin Zhichun, perhaps more than any other historians at the time, played active roles in the formation and development of world-historical studies within a Marxist framework. Their conversions to Marxist views shed light on an important and often neglected theme in the intellectual history of twentieth-century China: the formation of socialist belief.

In contrast to older intellectuals who had established influence prior to 1949, the new intellectuals usually hailed from humble beginnings in the academic world.[95] This was the case for both Tong Shuye and Lin Zhichun. Tong was born into a wealthy family in Zhejiang. Unlike

---

[94] *Neibu cankao*, June 16, 1957. Shen, "Cong Bo-Xiong shijian dao fanyoupai yundong," 17. Xie Yong, "1957 nian fanyouyundong shiliao de shouji yu pingjia" [The collection and evaluation of historical materials on the Anti-Rightist Campaign of 1957], in *Wushinian wuji erji*, 334–335.

[95] Huaiyin Li discusses how a younger generation of Chinese historians who grew up from the 1920s to the 1940s tended to be more enthusiastic about applying Marxist ideology to historical studies during this period. In contrast to the earlier generation of foreign returnees such as Lei Haizong and Wu Mi, these scholars were often less professionally

professional historians in the Republican period, he had neither received a decent college education nor earned a prestigious foreign postgraduate degree. He started his academic career as a research assistant to the historian Gu Jiegang in the 1930s. The latter discovered Tong's talent and asked him to edit the last volume of his famous book series *Debates on Ancient History (Gushibian)*. Before the revolution, Tong's research interests were primarily in ancient Chinese history and geography. Without an accredited degree, Tong was unable to obtain a permanent position at a university in the Republican period.[96] Instead, he took part-time jobs and taught at various places.

After the revolution, Tong's academic career underwent a major shift. He was invited to Shandong to teach at the newly founded Shandong University in Qingdao, where his friend Yang Xiangkui worked.[97] Yang (1910–2000), already an active Marxist historian at the time and an influential figure at the institution, helped Tong secure this position.[98] Tong arrived in Qingdao on September 10, 1949 and found a very active atmosphere of Marxist learning on campus. The president of the university, Hua Gang (1903–1973), was a veteran Marxist scholar in historical studies. His book on the history of the great Chinese revolution from 1925 to 1927, published in 1931, was an early attempt to apply Marxist historical materialism to the study of modern Chinese history and had wide influence among early party members. Starting as a scholar himself, Hua Gang was aware of the needs and wants of his fellow intellectuals. He treated scholars like Tong Shuye with respect.[99]

As one of the early socialist institutions of higher learning founded by the party-state, Shandong University gathered a strong team in the Department of History in the early 1950s, including eight reputable professors: Yang Xiangkui, Tong Shuye, Huang Yunmei (1898–1977), Zhang Weihua (1902–1987), Zhao Lisheng, Zheng Hesheng (1901–1989), Chen Tongxie (also a world historian; 1898–1970), and Wang Zhongluo (1913–1986). Campus-wide, seventeen professors reached the full professor level in the field of humanities before the Cultural Revolution. Among them, Feng Yuanjun (1900–1974) and Lu Kanru

---

trained and occupied lower status in the academic hierarchy. Li, *Reinventing Modern China*, 133.

[96] Tong Jiaoying, *Cong lianyu zhong shenghua: Wo de fuqin Tong Shuye* [Rising over purgatory: My father Tong Shuye] (Shanghai: Huadong daxue chubanshe, 2001), 149.

[97] Before 1958, the university was located in Qingdao. After Cheng Fangwu took over as leader, the university was relocated to Jinan.

[98] Tong, *Cong lianyu zhong shenghua*, 145.

[99] Tong, *Cong lianyu zhong shenghua*, 145–149; Liu Guangyu, "Hua Gang yu *Wenshizhe*" [Hua Gang and (the journal) *Literature, History and Philosophy*], *Chuban shiliao* [Historical sources on publishing], no. 4 (2006): 4–11.

(1903–1978) studied in France; Chen Tongxie, Wu Fuheng (1911–2001), Wu Dakun (1916–2007), and Huang Jiade (1908–1993) studied in the United States; Yin Menglun (1908–1988) studied in Japan; Xiao Difei (1907–1991) and Zhao Lisheng graduated from Tsinghua University; Zhang Weihua graduated from Yenching University; and Wang Zhongluo was considered to be a close disciple of Zhang Taiyan, the leader of the last generation of Classical Studies scholars, and later served in the first national history discipline review committee for the State Council. The atmosphere was both diverse and cosmopolitan.

As a veteran party cadre, Hua Gang was active in spreading communist ideas on campus. Thanks to his established position as a party ideologue, he constantly delivered lectures and organized ideological studies among scholars. This was a rare opportunity when accessibility to ideology education was scarce.[100] By September 1952, for instance, there were only 24 political ideology teachers along with 20 teaching assistants in the 7 higher education institutions in the entire region of Northwestern China, with a total student population of near 9,000, not without saying that 10 out of these 20 teachers were unable to fulfill the teaching duty for various reason.[101] As a result, at a time when people had little acquaintance with Marxist ideology, scholars at Shandong University enjoyed a privileged position of and a pioneering role in acquiring the latest messages sent from the party; indeed, Gu Jiegang at times had to ask his student Tong Shuye to send his lecture notes to Shanghai in order to pass the party examinations during ideological campaigns. The latter was keen on studying the new ideology and became one of the early Marxist converts.

Nationwide, Shandong University was one of the most active centers of Marxist historical studies. Another was Northeast Normal University in Changchun, where Lin Zhichun had held a position in history since 1950. Northeast Normal University was among the first universities established by the CCP. Its history can be traced back to the Civil War period when Zhang Xuesi (1916–1970), brother to the famous warlord Zhang Xueliang (1901–2001), founded Northeastern (Dongbei) University in Benxi, Liaoning. After the revolution, it gained its current name and was eventually relocated to Changchun, the capital of Jilin province and the

---

[100] Zhu Yujin, "'Jiuquan wenxun yi xinran!' Huainian Hua Gang tongzhi" ["Pleased to hear news from the afterworld!" Remembering Comrade Hua Gang], *Dushu* [Reading], no. 11 (1980): 110.

[101] "Zhonggong zhongyang pizhuan Xibeiju guangyu peiyang gaodeng, zhongdeng xuexiao MaLiezhuyi shizi de jihua" [The plan by the Northwestern Bureau concerning educating college and secondary school teachers in Marxist-Leninism commented and forwarded by the CCP Central Committee], *ZZWX*, 10:176–177.

former New Capital of the Japanese puppet stage Manchukuo. In the 1950s, like Shandong University, it was a key site for socialist education in North China and was staffed with revolutionary cadres. The founding president of the university, Zhang Ruxin (1908–1976) was a veteran scholar of the Chinese revolution; as Mao Zedong's secretary, he first coined the term "Mao Zedong Thought."[102] After Zhang's tenure, Cheng Fangwu, a participant of the Long March and a veteran party intellectual, succeeded to the position in 1952.[103]

Compared to Tong, Lin Zhichun was even less well known in historical studies before 1949. Lin was born in Fujian and graduated from Daxia University, a lower-tier college in Shanghai and a spin-off of Amoy University from Xiamen, in 1941.[104] After that, he taught at several colleges and local schools in Shanghai, Shenyang, and Fuzhou. He was promoted to associate professor in history at Daxia University. After the establishment of the PRC, he was transferred to Changchun to teach at Northeast Normal University in the fall of 1950. Lin was already a leftist scholar before 1949.[105] Now, with institutional support, Lin arduously learned about Marxism-Leninism. Thanks to his rare language ability in Russian, he became a star among the new Chinese Marxist historians of world history in the context of China's "leaning to one side" in the early 1950s.

Because the influence of Marxist ideology faded after the collapse of the Soviet Union and the sea change in East Europe in the early 1990s, it has become increasingly difficult for scholars to understand why and how intellectuals would accept Marxism under an earlier socialist regime. The cases of Lin Zhichun and Tong Shuye offer some answers to these questions. As we have seen, for each individual, turning into a Marxist historian was a story tinged with belief, fear, and a sense of opportunity.

The growth of interest in Marxist-Leninist theory was a slow process. For the field of world history, Marxism-Leninism played a radical role in breaking the old disciplinary boundaries in the past academic structure and presented an opportunity for its development. Neither Tong Shuye

---

[102] Gao Hua, *Hongtaiyang shi zenyang shengqi de?* [How did the red sun rise up?], (Hong Kong: Chinese University of Hong Kong Press, 2000), 606–607; Daniel Leese, "Mao the Man and Mao the Icon," in *A Critical Introduction to Mao*, ed. Timothy Cheek (Cambridge: Cambridge University Press, 2010), 225.

[103] Cheng Fangwu was vice president of Renmin University in Beijing from 1950 to 1952. Zhang and Song, "Cheng Fangwu nianpu," 89.

[104] Daxia University was a private university in Shanghai, founded in 1924 as a result of disputes within Amoy University. Yeh, *The Alienated Academy*, 102–103. In 1951, as part of the restructuring of the system of higher education, the university was merged into East China Normal University.

[105] Lin Zhichun, "Sixiang zizhuan" [Autobiography of thought], February 10, 1951, Lin Zhichun Personnel Archives.

nor Lin Zhichun was a Marxist historian prior to 1949. Lin held a sympathetic view toward the revolution. Interestingly enough, his real exposure to communist ideas was through his passion for foreign-language studies. From 1937 to 1938, Lin studied English with Lu Maoju, a possible underground party member who later died in the Nationalist Party's concentration camp in Shangrao.[106] His English-language essays published in a Shanghai newspaper in the late 1940s reflected a leftist influence. In them, Lin drew a historical analogy between ancient Chinese history and modern politics, calling the Chinese communist revolution a peasant revolution and the Nationalist rule a falling dynasty.[107] In contrast, Tong Shuye was not outspoken about his political views and seems to have been less interested in politics, although he somehow recognized historical materialism as a viable historical methodology according to his later recollections.[108]

After 1949, the party was in urgent need of Chinese intellectuals who were willing to work with Marxist ideology. Yet there were few places where people were able to acquire such information, since venues of information between the party and intellectuals were still limited. The influence of the party in many aspects was minimal.[109] A sense of confusion about Marxism existed among many members of the educated class in the early 1950s. Both Tong and Lin worked at the centers of Marxist education, where Hua Gang, Zhang Ruxin, and Cheng Fangwu were the spokesmen for the party to intellectuals. Through them, Tong and Lin were able to keep up with the latest messages from the party.

At Shandong University, for instance, Tong quickly developed a very close and trusting relationship with President Hua Gang, who had a charming personality.[110] One anecdote confirms this. In 1954, after hearing that Winston Churchill had been reelected as prime minister in the United Kingdom, Tong, believing Churchill was a warmonger, panicked and ran to Hua's house. On his arrival, he shouted to Hua, "I have a question. You don't have to analyze it, but just give an answer." "What's the matter?," the latter responded. Tong asked: "Churchill has stepped into power. Will there be a world war?" "Of course not!" On hearing the answer, Tong turned around and left. Because of this abiding trust, Tong turned into an eager learner of Marxist theory, as evidenced by another

---

[106] Lin Zhichun, *Geren jianli* [Autobiography], ca. 1954, Lin Zhichun Personnel Archive.
[107] C. C. Lin, "China's Peasant Revolutions," *The China Weekly Review* 112, no. 6 (January 8, 1949): 144; "The Kuo Min Tang and Chinese Dynasties," *The China Weekly Review* 112, no. 13 (February 26, 1949): 315–316.
[108] Tong, *Cong lianyu zhong shenghua*, 63–65.
[109] Jeremy Brown and Paul Pickowicz, eds, *Dilemmas of Victory: The Early Years of the People's Republic of China* (Cambridge, MA: Harvard University Press, 2007), 8.
[110] Tong, *Cong lianyu zhong shenghua*, 172–173; Huang Miantang, "Huainian Tong Shuye xiansheng" [Remembering Mr. Tong Shuye], *Wenshizhe*, no. 6 (1998): 25.

famous anecdote showing his passion for studying Marxism. As the leader of the university, one of Hua's responsibilities included updating the campus community with the latest political issues. He did so by offering public talks. He was, however, not always available to all the campus branches due to a heavy administrative workload. So, people would simply ask Tong, a man with an extraordinarily memory, to attend Hua's earlier talk and to recite the whole speech. Tong paid so much attention to the lectures that he could remember every detail. His attention to detail was so great that, when he repeated the lectures, he would even mimic Hua's coughs.

While embracing Marxism, Tong severed his ties with the previous generation of historians. The correspondence with his old teacher Gu Jiegang documents this dramatic change in his thought. On February 5, 1951, Tong reported to his master on his recent study of Marxist-Leninist historiography. He wrote, "Half the courses I taught during the past year were about Marxism-Leninism. [I] have already made some good initial progress on studying Marxist-Leninist historiography."[111] He then boasted of his ambitious plan to coauthor, with Yang Xiangkui, a 2 million–character general history of China based on historical materialism.[112] Four months later, Tong wrote another letter to Gu addressing the critical issue of historical methodology.

By 1952, Tong had openly criticized textual criticism as an approach to historical analysis, one that was followed by his own teacher Gu Jiegang. In a published essay, Tong classified the old research method as bourgeois historiography and maintained that it had already lost its historical significance during the later stages of the war with Japan.[113] Roughly during the same time, Tong wrote to Gu in private, pointing out that, although his teacher's method in history already contained some basic elements of dialecticism (an important element in historical materialism), Gu was unable to further develop his methodology up to the full level because of his class standing. The only way to reform it was to embrace Marxism-Leninism. He urged his master to study Marxism-Leninism more. Because of the private nature of this communication, it is safe to argue that Tong had embraced Marxism as a historical method.[114]

---

[111] Gu Jiegang, *Gu Jiegang dushu biji* [Gu Jiegang's reading notes] (Taipei: Lianjing, 1995), 5: 2705.

[112] Gu, *Gu Jiegang dushu biji*, 5:2711.

[113] Gu, *Gu Jiegang dushu biji*, 5:2791–2792. It is interesting to point out that conservative scholars like Lin Tongji and Lei Haizong made a similar critique of textual criticism during the same time.

[114] Gu, *Gu Jiegang riji*, 7:346, 347.

This transformation to socialist belief also took place for Lin Zhichun at Northeast Normal University, where Cheng Fangwu urged faculty members to study Marxism. In the first meeting with the university administrative staff after his arrival on October 21, 1952, Cheng said that one of his main tasks was to implement a systematic Marxist-Leninist education at the school. Shortly after this, he announced the establishment of four Marxist ideological *jiaoyanshi* and took responsibility for the unit on Marxism-Leninism.[115] This immersion in ideological education expedited Lin's acceptance of Marxism.

Although some new intellectuals probably did seriously accept Marxism as a belief, fear still played a crucial role in spreading the ideology. The People's Republic, which Mao frankly described as "the people's democratic dictatorship," was a regime of terror for many of its dissidents. This revolutionary ideal was based on a binary opposition between friends and enemies, and one can clearly see that the party had gradually institutionalized this opposition in the early 1950s.[116] In a state of emergency (in some cases, self-perpetuated), the party-state claimed the legitimacy of adopting any and all possible means to eliminate potential oppositions. The consequences were severe for those who were to be categorized as enemies of the party. Most intellectuals were uncertain about their position in the friends/enemies binary because of their ambiguous connections to the previous regime. This fear of being categorized as enemies dominated their social and political lives. It also played into academic discussions and jeopardized the autonomy of the community. This was especially true of Tong, who, torn apart by great psychological pressure during the various campaigns, lost his sanity on several occasions.

Tong was a unique figure. He was a talented man and had an extraordinary ability to memorize academic sources. He was also able to swiftly identify problems in the existing literature. As a scholar, he did not waste his talent; his research covers not only ancient Chinese and world history but also the history of painting and ceramics. Moreover, he was a good painter and a connoisseur of antiques. Deng Tuo (1912–1966), a top-level party intellectual who once served as deputy major of Beijing, admired Tong's skills in evaluating antiques (especially ceramics and paintings) and often called for his help.[117] Despite his accomplishments, Tong had suffered from what is now known as obsessive compulsive disorder since childhood, and he approached his own problems in an

---

[115] Zhang and Song, "Cheng Fangfu nianpu," 89.
[116] For more on the enemy/friend binary, see Dutton, *Policing Chinese Politics*.
[117] Tong, *Cong lianyu zhong shenghua*, 173.

equally scholarly manner. In order to understand his psychological condition, he taught himself psychology and eventually published a book on the topic. In the book, Tong argues that, unlike other mental health diseases, compulsion was a psychological disorder that the patient themselves were fully aware of.[118] In his case, he could not help being scared by the many trivial things in his personal life, let alone more serious fears such as political campaigns.[119] For instance, his friend and colleague Lu Yao once concluded that Tong had six fears: unemployment, thunder and lightning, airborne attacks, contagious diseases, cancer, and political campaigns. Another of his students added two more: earthquakes and Chiang Kai-shek's counterattack on the mainland. His political fears played into his mental condition and eventually drove him to temporarily lose his sanity in the mid-1950s, during the Anti-Hu Feng (1902–1985) and the Cleansing Counter-Revolutionary campaigns.[120]

The Anti-Hu Feng Campaign of 1955 was the product of academic politics. Starting with an academic discussion among a small group of literary scholars, it quickly developed into a nationwide political campaign that also swept across the Shandong University campus. Tong's patron, Hua Gang, was accused of being a member of the counterrevolutionary group and thrown into jail.[121] Tong was soon exposed to a subsequent campaign that took place almost simultaneously, the Campaign to Suppress Counterrevolutionaries (*Sufan*).[122] In contrast to the relatively small-scale Anti-Hu Feng Campaign, the *Sufan* was aimed at escalating the former into a mass movement. Orders from the high-level party organization named three counterrevolutionaries in the Department of History, and Tong was one of them. The rumor was that Tong had killed 1,000 party members in just one night during the Republican period.[123]

The incident was almost tragically funny because of his well-known fear of almost everything, and no one really believed that Tong could have

---

[118] Tong Shuye, *Jingshenbing yu xinli weisheng* [Mental illness and psychological health], 171. Cited in Tong, *Cong lianyu zhong shenghua*, 7.

[119] Lu Yao and Hu Xiaozhong, "Tong Shuye zai Shandong daxue" [Tong Shuye at Shandong University], *Shandong daxue bao* [Shandong University newspaper] 1741 (February 25, 2009), 6.

[120] Hu Feng was a Chinese writer and art theorist who was active in the League of Left-Wing Writers during the 1930s. His outspoken nature caused clashes with several other Marxist writers and eventually led to his prosecution in the 1950s.

[121] Scholars are still debating the CCP's motive in launching the Anti-Hu Feng Campaign. Either way, the campaign indicated the intense internal tensions that existed among left intellectuals. Kirk Denton, "The Hu Feng Group: Genealogy of a Literary School," in *Literary Societies in Republican China*, ed. Kirk Denton and Michel Hockx (Lanham, MD: Lexington Books, 2008), 413–473.

[122] For a general introduction on this campaign, see Strauss, "Morality, Coercion and State Building," 908–910.

[123] Zhao, *Lijintang zixu*, 160.

committed such a crime. Initially, Tong himself also refused to admit it. On July 29, 1955, he wrote a letter to the party branch to rebuke the accusation.[124] Some cadres, however, continued to press him.[125] Two days later, the psychological pressure overwhelmed his defenses and caused him to have a mental breakdown. In a state of insanity, he wrote a petition to the party admitting that he belonged to a "counter-revolutionary underground organization." This organization, he reported, was financially supported by American intelligence bureaus and had long been secretly operating on the mainland. With branches all over China, the chief director was Gu Jiegang (his mentor); the director of the Shanghai branch was Yang Kuan (his friend; 1914–2005); the director of the Shandong branch was Wang Zhongluo (his colleague who often cooked fried rice for him); the director of the Northeast branch was Lin Zhichun (his debate opponent); and, in addition, Tong himself and his friend Zhao Lisheng were members of this organization.[126] Thanks to Tong's friends' help, this petition was never made public and did not cause further political repercussions.[127] Be that as it may, the incident clearly shows how fear shaped behavior, while underscoring the political and professional context of socialist life in the 1950s.

This sense of fear not only dominated Tong's personal life but also changed the course of his academic research. Lu Yao remembers an anecdote that best captures how political concerns influenced Tong's academic choices. Lu recalled that, at the beginning of a debate on the Asiatic mode of production, Tong had proposed that Chinese feudal society had started under the Western Zhou dynasty.[128] During the debate, he revised his thesis and argued that the Wei–Jin period was the beginning point of Chinese feudal society. Tong was ardent about his new perspective, especially after this view was confirmed by the renowned Marxist historian Shang Yue (1902–1982). Shang was director of the Chinese history *jiaoyanshi* at People's University, then the center of socialist higher education. Tong, however, soon panicked after hearing Yang Xiangkui's comment that this perspective contradicted Mao's personal view on the issue. Tong continually asked Lu

---

[124] The letter was included in his biography written by his daughter, Tong Jiaoying. Tong, *Cong liangyu zhong shenghua*, 205–206.

[125] It was probably due to a personal feud. Tong Shuye was not a popular character in the department by any means, as his conflict with Sun Sibai shows. Tong, *Cong lianyu zhong shenghua*, 176–180.

[126] Most of the names on this list were Tong's acquaintances. Zhao, *Lijintang zixu*, 162. The details of this document were not, however, included in the biography written by his daughter.

[127] Zhao, *Lijintang zixu*, 162.   [128] See Chapter 4.

what to do since his conclusion was different from Mao's.[129] Under increasing political pressure after the Anti-Rightist Campaign, Tong eventually gave up the discussion of the nature of ancient societies.[130]

In the discussion of socialist life during the 1950s, Tong Shuye might be a rare case due to his unique personality. His story, however, does reflect the collective experience of fear among a whole generation of Chinese intellectuals. This fear of deviating from the official ideology was an important factor that affected Chinese intellectuals' thinking during this period; moreover, it affected the way in which historians conceptualized issues that were contingent on the party's guidelines.

Although fear and belief were important factors in their conversion to Marxism, it would be difficult for us to fully make sense of Tong's and Lin's embrace of Marxism in the early 1950s without also considering opportunism. In the case of Tong, the establishment of the new government changed his life trajectory. Prior to 1949, he was merely a part-time teacher who was unable to secure a permanent position in Shanghai. After 1949, he received a professional position in the Department of History and the Research Institute of History and Languages at Shandong University. Within the university, he was a faculty representative in the Committee of Academic Affairs on behalf of the School of Arts. He was also invited to become a member of the Qingdao Municipal Committee on the Management of Antiquities, as well as editor for the famous academic journal *Literature, History, and Philosophy*, known as *Wenshizhe*. Tong thrived after his transition from a part-time college teacher to a well-established university professor.[131]

Lin Zhichun was also a beneficiary of the new state. After the People's Republic, through his active service, he was able to rise from being a lesser known scholar to recognized as the "founding father of ancient world-historical studies." After restructuring China's higher education system, most schools had to follow the Soviet model and to establish world history *jiaoyanshi* from scratch.[132] Therefore, the party organized national programs to cultivate a new workforce for the field. In the fall of 1955, the Chinese government organized an advanced seminar on ancient world history at Northeast Normal University in Changchun.[133] It selected twenty-eight young faculty members from twenty-eight universities and

[129] Lu and Hu, "Tong Shuye zai Shandong daxue," 6.
[130] Tong, *Cong lianyu zhong shenghua*, 292–293.
[131] Tong, *Cong lianyu zhong shenghua*, 147.
[132] For a more detailed explanation, see Chapter 5.
[133] Zhou Qidi, "Gudai Nanya" [Ancient South Asia], in *Shijie gudai wenmingshi yanjiu daolun*, 179. The opening ceremony for this seminar was held in November 1955 and was attended by the president of Northeast Normal University. Zhang and Song, "Cheng Fangwu nianpu," 91; Wang Dunshu, "Lin Zhichun he Zhongguo shijie gudaishi xueke de jianshe

Table 4 *Participants of the 1955–1957 Ancient World History Seminar*

Name	Institution	Place
Chen Youqiang陳有鏘	Shanghai Teachers College	Shanghai
Chen Wenming陳文明	Shanxi University	Taiyuan, Shanxi
Fang Huilan方廻瀾	Central China Teachers College	Wuhan, Hubei
Cui Lianzhong崔連仲	Liaoning Teachers College	Dalian, Liaoning
Huang Yingxian黄英賢	South China Teachers College	Guangzhou, Guangdong
Li Changlin李長林	Hunan Teachers College	Changsha, Hunan
Li Chunyuan李春元	Fudan University	Shanghai
Li Zutang李祖唐	Guizhou University	Guiyang, Guizhou
Liu Wenpeng劉文鵬	Northeast Normal University	Changchun, Jilin
Liu Yongkun劉永坤	Henan Teachers College	Kaifeng, Henan
Liu Jiahe劉家和	Beijing Normal University	Beijing
Liu Songtao劉松濤	Nanchong Teachers College	Nanchong, Sichuan
Lu Mantang陸滿堂	East China Normal University	Shanghai
Luo Jingtang羅景唐	Henan Teachers Specialized School	Kaifeng, Henan
Ma Chaoqun馬超群	Kunming Teachers College	Kunming, Yunnan
Mao Zhaoxi毛昭晰	Hanzhou University	Hangzhou, Zhejiang
Ren Fengge任鳳閣	Xi'an Teachers College	Xi'an, Shaanxi
Suo Ruole索若勒	Inner Mongolia Teachers College	Hohhot, Inner Mongolia
Tu Houshan涂厚善	Central China Teachers College	Wuhan, Hubei
Wang Chang王暢	Jiangsu Teachers College	Suzhou, Jiangsu
Wang Chongyue王崇岳	Shandong Teachers College	Jinan, Shandong
Wu Pingfan吳平凡	Xinjiang University	Urumqi, Xinjiang
Yan Pei嚴沛	Guangxi Teachers College	Nanning, Guangxi
Yu Naikang余乃康	Anhui Teachers College	Wuhu, Anhui
Zeng Duhong曾度洪	Guangxi Teachers College	Nanning, Guangxi
Zhang Dianji張殿吉	Hebei Teachers College	Xuanhua, Hebei
Zhou Yitian周怡天	Peking University	Beijing
Liu Ruohan劉若翰	Kunming Teachers College	Kunming, Yunnan

teachers colleges across China and sent them to Changchun to receive two years of training on ancient world history from Soviet advisors (for a complete list, see Table 4; and, for the origins of students, see Figure 4).

This seminar adopted Russian textbooks and offered courses by Russian instructors in Russian. The language became a big hurdle, as it was inaccessible to most students. Lin studied some Russian while in Shanghai, so he was assigned to assist Soviet specialists in the program. This was not an easy job, as the relationship between Chinese students and Russian specialists was a politically sensitive issue. Working diligently, Lin played a constructive role in facilitating communication

yu fazhan" [Lin Zhichun and the establishment and development of the Chinese discipline of ancient world history], *Shijie lishi* [World history], no. 2 (2000), 122.

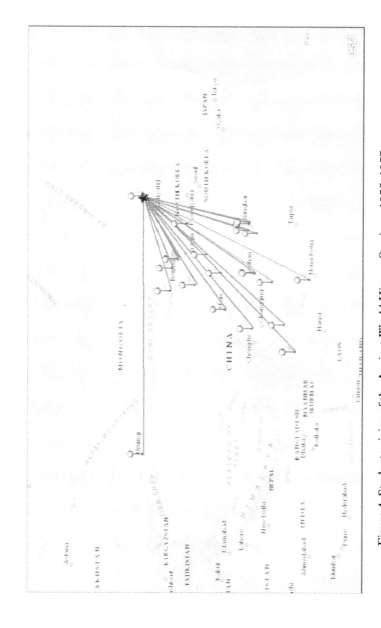

Figure 4 Student origins of the Ancient World History Seminar, 1955–1957

between the two sides. On some occasions, he allowed students to challenge Soviet views. Meanwhile, Lin seized the opportunity and worked with students to translate some Russian textbooks and primary sources for publication. Their work was collected into *The Selected Sources on Ancient World History* (*Shijie gudaishi ziliao xuanji*), coedited in the name of the Departments of History of Beijing Normal University and Northeast Normal University.[134] Through this, Lin developed strong bonds with many students during those two years, and he continued to maintain these relations during the subsequent four decades.[135]

The state initiative also changed the landscape of ancient world history in China. Graduates from this program became leading scholars on various topics. To name just a few, Mao Zhaoxi (1925–2020) became a leading expert on the histories of primitive society, Liu Wenpeng (1931–2007) on ancient Egyptian history, Cui Lianzhong (1925–) on ancient Indian history, and Liu Jiahe (1928–) on the comparative study of Chinese and Western historiography, and their influence persists today. Thus, one could argue that this program, to a certain degree, laid the foundation for the professional study of ancient world history, and Lin played a crucial role in this.

In the early People's Republic, the communist state launched a series of ambitious plans aiming at a total transformation in the field of history. The seminar on ancient world history was one of three programs that the government organized during the year. The other two included a seminar on the histories of East Asia and Southeast Asia at Northeast Normal University and a seminar on the history of the modern world at East China Normal University in Shanghai, both of which played a similar role in establishing the future development of the respective fields. State intervention became a decisive factor in the creation of a professional team of scholars in world history, and it laid the foundations for later development. Participants in the seminars developed common research interests during their time of study, and they continued to flourish in teaching and research in the next several decades. This collaborative model for historical studies became an important method for scholars in the field, lasting up to the 1990s.

In a 1975 interview, which was published as "Body/Power" from his influential book *Power/Knowledge*, Michel Foucault reflected on the state apparatus's role in knowledge production. Using the failure of the Soviet Union as a case, he argues:

---

[134] Zhou, "Gudai Nanya," 179.
[135] Wang, "Lin Zhichun he Zhongguo shijie gudaishi xueke de jianshe yu fazhan," 122. For more on the change in Chinese attitudes toward Soviet specialists, see Stiffler, "Sulian zhuanjia zai Zhongguo Renmin daxue (1950–1957)," 11–20.

Although the ultimate goal for socialist revolution is to undermine the State apparatus, in the battle against the Bourgeois State as the class struggle still lingered after the establishment of a proletariat dictatorship, the Marxist revolutionary party had to borrow the same "mechanisms of hierarchies and organizations of powers" from their rival. In order to continue to operate the State apparatus, the revolutionary party had to rely upon technicians and specialists from the old class. This caused the failure of the revolutionary process.[136]

Foucault claimed that the persistence of the influence of the old elites led to the eventual dissolution of the Soviet Union. This led him to question the role of the state apparatus in a modern society. Foucault continues:

I don't claim at all that the State apparatus is unimportant, but it seems to me that among all the conditions for avoiding a repetition of the Soviet experience and preventing the revolutionary process from running into the ground, one of the first things that has to be understood is the power isn't localised in the State apparatus and that nothing in society will be changed if the mechanisms of power that function outside, below and alongside the State apparatuses, on a much more minute and everyday level, are not also changed.[137]

In light of Foucault's theoretical overview, the Chinese party-state's effort to control historical thought reveals that it was only partially successful. In contrast to the past prevailing view that emphasized the control of the authoritarian state, often dubbed totalitarian, the evidence cited here proposes that states have only a limited ability to control people's thoughts. Indeed, the conflict between Wu Mi and Wang Xingyun, for example, suggests that state efforts to dominate people's minds may stimulate compliance as well as resistance. This may be particularly the case when state influence endangers the ultimate autonomy of intellectual communities.

This research also sheds light on our understanding of professionalization in modern China because it is a vital link between institutions of knowledge prior to the establishment of the PRC and those that emerged later. "Professionalism," as Peter Novick defines it, "includes a common list of criteria of a profession: institutional apparatus (an association, a learned journal), standardized training in esoteric skills, leading to certification and controlled access to practice, heightened status, autonomy."[138] It is interesting to see that professionalization took place not only in Europe and in the United States but, beginning in the 1920s

---

[136] Michel Foucault, "Body/Power," in Foucault, *Power/ Knowledge: Selected Interviews and Other Writings 1972–1977*, ed. and trans. Colin Gordon, Leo Marshall, John Mepham, and Kate Soper (New York: Pantheon Books, 1980), 60.

[137] Foucault, "Body/Power," 60.

[138] Peter Novick, *That Noble Dream: The "Objectivity Question" and the American Historical Profession* (Cambridge: Cambridge University Press, 1988), 48.

and 1930s, also in China. The process in Chinese historiography took on four forms: (1) the institutionalization of historians; (2) state regulation and standardization of history education; (3) the creation and consolidation of academic leadership; and (4) the formation of voluntary, common-interest groups among autonomous intellectuals.

As a high modernist state, the early People's Republic attempted to control knowledge production by an emerging group of professional historians. Yet the professionalization process had a double impact. In order to achieve its high modernist goal, the socialist state adopted professionalization as well as specialization as tools to control the physical bodies and mental processes of Chinese intellectuals. It imposed these through relocating individuals, restructuring the system, and introducing new control regimes (such as the teaching and research unit system). However, professionalization could sometimes justify the pursuit of intellectual autonomy – even within the rhetoric of the authoritarian state. By invoking professionalization, Chinese intellectuals could draw a boundary between politics and academics in an effort to protect their academic authority. In doing so, they gradually developed strong solidarity in response to the penetrating influence of the state. Although this solidarity was repeatedly challenged in the Maoist era, it escalated into a strong nationalist sentiment in the post-Mao era. This dynamic would affect the writing of world history in China for the remainder of the twentieth century. It is a story of conflict and change; and it is one that would have profound repercussions in shaping China's history and identity within a global context to this day.

4   The Forced Analogy
Control, Resistance, and World History in the 1950s

On November 13, 1954, the History Department of Shandong University held a symposium on the periodization of ancient Chinese history. Historian Tong Shuye delivered a report on the current state of research on this issue. His colleagues followed with a discussion. Tong's report was a weak piece. He was less confident than he had always been in the past; for his presentation, he had revised his thesis in order to follow the line of mainstream Soviet historiography. This humble piece was, however, not well received among his colleagues, most of whom were ancient Chinese historians.

For scholars in the audience, the main problem with Tong's report was his use of the so-called forced analogy between China and other ancient civilizations. Zhang Weihua commented that Tong had cited too many foreign sources and too few Chinese ones, which gave people the wrong impression that it was not really about China. Admittedly countries in general had demonstrated some common characteristics during the process of development. He, however, contended, "If [one] wants to explain the problem regarding the nature of ancient Chinese society, ... [one] must mainly point out the characteristics of China's own development."[1]

Zhang's critique was echoed by Lu Qiaonan (pseud. Zhenhua, 1911–1979), who had already raised the point that Tong had relied too much on world history to study ancient Chinese society. Lu commented that he felt Tong's report was satisfactory but insufficient, which was a polite rejection in Chinese academic jargon. Although Lu granted that Tong had been the first one among his colleagues to realize the significance of Oriental studies (the study of ancient Asia, Middle East, and North Africa) and that he had made an effort to do research in that area, Lu was not fully convinced by Tong's comparative approach. Lu pointed out that Tong listed many social phenomena in world history in his report. It certainly showed that Tong was very knowledgeable about world history,

---

[1] "Zhongguo gushi fenqi wenti zuotan jilu" [Minutes of the symposium on the periodization of ancient Chinese history], ed. Xiao Ou, *Wenshizhe*, no. 1 (1955): 55.

128

but Lu asked, "How much does it [i.e., listing phenomena in other ancient societies in world history] contribute to solving the problem of periodization in ancient Chinese history?" He continued, "If such a listing can result in deciding the nature of ancient Chinese society, it is then tantamount to using world history to predetermine Chinese history."[2]

Not only scholars but also students joined the criticism of Tong's world-historical approach. Wang Zhifang, the only student recorded in the minutes to have spoken at the symposium, questioned his professor's theoretical framework. Following the Chinese scholarly tradition, Wang humbly stated that, as a student, he knew too little about this issue and thereby was in no position to either support or oppose Tong's thesis. After raising two questions about the details in Tong's report, Wang did, however, challenge the core of his teacher's methodology, saying that it was certainly helpful to study Chinese history in a world-historical context but scholars must rely on historical facts about the development of Chinese history in order to solve an important problem like this. He continued, "In other words, although [one] needs to be aware of universal principles, [one] must pay attention to the special nature of China."[3]

The criticism of Tong's world-historical approach in studying ancient Chinese society was to a certain degree justifiable. During the discussion, Tong's attempt to explain China as parallel historically with other ancient "Oriental" societies such as Babylon indeed sounded a little arbitrary, and his claims such as that "the first transitional period in ancient Egyptian history was almost exactly the same as China's 'feudal' system" seemed far-fetched.[4] The same accusation, however, can also be applied to those scholars who criticized Tong's approach. To wit, how could one even know that a particular feature of Chinese history was special without placing it within a world-historical context?

Perhaps the criticism of Tong's work was largely personal. Tong indeed had an awkward relationship with some of his colleagues, especially Zhang Weihua. Both Zhang and Tong used to work for Gu Jiegang as research assistants. Zhang's relationship with Gu deteriorated in the 1940s, whereas Tong remained close to his teacher during the 1950s.[5] It is hard to say how this affected the relationship between Zhang and

[2] Xiao Ou ed., "Zhongguo gushi fenqi wenti zuotan jilu," 54.
[3] Xiao Ou ed., "Zhongguo gushi fenqi wenti zuotan jilu," 56.
[4] Tong Shuye, "Zhongguo gushi fenqi wenti de taolun," in *Tong Shuye gudai shehui lunji* [Collection of Tong Shuye's works on ancient society], ed. Tong Jiaoying (Beijing: Zhonghua shuju, 2006), 240.
[5] For instance, Gu Jiegang stayed at Tong's home while on vacation in Qingdao in 1956, and Tong's wife cooked for him every day for more than a month. Tong, *Cong lianyu zhong shenghua*, 192.

Tong, since Tong had make a failed attempt to repair the relationship between Gu and Zhang two years earlier in 1952.[6] Three years later (1957), Zhang attacked Tong and Zhao Lisheng in front of students. He dismissed the latter two as belonging to "the school of theory," which was considered to be an insult in Chinese academic jargon of the time.[7] Zhao left Shandong University that year due to increasing pressures that resulted as the Anti-Rightist Campaign unfolded. Tong almost followed. Nevertheless, we have little information about Tong's relationship with other participants in the discussion. At that time he still seemed to be getting along with Zhang. It is doubtful that the criticism of Tong's work was highly personal.

To further understand this exchange, we need to place the criticism of Tong's world-historical approach in the context of the tension between the party-state and Chinese intellectuals in the early 1950s. In so doing, we can see that the resistance to the world-historical approach introduced from the Soviet Union and based on Marxist-Leninist ideology was commonly shared within the intellectual community.

The 1950s was a period of great change in twentieth-century Chinese intellectual history. As previous chapters have discussed, increasing ideological control redefined relationships among individuals in academic circles and gave rise to a new generation of world historians who were willing to work with the communist state to uplift their own social standing. In this chapter, we will further examine the writings of these world historians. In a field whose development was nurtured by the party-state, new scholars adopted the theoretical weapon of Marxism-Leninism and knowledge of world history to assert their position in the system of knowledge production. They challenged scholars of the older generation who had achieved authoritative positions in the system prior to the revolution. Compared with the new generation, the older generation was at a disadvantage in defending its position in a field such as world history. First, most scholars were less familiar with world-historical knowledge, since only a few Chinese historians prior to the People's Republic had conducted research in this field. Second, a large number of intellectuals in the Republican period had been educated in Europe or the United States and favored Euro-American scholarship over Soviet research. Thus, most of them were less motivated or even resentful at having to study and apply Marxism-Leninism in their work. Under certain circumstances, where control was relaxed a bit, this latent resistance became visible. In contrast, new scholars who had little baggage from the past were eager to learn from Soviet historiography and actively applied it in

---

[6] Tong, *Cong lianyu zhong shenghua*, 194.   [7] Gu, *Gu Jiegang riji*, 8:280–281.

their studies. Constantly seeking comparisons and common patterns between China and the rest of the world, these young world historians insisted on the universality of historical materialism and were eager to rewrite world history through the staged development of economic productivity.[8]

Finding it impossible to challenge the state ideology under the current tightened controls, those "old" historians found a subtle but efficient way to protect their own control over knowledge production – they would emphasize cultural differences. If China were a "unique" case in world history, then Marxism as a foreign ideology would not be applicable to the study of its history. In other words, Chinese exceptionalism became a tool by which historians attempted to exclude the external influences from the communist state on historical writing. The field of world history was caught up in the intense scholarly politics that placed the consensus of a common humanity in conflict with the assertion of cultural difference. The end result of this contention – the separation of world history from the general field of historical studies – would appear more prominently in later years. Yet, despite all the drawbacks, China's new world historians in the 1950s, as the debates on the Asiatic mode of production will show, had identified some key challenges in integrating China's past within a world-historical context. From a Eurocentric view of space to a teleological sense of time, these historians were exploring alternatives to put China on an equal footing with its foreign counterparts. These experiments would later serve as a new foundation for the development of world-historical research in post-Mao China.

For the party-state, world history is political because it provides an ideological foundation for and a roadmap to the communist revolution. As a complex ideological system, Marxism emerged from the nineteenth-century European critique of laissez-faire capitalism. It holds a materialist interpretation of history, a dialectical view of social change, and an analysis and critique of the development of capitalism. In its original theory, the theoretical thrust was based on the concept of alienation (*Entfremdung*), a starting point of Karl Marx's sojourn between his study of politics and history. Struck by the cruel conditions of workers' lives in nineteenth-century Europe, Marx believed that workers in a modern society had lost their basic dignity and essence as human beings. Determined to decode the historical process of how human beings had lost their self-consciousness, he argued that changes in modes of

---

[8] As Huaiyin Li points out, one of the central premises in Chinese Marxist historiography is to prove China was "no exception to the universal pattern of social evolution." Li, *Reinventing Modern China*, 16.

production had transformed human beings into dispirited subjects in a capitalized society. He therefore adopted historical materialism and developed a deterministic interpretation. In other words, he believed that relations of production predetermined the social existence of man. His interest in human consciousness and historical materialism created a deep tension in his larger ideological framework; that is, he had a problem "reconciling the consciousness and practical political activities of man with a theory of historical inevitability."[9]

After the Russian Revolution of 1917, Marxism became the guiding ideology for the socialist movement around the world. From theory to practice, Marxism became increasingly canonized and lost its complexity in exchange for simplicity. In the People's Republic, ideologues grasped Marxism according to three sets of doctrines: its philosophy based on dialectical materialism and historical materialism, its political economy, and its scientific socialism. With a strong sense of historical determinism, they asserted that the triumph of the communist revolution was an inevitable result of social dynamics (in the form of class struggles) that was propelled by the fundamental dynamics of the staged economic progression. In other words, the fundamental principles manifested in history predetermined the future of the world.

The introduction of Marxism to China was marked by constant discussions and debates among Chinese intellectuals. As a critical source of Marxism, socialist thought was introduced into China as early as the opening of the twentieth century.[10] For a fairly long time, it received little attention among mainstream Chinese intellectuals; indeed, some of whom were more attracted to anarchism, which promised a quicker transformation of society, for, as scholars argue, China lacks a tradition of historical materialism and therefore it was quite difficult for Chinese theorists to fully embrace it when Marxism first arrived in China. Li Dazhao (1888–1927), one of the two cofounders of China's Communist Party, took a critical view of Marx's historical materialism before 1919. In his famous essay "My View of Marx," he was hesitant about accepting historical materialism. Even later, when he announced his conversion, he did not give up his emphasis on ethics in society and showed little interest in further decoding the economic conditions to define a class as orthodox Marxist scholars did.[11]

---

[9] Maurice Meisner, *Li Ta-chao and the Origins of Chinese Marxism* (Cambridge, MA: Harvard University Press, 1967), 136.
[10] The earliest appearance of Marx's name in Chinese sources was in 1905. Fung, *The Intellectual Foundations of Chinese Modernity*, 194.
[11] Meisner, *Li Ta-chao and the Origins of Chinese Marxism*, 146, 154.

The dedicated interest of Chinese intellectuals in Marxism-Leninism grew in the wake of the Russian Revolution of 1917 and May Fourth Movement of 1919. At this time, intellectuals began to seek an all-embracing answer to problems in Chinese society. As a complex ideological system, Marxism offered both a political solution to existing problems in society and a historical interpretation of their origins. In the wake of the New Culture Movement, it was more appealing to doers than to thinkers.[12] Early Chinese Marxist converts in China, inspired by the victory of the October Revolution in Russia, believed that a Soviet-style revolution would be a great opportunity to expedite social transformation. In contrast to their enthusiasm for adopting Marx's class struggle as their guiding philosophy, they were less interested in applying historical materialism; thus, they largely ignored this theoretical tension in Marx's philosophical system.

Yet, in the later periods, this theoretical issue became a source of tension; in particular, scholars who opposed Marxism often wondered whether China, seen as a backward and stagnant country, was ready for a socialist revolution. This critique appealed to many people. According to orthodox Marxist theory, economic conditions predetermine society's nature and therefore regulated its fundamental contradictions. Taking modern capitalist society as an example, Marxists believed that the fundamental contradiction was the struggle between the proletariat and bourgeois classes and that this was predetermined by the economic nature of this stage of world-historical development. What if, however, the society is not yet at the stage of capitalist development? During the late 1910s and the 1920s, since there was only rudimentary modern industry in China, many believed that capitalism was not a dominant mode of economic production. If they were right, then the goal for the revolution should be to propel capitalist development instead of communist revolution.

The early Marxist Li Dazhao prematurely offered an answer to this critique. He argued that the current integration of world-economic systems had transformed the nature of Chinese society to such an extreme that the entire Chinese nation had become part of the world proletariat.[13] Through this creative interpretation of the concept of "class," he circumvented the economic determinism that prevented China from participating in the socialist revolution initiated in the Soviet Union. While Li demonstrated a remarkable awareness of the extent of China's twentieth-century integration into world history, his belief that the Chinese people constituted a single unified class apparently contradicted the original

---

[12] Meisner, *Li Ta-chao and the Origins of Chinese Marxism*, 136.
[13] Meisner, *Li Ta-chao and the Origins of Chinese Marxism*, 144.

thinking of Karl Marx. It not only neglects the multiethnicity of the Chinese state but also deviated from Marxist historical materialism that emphasizes the role of economic foundations in shaping class reality.

Be that as it may, Li's creative interpretation of the nature of class shows that Chinese Marxists attempted to circumvent the deterministic nature of historical materialism at an early stage in the communist movement when they had to apply Marxism as a foreign ideology to China's reality.[14] However, as the social revolutionary movement progressed in the mid-1920s, and especially after its setback in the Shanghai Massacre of leftists by the Nationalists in 1927, it became an urgent task for Chinese Marxist-Leninists to assert that a communist revolution was a legitimate cause for Chinese revolutionary movements, as the counterrevolutionaries stressed that Chinese society had a unique social structure to which Marxist theory was not applicable. The key issue was whether the nature of Chinese society fit the teleological agenda projected by Marxist historiography. Since it revolved around the issue of the nature of Chinese society, scholars started to study and discuss Marxist historiography seriously.[15]

The debate over the nature of Chinese society originated among communists outside China, too. To them, determining which stage China occupied in the five-stage Marxist-Leninist theory of world history was the focus rather than whether the theory was relevant to China. This interest grew out of the Communist International Movement that originally emanated from Moscow in the mid-1920s. Early on, the Soviet leader Joseph Stalin and his opponents had conflicting visions for the revolution in China. Stalin and his ideologues believed that contemporary China was predominantly a feudal society, "with imperialism supporting (or perpetuating) the feudal social structure in China."[16] In contrast, Leon Trotsky (1879–1940) and his followers adhered to the argument that "China was predominantly capitalist, with imperialism, by its very nature, helping the development of capitalist forces in Chinese society (or, more often, among the bourgeoisie)."[17] Because historical materialism played a crucial role in the activist philosophy of the Communist Party, this debate had a noticeable impact on the trajectory of the Chinese revolution. In theory, if Chinese society had a feudal nature, then the social and economic revolution led by the Chinese bourgeoisie, represented by Sun Yat-sen (1866–1925) and his Nationalist Party, was a necessary stage before China could enter into the phase of socialist revolution. This was

---

[14] Arif Dirlik, *The Revolution and History: Origins of Marxist Historiography in China, 1919–1937* (Berkeley: University of California Press, 1978), 59.
[15] Dirlik, *Revolution and History*, 90–94.   [16] Dirlik, *Revolution and History*, 72.
[17] Dirlik, *Revolution and History*, 72.

the policy that Moscow followed with regard to the Chinese revolution. It demanded that the CCP play only an auxiliary role in the current stage of the Chinese revolution. Alternatively, if Chinese society were already capitalist by nature, then the current revolution in China would have to be a proletarian one and the CCP should assume leadership. Therefore, Trotsky and his supporters diverged from Stalin's China policy of supporting the Nationalist Party. They demanded a more radical approach toward the Chinese revolution that included support for urban uprisings.

The debate in Moscow apparently had an impact on intellectuals and political activists in China in the late 1920s. Revolving around the basic themes in the Soviet debate, three groups contested the nature of Chinese society through the lens of historical materialism: leftist Nationalist intellectuals, whose leading advocate was Dai Jitao, a major ideologue in the Party; the CCP intellectuals who followed Stalin's view; and the Chinese Trotskyites. During this debate, Chinese Marxists gradually realized that the thesis about the premature nature of Chinese society for communist revolution had become increasingly detrimental to the communist movement in China. They had to respond to the challenge by carefully studying and appropriating Marxist-Leninist historical materialism. They were forced to realize that the meanings of certain crucial historical concepts like "feudalism" and "slave society" were vague in the Chinese historical context.[18] The debate over the nature of contemporary Chinese society had gradually turned into a discussion of historical issues. As a result, three topics increasingly seized the attention of scholars: feudalism, slave society, and the Asiatic mode of production. In 1949, those issues remained unresolved.

The very fact that Chinese historians chose to engage in a vigorous discussion on the Asiatic mode of production reflects the intricate dynamics between state control and intellectual resistance in the production of historical knowledge in the early 1950s. To a high modernist state like the People's Republic, the charm of the Marxist paradigm in historical writing was its simplicity. It provided a straightforward paradigm that was easy for the few, select and professional revolutionary cadres to adopt to mobilize the masses. Reception of the Marxist historical paradigm in this country, however, was not an easy process. It was followed by a series of heated discussions and debates among Chinese scholars. After all, Marxism was a foreign theory. For those who believed in cultural difference such as Lei Haizong, it was problematic to accept this European

---

[18] For a recent discussion on how certain key concepts shaped the contours of the history of twentieth-century China, see Rebecca Karl, *The Magic of Concepts: History and the Economic in Twentieth-Century China* (Durham, NC and London: Duke University Press, 2017).

ideology. Thus, it became a mission for state ideologues to prove not only that China followed the same dynamics of development as the rest of the world but also that Marxism was applicable to China. By contrast, as the cost was too high if non-Marxist historians directly challenged the validity of Marxism, the best way to address this was to point out the complex reality that contradicted the simplistic formula in Marxist historiography. The relationship between China and the rest of the world became a political issue in the early People's Republic.

This debate also spoke to the interest of the general field of historical studies where Chinese intellectuals focused on five issues in which to engage a lively conversation within the framework of Marxist ideology. These issues were the periodization of ancient history, the formation of the Han nationality, the role of Chinese "peasant wars" in Chinese history, incipient capitalism in traditional China, and landownership in feudal China.[19] These discussions, known as "the five golden flowers" (*wuduo jinhua*), represent the subtle and yet pervasive tensions between the Marxist model of historical determinism and other models of historical interpretation.[20] The Chinese world historians' debate on the Asiatic mode of production (AMP) in the 1950s was an important episode in the discussions about periodization in ancient history. Transcending national interests, the central issue in this debate was how to address historical time within global space, a topic that was shared by both late Qing and Republican world history writers.[21]

The Stalinist Marxist conception of time was a five-stage, linear process, predetermined by the evolution of economic productivity: from primitive, to slave, to feudal, to capitalist, and finally to socialist societies as shown in Table 5. This view dominated world history education in the "socialist bloc," including China in the 1950s, and socialist leaders used it to promote a communist revolution on a global scale. Yet this five-stage periodization of world history was derived from European history. Today, many historians in the non-Western world deem it Eurocentric. Yet, even at that time, some scholars recognized the problem. Lei Haizong, for one, questioned whether a slave society had ever existed in Chinese history. The Communist Party in China could not tolerate this train of thought, that is, accepting it would undermine the validity of Marxist historical

---

[19] Q. Edward Wang, "Between Marxism and Nationalism: Chinese Historiography and the Soviet Influence, 1949–1963," *Journal of Contemporary China* 9 (2000): 96.

[20] Wang, "Between Marxism and Nationalism," 98; Like in ancient history, periodization was also a central concern and a heated topic for discussion among historians of modern China. Li, *Reinventing Modern China*, 111.

[21] Karl, *The Magic of Concepts*, 41.

Table 5 *Debate on the Asiatic mode of production in the early 1950s*

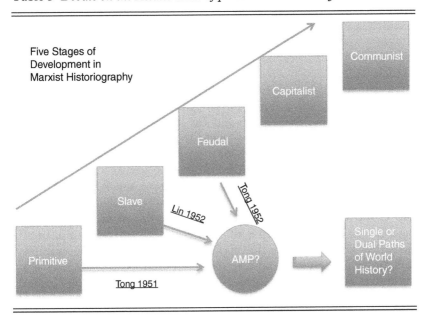

theory as an organic whole. Specifically, if the beginning stage of slavery was missing, the entire system would collapse.

This became more confusing with the supposition that Karl Marx might have suggested that Asian societies were following an alternative path to development (or, for better or worse, stagnation) in world history. He once wrote, "In broad outline, the Asiatic, ancient, feudal, and modern bourgeois modes of production may be designated as epochs making progress in the economic development of society."[22] What does "the Asiatic" mean? Marx never offered a definite answer. The ambiguity in Marx's own writing invited heated discussions among friends and foes of the communist movement.

The Asiatic mode of production was also a focus of attention among Chinese scholars. Here, again, the Marxist classics are unsuitable, which left the party-state without a clear blueprint to follow. Ironically, ambiguity in Marxist original theories generated, to a certain degree, free discussion. Some scholars argued that the AMP was an alternative stage in

---

[22] Karl Marx, *A Contribution to the Critique of Political Economy* (Chicago: C. H. Kerr, 1904), 21.

human development and that it represented a unique Eastern path in world history. Others, especially more orthodox Marxists, adamantly defended the universal nature of Marxist historiography. As they debated, scholars would contend that the AMP was merely a variation of one of the stages in world-historical development (primitive, slave-owning, or feudal societies).

The Chinese debate echoed Stalinist-era discussions in the Soviet Union. At that time, mainstream scholars argued that the AMP was merely a variation of slave society and was at a lower level of development compared to the classical slave society represented by Greece and Rome.[23] V. V. Struve (1889–1965), an authority on Soviet Oriental studies, claimed that all Eastern countries experienced a stage of slave-owning society, which was soon reaffirmed by a specialist on Sumer, A. I. Tyumenev. For decades, Soviet scholars were able to "affirm the unity of the universal historical process, leaving no ground for 'Europe-centered' and 'Orient-centered' concepts of universal history."[24] Dissenting voices were excluded from the discussion. For example, there was no interest in the position of the one-time Marxist but later anti-communist Karl Wittfogel (1896–1988). Wittfogel believed that Oriental Despotism was not an Eastern alternative to the early social stage of slavery; rather, he identified it as a permanent condition of stagnation.[25]

Being aware of the Soviet discussion and propelled by their own agendas, Chinese historians engaged in debates on the AMP three times: in the 1920s to 1930s, the 1950s, and the 1980s to 1990s. Scholars have discussed the context and content of these debates, especially the ones that took place in the 1920s to 1930s and those in the 1980s and 1990s. In contrast, scholars have rarely discussed the AMP debate of the 1950s. This lack of attention may be due to the fact that a significant part of the discussion took place primarily among world historians, a community that is often neglected in Chinese intellectual history.[26] As I will show in this chapter, a careful analysis of the 1950s debate within the context of the state control of historical research and its subtle resistance discloses

---

[23] I. M. Diakonoff, ed. *Early Antiquity*, trans. Alexander Kirjanov (Chicago: University of Chicago Press, 1991), 10.

[24] Diakonoff, *Early Antiquity*, 7.

[25] Karl Wittfogel, *Oriental Despotism: A Comparative Study of Total Power* (New Haven, CT: Yale University Press, 1957), 402.

[26] Karl, *The Magic of Concepts*, esp. chapter 2; Joshua Fogel, "The Debates over the Asiatic Mode of Production in Soviet Russia, China, and Japan," *American Historical Review* 93, no. 1 (1988): 58. Zhang Guangzhi, *Zhongguo gushi fenqi taolun de huigu yu fansi* [Reflection on past debates over the periodization of ancient Chinese history] (Xi'an: Shaanxi shifan daxue chubanshe, 2003), 123–124. Timothy Brook organized and translated some major articles from the debate in the 1980s. See Brook, ed., *The Asiatic Mode of Production in China* (Armonk, NY: M. E. Sharpe, 1989).

that quite a lot took place at this overlooked moment. In particular, we can observe the dynamic formation of the Chinese worldview in the process of introduction, translation, and appropriation of Marxism in China. More importantly, in this round of discussion, world historians for the first time appeared prominently in Chinese academia as a professional group. Scholars such as Lin Zhichun and Tong Shuye, with their knowledge of world history, contributed much to this discussion. In this regard, the debate in the 1950s shows both continuity and change in the development of Marxist historiography. Deliberations continued to feature issues similar to those in the earlier debates, such as the nature of ancient Chinese society; however, by placing China's ancient past within a world-historical context, it transcended the scale of the discussion of those issues.

The change in usage of the concept "ancient history" indicates the rise of global consciousness in historical studies in the early People's Republic. In the Republican period, historians often referred to this period as "ancient *Chinese* history." In the 1950s, historians started to use the term "ancient history" to address the entire world, following the Soviet convention in the field. This was an attempt to call for a balanced presentation of the past of all countries in history, as Soviet historians felt that "Soviet students must know the past history of these countries [such as India and China] as well" and should abandon the "exclusive concentration on Europe."[27] The establishment of an equivalence between "ancient world history" and "ancient history" promoted a global view among Chinese scholars just as it had among their Soviet counterparts. During the 1950s, young scholars preparing to be world historians were required to study a broader spectrum of the ancient world that included not only Chinese but also non-European civilizations. As a result, many of them considered ancient Chinese history to be a crucial part of their studies. Unimpeded by notions of a clear-cut boundary between China and the world in the world history discipline, these young world historians in the 1950s wrote extensively and comparatively about ancient history. This new development evolved out of the debate over the AMP.

This debate started with Tong Shuye's 1951 article in the prestigious journal *Literature, History, and Philosophy*.[28] In it, Tong critically reviewed the existing scholarship and challenged four common positions defining

---

[27] Graham, "The Significant Role of the Study of Ancient History in the Soviet Union," 91.
[28] Tong Shuye, "Lun Yaxiya shengchan fangfa" [On the Asiatic mode of production], *Wenshizhe* 1, no. 4 (1951): 14–17, cited in Tong, *Tong Shuye gudai shehui lunji*, 187–96; Wang Qingjia, "Shijieshi lilun, fangfa ji waiguo shixueshi de yanjiu gaishu" [A survey of research on the theory and methodology of world history as well as on the history of foreign historiography], in *Jianguo yilai shijieshi yanjiu gaishu*, 29.

the term "Asiatic mode of production" in the work of Russian and Japanese scholars. He then proposed that the AMP referred to primitive communism, a position held by the renowned Marxist ideologue Guo Moruo.[29]

The article was soon refuted by another world history scholar, Lin Zhichun, who considered the AMP to be a lower stage of development in a slave society. Thanks to his collaboration with Russian scholars, Lin was quite confident in his knowledge of Soviet scholarship and argued that Tong's article was based on obsolete work. He pointed out that, according to the contemporary, mainstream view in the Soviet Union, Asiatic society was a variation of a slave society in the Orient.[30] To prove this point, Lin cited the latest developments in historiography in the Soviet Union, especially *The History of the Ancient Orient* by V. I. Avdiev, which was being translated into Chinese at that time. Lin concluded that, although debate on the AMP was quite active in the Soviet Union in the 1930s, Soviet scholars had already reached a consensus over the course of the past decade that Asiatic society was "a lower stage of slave society."[31]

Pointing to the significant role of primary sources in historical studies, Lin criticized Tong's neglect of Marx's original work, *A Contribution to the Critique of Political Economy*, especially the section on "Forms Which Precede Capitalist Production."[32] Only in this document, Lin argued, could one find a detailed discussion of the issue of the AMP by Karl Marx. Scrutinizing the text word by word in a way similar to how previous classical scholars perused Confucian canons, Lin claimed that the ancient world was divided into two parts: "the ancient Orient (or the Asiatic society)," which included the area from Egypt to China, and the classical world (centered on the Mediterranean). The spatial divide was also invested with temporal meaning. In comparison, he observed, "The ancient Orient evolved early (the Bronze Age was a slave society), but it developed slowly (in accordance with being a lower stage of development); the classical world evolved late (the Iron Age), but developed quickly (as is typical of the slavery stage)."[33] However, if the ancient Orient and the classical world represented two different stages in the development of slavery in the ancient world, how then could one explain the hierarchy of the development? Lin seems to have adopted a geographically

---

[29] Tong, "Lun Yaxiya shengchan fangfa," 188.
[30] Rizhi, "Yu Tong Shuye xiansheng lun Yaxiya shengchan fangfa wenti" [Discussing the Asiatic mode of production with Mr. Tong Shuye], *Wenshizhe*, no. 2 (1952): 20.
[31] Rizhi, "Yu Tong Shuye xiansheng lun Yaxiya shengchan fangfa wenti," 20.
[32] In particular, Karl Marx, "Pre-Capitalist Economic Formations," in *A Contribution to the Critique of Political Economy*.
[33] Rizhi, "Yu Tong Shuye xiansheng lun Yaxiya shengchan fangfa wenti," 22.

deterministic view to explain the difference between the Orient and the Occident.[34] He asserts that, as China was located in the Orient, "We certainly do not have the environment of the Mediterranean, [so] we should not assume that a similar slave society existed [in China]."[35]

Lin eventually turned to the question of how to regard Soviet scholarship, which was a sensitive issue at the time. As the party-state called for learning from the Soviet Union, historians were forced to reform historical teaching and research according to the Soviet standards. Many resented this change. Lei Haizong's criticism was merely one example out of many, as discussed in Chapter 3. Yet the new-generation world historians like Lin were more willing to embrace it. In his view, since so much research about ancient Oriental slave society had been carried out in the Soviet Union, would it not be better for scholars in China to utilize it rather than studying the issue from scratch?[36] Steadily and cautiously following Soviet scholarship, Lin submitted to the assertion that ancient Chinese society had remained at a stage of development that was lower than that of Western classical antiquity. In arguing for maintaining the state's policy, Lin's knowledge of Russian and his awareness of the latest scholarship from the Soviet Union allowed him to play the upper hand in the debate.

In response, Tong spoke to Chinese historians' national pride, resisting the assertion that the West was more advanced than the East from the ancient times on. In his next article, which was published in 1952, Tong questioned the validity of the Soviet scholarship and the way in which Lin studied Marxist doctrine. In contrast to Lin's thesis, Tong argued that the "Asiatic society in the Orient" was not belated in its development. On the contrary, he asserted that not only did it already contain some features of feudalism but it also overall belonged to the next stage of social development. In short, the East had not been left behind; rather, it was the frontrunner in ancient world history.

Tong acknowledged his disagreement with Soviet scholars. He traced Lin's thesis to the Soviet authority V. V. Struve, but he disagreed anyway. Tong claimed that, since Marxism is a progressive discipline, it entailed

---

[34] Lin Zhichun had already studied Toynbee prior to the 1950s, and he was interested in historical geography when teaching in Shanghai. Both factors suggest that he tended to use geographical determinism to explain the difference between West and East. For his early interest in historical geography, see Lin Zhichun, "Shijing dili yanjiu" [A study of geography in the Book of Poetry], *Jiaoyu yu wenhua (Fuzhou)* [Education and cultural (Fuzhou)] 1, no. 1 (1945): 51–56. For his review of Arnold Toynbee, see Lin Zhichun, "Wenming zhi yuanshi" [The origins of civilizations], *Dushu tongxun* [Reading newsletter], no. 148 (1948): 4–9.

[35] Rizhi, "Yu Tong Shuye xiansheng lun Yaxiya shengchan fangfa wenti," 22.

[36] Rizhi, "Yu Tong Shuye xiansheng lun Yaxiya shengchan fangfa wenti," 22.

a progressive view of historical studies. The problem was Lin's conception of slavery. Two issues came to Tong's attention: the existence of a sizable source of free labor in the production regime of Asiatic society and Lin's further division of slavery into two stages.[37] For one, what defined slavery? As classic Marxism often distinguishes slavery from free labor, Tong asked whether one could call it a slave society if a large percentage of free labor was present. (At the time, there was a consensus about this among scholars – including Lin Zhichun.) Equally bewildering, Tong noticed that Lin, following the Soviet scholar Struve, divided slave society into two periods, which deviated from the orthodox view of the five stages of social development.[38] If the stage of slave society could be divided by spatial difference, then what about the stages of other modes of production, say, feudalism?[39] Therefore, Tong concluded that the AMP should retain only one mode of production, not a variation, and that this mode of production was feudalism because its dominant workforce consisted of free people. The term "Asiatic" was not a spatial one, as suggested by Lin, but rather a temporal one in Marx's original meaning, according to Tong.

The Three-Antis Campaign took place at Shandong University in March 1952 and affected Tong Shuye and his colleagues. His close friend Zhao Lisheng, for instance, had to conduct self-criticism in front of the entire campus community.[40] Scared of being accused of deviating from official ideology, Tong became very cautious about his argument. In a subsequent article published in September, he wavered. He said, after reading Soviet scholarship, he felt less confident about his own views and acknowledged that the consensus among Soviet historians was indeed that Oriental society was a slave society.[41] Tong, however, did not totally give up his opinions. He politely asked readers to reconsider the "Soviet" position. He pointed out the discrepancy in Soviet and Chinese historical pedagogies. He pinpointed the essence of the problem as follows: World history courses generally relied on Soviet world history textbooks. These textbooks claimed that Chinese slave society lasted to the end of the Han dynasty. In contrast, courses in Chinese history relied on Chinese textbooks. These textbooks often identified a slave society before the Shang dynasty, and historical facts seemed to confirm this view. Tong

[37] Tong, "Da Rizhi xiansheng lun Yaxiya shengchan fangshi wenti" [In reply to Mr. Rizhi's "On the Asiastic mode of production"], in *Tong Shuye gudai shehui lunji*, 198.

[38] Tong, "Da Rizhi xiansheng lun Yaxiya shengchan fangfa wenti," 200.

[39] Tong, "Da Rizhi xiansheng lun Yaxiya shengchan fangfa wenti," 201.

[40] Zhao Lisheng, "Wo de chubu jiantao," 30–33.

[41] Tong, "Guanyu Zhongguo gudai shehui xingzhi de wenti" [Concerning the question of the nature of ancient Chinese society], *Wenshizhe*, no. 5 (1952): 39–42; in *Tong Shuye gudai shehui lunji*, 204.

apparently favored the second view. Yet, owing to political pressure, he cautiously admitted that this was an unsolved issue; without affirmatively asserting his own position, he humbly compiled a list of primary sources to support the second view.[42]

Chinese Marxists gradually realized the significant role of cultural and historical comparison in this debate. In the wake of the restructuring of the higher education system, Tong was assigned to teach ancient world history. This change allowed him to develop a world-historical approach and adopt a comparative methodology. To contextualize China's historical development without referencing the West, he chose ancient Babylon (by which he meant from the times of Sumer to Old Babylonia) as a case for comparison.[43] He identified four common features in Asiatic societies and compared these to European counterparts: (1) residual supply of free labor; (2) lack of dominance of slave-based production; (3) autocratic strengthening in conjunction with bureaucratic expansion; and (4) the "apparent existence" of a "feudal-like" mode of production.[44] Tong politely suggested that there might be two lines of thinking on the issue: the Soviet view identified the AMP as a lower stage of slave society, while the Chinese view identified it with feudal society. Refraining from directly challenging the Soviet view during the political campaigns, he implied that it would still be possible to adopt the Chinese view. He further explained how this might work. If ancient China had a feudal society, it could be understood as having two stages corresponding to the divisions of the Eastern Zhou dynasty: lord feudalism (*lingzhu zhi*) during the Spring and Autumn period and landlord feudalism (*dizhu zhi*) during the Warring States period.[45] This view accorded with one that Tong had mentioned in private correspondence with Gu Jiegang in 1951.[46] He probably realized that he was fabricating an arbitrary spatial divide between the East and the West. The alternative comparative framework he proposed prior to concluding the article was probably a cursory attempt to correct this. In this outline, he suggested that all ancient societies followed similar paths to social development. Initially, there was a period of monarchy; and then class conflicts between plebeians

[42] Tong, "Guanyu Zhongguo gudai shehui xingzhi de wenti," 204.

[43] Tong Shuye, "Cong gudai Babilun shehui xingtai renshi gudai 'Dongfang shehui' de texing" [Understanding the special nature of ancient 'Oriental societies' from the social conditions of ancient Babylonia], in *Tong Shuye gudai shehui lunji*, 216.

[44] Tong, "Cong gudai Babilun shehui xingtai renshi gudai 'Dongfang shehui' de texing," 234–35n1. Soviet scholars believed that ancient Babylon was a perfect case study to examine ancient Oriental societies.

[45] Tong, "Cong gudai Babilun shehui xingtai renshi gudai 'Dongfang shehui' de texing," 232.

[46] See Chapter 3. Tong Shuye had formulated this view as early as February 5, 1951.

and patricians led to the decline of monarchical power, which was replaced by democratic politics. After reaching the highest level of development, ancient societies eventually collapsed into chaos.[47] Because it focuses entirely on political development without any consideration of economic factors, such a framework is an astonishing deviation from historical materialism. Rather, it sounds more like the cultural history Lei Haizong proposed in the 1930s or even the dynastic cycle thesis in traditional Chinese historiography. This model of thinking was quickly abandoned in subsequent debates about the AMP during the 1950s. However, it reemerged in the post-Mao era when it was resumed by Tong's debate opponent Lin Zhichun.

As the 1950s progressed, debates over the AMP continued, and both sides slightly adjusted their positions and arguments. Today's scholars may find this process puzzling, but spatial and temporal relations between the East and the West remained a central concern for Chinese scholars in the 1950s. For instance, in 1953 Tong visited Beijing and had a meeting with Shang Yue (1902–1982), a celebrated Marxist historian at People's University. After their discussions, Tong announced that he had changed his thesis and had accepted Shang's thesis that the transition from a slave society to a feudal society took place during the Wei–Jin dynasties.[48] After this brief change, Tong soon reverted to his original thesis.[49] Meanwhile, Lin was busy translating the latest Soviet scholarship. He was more consistent in his view that the Oriental society was a lower stage of the slave society. In 1953, he translated and introduced the latest theory from the Soviet Union regarding the two stages of development in a slave society. In doing so, Lin attempted to confirm his earlier argument in the debate by reciting Soviet authorities.[50] From 1955, he began to take part in the National Seminar of Ancient World History in Changchun. By participating in this, he contributed to educating a generation of young scholars in ancient world-historical studies.

The political atmosphere changed in early 1956 and allowed an opportunity for Chinese historians to engage in international discussions with Soviet scholars. After the Soviet leader Nikita Khrushchev's (1894–1971) secret report calling for the elimination of Stalin's influences, Mao Zedong

---

[47] Tong, "Cong gudai Babilun shehui xingtai renshi gudai 'Dongfang shehui' de texing," 233.
[48] Lu and Hu "Tong Shuye zai Shandong daxue"; Tong, "Zhongguo gushi fenqi wenti de taolun," 239.
[49] Lu and Hu, "Tong Shuye zai Shandong daxue."
[50] Rizhi, "Nuli shehui zhi liangge jieduan yu liuge shiqi" [Two stages and six periods of slave society], Lishi jiaoxue [History pedagogy], no. 3 (1953): 13–17.

responded with a critical examination of the mechanical copying of Soviet experience and instructed Chinese scholars to reevaluate Soviet scholarship. This reinvigorated discussion of the AMP. In the same year, Tong Shuye published another article in the first issue of the newly founded journal *Historical Research* (*Lishi yanjiu*). In his article, which was dedicated to the issue of foreign slavery, Tong reverts to the original thesis he proposed in 1951.[51]

Together with his other works on the nature of Oriental society, Tong initiated discussion of the nature of ancient Mesopotamian society among Chinese historians. This again was soon refuted by Lin. Publishing in the same journal in December, Lin accused his opponent of having used out-dated secondary sources and of being confused about scholarly ideas. He argued that Tong's article was hinged on two hypotheses: the early development of feudalism in Asiatic societies in general and the feudal nature of ancient Babylonian society in particular. The former was a theoretical asser-tion and the latter was a historiographical assumption.[52] Lin invoked Marx's and Engels's original works, the latest Soviet scholarship, and primary sources from ancient Greece and Mesopotamia. He pointed out that both of Tong's theses were based on shaky ground. Lin returned to the seeming tension between Marxist theory and ancient sources concerning the extent slavery dominated economic production in ancient societies.[53] The concept of *zhudao* (leading element) was essential to his reasoning. He argued that, although slaves might not have been the majority of the workforce in terms of their number, nevertheless, they led the direction of change in this society. In other words, one must ask, what was the most progressive direction of change in a historical period?[54] By taking the perspective of change, Lin establishes a circular argument: because Asiatic societies were slave societies, their dominant mode of production must have been based on slavery; and

---

[51] The journal was founded in 1954 by the Zhongguo lishi wenti yanjiu weiyuanhui [Chinese research committee on historical problems] of the Central Committee of the CCP and soon became the most authoritative academic journal in historical studies. For more information on the founding of this journal, see Zhang Jianping, *Xin Zhongguo shixue wushinian* [New China's historiography (of the past) fifty years] (Beijing: Xueyuan chubanshe, 2003), 36. Tong Shuye, "Cong zudian zhidu yu lishu nongmin de shenfen tantao gu Babilun shehui de xingzhi" [Investigating the nature of ancient Babylonian society from the tenancy system and the social status of subordinate peasants], *Lishi yanjiu* [Historical research], no. 5 (1956): 17–36.

[52] Rizhi, "Women zai yanjiu gudaishi zhong suo cunzai de yixie wenti (ping Tong Shuye zhu 'Cong zudian zhidu yu lishu nongmin de shenfen tantao gu Balilun shehui de xingzhi')'" [A few problems in the study of ancient history (a critique of Tong Shuye's "Discussing the nature of ancient Babylonian society from the [angle of the] tenancy system and the social status of subordinate peasants")], *Lishi yanjiu*, no. 12 (1956): 1.

[53] Rizhi, "Women zai yanjiu gudaishi zhong suo cunzai de yixie wenti," 13–14.

[54] Rizhi, "Women zai yanjiu gudaishi zhong suo cunzai de yixie wenti," 12.

because their dominant mode of production was based on slavery, Asiatic societies must have been slave societies.

Lin gave yet another reason for scholars to be wary of Tong's thesis. He pointed out that the latter's works had already received attention from scholars in the Soviet Union. In particular, Tong's article on the periodization of ancient history in China had been introduced into the Soviet Union and was published in the most prestigious journal, *Vestnik Drevnej Istorii (Journal of Ancient History)*.[55] Lin worried that, if Tong continued to spread his "wrong" ideas, it might jeopardize relations between the two countries. In contrast, Tong was excited about the opportunity to publicize his alternative views – especially since Mao had warned against simply copying from the Soviet Union.

Socialist scholars around the world had indeed been paying attention to Tong's proactive discussion on ancient world history. A major venue where Tong published, the journal *Literature, History, and Philosophy*, temporarily ceased publication from January 1959 to August 1961. When this happened, scholars from Japan, Vietnam, and Hungary made inquiries about Tong's recent works through Chinese embassies and other channels.[56] Soviet scholars were interested, too. On December 3, 1956, a Russian scholar, Uliyanov Andrey Iosifovich, sent a letter to Tong in which he introduced a recent discussion on the nature of slavery in Oriental societies (including China) and initiated the exchange. He said that his colleague Semyonov (his original Russian first and middle names are missing) had recently put forward an argument that slavery had not achieved a dominant position in ancient Oriental countries; rather, the social structure in those countries was built on the coexistence of two socioeconomic structures: slavery and feudalism.[57] Tong was very excited about this message. On February 1 of the following year, he replied to his Soviet colleagues in a lengthy open letter (more than 20,000 characters in Chinese). In the letter, he explained his positions on many issues regarding the nature of ancient Oriental societies in detail. He also pointed out his main difference with Semyonov; in particular, Tong was not against the Stalinist five-stage schema.

To understand this exchange, we have to place it within the context of Cold War politics. It took place in late 1956 and 1957 when the Soviets were critically reexamining Stalin's legacy during the time of de-Stalinization. The

---

[55] The introduction to Tong Shuye's article was published in the fourth issue in 1955. Rizhi, "Women zai yanjiu gudaishi zhong suo cunzai de yixie wenti," 2.

[56] Tong, *Cong lianyu zhong shenghua*, 175.

[57] Tong Shuye, "Yu Sulian zhuanjia Wu An Yuesefuweiqi shangque Zhongguo gushi fenqi de wenti" [Discussing the periodization issue in ancient Chinese history with Soviet specialist Wu An Yuesefuweiqi (original Russian name missing)], in *Tong Shuye gudai shehui lunji*, 331. I am grateful for Anna Belogurova's help in transcribing these Russian names from Chinese characters.

political change allowed Soviet scholars to challenge the rigid five-stages thesis that Stalin had laid out in the 1930s. In a sense, Semyonov's thesis reflects this change as he basically argued that the AMP was an alternative to Stalin's five-stage thesis, which did not apply to non-Western societies. There were signs of China loosening its ideological reins as well. Tong, however, was very cautious and stopped short of totally abandoning the Stalinist view of world history. The Chinese government never entirely gave up Stalin's legacy, even during the Hundred Flowers Campaign (for more on this campaign, see Chapter 3). Tong had no intention of abandoning the orthodox ideological system. The bottom line was that the AMP was not an alternative to Stalin's five-stage model.

Acknowledging the difference, Tong agreed with Semyonov in recognizing the coexistence of the elements of slave and feudal systems in some ancient societies.[58] He insisted on his previous position that the AMP represented the rural communal system (*nongcun gongshe zhi*), which was a variation of the "feudal" system like the one in India.[59] Having analyzed the concept of "the ancient Orient," he confirmed that it contained both slave-owning and feudal elements. The two elements were constantly in competition, and one of them was always dominant. He concluded that the term "ancient Orient" did not describe historical time in line with any mode of production; rather, it was a spatial concept. Such a society could be either a slave society or a feudal society; scholars should decide which one of the modes of production was dominant in these Asiatic societies.[60] Meanwhile, Tong and many other Chinese scholars argued that ancient Oriental societies had developed into feudal societies much earlier than their Occidental counterparts. The next question, then, was how to explain the early development of the ancient Oriental feudal system. The key question was as follows: If societies followed similar trajectories in the ancient world, how could some Oriental societies such as China have achieved the next stage of development far in advance of Europe?

In solving this theoretical challenge, Tong revised orthodox Marxist doctrine and argued that slave and feudal modes of production in fact shared some common features. He explained that neither Marx nor Engels had regarded feudalism as the next stage of development after slavery; in fact, feudalism could derive directly from primitive society.[61] Referring again to

---

[58] Tong, "Yu Sulian zhuanjia Wu An Yuesefuweiqi shangque Zhongguo gushi fenqi de wenti," 305.
[59] Tong, "Yu Sulian zhuanjia Wu An Yuesefuweiqi shangque Zhongguo gushi fenqi de wenti," 306–307.
[60] Tong, "Yu Sulian zhuanjia Wu An Yuesefuweiqi shangque Zhongguo gushi fenqi de wenti," 308.
[61] Tong, "Yu Sulian zhuanjia Wu An Yuesefuweiqi shangque Zhongguo gushi fenqi de wenti," 313.

the historical context, after comparing the conditions of ancient societies in the East and West, Tong argued that a huge jump was not required for a society to transition from slavery to feudalism in terms of productivity. How was this discussion related to China? Tong further explained his view of ancient Chinese society in a world-historical context. On one hand, he argued that China, like any other ancient Oriental society, had some unique characteristics in its development – most importantly, its early development and maturation of feudalism. On the other hand, he argued that China also followed the common trajectory of development: there had been a stage of collapse in the primitive communal system, followed by the development of slavery, and then by a classical commodity economy. Tong believed that there was a "classical period" in every ancient civilization including Egypt, Mesopotamia, India, China, Greece, and Rome.[62] After the Cultural Revolution, Lin Zhichun and his team would once again elaborate on this argument for classical antiquity as a global concept.

In hindsight, Tong Shuye took pains to place China specifically, and ancient Oriental societies in general, within a world-historical paradigm that developed according to the European experience. Because he considered China to be part of the Oriental world, it was, therefore, part of the world. In contrast, according to the orthodox view of Marxist historiography as introduced by Lin Zhichun, China, along with other non-European countries, was in a position that was intrinsically inferior to Europe since the very beginnings of their histories and from which they were unable to generate a system that could match Europe. As a Chinese scholar, Tong wanted to show that China as well as other Oriental societies such as Babylon and India had not been left behind by Europe. On the contrary, it might well be that they were more advanced than the West in the first place. At the same time, as a Marxist historian, he was hesitant to challenge the overall position of the five-stage thesis; as such, he had to soften his tone, saying that there was not much difference between slave-owning and feudal systems. In this way, he placed both the Orient and the Occident within a common stage of human development.

The debates between Tong and Lin were part of the wider discussion on historical periodization in the early People's Republic.[63] This discussion mobilized almost the entire scholarly community. Scholars from a range of fields, including the economist Wu Dakun and the historian

---

[62] Tong, "Yu Sulian zhuanjia Wu An Yuesefuweiqi shangque Zhongguo gushi fenqi de wenti," 324. Ironically, Lin Zhichun took over Tong's thesis and further developed it in the 1980s. See Chapter 5.

[63] He Gaoji, "Wo dui gudaishi yanjiu zhong jige wenti de kanfa" [My views concerning several questions in the study of ancient history], *Wenshizhe*, no. 9 (1956): 22–26.

Guo Moruo, contributed to the debate. Unlike in the Republican period, when world history remained a teaching field, world historians like Tong and Lin for the first time not only participated in but also introduced new topics to this significant discussion. World history was thus developing into a research field. At the same time, the debate also had a direct impact on the development of the field. During this time, Lin worked with a team of young scholars at the Ancient World History Seminar in Changchun. They translated a series of sources from Soviet scholarship on primary sources to advance his thesis.[64]

The debate between the two lasted for another year or so until the Anti-Rightist Campaign in 1957. Tong was still interested in the topic in the subsequent years of political radicalism, but he no longer could find any place to publish his work. During the Cultural Revolution, he lost his teaching position and suffered from political violence. He died of ill treatment as a "class enemy." Lin survived; however, it was only after the Cultural Revolution that he was able to resume the discussion.

The past discussions on the AMP have recently been revived and caught scholars' attention through Rebecca Karl's fascinating book on historical concepts. In it, she asserts that the AMP as a historical concept had already "died an appropriate death in the 1930s and should remain dead." Yet the question remains why this "zombie-like" term went through repeated resurrections at various intervals of the twentieth century.[65] Examining the AMP debate in the early People's Republic, I argue that it was a significant moment in the development of the discipline of world history. The "resurrection of the zombie" allowed Chinese scholars to ask new and meaningful questions on Chinese and world histories despite the ideologically charged language: whether human societies followed a universal path and common stages in their development. Focusing on the economic history of ancient society, this debate contained several seemingly disjunctive but actually connected threads.

The first is about how to understand the translated Soviet Marxist historiography. In the 1950s, as the party-state embraced the policy of "leaning to one side" and urged historians to follow, the pressure to follow Soviet standards of historical teaching and research was high. Yet resistance was subtle but noticeable. In the early stages of the debate, Tong contended that one needed to regard Marxism as an evolving ideological system and to avoid engaging problems in a mechanical way.[66] This view

---

[64] Liu and Liao, *Shijie gudai wenmingshi yanjiu daolun*, 17–18.
[65] Karl, *The Magic of Concepts*, 42.
[66] Tong, "Guanyu Zhongguo gudai shehui xingzhi de wenti," 202–210.

allowed scholars to discuss interpretations of Marxism-Leninism by underscoring its dynamic nature. Likewise, if the original Marxist theory was not completely perfect and still needed developing, it was certainly possible to challenge the unoriginal Soviet interpretation of Marxism.[67] Hence, Tong was able to disagree with Soviet specialists, questioning the "direct copying" of Soviet scholarship.[68]

Second, this debate continuously nurtured research on specialized topics in world history such as the status of helots in Sparta, the caste system in ancient India, and the economic nature of Babylonian society. Within the framework of cross-cultural reference and comparison, Tong identified the similarity between Mesopotamia and Sparta and argued that the latter was another example of the early development of feudalism. Key to his argument was how to interpret the helots (classical Greek: Εἵλωτες). These were people who made up most of the population of Laconia and all of Messenia (areas of Sparta). Their exact status was disputed in antiquity: according to Critias, they were "especial slaves," whereas, to Pollux, they occupied a status "between free men and slaves." Marxist historians, following Engels, often refer to them as "serfs." Tied to the land, the helots primarily performed agricultural work that economically supported Spartan citizens. Helots were routinely mistreated, humiliated, and even slaughtered.

In examining the ambiguous nature of the helots between slaves and serfs, Tong identified similar modes of economic production in ancient Sparta, Mesopotamia, and China. He was able to present the argument that there existed alternatives to the prototype of a slave society represented by Western classical societies. In contrast, Lin believed that the helot system was merely a variation of a slave economy. By downplaying the difference between China and other parts of the world, he argued that a slave society was a universal stage in ancient history. Regardless of what positions Tong and Lin took, their debate is significant in showing that world historians had begun to develop serious research interests in topics that previous scholars in China had rarely taken on, such as Mesopotamia and Egypt. To include non-European areas in the study of world history was a great achievement in the development of this field in the 1950s, and it was an important building block for the development of the field after the Cultural Revolution.

---

[67] Tong's argument echoed that of Soviet scholar L. I. Mad'iar. See Anne Bailey and Josep Llobera, eds., *The Asiatic Mode of Production: Science and Politics* (London: Routledge and Kegan Paul, 1981).

[68] Tong Shuye, "Lun nuli zai Babilun de diwei he daiyu" [On the social status and treatment of slaves in Babylon], *Xueshu yuekan* [Academic monthly], no. 5 (1957): 46–54; no. 6 (1957): 69–75.

Third, scholars who sided with both Lin and Tong touched on a fundamental issue regarding the consensus of a common humanity in this debate: the temporal and spatial nature of ancient societies. According to Lin and his followers, the AMP was a temporal regime and a lower stage of slavery when compared to the classical slavery in Greece and Rome. This thesis fit the five-stage model in Soviet historiography; using this model, China and other Oriental societies were placed in a perpetual position of belatedness to Europe. In contrast, scholars like Tong believed that the AMP was a spatial regime. Tong had made it very clear that "the Asiatic" or "the Oriental" mentioned in the works of Karl Marx and Friedrich Engels had limited spatial confines just like "China" and "India." These terms did not register any specific temporary meaning as a mode of production.[69]

We can see that scholars on both sides shared a similar experience in having recently shifted their research areas from Chinese history to world history and of accepting the consensus of a common humanity. However, they drew divergent conclusions, according to how they interpreted primary sources and imported theories from the Soviet Union. Yet, like Tong's criticism of Lin's "direct copying" of Soviet Marxist historiography onto Chinese history, resistance to the application of Soviet theory to Chinese history was consistent throughout the 1950s.

Despite the abovementioned developments in the field, world-historical research in the early People's Republic remained marginal in the broader field of historical studies. In contrast to Chinese history, historians constantly relegated world history to a lower status in Chinese academia. During the Hundred Flowers Campaign, for instance, Yang Renpian expressed disappointment: "Our science is backward, so certainly we cannot ask all the disciplines to develop at the same pace. We should form a list [for things to be developed]. Why don't [we] just place world history at the end of the list, as long as we don't leave it out?"[70] Unlike Tong and Lin, Yang was one of the few prominent world historians in China before 1949. He had studied at the University of Oxford, and he originally worked on the history of the French Revolution. In the mid-1950s, he called for the organization of professional academic institutions for world-historical studies in China. This essay got him into trouble. He was labeled a rightist in the subsequent Anti-Rightist Campaign. Although he was allowed to continue to teach at Peking University, he had to change his research focus to Africa in 1959.

[69] Tong, "Lun Yaxiya shengchan fangfa," 188.
[70] Yang Renpian, "Yao zhongshi shijie shi" [On the need to pay attention to world history], *Renmin ribao*, May 10, 1957. For information on his early life, see Cao Juren, *Wo yu wo de shijie* [Me and my world] (Beijing: Renmin wenxue chubanshe, 1983), 240–244.

At any rate, we should not overstate Yang's pessimism. In contrast to its marginal status in the Republican period, in the early People's Republic, world history was at least beginning to develop into a specialized research field. Rather, it was the poor reception of world-historical scholarship in the general field of historical studies that Yang and his colleagues found frustrating. At that time, Chinese historians by and large showed little appreciation for their work.[71] As we also saw at the beginning of this chapter, Tong Shuye's world-historical approach to solving periodization in Chinese history was encountered with great resistance. This resistance is indicative of the conflicting historical methodologies of Chinese history and world history; but that is not all. The changing social and political environment at the time certainly contributed to the tension and, perhaps, was an even greater source of the problem.

---

[71] Zhou Gucheng, "Lun Xiya gushi de zhongyao xing" [On the importance of the ancient history of West Asia], in *Zhou Gucheng shixue lunwen xuanji* [A selective collection of Zhou Gucheng's essays on historiography] (Beijing: Renmin chubanshe, 1982), 152.

5 Imagining Global Antiquity
Continuity, Transformation, and World History in Post-Mao China

In the late 1980s, William Brashear, an Oberlin graduate and an ancient Egyptian papyrologist based in Berlin, had the rare chance to teach in Changchun, an "austere and dreary industrial city . . . 500 km. due west of Vladivostok."[1] For global travelers of the time, Changchun was not a choice place to stop along the Trans-Siberian rail route. To his surprise, he found that it was home to China's rising center in ancient world-historical studies, the Institute for the History of Ancient Civilizations (IHAC), and it was already "producing China's first generation of locally trained scholars competent in the ancient languages of the West." At this small institute, Chinese students were learning not only subjects including "Latin, Greek, and Greek and Roman history, but also the spate of course offerings in Egyptology, Hittitology and Assyriology."[2]

The founding director of IHAC was Lin Zhichun, who was about to celebrate his seventy-sixth birthday. Zhu Huan (1926–2020), a medieval Russian historian and a revolutionary veteran, was directing the program with the assistance of Yang Zhi,[3] the deputy director and China's first Assyriologist to have received a PhD degree from the renowned Oriental Institute at the University of Chicago. They were joined by Yang's Canadian-born husband, David Jacobson (aka Yang Dawu), and Latin professor Han Jingtao (aka Jing Tao or Andrew Jing-tao, 1919–). Han Jingtao was an ordained Roman Catholic priest who had received his training in Quebec and Strasbourg in the 1930s. Owing to his loyalty to the Vatican, he had been a prisoner of the Chinese state. Along with this impressive list, several foreign professors taught some twenty-five students selected from across China. After two years in Changchun, Brashear was optimistic about the future of the center. As he predicted, "Given the chance, China will one day undoubtedly produce on a regular

---

[1] William Brashear, "Classics in China," *The Classical Journal* 86, no. 1 (1990): 73.
[2] Brashear, "Classics in China," 74.
[3] Her given name 炽 is officially pronounced as *chi*, but people commonly pronounce it as "zhi."

basis scholars just as competent in our classic literary heritage as her present-day musicians in our musical one."[4]

The late 1980s prior to the Tiananmen Incident were a moment of rapid change in China's academia. A group of intellectuals who were born prior to the revolution advocated for a renewed discussion on liberal democratic ideas, which had been interrupted by the Cultural Revolution. The issue of humanism in and beyond the Marxist tradition became a central focus of this so-called New Enlightenment Movement.[5] This general change in the intellectual milieu also affected the field of world history, as scholars again demonstrated a keen interest in engaging in some globally significant discussions. The founding of IHAC reflects an interesting global moment in China's world-historical studies. At that time, the fusing of China's socialist legacy with Western ideas opened up a new perception of China's position in the globalized past. Leaving the Marxist framework aside, world historians started to give way to their nationalist emotions in their research in the 1990s. This chapter is the story of this development.

From the 1960s to the late 1970s, radical political campaigns inter-rupted the development of historical studies in China and brought disas-trous experiences to Chinese historians. For example, consider what happened to the individuals discussed in the previous chapters: Lei Haizong died of a kidney ailment in 1962 before the Cultural Revolution. In the early stages of the revolution, Tong Shuye suffered greatly and died of ill treatment in 1968. Later that same year, the renowned Marxist historian Jian Bozan committed suicide after being criticized and tortured. Tong Shuye's close friend Zhao Lisheng lost his daughter while in political exile. Wu Mi was tortured and beaten. He lost the vision in his right eye and was unable to live on his own. He managed to survive the movement but passed away in 1978. Gu Jiegang was also affected and seriously contemplated committing suicide. He survived the chaotic decade as Prime Minister Zhou Enlai (1898–1976) nominated him to take charge of a state-sponsored project to edit the official history of the twenty-four dynasties.[6]

However, some were less affected by the unsettling times. Chen Hengzhe, for instance, withdrew from active public engagements after 1949 and she lived through the turbulent years relatively peacefully. She passed away in 1976 at the age of eighty-six. Lin Zhichun was somewhat able to maintain his research agenda during the radical years, in spite of his struggle to find venues to publish his research outcomes. When radical

---

[4] Brashear, "Classics in China," 78.   [5] Li, *Reinventing Modern China*, 170–171.
[6] Gu, *Gu Jiegang riji*, 9:299.

ideological control was momentarily lifted, he managed to publish here and there. In 1973, for instance, he edited a college world history text-book and published an essay on primitive society.[7] After the political chaos subsided, thanks to his continuous work, Lin was able to return immediately to a productive academic life, producing a world history textbook in 1979. For the entire field, the "return to normalcy" started in 1978, and the recovery was surprisingly speedy. As a matter of fact, the few years between the late 1970s and early 1980s witnessed not only recovery but also a series of developments in world-historical teaching and research.

The return to normalcy started with the reinstating of world history in secondary education curricula. In 1978, the Ministry of Education issued a tentative draft outlining pedagogy for teaching middle school and high school history. World history officially returned to the senior high school curriculum. In 1986, world history became a required subject for the national junior high curriculum.[8] Along with the revival of world history education in the secondary education system, Chinese higher education institutions resumed world history courses at the college level, even though it was still a marginal subject in curricula. By the mid-1980s, only 3 universities (Peking University, Nankai University, and Wuhan University) out of 300 higher education institutions in China offered world history majors in their undergraduate programs.[9] Meanwhile, a little more than twenty higher education institutions had faculty members who engaged in teaching and research in world history, which laid the groundwork for further development.

Along with the recovery of world history pedagogy, the development of world-historical research almost simultaneously took off in 1978. As an essential part of the professionalization process, the development of this field required building up an array of academic infrastructures, namely library collections, professional institutions, academic journals, and research organizations.

First of all, the decade after 1978 witnessed the establishment of professional research organizations and institutions of world history. The *jiaoyanshi* system established in the 1950s laid the foundations for individual research. Yet the scope of exchange among scholars across the field was still limited. Researchers were scattered in their own academic

---

[7] Lin Zhichun, "Yuanshi qun wenti biannian tigang" [Outline for chronicling the primitive groups issue], *Jilin shifan daxue xuebao* [Journal of Jilin Normal University], no. 2 (1973).

[8] Tan Dong and Hu Zhongbo, "Shijieshi zai zhongxue lishi jiaoxue zhong de diwei tantao" [A discussion on the role of world history in high school history education], *Zhongxue lishi jiaoxue* [Secondary school history pedagogy], no. 8 (2002): 30.

[9] Chen, *Jianguo yilai shijieshi yanjiu gaishu*, 5.

departments. They had yet to form national organizations for world-historical studies. There was also a lack of specialized academic journals for the field, though academic journals and newspapers, such as *Literature, History, and Philosophy, Historical Research*, and *Guangming Daily*, occasionally published works on world history. This situation changed quickly in the late 1970s.

New organizations were established after a meeting on the national development of the discipline of world-historical studies, which was held in Beijing from April 17 to April 24, 1979. During the event, scholars agreed to establish a national association of world-historical studies. Liu Simu (1904–1985) was nominated convener of the association. Liu was director of the World History Institute affiliated with the Chinese Academy of Social Sciences (CASS), the highest-level national research institution. As part of the proposal, branch organizations on world-historical studies were soon established later in that year. In May, the Chinese Research Association of Medieval World History was founded in Chongqing. The Harvard-trained historian Wu Yujin (1913–1993) was elected secretary of the association.[10] In August, the Chinese Research Association of Ancient World History was founded in Changchun and Lin Zhichun was selected as the first secretary of that organization.[11] Several years later (1984), the Chinese Research Association of Modern World History was also established in Shenyang. The establishment of these national research associations for the various sectors signaled further specialization in world-historical studies.

During this transition, the World History Institute gradually shied away from its political mission as a national think tank and gradually embraced a more active research agenda. It followed the trend of specialization by establishing new research branches such as the Research Unit of Ancient and Medieval World History in 1978. It also launched the first professional journal fully devoted to world-historical studies, *World History (Shijie lishi)*.[12] After years of development, Chinese world historians finally had their own platform to publish their research. This was a milestone in the development of world history. In subsequent years, *World History* remained the flagship world-historical research journal in

---

[10] The teaching and research of ancient world history and medieval world history are often conducted in a combined teaching and research unit in Chinese higher education institutions. Therefore, it is conventional to consider them as belonging to the same subfield.

[11] Meng Zhongjie, "Shijieshi xueke fazhan 30 nian dashiji (1978–2008) (shang)" [Chronicle of the 30-year development of the world history discipline (Vol. 1)], *Lishi jiaoxue wenti* [Questions in world history pedagogy], no. 1 (2009): 105.

[12] Wang Lixin, "Guanzhu xianshi: wo kan shijie lishi" [Paying attention to reality: My view of *World History*], *Shijie lishi* [World history], no. 6 (1998): 67.

China. With increased research interest, the institute further launched a series of academic journals devoted to introducing and translating foreign scholarship in world-historical studies in the late 1970s and early 1980s, including *Shijieshi yanjiu dongtai* (*Latest Information on World-Historical Research*) (1979), *Shijie lishi yicong* (*Translation Series on World History*) (1979–1980), and *Waiguoshi zhishi* (*Knowledge of Foreign History*).[13] With a renewed aspiration to know "the world," world history became desirable knowledge not only for professional researchers but also for general readers.

To meet the rising interest in world history, the Commercial Press launched a massive translation project in 1981: the World Academic Classics Series in Chinese Translation.[14] By 2011, the press had produced 12 series and 500 titles of "world classics." It was already planning the thirteenth series, which would include another forty titles. Some scholars compare this series with the Loeb Classical Library collection, complaining about the small number of ancient sources that this includes.[15] The Commercial Press series, however, is an impressive achievement – especially if compared to Western scholars' limited efforts to translate ancient Chinese classics. The majority of significant works in Chinese historiography are yet to become fully available in English-language translations, including the *Records of the Grand Historian* (*Shiji*) and most dynastic histories of China. This asymmetrical exchange of knowledge between China and the West had already raised eyebrows among scholars.[16]

Aside from the increase in translations of primary sources, world historians were updating Chinese readers with the latest world-historical scholarship from abroad in the 1980s. They gradually shifted the early emphasis on the Soviet Union to Western countries. Translation in ancient world history provides a good example. Still holding an interest in historical materialism, Chinese historians first looked to Western

---

[13] Chen, *Jianguo yilai shijieshi yanjiu gaishu*, 6; Meng, "Shijieshi xueke fazhan 30 nian dashiji," 105–106.

[14] The Commercial Press was one of the most influential book presses in China over the course of the twentieth century. For more on the history of its early development in Shanghai, see Reed, *Gutenberg in Shanghai*; as for the translation project, also see Q. Edward Wang, "Encountering the World: China and Its Other(s) in Historical Narratives, 1949–89," *Journal of World History* 14, no. 3 (2003): 333. Earlier translations in this project, as Wang points out, started in the early 1950s. Yet systematic translation efforts started in 1981.

[15] The Loeb Classical Library collection, now published by Harvard University Press, is considered by many to be one of the most authoritative English-language translation series for ancient Greek and Roman works.

[16] Paul Cohen, "The Asymmetry in Intellectual Relations between China and the West in the Twentieth Century," In *Ershi shiji de Zhongguo yu shijie lunwen xuanji* [Selected essays on China and the world in the twentieth century], Vol. 1, ed. Zhang Qixiong (Taipei: Academia Sinica, 2001): 61–93.

authors who specialized more or less in economic history. These included figures such as Michael Rostovtzeff (1870–1952), Sir Moses I. Finley (1912–1986), and G. E. M. de Ste. Croix (1910–2000), most of whom were left-leaning historians at the time.[17]

Within the context of these changes, the study of world history in China began to recover quickly. Within the field of ancient world history, the first achievement was the publication of a new textbook. In 1979, the People's Publishing House, the country's leading state publisher, published Lin Zhichun's *An Outline of Ancient World History* (hereafter *Outline*).[18] Like the 1962 edition of the world history textbook, the 1979 edition was a significant landmark in the development of world-historical studies in China. It was also the product of collective work. Participants in this project included eight faculty members from six universities and colleges. Following the norm of the time, Lin did not list names in the book; rather, he credited it to the editing team – but most of the contributors to the volume seem to be from the 1955–1957 Ancient World History Seminar in Changchun, including Mao Zhaoxi (Hangzhou University), Zhou Yitian (Peking University), Liu Jiahe (Beijing Normal University), Cui Lianzhong (Liaoning University), and Liu Wenpeng (Tongliao Teachers College), and all of them became leading authorities in their own fields in later years. Northeast Normal University (which temporarily changed its name to Jilin Normal University) was the only school that contributed three participants to the project, including the principal investigator, Lin Zhichun. Unlike previous textbooks, this new book not only contained a survey of ancient civilizations but also made a theoretical attempt to reorient the study of ancient world history and shape the future trajectory of the field. Based on the latest scholarly literature and archaeological evidence, the textbook's editors engaged in some fundamental issues in the study of ancient world history that previous Marxist scholars in China had not resolved. This proposal revived and inspired several important debates in the 1980s,

---

[17] G. E. M. de Ste. Croix, *The Class Struggle in the Ancient Greek World from the Archaic Age to the Arab Conquests* (London: Duckworth, 1981); *Guanyu yuanshi Jidujiao dui caichan he nulizhi de jige xin guandian* [Several new views regarding proto-Christian views of property and slavery], trans. Yu Ke and Wu Shuping (Tianjin: History Department of Nankai University, 1988). This text is a selective translation of de Ste. Croix's *The Class Struggle in the Ancient Greek World from the Archaic Age to the Arab Conquests*; a copy of this manuscript is held in the IHAC library collection in Changchun.

[18] Shijie shanggu shigang bianxiezu [Editorial unit for ancient world history], ed., *Shijie shanggu shigang* [Outline for ancient world history] (Beijing: Renmin chubanshe, 1979). Considering the timing of this publication, it is safe to say that the participants had already begun editing this book before 1978. The textbook contains two volumes; the second volume was published in 1981.

which included discussions on the Asiatic mode of production (AMP), the city-state (*polis*), and the "Labor Created Man" thesis.

The debate on the AMP among world historians in the 1980s to some extent was a return to the interrupted debate that took place between Tong Shuye and Lin Zhichun in the 1950s. In the 1979 textbook, editors under the leadership of Lin made an attempt to conclude the previous debates by inserting a long excerpt concerning the issue. In it, they reiterated Lin's previous proposition that "Asiatic" was a temporal concept for a historical developmental stage rather than a spatial category designated specifically for non-European regions. Yet they substantially revised Lin's earlier argument and realigned the AMP with the last stage of a primitive society, instead of as a lower stage of a slave society.[19] They continued to believe that the AMP was a universal stage of human development, stating: "The Asiatic (Oriental) and the Ancient (Classical) types of property ownership (or, modes of production) are two stages that follow one another, not one stage that existed in the East and West in parallel."[20]

The new perspective almost immediately inspired discussions among world historians. The first convention of the Chinese Research Association of Ancient World History took place in Changchun from August 23 to August 29, 1979. During the meeting, editors of *Outline* introduced this view. It received mixed responses. Some scholars argued that Karl Marx and Friedrich Engels had already abandoned this concept after the 1870s;[21] others thought that pairing the AMP with primitive society contradicted the true teachings of the communist founding fathers. For them, the AMP was merely a transitional stage in the East, a spatial concept instead of a universal stage of human development.[22] In the following year, Lin and his colleagues continued this discussion. In a polemical article, they announced: "Any attempt to parallel 'Asiatic' with 'Ancient' and to dichotomize 'the Ancient East' and 'the Classical World'" deviated from Marxism.[23] The concept "Asiatic" remained an

---

[19] *Shigang*, 286–287.   [20] *Shigang*, 19–20.

[21] Wang Dunshu and Yu Ke, "Guanyu chengbang yanjiu de jige wenti – jian ping *Shijie shanggu shigang* guanyu chengbang he diguo de guandian" [Several issues regarding the study of city-states – and a critique of the point of view on city-states and empires in *An Outline of Ancient World history*], *Shijie lishi* [World history] no. 5 (1982): 48–57.

[22] Liao Xuesheng, "Zhongguo shijie gudaishi yanjiuhui juxing diyici daibiao dahui" [The first representative conference of the Chinese Research Association of Ancient World History], *Shijie lishi* [World history], no. 6 (1979): 92. The second view seems to resonate more with Tong Shuye's argument in the 1950s.

[23] Shijie shanggushi shigang bianxiezu [Editorial unit for *An Outline of Ancient World History*], "Yaxiya shengchan fangshi: bu chengwei wenti de wenti" [The Asiatic mode of production: A problem that does not constitute a problem], *Lishi yanjiu* [Historical research], no. 2 (1980): 3.

original concept in Marxist theory.[24] In spite of conflicting views, scholars agreed that this topic deserved further discussion, which led to conferences on the topic in Changchun in 1978, Tianjin in 1979, and the national conference in Tianjin on April 21–27, 1981.[25] At these conferences, the revisionist view continued to receive challenges from world historians. Discussion on the topic had already produced around sixty articles by 1985 and lasted through the rest of the 1980s.[26] Yet the general trend suggests that an increasing number of scholars began to advocate for representing the AMP as a bifurcated path of development between East and West. The consensus of a common humanity based on historical materialism seems to have gradually given way to a belief in cultural differences.

As with the resumption of the debate on the AMP, the 1980s were a time when Chinese scholars of world history began to rethink the various relationships that have linked the East and West throughout history. Issues from the past still framed ongoing debates. At the same time, historians were exploring new alternatives to reconciling this fundamental question in world history. Wu Yujin's new definition of world history is indicative of this nuanced relationship between the past legacy and the new thinking. Like past Marxist historians, Wu celebrated the integration in world history. To him, historical synthesis in world-historical studies should take place in both vertical and horizontal dimensions, as world history results from the interaction of both processes.[27] The horizontal dimension is an interaction of diverse modes of production that transforms social formations across space. The vertical dimension refers to the objective progression of economic development over time. Accordingly, connections gradually emerge from isolated regions, bridging previously dispersed entities with the end result of an integrated world.[28] In world history, this is often called "the history of the integrated world" (shijie zhengti de lishi). Wu's interpretation of world history

---

[24] Shijie shanggushi shigang bianxiezu, "Yaxiya shengchan fangshi," 8–11.

[25] Prior to the national conference, Peking University and Jilin Normal University held a conference on this issue in Changchun in 1978 and Nankai University held one in Tianjin in 1979. Meng, "Shijieshi xueke fazhan 30 nian dashiji," 106.

[26] Yu Ke, "Shijie gudaishi yanjiu gaishu" [An overview of the study of ancient world history], in Jianguo yilai shijieshi yanjiu gaishu, 124.

[27] For more on Wu Yujin and his contribution to world-historical studies in China, see Xu, "Reconstructing World History in the People's Republic of China since the 1980s," 329–334.

[28] Wu Yujin, "Zongxu" [Preface], in Shijie lishi, Gudaishi bian, shang juan [World history, Vol. 1: ancient world history], ed. Wu Yujin and Qi Shirong (Beijing: Gaodeng jiaoyu chubanshe, 1995), 9–10.

gradually became the dominant view among Chinese world historians in the 1980s and remains so even today.[29]

While world historians were forming a new consensus on the concept of world history, the general field of historical studies in the 1980s was undergoing a profound transition. With the gradual decline of historical materialism, an increasing number of historians began to embrace nationalistic sentiments. The discourse of modernization provided a crucial link in this transition.

As a temporal concept, modernity registers a teleological path in world-historical development from the "backward" traditional times to the "progressive" modern societies. Despite the fact that Chinese Marxists disagreed with Western scholars on many other issues, by the 1980s they came around to acknowledging that, after many years of political instability and economic stagnation, China had been left behind by "advanced countries." In order to catch up, the communist government launched a radical modernization project, the "four modernizations" that included goals to strengthen the fields of agriculture, industry, national defense, and science and technology. As for modernization, Chinese intellectuals had already started debating this concept in the Republican period. Chinese prime minster Zhou Enlai proposed a modernization policy in 1963, but it was not until 1978 that it was fully carried out under the guidance of Deng Xiaoping (1904–1997).[30] Modernization gradually became the catchword for Chinese social development of the time.

This modernization mindset profoundly affected the study of world history. In 1979, Chen Zhihua (1934–), a scholar based at the World History Institute of the CASS called for the study of world history to serve China's Four Modernizations movement, although he paradoxically stressed the urgency to "liberate thought" from politics in academic study and refuted the assertion of history as only a tool for political goals.[31] What was the value of world history for China's modernization? Chen believed that it could help China "predict" problems in its development. Thinking within the linear, teleological framework of historical materialism, like many scholars, Chen believed that China's modernization was a movement to "catch up" or even replicate the development process that "advanced" nations had already experienced. Thus, world history offered lessons for China's belated development. In other words, in the past of Western countries, China could find its future. Still

---

[29] Wu Yujin, "Shijie lishi" [World history], in *Zhongguo dabaike quanshu* [Encyclopedia Sinica] (Beijing: Zhongguo dabaike quanshu chubanshe).

[30] Li, *Reinventing Modern China*, especially chapter 2, 33–73.

[31] Chen Zhihua, "Shijieshi yanjiu yu sige xiandaihua" [World-historical studies and the four modernizations], *Shijie lishi* [World history], no. 5 (1979): 3–8.

operating with the mindset of the later stages of Cold War politics, Chen did not forget to stress that world history was an important tool for carrying out China's international strategies. Studying world history, especially the histories of international relations and the two world wars, would allow China to better understand the international scene. Thus, it would be in a better position to achieve the stated goal of its diplomacy, to "oppose hegemonism and preserve international peace."[32] Culturally speaking, the development of world history as part of the modern knowledge system was a useful parameter to measure the progress of science in and the culture of the Chinese nation. It was significant for educational purposes as well, especially because world history was a useful tool to cultivate a "correct" worldview among China's younger generations.[33]

Chen further spoke to the debate on the relationship between China and the rest of the world and between the ancient and the modern. Mao Zedong regarded history as the handmaiden of political ideology. In the late stages of the Cultural Revolution, he called for projects to "make the past serve the present" and to "make foreign things serve China."[34] Such a utilitarian view of history created a problem for the healthy development of world history studies. Sensing the problem, Chen explained that the study of ancient history was still useful for China's four modernizations since history was an integrated process and many historical events in modern history had their roots in the earliest past. Yet he was reluctant to challenge Mao's position. He agreed that these slogans were still valid and that they did not contradict the four modernizations. In principle, modern and contemporary histories would serve the real struggles more than ancient history, he admitted.

To clarify, the term "real struggles" is Marxist jargon that refers to class struggles that propelled the progression of a society. The word "struggle" does not contain any negative meaning, because Marxists believe that struggles underpin the dynamics of society and propel societal progress. Focusing on the contemporary concerns, Chen claimed, "It is necessary to emphasize modern and contemporary histories."[35] Still caged in the Maoist conceptual framework, historians like Chen emphasized world-historical research on the modern period over the ancient.

Yet, unlike earlier world historians who insisted on the common nature of humanity, Chen and other world historians in the 1980s had abandoned this universalism and stressed the mission to serve the Chinese nation-state. The obsession with modernity led to the rise of nationalism.

[32] Cold War rhetoric was still visible in Chinese discourse of the 1980s.
[33] Chen, "Shijieshi yanjiu yu sige xiandaihua," 4–5.
[34] Writing shortly after the Cultural Revolution, Chen was still using Maoist terms.
[35] Chen, "Shijieshi yanjiu yu sige xiandaihua," 5.

As Prasenjit Duara has observed, the Enlightenment project in Europe shaped a linear, evolutionary view of time that measures each country's level of development in accordance with how far it has progressed toward becoming a nation-state.[36] In China, world history had become increasingly drawn into the service of the rise of Chinese nationalism. Chen makes this point very clear:

An important precondition to realize the four modernizations is to improve the level of science and culture of our whole nation ... The science and culture of socialism is a development based on a critical inheritance of the whole cultural legacy that the entire human race has created ... It is hard to imagine, if [we] know little about world history, or even know none, [we] can achieve this goal. It is also *hard to imagine*, if [we] do not study world history seriously and cannot command the scientific and cultural fruits of the entire human race that *our nation could enter into the front ranks among the world's civilized peoples*. (My emphasis)[37]

The emphasis on the connection between world-historical knowledge, the modernization project, and the revival of the Chinese nation became the keynote in Chinese historiography in the 1980s. This important change had a noticeable impact on Lin Zhichun as well.

From a steadfast follower of the Soviet Marxist historiography, Lin gradually became outspoken about the goal of world-historical studies as being in service to the Chinese nation. In 1985, he coauthored a petition to the government along with two other prominent world historians, Zhou Gucheng and Wu Yujin. In it, he reiterated the connection between the study of ancient world history and China's modernization.[38] According to Lin, the crucial link between these two was professionalization. He contended that the study of ancient civilizations was a modern scientific discipline in which professional scholars commanded specialized expertise (especially ancient languages) to discover lost civilizations and identify the origins of human society. It was important for China today because it was also a tool for the nation-building project. For instance, one could use it to highlight China's long history and celebrate the early achievements of Chinese civilization in order to cultivate national pride. Yet the current study of ancient world history in China was so backward that it failed to achieve these goals. He pointed out that Chinese scholars must be able to compete with their foreign counterparts. To do this, they needed a command of ancient, non-Chinese scripts that

[36] Duara, *Rescuing History from the Nation*, 33.
[37] Chen, "Shijieshi yanjiu yu sige xiandaihua," 4–5.
[38] Zhou Gucheng, Wu Yujin, and Lin Zhichun, "Gudian wenming yanjiu zai woguo de kongbai bixu tianbu" [The void in the study of ancient civilizations in our country must be filled], *Shijie lishi* [World history] (1985): 1–3; reprinted in *Journal of Ancient Civilizations*, no. 1 (1986): 3–11.

was as deft as their command of ancient Chinese. The lack of development in the study of ancient civilizations could and must be filled. To achieve this goal, the government's support was essential. After all, China as a "backward country" needed to catch up in all areas, including the professional study of ancient history. The petition eventually gave birth to the IHAC. I will look more closely at this later in this chapter.

From promoting radical revolutions to launching modernization campaigns, the communist government gradually shifted its direction in the 1980s. In accordance with this change, some party leaders began to realize the essential importance of having expertise in China's social, economic, and even political developments. They gingerly loosened some of their ideological control over historical studies. Historians seized the fleeting opportunity to engage in more open discussions on certain issues, and some started to question the validity of Marxism-Leninism in historical studies. Yet the ideological pressure persisted. In a subtle way, historians had to choose topics carefully and avoid direct confrontations with core issues in Marxist ideology.[39] In the field of world history, the most profound challenge came from a place that one would hardly have anticipated today – the history of primitive society. Historians conducted a lively discussion on the thesis of "Labor Created Man," a topic with seemingly little relevance to contemporary intellectual life.

The origin of human beings, to be sure, was a question on which traditional Marxist scholars had already reached a conclusion. In 1876, Friedrich Engels (1820–1895) argued that an essential transition from apes to humans was the "liberation" of hands, which was achieved through the process of labor.[40] This thesis was translated into Chinese as early as 1928 and spread among the communists during the Yan'an era. Often referred to as "Labor Created Man," the state actively promoted this thesis in its propaganda after the revolution.[41] Because of its self-claimed origins in modern biology, it reinforced the assertion that Marxist theory is a scientific and universal knowledge system and introduced labor as a key component of the common nature of humanity. In 1953, Pei Wenzhong (1904–1982) and Jia Lanpo (1908–2001) coauthored a short brochure entitled *Labor Created Man*. Both authors were renowned scholars and high-level CCP propagandists. Pei Wenzhong is

---

[39] Li, *Reinventing Modern China*, 172.

[40] This was from Engels's works. Friedrich Engels, *The Part Played by Labour in the Transition from Ape to Man* [Anteil der Arbeit an der Menschwerdung des Affen], 1st English ed. (Moscow: Progress Publishers, 1934).

[41] For more detailed discussion of the introduction and early spread of Engels's thesis, see Sigrid Schmalzer, *The People's Peking Man: Popular Science and Human Identity in Twentieth-Century China* (Chicago: University of Chicago Press, 2008), 60–62.

credited as a founding figure of anthropology in China. In 1928, he discovered the Peking Man skull, which was commonly regarded as the origin of the Chinese human race. He received his PhD from the University of Paris in 1935 and held many high-level positions after the founding of the People's Republic. In 1953, he was a cadre in the Ministry of Culture in charge of social cultural affairs, museums specifically. Jia Lanpo also participated in the famous Zhoukoudian excavation where the Peking Man skull was discovered. Like Pei, he was an experienced paleontologist and in charge of many key excavations in the early People's Republic. In this brochure, which was clearly written for a general audience, the authors gave a simplistic and polemical introduction to the presumably essential role that labor played in the formation of the human race. Following the party rhetoric, they celebrated Charles Darwin's (1809–1882) theory of evolution as a "lethal" blow to "superstitions/feudal thoughts" in the West. However, Darwinism had a fatal flaw, as it was unable to provide a satisfactory explanation for the process by which apes evolved into humans. Labor, as Engels successfully proved, was the missing link in this transition.[42] In the closing pages of the brochure, they identified the claim of multiple origins of humankind as an assertion proposed by "reactionary Euro-American scholars."[43] By doing so, they stressed a common origin of humankind and the universality of Marxist ideology. Using paleontology as a tool for ideological indoctrination, they strengthened the connection between academics and politics.

Engels's thesis was further appropriated during the Cultural Revolution. During the later stages of the Cultural Revolution, radical groups led by Jiang Qing (1914–1991) and Kang Sheng recruited university professors to write newspaper and journal articles as well as propaganda brochures to popularize their political agenda. These college professors usually conducted group work in writing and published under pseudonyms. For instance, the writing group at the Central Party School adopted the name Tang Xiaowen (literally, "essays from the Party School"). The name first appeared in *Red Flag* in 1972. In 1973, the writing group published a brochure with the same title, *Labor Created Man*. In the context of ideological conflicts in the late phase of the Cultural Revolution, it underscored the polemics of the "Labor Created Man" thesis. Similar to many works during the time, the group claimed that the debate on the origins of humankind mattered because it was

---

[42] Pei Wenzhong and Jia Lanpo, *Laodong chuangzao le ren* [Labor created man] (Beijing: Zhonghua quanguo kexue jishu puji xiehui, 1953), 1–2.

[43] Pei and Jia, *Laodong chuangzao le ren*, 17–19.

a struggle between idealists and materialists, a class struggle fundamental to the world revolution; it was thus a crucial component of the communist ideology. They summarily classified those who believed that God created humankind as idealists and classified those who believed that labor created humans as materialists.[44] They then connected the concept of labor to practice, a central concept in Mao Zedong's ideological system.[45] As a result, the "Labor Created Man" thesis became an issue through which one had to show not only belief in Marxist mentors but also loyalty to the great leader of the Chinese revolution.

Canonized into Chinese communist doctrines, the "Labor Created Man" thesis was put into wide circulation in Mao's China.[46] It shaped some fundamental concepts in Chinese communist worldviews with its emphasis on the essential role of labor in shaping human consciousness. Based on this, communists in China, for instance, believed that labor should be a critical component in criminal reform. According to this view, criminals could be brought back to their true human nature only through the process of labor.[47] Li Zehou (1930–), a prominent thinker in the 1980s, also thought highly of the role of labor in human consciousness. He regarded it as the source of aesthetics. Not only did labor create humanity; it also created beauty.[48] As such, this thesis flourished in Chinese communist arts and literature, too.

The "Labor Created Man" thesis carried strong rhetorical power; but it is a false conception of nineteenth-century biology. In the 1980s, Chinese scholars discovered that the thesis contradicted Charles Darwin's original theory. This is because the latter underscored the role of natural selection in the process of random biological mutations – not conscious effort. The use or disuse of certain parts of living organisms could not cause genetic changes in a biological organism. Therefore, labor could not have had a direct impact on human evolution. Engels's thesis, as scholars in the 1990s would point out, was actually more in line with French naturalist Jean-Baptiste Lamarck's "use and disuse" thesis, which had been widely criticized by Darwinists. Besides the biological discussion, even judged on the grounds of simple logic, the "Labor Created Man" thesis was more or less like a chicken-and-egg question: If labor created mankind, then what created labor? Can animals practice labor? If so, then why did

---

[44] Tang Xiaowen, *Laodong chuangzao le ren* [Labor created man] (Beijing: Renmin chubanshe, 1972), 4–5.

[45] Tang, *Laodong chuangzao le ren*, 39.   [46] Schmalzer, *People's Peking Man*, 5–6.

[47] Klaus Mühlhahn, *Criminal Justice in China: A History* (Cambridge, MA: Harvard University Press, 2009), 149–151.

[48] Li Zehou, *Meixue sijiang* [Four lectures on aesthetics] (Beijing: Sanlian, 1989), 67.

animals not evolve into humans? If not, then at what stage did humans (or apes) diverge from animals?

Perhaps the editors of the 1979 textbook sensed the theoretical weakness in the thesis. They made efforts to revise it, but as the thesis was still highly influential in China, they followed an indirect approach. They argued that the term that Engels used in his thesis "die Menschwerdung" was equivalent to "die werdenden Menschen," both meaning "man-in-formation." Taking on this point, they argued that there were two kinds of labor. One was the labor of the man-in-formation, and the other was the labor of the fully formed man. Based on the ability to use tools, they further differentiated fully formed man from man-in-formation. The latter, not being fully human, was not yet able to make tools. Instead, the man-in-formation only used tools that were available in nature.[49] Thus, the editors argued that the "man" that Engels designated in the "Labor Created Man" thesis was man-in-formation.[50]

Some scholars regarded the revisionism in the 1979 textbook as a sign of a latent challenge to Marxist orthodoxy.[51] They insisted that Engels's definition of labor was crystal clear and that there was no need to distinguish the labor of the man-in-formation from the labor of the fully formed man. Both were labor after all.[52] Others emphasized the difference between social and natural sciences, asserting that the "Labor Created Man" thesis was a topic in social sciences and thus the natural selection theory, belonging to the natural sciences, did not apply.[53] The debate continued into the next decade.

In the 1990s, despite the temporary setback of the Tiananmen Incident of 1989, scholars continued to critically examine the Marxist legacy in historical studies. A key development in the intellectual history of the time was a "Realistic Revolution," in which cultural critics and postsocialist thinkers rejected the legacy of the radical revolutionary movements of the twentieth century and called for a gradual and pragmatic approach to social changes.[54] In world history, some also directly challenged the revolutionary orthodoxy. In 1994, a young scholar in Zhejiang, Gong Yingyan (1961–), resumed the discussion

---

[49] *Shigang*, 1–4.   [50] *Shigang*, 2.

[51] The editing team summarized the main arguments of the textbook and published them in 1977.

[52] Lu Wenzhong, "Guanyu renlei qiyuan de jige wenti" [Several questions regarding the origins of humans], *Jilin shifan daxue xuebao*, no. 2 (1978): 39–43.

[53] Xue Wanren, "Laodong chuangzao le ren" [Labor created man], *Shenyang shifan xueyuan xuebao* [Journal of Shenyang Teachers College], no. 2 (1982); cited from Yu, "Shijie gudaishi yanjiu gaishu," 116.

[54] Els van Dongen, *Realistic Revolution: Contesting Chinese History, Culture, and Politics after 1989* (Cambridge: Cambridge University Press, 2019).

of the "Labor Created Man" thesis.[55] Teaching at Hangzhou University (now part of Zhejiang University), Gong acknowledged the previous generation's contribution to the study of this topic, including that by Mao Zhaoxi, his senior colleague in the school, and the members of the 1979 textbook editing team led by Lin Zhichun. Yet he furthered the discussion in light of modern biological science. In this flamboyant essay, not only did he connect the "Labor Created Man" thesis to Lamarck's "use and disuse" thesis but he also discredited its scientific value. In opposition to the assertion that the thesis "became a key to the riddle of human origins" as it "liquidated the idealism in the field of [the study] of human origins, [and thereby] fundamentally solved the difficult question of the transition from ape to man,"[56] Gong claimed that, as science was always moving forward, it was both dogmatic and nonsensical to hold on to Engels's thesis as a universal truth. He pointed out that Engels himself had proposed this thesis with some caution, as the latter wrote, "It is the prime basic condition for all human existence, and this to such an extent that, in a sense, we have to say that labor created man himself." The phrase here "in a sense" seems to signal the tentative nature of this thesis.[57]

This article provoked another round of discussions during which Gong eventually launched a full-fledged attack on Marxist doctrines. As in the 1980s, some doctrinarians stretched the limits of the differences between the natural sciences and the social sciences in making sense of Marxist ideology. These scholars claimed that the debate on the "Labor Created Man" thesis was not one of a biological issue but a philosophical and political one.[58] In response to such an assertion, Gong lambasted the state of historical studies in China. In particular, he stated, "[During] the lengthy history of the past two millennia, the hermeneutics of Confucian classics that focused on illuminating the deep meaning from sublime words dominated the academics of ancient China; natural science was considered a petty craft and was looked down upon." He thus concluded, "The thought model [of Chinese academics] lacked a logical system of argumentation and was more prone to ambiguous

---

[55] Gong Yingyan, "Guanyu 'laodong chuangzao ren' de mingti" [On the thesis 'labor created man'], *Shixue lilun yanjiu* [Historiography Quarterly], no. 2 (1994): 26.

[56] Gong, "Guanyu 'laodong chuangzao ren' de mingti," 25.

[57] Gong, "Guanyu 'laodong chuangzao ren' de mingti," 25.

[58] Han Minqing, "Shi shengwuxue wenti, haishi lishiguan wenti" [Is it a question of biology or historical view?], *Zhexue yanjiu* [Philosophical studies], no. 4 (1995): 11–19; Su Zhihong and Hao Lidan, "Dui 'Guanyu (Laodong chuanzao ren) de mingti' de zhiyi" [Questioning (the article) "On the thesis that labor created man"], *Shixue lilun yanjiu*, no. 2 (1995): 35–40, and 13.

comparisons."[59] In other words, to him, those who insisted on the "Labor Created Man" thesis today were exactly like those who had followed the hermeneutical tradition in the past. Gong blamed this hermeneutical tradition in scholarly research for the stagnation in scientific developments in China. He further pointed out that, as Engels was eager to follow the latest scientific developments even a century ago, Chinese scholars today needed to keep themselves up to date with the latest in the current state of knowledge. Only by doing so could the Chinese nation catch up with the rest of the world and attain the place that it deserved in international academic rankings.[60] The defense of academic objectivity and the promotion of nationalist sentiment paradoxically converged on this passionate discussion over a topic drawn from seemingly apolitical paleontology.

As such, the "Labor Created Man" thesis placed the history of the ancient world on the frontline in the development of Chinese historiography in the 1980s and 1990s. Its unfolding is indicative of increasing doubt within academic circles concerning Marxism as a valid theoretical system. Scholars started to cautiously raise questions and eventually made an open statement that Engels's thesis was based on an outdated knowledge system. By the 1990s, it was time to abandon it. Interestingly enough, discussions on topics in ancient world history once again became harbingers of change. Despite the ruptures in historical methodologies and political ideologies, these grew out of the old frameworks that the world historians Tong Shuye and Lin Zhichun had already laid out in the 1950s.

The debate on ancient city-states was one of the featured topics. To a certain degree, this topic was a reincarnation of the AMP discussions in post-Mao China. In the 1979 textbook, discussion of the AMP still operated within the framework of Marxist historiography. Many of its basic terms such as "slavery," "feudalism," and the "Asiatic mode of production" were derived from the original works of Karl Marx and Friedrich Engels; by contrast, Engels did not use the term "city-state" in his influential piece *The Origins of the Family, Private Property, and the State*; indeed, in his posthumous works, the word "polis" appears only one and without much context as to its signification.[61] The discussion on

---

[59] Gong Yingyan, "Rang women jiaota shidi de maixiang xin shiji: Zhili xingzou ji women de xueshu" ["Walking Erectly" and our researches (original English title)]," *Shixue lilun yanjiu*, no. 1 (1996): 70.

[60] Gong, "Rang women jiaota shidi de maixiang xin shiji," 70.

[61] Lin Zhichun [Rizhi], "Chengbang yu chengbang lianmeng" [City-states and city-state federations], in *Gudai chengbang shi yanjiu* [Study of the history of ancient city-states] (Beijing: Renmin chubanshe, 1989), 3.

city-states did not point to ambiguity so much as to inadequacy in classical Marxist historiography.

The 1979 textbook includes a discussion on ancient city-states. When the editors of the textbook revised their view of the AMP from the early stage of a slave society to the late stage of a primitive society, a question remained: In what way did the slave-owning society evolve? In other words, if slavery was a major stage of development in world history that could have lasted for thousands of years, how can we understand its dynamics of change? In the 1979 textbook, Lin and his colleagues argued that the transition from city-states (*chengbang*) to empires was a common path in slave-owning societies.[62] They explained that slave-owning city-states emerged after the collapse of communal society. In the beginning, these city-states had certain common characteristics. They were small in both population size and territorial scope, and they were congregated around cities or communal centers.[63] More importantly, they were not a unique case in the Greco-Roman world; rather, they represent a common stage of world-historical development from primitive society to slave society.[64]

The implications of this thesis were latently political, since they were discussing the roots of democracy and despotism. The editors believed that economic relations predetermined these political systems, which had little to do with cultural values. The latter was more or less shaped by ethnic, racial, or environmental factors. These scholars contended that a petty peasantry was the economic foundation of ancient city-states, on which a community of citizens (*gongmin*) came into being. The economic nature of the system predetermined civic values, and the East and West shared a common path to realizing these. Thinking within the framework of historical materialism, the editors believed that the bankruptcy of the petty peasantry was a natural consequence of class struggles in the ancient world. The demise of city-states was inevitable. Despotic empires eventually replaced city-states as the next step in the development of slave societies.[65]

It is quite clear that the editors of the 1979 textbook to some extent were already aware of the Oriental Despotism thesis that was in wide circulation outside of China during the past several centuries.[66] This

---

[62] The Chinese term *chengbang* combines the Chinese characters *cheng* (city) and *bang* (state), so it is a literal translation of "city-state" in English, which is a translation from the Greek word "polis (πόλις)."

[63] Scholars debated the differences and similarities between "city" and "communal center."

[64] *Shigang*, 25–26.   [65] *Shigang*, 27.

[66] Liao Xuesheng, "Guanyu Dongfang zhuanzhi zhuyi" [On oriental despotism], *Shijie lishi* [World history], no. 1 (1980): 89–93, and 96.

concept first appeared in 1758 in France. It soon became popular on the eve of the French Revolution, spreading among intellectuals on the European Continent.[67] Influenced by this thesis, generations of scholars in the West from G. W. Hegel to Karl Wittfogel believed that despotism was central to the political nature of the Oriental society. Owing to Hegel's heavy influence on Karl Marx's conception of the Orient, Chinese historians in the 1980s were reluctant to openly criticize him. They directed their criticism at Karl Wittfogel, a former German Marxist who fled to the United States after World War II and subsequently became a staunch anticommunist. In his 1957 publication *Oriental Despotism*, Wittfogel drew on Karl Marx's sketchy discussion of the AMP and put forth an assertion that Oriental society was intrinsically despotic in its political nature. Wittfogel held a view of environmental determinism, believing that Asiatic societies commonly relied on the operation and regulation of irrigation systems. In order to manage these systems, the state had to establish centralized and powerful bureaucratic apparatuses, which inevitably led to the emergence of despotism. *Oriental Despotism* provoked heated discussion among Chinese historians, though many of them seemed to agree that democracy was absent in Oriental societies.[68]

The Oriental Despotism thesis incited protest from Lin Zhichun and his colleagues, too. They admitted that, while ancient Greek and Roman authors such as Herodotus, Aristotle, and Cicero described despotic empires in the East in their times, they failed to document the existence of city-states in the area.[69] In the 1979 textbook, Lin and his colleagues argued that the earliest democracy and bicameral politics did not derive in Europe. They actually originated in Sumer, an ancient city-state in Mesopotamia.[70] From democracy to despotism, the East and the West followed a common path. In this way, Lin Zhichun and his team

---

[67] Marian Sawer, *Marxism and the Question of the Asiatic Mode of Production* (The Hague: Springer, 1977), 4–12.

[68] Karl Wittfogel, *Oriental Despotism: A Comparative Study of Total Power* (New Haven, CT: Yale University Press, 1957). For Chinese scholars' critique of the Oriental Despotism thesis in the 1980s, see Liao Xuesheng, "Guanyu Dongfang zhuanzhi zhuyi." In the 1990s, Liao continued to criticize the historiographical foundation of Wittfogel's works by analyzing the latter's sources for ancient Greek history. Liao Xuesheng, "Weitefu de 'Dongfang zhuanzhi zhuyi' yu gudai Xila de lishi" [Wittfogel's "Oriental Despotism" and ancient Greek history], *Shixue lilun yanjiu* [Historiography Quarterly], no. 1 (1992): 29–37.

[69] *Shigang*, 28.

[70] *Shigang*, 28. They cited the famous Assyriologist Samuel. N. Kramer (1897–1990) to support the argument. S. N. Kramer, *From the Tablets of Sumer: Twenty-five Firsts in Man's Recorded History* (Indian Hills, CO: Falcon's Wing Press, 1956), 26–31; *History Begins at Sumer: Thirty-Nine Firsts in Man's Recorded History* (Garden City, NY: Doubleday Anchor Books, 1959), 29–34.

constantly made cross-cultural references. They claimed, for instance, that Indian kinship organizations were not much different from the ones among the Greeks, Romans, and Teutons. Thus, historians could use historical materials from one ancient culture to study another. Going even further, they made the bold claim that the most typical imperial despotism was developed not in the East but in the West – independent of Oriental influence. This was the Roman Empire.[71]

Following Lin's pioneering work, Chinese historians came to a realization about the significance of ancient city-states and passionately discussed them in the 1980s.[72] The Chinese Research Association of Ancient World History organized three national conferences to discuss this topic (in 1980, 1982, and 1983). These discussions were gradually narrowed down to some key elements in the relationship between East and West in world history. In these debates, Chinese historians developed a more nuanced understanding of important concepts such as "city-state, " "empire," and "republic."[73] The discussion continued through the rest of the 1980s and transcended the scope of world-historical studies. In 1982, Chen Minzhi and Wu Jinglian (1930–) collected and posthumously published Gu Zhun's reading notes on Greek democracy.[74] In the context of the rise of neoliberalism in 1980s China, this publication on ancient city-states would have a profound impact on the popular understanding of China's cultural and political tradition in the coming decades.

Gu Zhun (1915–1974) was not a historian.[75] Born into a poor family in Shanghai, he taught himself to become an accountant at the age of fifteen. In 1930, he edited a textbook on accounting, *Bank Accounting (Yinhang*

---

[71] *Shigang*, 29.

[72] For example, Kong Lingping positively reviewed the thesis and Zuo Wenhua challenged it. Kong Lingping, "Shijie gudaishi yanjiu de xin chengguo" [New fruits of ancient world-historical studies], *Lishi yanjiu* [Historical research], no. 1 (1980); Zuo Wenhua, "Guanyu nuli shehuishi de jige wenti" [Several issues concerning the social history of slavery], *Jilin daxue xuebao* Journal of Jilin University], no. 2 (1980): 98–103.

[73] Wang Dunshu, "Luelun gudai shijie de zaoqi guojia xingtai: Zhongguo gushi xuejie guanyu gudai chengbang wenti de yanjiu yu tantao" [A brief disquisition on forms of early states in the ancient world: Research and discussion on the issue of ancient city-states in the field of ancient history in China], *Shijie lishi* [World history], no. 5 (2010): 116–125.

[74] Gu Zhun, *Xila chengbang zhidu: du Xila shi biji* [Greek city-state system: Notes from reading Greek history] (Beijing: Zhongguo shehui kexue chubanshe, 1982). Chen is Gu Zhun's biological father's family name, but Gu Zhun went by his mother's maiden name. For more on Gu Zhun's life, see Wen-hsin Yeh, *Shanghai Splendor: Economic Sentiments and the Making of Modern China, 1843–1949* (Berkeley: University of California Press, 2007), 196–204; for Chinese intellectuals' critical assessment of Gu Zhun's relationship with Hegel, see Gloria Davies, *Worrying about China: The Language of Chinese Critical Inquiry* (Cambridge, MA: Harvard University Press, 2007), 157–158.

[75] Liao Xuesheng, "*Xila chengbang zhidu* duhou" [After reading *System of the Greek City States*], *Shijie lishi* [World history], no. 4 (1984): 87.

kuaiji) that was widely adopted by universities and colleges in Shanghai. In the same year, Gu started to accept communist ideas. He became a party member in 1935 and actively participated in the communist revolution in the following years. After the revolution, he was promoted to director of the Shanghai Finance Bureau and of the Shanghai Tax Bureau in 1949, two crucially important offices in China's economic center. Yet, during the Three-Antis Campaign, he was accused of being a rightist and demoted to the Institute of Economic Research in Beijing in 1956. In the subsequent political movements, he was twice labeled a rightist in 1957 and 1965, respectively. He and his family were severely persecuted during the Cultural Revolution that followed. Under political pressure, his wife of more than thirty years had to divorce him. She soon committed suicide. His five children were forced to cut off family ties with him. On top of that, he was diagnosed with terminal cancer in the 1970s.

Democracy was the topic that got Gu and his family into trouble. Even in the context of political chaos and family tragedy, he never gave up his study of this topic. During the last year of his life (1974), he continued to search for the answer to the question, which he posed as, "What should Nora do after leaving home?"[76] Nora is the protagonist in Henrik Ibsen's (1828–1906) three-act play *A Doll's House* (1879). The play follows Nora's gradual development from the status of a housewife, dependent on her husband, to living as an independent woman who, in seeking her own identity, chooses to leave her home. When it was originally published, the play reflected the intense conflicts between individual freedom and traditional values in the women's movement in late nineteenth-century Europe. Lu Xun first introduced the play to China, where it subsequently gained significant notoriety. In a talk at Beijing Women's College on December 26, 1926, Lu Xun asked, "What happens after Nora leaves home?" In this talk, he stated that there were only three things that a Chinese Nora could do if she left home: starve, live an immoral life, or return home to her husband. In other words, it would be a continuous struggle even if Nora chose to leave home, as the social and political conditions that suffocated Chinese women had not yet changed. After the victory of the communist revolution, Gu asked a similar question: "What happens after a proletarian party seizes power?" He was deeply concerned with the future of the Chinese revolution, as he was worried that the

---

[76] Jonathan Spence, *The Gate of Heavenly Peace: The Chinese and Their Revolution 1895–1980* (New York: Penguin, 1981), 254–255. Here, Gu Zhun metaphorically uses Nora to ask how a liberated subject continues to seek its own fate.

revolutionary party would eventually lose sight of its original goals in pursuit of true democracy. What is true democracy? To Gu, this was not only a question of contemporary politics but also a question of historical contingency. Searching for an answer, he surveyed Western and Chinese history in an attempt to identify the historical origins of postrevolutionary China's political problems. His collection of reading notes on ancient Greek city-states represents the unfinished product of this project.

Not being a professional historian, Gu worked with secondary sources such as translated Greek works and Soviet textbooks. He took notes on ancient Greek history in preparation for a larger project. The ideas he inscribed into these notes were not unfamiliar to Chinese readers in the 1980s; indeed, they believed that Gu made great contributions not only to Greek history but also to political philosophy. Yet, unlike Lin Zhichun and his team, Gu argued that the city-state system was a unique legacy of Western history and it did not exist in ancient China or other Oriental societies.[77] Historically, the West was outgoing, diverse, and held legal institutions in high esteem.[78]

As such, Gu stressed the fundamental cultural differences between East and West.[79] He argued that it would be a mistake to compare Greek city-states to the small kingdoms that populated China during the Spring and Autumn period, since these small kingdoms were not fully independent.[80] More importantly, unlike democratic Greek cities, neither popular sovereignty nor direct democracy existed in ancient China.[81] He hinted that democracy was a historical tradition; in its absence, China suffered from despotism throughout its history. Like previous thinkers, including Zhou Weihan and Lei Haizong, Gu returned to the history of the Three Dynasties especially the Spring and Autumn and the Warring States periods. As he contended, this was "a critical moment for historical change" in Chinese history; yet the change was predetermined by history. According to Gu, "[The] tradition of 'divine bestowal of rulership' that [began in the period from] the Shang Dynasty through Western and Eastern Zhou had already predetermined that only absolute despotism would achieve the unification of China, and [only

[77] Cui Zhiyuan, "Bijiao lishi yanjiu de yige changshi: Gu Zhun *Xila chengbang zhidu* pingshu" [An attempt at comparative historical study: A review of Gu Zhun's *Greek City State System*], *Dushu*, no. 4 (1984): 34–35; Gu, *Xila chengbang zhidu*, 22–24.

[78] Cui, "Bijiao lishi yanjiu de yige changshi," 35–38. Gu claimed that Greek city-states were a unique case in world history. Liao Xuesheng pointed out that Gu failed to respond to the thesis concerning the deep cultural roots of Oriental Despotism. Liao, "Duhou," 87.

[79] For a scholarly discussion of Gu Zhun's view of ancient Greece, see Zhou, "Greek Antiquity, Chinese Modernity, and the Changing World Order," 112–114.

[80] Gu, *Xila chengbang zhidu*, 9.   [81] Gu, *Xila chengbang zhidu*, 10.

absolute despotism could] continue to develop and spread Chinese civilization." Continuing, he states, "Although this despotism dragged China into a long period of stagnation or limited [its] development, it was history, and there was nothing to regret in history."[82]

Gu's world-historical critique of Chinese tradition was well received among Chinese scholars in the 1980s. Wu Jinglian, the coeditor of Gu's posthumous work, was his junior colleague at the Institute of Economic Research. During the Cultural Revolution, Wu and Gu read about Greek history together. In the 2000s, he became the leading voice for marketization and a major advisor on China's economic reform. The book's success at the time, in a way, is indicative of the emergence of the belief in cultural difference between China and the West among Chinese intellectuals in the 1980s.[83]

This cultural fad eventually crystalized into the six-episode television series *River Elegy* (*Heshang*) in 1988. In this documentary, the scriptwriters criticized the Chinese tradition with its strong sense of cultural determinism. They generalized that the nature of Chinese civilization was of a "Yellow civilization," which was inward, stagnant, and lacking momentum for change. By contrast, Western civilization, they argued, was "blue," which was open to the ocean and thus outgoing, progressive, and dynamic. The documentary echoed Gu Zhun's view that China's present-day lack of democracy was a problem deeply rooted in China's past. The only way for China to modernize was for it to give up its traditional culture. The series was broadcast twice on China's Central Television (CCTV) in 1988, a sensitive moment leading to the Tiananmen Incident of 1989. After the crackdown, the CCP blamed this sort of cultural iconoclasm for provoking political upheavals in China, accusing *River Elegy* of contributing to the outbreak of massive protests in 1989.[84]

Joining the vibrant discussion on city-states, Lin Zhichun mobilized his former students and launched another research project, which led to the publication of *The Study of the History of Ancient City-States* in 1989.[85] In this project, Lin and his team combined theoretical inventions with detailed case studies to argue that the city-state was a common stage in world-historical development. Lin and his colleagues had proposed a similar argument in the 1979 textbook. In the 1989 publication, they

---

[82] Gu, *Xila chengbang zhidu*, 143.

[83] For example, Cui, "Bijiao lishi yanjiu de yige changshi," 33.

[84] Jing Wang, "*Heshang* and the Paradoxes of the Chinese Enlightenment," in *High Cultural Fever: Politics, Aesthetics, and Ideology in Deng's China* (Berkeley: University of California Press, 2003), 118–136, esp. 308n1.

[85] The Chinese title of this book is *Gudai chengbang shi yanjiu*.

applied it to Chinese history. In this process, they formally abandon slave society as the central focus of ancient world-historical studies. As I have discussed, this view derived from the Soviet historiography and had dominated Chinese historiography over the course of several decades.

The 1989 book exhibits an extensive scope of collaborative research. As a comparative study of city-states, it contains two parts. The first part has four chapters, all of which are written by Lin (the last one with the assistance of his student, [Chai] Xiaoying). It provides a general discussion of the definition, theory, and periodization of city-states in the ancient world. The second part consists of ten case studies, each of which constitutes an individual chapter and is composed by a specialist on the topic. These case studies cover a wide range of topics, including the origins of humankind, the transition from primitive to civilized ages, ancient Egyptian kingdoms, Sumerian city-state leagues, Indian city-states, a brief history of the Greek city-state Argos, a discussion of Athenian democracy from the sixth to the fourth century BC, the origin of Rome as a city-state, the rise and development of Chu,[86] the founding of Zhou and its relations with other regions, and a preliminary study of oracle-bone records of the Xia people. These case studies not only substantiate Lin's hypothesis on the world-historical concept of city-states but also use this concept to reexamine ancient Chinese history. Lin's thinking is clearly imprinted on the book, and its assertions reflect his intellectual development. In his early works, he argued that city-states were a common stage of early civilizational development and that the political systems associated with them were democratic by nature. In this collection, he reiterates this thesis, asserting, "Despotism was absent in the age of city-states, and despotic politics was not even known to [the people of that time]."[87] This was the case in China and in the West, he insists.

An important implication of this assertion is that it shows that the ancient Chinese historical record has acquired world-historical significance. Lin explains that, among ancient civilizations – the Indus River or the Harappan civilization in India, the Aegean or the Cretan Mycenaean civilization in Greece, and the Sumerian or Akkadian civilization in Mesopotamia – few left much of a record for the people of today. Similarly, the Mayan civilization was destroyed by Spanish invaders.[88] Some parts of these ancient sites still remain to be discovered by archaeological excavations. In contrast, as Lin believed, Chinese civilization was

---

[86] Chu was an ancient state in early China. It was a major power in the Eastern Zhou period.
[87] Rizhi, *Gudai chengbang shi yanjiu*, 3.
[88] The Indus Valley Civilization was a Bronze Age civilization located in the western region of South Asia. Its high point is estimated to have been from 26 BC to 19 BC.

the only ancient civilization that continuously had a written record. This record is a valuable reference to help world historians in China and beyond to study ancient city-states in other cultural regions.[89]

Yet the evidence for the very existence of "democratic" city-states in the earlier periods is often buried in Chinese sources; thus, the false conviction that China had remained a "despotic" empire since the beginning emerged.[90] According to Lin, this was a problem of historiography. He blames the dynastic historical tradition for overlooking this important historical fact. Later-generation historians distorted the historical record and projected the concept of grand unification onto early Chinese history in order to serve the monarchy.[91] To prove this point, Lin critically reexamined early Chinese historiography.

For Lin, classical antiquity in China refers to the second part of the Zhou dynasty that includes the Spring and Autumn and the Warring States periodis. During these eras, China gradually emerged from being a decentralized feudal-like state to a unified empire. According to the traditional narrative, the Zhou household acted as the common lord over the entire Chinese territory, the *tianxia* (or, in other words, the scope of the entire world known to the Chinese at that time). Lin challenged this narrative by claiming that there was no centralized power among the various states in the Spring and Autumn period and that Confucius's grand unification was actually a later invention.[92] Lin's ambitious plan to reorient the historical narrative of ancient Chinese society was not new, to be sure. The famous Chinese historian Gu Jiegang had already initiated the movement to critically reexamine fabrications in ancient Chinese historiography back in the 1920s. Tong Shuye, Lin's debate opponent in the 1950s, was Gu's capable assistant in the later stages of this movement in the 1940s. Questioning the authenticity of the ancient Chinese historical record is an intellectual stream that continues today.[93] What was new was Lin's attempt to apply the world-historical concept of the city-state to ancient Chinese historiography. To prove its existence, he raised doubts about the relationship between Zhou and other feudal states.

In regard to the status of Zhou, Lin argued that a league of city-states existed in this period and the Zhou household was the nominal leader of the

---

[89] Rizhi, "Chengbang yu chengbang lianmeng" [City-states and the leagues of city-states], in *Gudai chengbang shi yanjiu*, 4.

[90] Rizhi, "Chengbang yu chengbang lianmeng," in *Gudai chengbang shi yanjiu*, 20.

[91] Rizhi, *Gudai chengbang shi yanjiu*, 52.

[92] Rizhi, *Gudai chengbang shi yanjiu*, 21, 20, 52.

[93] For instance, Liang Cai argues that the grand unification, commonly regarded as Confucius's idea, was rather a later fabrication to serve the purpose of consolidating monarchical power by Emperor Wu of Han (r. 141–87 BC). Liang Cai, *Witchcraft and the Rise of the First Confucian Empire* (Albany: State University of New York Press, 2014).

league. However grand the scope that the Zhou federation claimed to have, the Zhou state was still one among others. The relations among them were rather equal.[94] The loose league of independent states was a confederation of city-states. Empires would emerge from the collapse of these city-states in the later stages of the ancient world. In China, this city-state stage ended with the emergence of the "Warring States" era after the Spring and Autumn period.[95] Applying this hypothesis beyond China, Lin offered a world-historical survey of political systems in ancient city-states. He categorized city-state politics into the following three levels: At the first level was the assembly of citizens. Lin argued that city-states were the first form of political unit in civilizational history. They were composed of the entire body of citizens, who assembled to execute power. In ancient Greece and Rome, members of city-states were called "citizens." In China, they were called *bangren, guoren* or *zhong*. In Sumer, a meeting of citizens was called *unkin*, and, in India, it was called *sabha*. Like their counterparts in ancient Greece and Rome, these citizens also enjoyed privileges in their own city-states. In other words, Lin concluded that citizens were the masters of the city-states.[96]

At the second level was the council of *zhanglao* (elders). *The Epic of Gilgamesh* contains the earliest record of such an institution.[97] In China, the earliest record can be found at least in the "Pan'geng," a chapter in the *Book of Documents (Shangshu)* that records the story of an ancient king named Pan'geng who revived the falling Shang dynasty by relocating his people. Lin argued that the document offers information on both the assembly of citizens and the council of elders. The *boule* in Athens, *Gerousia* in Sparta, and *Senatus* in Rome performed similar duties, as well as the *Samiti* in ancient India.[98] In classical Chinese, the elders in the council were called *zhu dafu*.[99]

At the third level was the leadership of the state. Lin identifies the existence of a separation of political, religious, and military powers among all early city-states. Sumer, ancient Greece, and ancient China followed almost the same division of the power structure within which power was distributed among the three levels (see Table 6).[100].

---

[94] Rizhi, *Gudai chengbang shi yanjiu*, 21.   [95] Rizhi, *Gudai chengbang shi yanjiu*, 24.
[96] Lin Zhichun focused on ancient Chinese sources that mention *guoren* and *zhong*. He discovered more than 300 references to these terms in the 3 commentaries of the *Chunqiu* [Spring and Autumn Annals]: *Zuozhuan, Guliang zhuan*, and *Gongyang zhuan*. He also used the *Zhouguan*, also called the *Zhouli*. Rizhi, *Gudai chengbang shi yanjiu*, 29.
[97] Rizhi, *Gudai chengbang shi yanjiu*, 37.   [98] Rizhi, *Gudai chengbang shi yanjiu*, 37.
[99] Lin Zhichun claims to have discovered dozens of records of *zhudafu* in the commentaries on the *Chunqiu*. Rizhi, *Gudai chengbang shi yanjiu*, 40.
[100] However, Lin admits that at different stages of city-state development there were variations in the power distribution. In some cases, there might be only two of these positions in the record. Rizhi, *Gudai chengbang shi yanjiu*, 47.

Table 6 *Separation of powers in ancient city-states*

States	Political Power	Religious Power	Military Power
Sumer	Ensi	En	lugal
Athens	*archon* (ἄρχων)	*basileus* (Βασιλεύς)[101]	*polemarchos* (πολέμαρχος)
Ancient China	*qing* 卿	*jun* 君	*wang* 王

Alongside reconstructing a global structure for the political systems of early city-state, Lin also analyzed the differences between leagues of city-states and empires. He did not believe that any unified empire could have ever existed at this early stage of city-states. In his view, the record of ancient "empires" was merely about loose city-state confederations.

In critically interpreting and analyzing ancient sources, Lin eventually places ancient civilizations, Chinese and non-Chinese, within a common schema of political development, which, he concludes, had four common stages: first, the legendary period (primitive [proto]-democratic city-states); second, the epic era (primitive [proto]-monarchical city-states); third, the Spring and Autumn period (*gong-qing* city-states), as the highest achievement of ancient democracy, where, in China and Greece alike, the executive power of the state shifted from a king (*jun* in Chinese and *basileus* in Greek) to nonhereditary positions (such as *archon* or *polemarchos* in Greek and *gong* or *qing* in Chinese);[102] fourth, the Warring States era (the transition to empires).[103] Like Zhou Weihan, Lei Haizong, and Lin Tongji, Lin adopts Chinese periodization and applies it to other world civilizations. In doing so, he and his research team falsified the Oriental Despotism thesis through their claim that ancient democracy was not a European monopoly but actually existed in Asiatic societies as well.

The attempt by Lin Zhichun and his colleagues to establish city-states as a global stage in world-historical development was warmly received by fellow world historians in China. It inspired continued discussions and formed a common research focus in the field. In 1993, Nankai University (where Lei Haizong used to teach) organized the first international conference on ancient world history. The ancient city-state became a key topic in that meeting. Lin's thesis was echoed by a Taiwanese scholar, Du Zhengsheng, who shared a similar view that city-states existed in ancient

---

[101] The legendary king in Athens was called *anax* (ἄναξ). Lin argues that this term was quite similar to *di* (as in *sanhuang wudi*, the legendary rulers) in ancient Chinese history. Rizhi, *Gudai chengbang shi yanjiu*, 47.

[102] Rizhi, *Gudai chengbang shi yanjiu*, 78–79.

[103] Rizhi, *Gudai chengbang shi yanjiu*, 61.

China.[104] In 1993 and 1998, scholars from the CASS eventually published two collections on despotism, democracy, and republicanism in the ancient world. The editors of these two volumes toned down Lin's thesis. They argue that, although some democratic elements in ancient China can be identified, democracy and republicanism as political ideas were still by and large absent in Chinese tradition.[105] Scholars continue to discuss this topic today.

Meanwhile, a growing number of scholars became indifferent to the issue.[106] Some thought this was a question too general to discuss and the existing scholarship on the topic was too theoretically driven and therefore lacked historical depth; at the same time, they fell more in the line with Gu Zhun, insisting on the cultural differences among ancient civilizations.[107] All things considered, the shift of focus from the AMP to city-states exemplifies an important change that took place in the 1980s: the abandonment of the Marxist framework in ancient world-historical studies. In Lin's case, in late 1979, he referred to city-states as an early stage of slave society, but, by 1989, the term "slave" had quietly disappeared from his work.

The trend of leaving the Marxist paradigm continued in the 1990s. Historians like Lin Zhichun, earlier the champion of Marxist historiography, finally abandoned Marxist theory in world-historical studies during this period. The most vivid example was his statement that the adoption of feudalism in Chinese historiography was an error of translation and that China did not experience a European-style feudal stage in its historical development.

Starting in the early twentieth century, Chinese intellectuals and political activists had borrowed the European concept of "feudalism" (*fengjian zhuyi*) to describe the nature of "traditional" Chinese society. For communist leaders, feudalism was one of the fundamental causes of China's belated development and thus to completely eradicate the residue of feudal influences was a stated goal of the communist revolution. As a foreign concept, its application in Chinese history caused enormous confusion. To clarify its meaning, Chinese scholars had engaged in various debates over the course of the entire century. The debates on the AMP between Tong Shuye and Lin Zhichun in the 1950s were certainly

---

[104] Du Zhengsheng, *Zhoudai chengbang* [City-states in the Zhou dynasty] (Taipei: Lianjing, 1979).

[105] Shi Zhisheng and Liu Xinru, ed., *Gudai wangquan yu zhuanzhi zhuyi* [Ancient kingship and autocracy] (Beijing: Zhongguo shehui kexue chubanshe, 1993); Shi Zhisheng and Guo Fang ed., *Gudai minzhu yu gonghe zhidu* [Ancient democracy and Republican institutions] (Beijing: Zhongguo shehui kexue chubanshe, 1998).

[106] For example, Wang, "Luelun gudai shijie de zaoqi guojia xingtai."

[107] *Zhongguo shijie lishixue 30 nian*, 45–46.

part of these broader discussions. Back then, Lin was a steadfast defendant of the orthodox view from the Soviet Union. However, by the 1990s, amid the continuous liberalization of thought in China, Lin was ready to totally give it up. He announced that it was incorrect to translate the English term "feudalism" into *fengjian* in Chinese.

To prove this point, Lin starts with a survey of the history of translation. According to him, the term "feudalism" (*Feudalismus* in German and *le féodalisme* in French) was absent in classical Latin. It originated in the medieval Latin word *feodalis*.[108] The early English translator of Chinese classics, James Legge (1815–1897), never used the term "feudal" or "feudalism" to translate *fengjian* in classical Chinese. He apparently did not pair the two terms. Instead, the term *fengjian* in ancient Chinese history is more similar to the terms *apoikia* in ancient Greek and *colonia* in Latin, which should be more appropriately translated as "colony" or "colonization." It was a mistake in translation.

Lin blames Yan Fu (1854–1921) for this lapse. This famous Chinese translator at the turn of the twentieth century originally translated feudalism as the *fute* system or *fute fengjian* when translating Adam Smith's *The Wealth of Nations*. He continued using *fute* in 1903 while translating John Stuart Mill's *On Liberty*. Only after that did he switch to *fengjian* to translate feudalism in translating Edward Jenks's *A History of Politics*. The latter soon became the dominant Chinese translation for the term and replaced "*fute*" in translation.[109] Chinese scholars had blindly followed this change, which led to a state of confusion in historical studies.

Put in the context of the cultural and political environments of early 1990s China, Lin's thesis is both bold and significant. Its underlining message is that, if feudalism in China was a mistake in translation, then the past debates revolving around this issue such as the debates on social history and the AMP had all become meaningless. More important, it implies that the existing framework of Marxist historiography, which claimed to be a holistic whole, could be fundamentally flawed. Questioning "translingual practice," Lin eventually abandoned feudalism as a stage in world-historical development, if not the entire five-stage schema of historical materialism. Once known as a "red professor," Lin abandoned the Marxist framework of world history. Yet this transition paradoxically resurrected nationalism in his thought and then broke his belief in the common nature of humanity.

---

[108] Rizhi, "'Fengjian zhuyi' wenti (Lun Feudalism bainian lai de wuyi)" [Problems of the term "feudalism (*fengjian*)": An incorrect translation of the past one hundred years], *Shijie lishi* [World history], no. 6 (1991): 30.

[109] Rizhi, "Fengjian," 38.

The last attempt in Lin Zhichun's reconfiguration of the world-historical schema was to liberate China from the "Dark Ages." Derived from European experiences, this world-historical concept often referred to a broken link in civilizational development. Near the end of the twentieth century (1999), Lin published an important essay in which he proposes that, unlike the Middle East, Greece, and medieval Europe, China never experienced a hiatus in the development of civilization and thus had never experienced a "Dark Age." Therefore, China was the only civilization in the world that had a continuous stream of civilization.[110] In spite of having defended Marxist universalism in the 1950s, in this article Lin celebrates the uniqueness of Chinese culture – a position that is not unlike what Lei proposed in wartime China.

To prove this point, Lin names three "unique" aspects of Chinese culture: harmonious relations among different ethnicities, cosmopolitanism in worldviews, and continuity of political legitimacy. Lin starts with the concept of ethnic "brotherhood." He argues that, although the Han Chinese and their neighboring tribal peoples at times had conflicts, they eventually developed a fraternal-like relationship over time. This was probably because of original blood ties among ancient ethnic groups. For instance, the Wu and the Yue peoples in early Chinese history shared the same ethnic origins;[111] or it might have been due to constant cultural exchanges. Using the relationship between the Xiongnu and Han peoples as evidence, Lin argues that the Han Chinese were able to learn from their neighbors, and the latter in turn not only accepted Han culture but also eventually joined the confluence in Chinese civilization.[112]

Speaking about cosmopolitanism in Chinese worldviews, Lin asserts that there were practical rituals but no xenophobic religions in Chinese history. In 307 BC, King Wuling of Zhao (r. 325–299 BC) reformed his army by adopting a cavalry, a nomadic tactic of military affairs. Since the old clothing style of the Han people was not suitable for mounted warfare, he appropriated the style of cavalry uniforms used by the surrounding nomadic people, the Xiongnu. This story is often used to illustrate the dynamic cultural exchanges between the Han Chinese and their

---

[110] Rizhi, "Lun Zhong-Xi gudian shi shang de 'heian shidai' wenti" [On the issue of an "Age of Darkness" in Chinese and Western classical history], *Xueshu yuekan*, no. 1 (1999): 68–69.

[111] Rizhi, "Lun Zhong-Xi gudian shi shang de 'heian shidai' wenti," 70. One must point out that Lin's knowledge about ethnic peoples in China seems to be quite superficial if compared with recent scholarship on the issue. For instance, in her study on the Yue people, Erica Fox Brindley has argued that the Yue people were not a self-identified ethnic group but a special reference to a wide range of peoples living in the southern frontier, including today's Vietnam. Brindley, *Ancient China and the Yue*, 27.

[112] Rizhi, "Lun Zhong-Xi gudian shi shang de 'heian shidai' wenti," 71.

neighboring peoples. Lin cites it as an example to show that the Han Chinese were open-minded and ready to learn from other neighboring peoples.[113] While he admits that religious thinking such as Buddhism, Christianity, and Islam may not be found in Chinese thought, nevertheless, he asserts, "From ancient to medieval, the Chinese realm of thought was more tolerant of differences among various religions and philosophies than the Western was."[114] It is interesting to observe that, although Lin had probably never heard of Zhou Weihan and he was writing from a very different intellectual tradition, he actually shares Zhou's negative view of religion. Both of them seem to believe that religious differences were a primary source of disharmony in world history.

Lin then breaks the flow of his essay and inserts a bizarre political statement, announcing that any attempts to provoke ethnic conflicts in China were destined to be futile thanks to the harmonious relations among ethnic groups. After this statement, Lin returns to his thesis and argues that the third aspect was the continuity of political legitimacy. This tradition is rather more an ideal that Chinese people should cherish and nurture than a subject of scholarly research. He takes the concept of *geming* (commonly translated as "revolution") as an example. He starts with an almost mysterious depiction of the common origins of the Chinese nation. He asserts, "Over the course of thousands of years, from the legendary to historical [ages], [the Chinese] have been of one family in blood ties and cultural traditions regardless of political unity or fragmentation." After listing sayings in ancient Chinese documents, he claims, "From [our Chinese] ancestors, the noble virtue and benevolent governance of the Chinese people had be conceptualized and materialized by the teaching [of] great harmony among human beings."[115] As such, unlike the common thinking that *geming* represents overthrowing the ruling house and replacing it with another, Lin returns to its original meaning in classical Chinese and emphasizes *ming*, mandate in the change of governance. He argues that, since the very beginning of Chinese civilization, the mandate had been handed down from Confucius and Mencius to the leaders of peasants and workers in the modern communist revolution.[116] This blind belief in the continuity of Chinese civilization is indicative of the strong nationalistic emotions in

---

[113] Nicola Di Cosmo, *The Cambridge History of Ancient China: From the Origins of Civilization to 221 B.C.*, ed. Michael Loewe and Edward Shaughnessy (Cambridge: University of Cambridge Press, 1999), 960–961.

[114] Rizhi, "Lun Zhong-Xi gudian shi shang de 'heian shidai' wenti," 72.

[115] Rizhi, "Lun Zhong-Xi gudian shi shang de 'heian shidai' wenti," 73.

[116] Rizhi, "Lun Zhong-Xi gudian shi shang de 'heian shidai' wenti," 73.

historical writing. By the end of the twentieth century, Lin had transformed from an orthodox Marxist scholar to a nationalistic historian.

At the same time, generational politics continued to influence world
historians in China during the last two decades of the twentieth century.
The first-generation world historians after the revolution, such as Lin
Zhichun, had become "old." On the one hand, they were still active in the
field and producing interesting work such as Lin's discussion of city-states
in world history. On the other hand, a new generation of scholars emerged
after the 1980s. In contrast to their elders, these younger scholars had had
the opportunity to receive an education abroad and were more exposed to
Western works on the subjects of research during a time of opening up
and reform in China. To them, the Marxist legacy in world-historical
studies had become outdated and even irrelevant. They were not interested in old topics such as the AMP and city-states. Their research topics
became increasingly specialized and disaggregated. Common research
topics from the past started to disappear from the field.[117] As a result,
the research carried out by new scholars became less contingent on the
general trends of historical studies. The founding and development of the
IHAC in 1984 exhibits this trend.

IHAC is an independent body of teaching and research on ancient
world history. It is affiliated with Northeast Normal University and has
been located on that campus since its creation in 1984.[118] The institute
has its own library, office, and reading/reception room as well as the only
professional, multilingual journal in China fully devoted to topics in
ancient world history during the time, *The Journal of Ancient
Civilizations*. Initiated in 1987, this journal had produced 12 volumes
within a decade with an annual circulation of 200 copies and contributors
from all over the world.[119] The institute is operated through special
funding from the State Education Commission. The initial plan was to
relocate this institute to Beijing when the program became fully established. This, however, never materialized and to this day the institute still
resides in Changchun.[120]

In many respects, the inaugural IHAC project was similar to the
national Ancient World History Seminar in the 1950s.[121] As with the
1950s project, students were selected from universities across China to

---

[117] A similar trend can also be observed in the field of modern Chinese history as well as
among the intellectual circle in general. See Li, *Reinventing Modern China*, 29. Gloria
Davies, *Worrying about China*, 66.
[118] Brashear, "Classics in China," 74.
[119] William Brashear, "China Update 1997," *The Classical Journal* 94, no. 1 (October to
November 1998): 85.
[120] Zhu, "Chentong daonian Lin Zhichun xiansheng"; Brashear, "Classics in China," 74.
[121] For information about the project, see Chapter 3.

study in Changchun for three years and obtain a degree in one of four subjects: Hittitology, Egyptology, Assyriology, or Western Classics. Among the eighteen students who studied in Changchun from 1984 to 1987, three came from Northeast Normal University, five from Beijing Normal University, four from Fudan University, three from Wuhan University, two from Nankai University, and one from Peking University. After their studies, a handful of students were selected for advanced degrees.[122] Several of them would eventually have the opportunity to study abroad. Prior to 1989, IHAC had already sent six students to study Egyptology, Assyriology, and Classics abroad. These students went to Oxford, Yale, UCLA, Tübingen, Mainz, and the Sorbonne.[123]

Lin Zhichun played a crucial role in initiating the program. In order to obtain the state's support, he traveled to Wuhan and Beijing to seek support from senior scholars such as Wu Yujin and Zhou Gucheng. He also negotiated with Northeast Normal University concerning the founding of the institute. After its establishment, he managed to organize a strong team by inviting scholars like Yang Zhi and Han Jingtao to the institute. The former was the daughter of the famous translators and married couple Yang Xianyi (1915–2009) and Gladys Yang (aka "Dai Naidie" in Chinese, 1919–1999), who had just received a PhD degree in Assyriology from the University of Chicago, the first Chinese national to achieve such an honor. She was the deputy director of IHAC in the late 1980s.[124] Educated abroad and married to a Canadian husband, Yang was a scholar with a global vision. During her tenure, Yang organized several international campaigns to seek donations and support, which also promoted the visibility of the institute. Further to her efforts, the Deutsche Forschungsgemeinschaft (DFG) contributed 8,600 deutsche mark to fund the IHAC library, and the Netherlands Instituut Voor Het Nabije Oosten further improved it with 500 US dollars' worth of books. In addition, the Oriental Institute at the University of Chicago set up a special fund to help the institute. Chinese historians had been complaining about the lack of library collections for world-historical research since the Republican period. For the first time in Chinese history, these endowments allowed IHAC to establish a specialized and professional collection on ancient world-historical studies. During the last two decades of

---

[122] Brashear, "Classics in China," 76.   [123] Brashear, "Classics in China," 77.

[124] Already past the age of seventy, Lin Zhichun retired from the directorship of the IHAC in the late 1980s. Zhu Huan, a specialist in Russian medieval history, succeeded him. However, owing to her linguistic capability and having studied abroad, Yang Zhi was the Chinese scholar primarily responsible for contacting and hosting foreign experts at the institute. Brashear, "Classics in China," 74.

Figure 5 Lin Zhichun statue at the Northeast Normal University campus. Photo credit: Sun Jianing

the twentieth century, world historians from across China have visited the library to gather crucial materials for research.

The other scholar at the institute who had extensive connections with the West was Han Jingtao. This Catholic priest was directly ordained by the Vatican Church. As China had severed ties with the pope after the revolution, Han had been imprisoned in China from 1953 to 1980. Admiring Han's Latin-language ability, Lin lobbied the local government and managed to recruit Han as a lecturer in Latin. At IHAC, Han compiled several Latin textbooks and readers for students until his retirement in 1987. He remained visible in the early 1990s until his mysterious disappearance.[125]

Lin Zhichun played a crucial role in the IHAC project. Not only did he actively recruit scholars with expertise in ancient languages, but he was also eager to send students to study abroad. Using the personal influence he had accumulated in the earlier period, Lin lobbied the Ministry of Education and managed to seek funding. At a time when his salary was limited and his living conditions remained poor, he was so passionate about his mission that, in several cases, he even used his personal savings to subsidize students to study in Western countries pursuing advanced degrees in areas such as Assyriology, Egyptology, and Classics.

Judging by its outcome, Lin's initiative was a success. Among the students who received government funding to study in foreign countries, several later became leading figures in their respective fields. For example, Wu Yuhong received a PhD degree in Assyriology at Birmingham University in the United Kingdom and completed his postdoctoral work at the University of Pennsylvania. He became director at IHAC in the late 1990s. Gong Yushu received a PhD degree in Assyriology from the University of Munich and became professor of Assyriology at Peking University. Huang Yang received a PhD degree in Classics from the University of London and has been teaching as a professor of ancient Greek history at Peking University and Fudan University. Yet even with Lin's personal support, IHAC could not afford to send a greater portion of its students and graduates to study abroad. By way of compensation, IHAC managed to obtain funding from the government to invite foreign specialists to teach in Changchun.[126] In contrast to the specialists who came from the Soviet Union in the 1950s, most foreign experts in the 1980s came from Western countries. According to some incomplete statistics, thirty-five scholars taught at the IHAC from 1985 to 2007, among

---

[125] Brashear, "Classics in China," 75; it is quite clear that Han went to the countryside to continue preaching in the 1990s. For more information, see "Underground Bishop Calls for Church Unification, Meets Obstacles," in *Union of Catholic Asian News* (UCAN), www.u canews.com/story-archive/?post_name=/1996/09/18/underground-bishop-calls-for-churc h-unification-meets-obstacles&post_id=8157 (accessed February 4, 2018).

[126] In theory, each year the IHAC was allowed to hire four specialists from abroad. Selected specialists had to have at least an MA degree and the ability to teach courses on the Classics (both Latin or Greek language and history), Hittitology, and Egyptology. Regarding benefits, the IHAC offered round-trip airfares to Beijing as well as round-trip train fares to Changchun. *IHAC News*, January 25, 1988.

which eleven came from the United States, nine from Germany, four from the United Kingdom, two from Australia, two from Canada, and one each from Holland, Iraq, Sweden, France, Russia, South Africa, and Israel.[127] The director of the program passionately wrote in 1988 that a communication revolution had taken place in China and the world.[128] Scholars at IHAC were ready to become pioneers in steering the changes.

Despite the success of IHAC and the optimism of foreign observers, a period of historiographical crisis broke out in China from the late 1980s to the early 1990s. This had something to do with the social changes taking place in the political environment in the period of reform. At this time, the state embraced neoliberal doctrines and withdrew subsidization from academic departments, programs, and publishing houses, declaring that each had to find its own means of "creating income." With shrinking state subsidies, academic books became more expensive. Unable to afford to buy them, ordinary readers became increasingly nonchalant about historical studies. The sales of professional history books plummeted, which made it even more difficult for researchers to get published. Even though some historians did eventually manage to publish their work, the influence of their publications was minimal, as only a few scholars would actually read them. As for students, history majors were having trouble finding jobs. Many had to give up on their studies and look for work in other areas.[129] In the context of the crisis of historiography, the study of ancient world history encountered great difficulties, if not the greatest. A sense of frustration spread among the scholars and students at IHAC. The political circumstances of 1989 made the situation worse. As many college professors supported the democratic movement in China, they were severely punished and became disillusioned with the state of affairs in China. In the early 1990s, Yang Zhi left IHAC as well as academia for good, while her parents invited trouble by openly supporting the students' democratic movement in 1989. Along with her Canadian husband, Yang returned to Beijing and opened a private business. Han Jingtao faced increased state surveillance, as he spoke out in support of the movement, too. For these who were selected and sent abroad, many of them changed careers and never returned to China.[130]

---

[127] To be sure, because scholars sometimes move between countries, the statistics on the national origins of those scholars is, to some extent, arbitrary. At any rate, it sheds light on the international scope of the IHAC program. Sources for this statistic are taken from the IHAC website, http://ihac.nenu.edu.cn/experts/forexperts.html (accessed March 31, 2012).
[128] "A World to See," *IHAC News*, January 25, 1988, original title in English.
[129] Chen Qineng, "Zonglun," 11–12.
[130] Wu, "Laoshi! Zhaoliang wo rensheng de zhilu mingdeng."

Aside from the political circumstances, scholars and students abandoned the study of ancient world history for complicated reasons. As the 1990s are the recent past, we can only draw some preliminary observations. First, many IHAC students were not really interested in their subject of study, as they had been assigned to work on it in the first place irrespective of their personal interests. In the 1980s and 1990s, the Chinese higher education system still followed the old practice in the early People's Republic, under which the universities assigned majors to students based on their performance in the college entrance examinations; personal interest played only a minor role in the decision process.[131] Job prospects in the humanities were considered to be poor. Many students regarded it as the last choice for a college major. Yet since only a tiny portion of college applicants could eventually find a place at college, many had to accept any assigned major, including studying ancient world history.[132] Students found it difficult to develop a genuine interest in a major that was not their first choice. As William Brashear later recalled, students at IHAC in ancient language courses such as ancient Greek and Latin were similar to students of Latin everywhere who were "disinterested, unmotivated, lackadaisical" and often "openly [voiced] their resentment and antagonism."[133]

Second, opening up to the world has had mixed effects on the study of ancient world history. On the one hand, it introduced new ideas, methods, and sources to Chinese historians. On the other hand, in adopting "new paradigms" of research, scholars realized how far China's academic research had been left behind by its counterparts in the West. In order to catch up, teachers at IHAC set unrealistically high expectations for their students. In the 1990s, students, many of whom were still struggling with daily English conversation skills, had to take courses on ancient languages and cultures in English. They were also expected to gain a command of reading German and French.[134] They complained about the heavy schedule of study. More importantly, what did they have to gain from making herculean efforts to study "dead" languages like Egyptian hieroglyphs and Babylonian cuneiforms?[135]

---

[131] Students could apply for the opportunity to study one of only a few majors before the exams. However, most students wanted to study science, technology, engineering, and business, and universities were only able to accept a limited number of students for each of these majors. This meant that many students who had not achieved the highest scores were "adjusted" to less popular majors such as philosophy, literature, and history.

[132] For instance, in the late 1980s, some of the twenty-five students at the IHAC had been forced to give up on their first choice in choosing a major. Brashear, "Classics in China," 75.

[133] Brashear, "China Update 1997," 84.   [134] IHAC News (January 25, 1988): 2–3.

[135] IHAC News (January 25, 1988): 3.

Lin Zhichun's generation was different. For them, there were some intellectual incentives for studying ancient world history; the party *demanded* that historians reinforce Marxist ideology and historical materialism was an essential part of this. There was plenty of work to do, both in meeting this demand and in working around it. From the debates on the AMP to the discussions on city-states, world historians contributed to the discussion of key issues in historical studies. As this concern disappeared from the research agendas of the new generation, it led to a decline in the sense of relevance. This is the third reason for the crisis in the field.

One may consider this shift in research focus as a positive change for the field. After all, Chinese historians of the ancient world began to publish their works in leading journals outside China. They chose highly specialized topics and conducted meticulous research.[136] Yet, by doing so, they lost interest in some issues regarding master narratives of the world.[137] These professional historians quickly forgot and largely overlooked the works of earlier generations of world historians such as Zhou Weihan, Lei Haizong, Tong Shuye, and Lin Zhichun. At the same time, the anti-Eurocentric stance of the previous generation softened as an increasing number of scholars received an education in the West and published their work in English or German through Western-based academic journals and publishing organizations. As a result, scholars have observed an ironic resurrection of Eurocentrism in contemporary historians' works.[138] The history of world civilizations has increasingly become the history of the civilizations of the "Great Powers."[139] In a disaggregated

---

[136] To just name a few examples, Wu Yuhong, "Rabies and Rabid Dogs in Sumerian and Akkadian Literature," *Journal of the American Oriental Society* 121, no. 1 (2001): 32–43; Gong Yushu, "Die mittelbabylonischen Namen der Keilschriftzeichen aus Hattusa und Emar," *Zeitschrift für Assyriologie* 85, no. 1 (1995): 47–57; Huang Yang and Fritz-Heiner Mutschler, "Rome and the Surrounding World in Historical Narratives from the Late Third Century BC to the Early First Century AD," in *Conceiving the Empire: China and Rome Compared*, ed. Fritz-Heiner Mutschler and Achim Mittag (Oxford: Oxford University Press, 2008), 88–111.

[137] The drift away from "critical inquiry," as Gloria Davies identifies, was driven by increasing marketization as well as a "publish-or-perish" mentality among professional scholars. Davies, *Worrying about China*, 7.

[138] Xu, "Reconstructing World History in the People's Republic of China since the 1980s," 329–334; Spakowski, "National Aspirations on a Global Stage," 475–495. For instance, some historians have complained about the lack of research interest in "peripheral" or "minor" civilizations such as the study of the ancient Hittite Empire. This used to be a main research track at IHAC but it has now disappeared into thin air.

[139] When the IHAC was created in the 1980s, Hittitology was one of four majors. Today, however, only a handful of scholars in China still conduct research on the subject. In a review article in 2011, Li Zheng, a Hittitologist at Peking University, lamented the state of the field. See, Li Zheng, "Shijieshi yihuo shi daguo shi? Shijie wenming shi yihuo shi daguo wenming shi?: cong jinnian lai wenshi de guonei ban youguan zhuzuo zhong

history of the ancient world that neglects communication and exchange among civilizations, a "comprehensive and systematic narrative of the birth of human civilization and its development" has become only an empty promise.[140]

In analyzing the development of the field during the final two decades of the twentieth century, we can draw two tentative conclusions in this chapter. First, the gradual abandonment of the Marxist paradigm in historical studies, as reflected in the debates on the AMP, "Labor Created Man," and ancient city-states, broke the theoretical consensus among scholars in the field and increased the scale of scholarly exchange. Second, along with the continuing development of professionalization, the new generation of scholars in this field, some of whom studied abroad, have devoted themselves to empirical studies and have chosen highly specialized topics; to some extent, this has weakened the ties of ancient world history to other fields, especially ancient Chinese history. To be sure, both reasons presented in this chapter are circumstantial, as if the decline of the field was only caused by scholars in the field. However, in the Conclusion, I place the changes that took place in the field within the wider context of historiographical, social, and ideological development in twentieth-century China.

de shijie shanggushi bufen tanqi" ["History of World" or "History of Great Powers"? "History of World Civilizations of the World" or "History of Civilizations of Great Powers"?: From the Point of View of Ancient World History in Chinese Monographs and Textbooks; original title in English)], *Xi'nan daxue xuebao* [Journal of Southwest University] 37, no. 4 (July 2011): 201–209.

[140] Li, "Shijie shi yihuo shi daguo shi," 209.

Conclusion: World History and the Value of the Past

On March 25, 2017, Liu Ruiling attended the civil servant examinations in the municipality of Lüliang in Shanxi, after she graduated from a master's program in world history. She did an outstanding job and made it to the second round of interviews. Only 5 candidates out of 200-plus applicants achieved this goal. While she was getting ready for the next step, she found out that the Personnel Department of the municipal government had forfeited her candidacy. It accused her of "filling out false information" in her application as the job was advertised for students majoring in "history" instead of "world history." "World history," the municipal government thinks, is not "history."[1]

This incident provoked heated discussions in China's online forums and social media venues. It continues to point to a profound challenge in twentieth-century Chinese historiography: the growing tensions between world and national (in other words, Chinese) histories. Although world historians over the course of the twentieth century attempted to bring a world-historical perspective to the ordinary Chinese people, many of them today still assume that only "national" history is relevant to them. World history is not "Chinese."

In this concluding chapter, I first offer an overview of the changing conception of world history in China. I do so through a survey of four generations of historians whose collective efforts led to the establishment of world history as a professional field in teaching and research over the course of the twentieth century. To be sure, each generation faced profound changes in Chinese society, culture, and politics. Yet all of them were attempting to help the Chinese people come to a better understanding of their country's position in the world. In the opening decades of the twenty-first century, the end result is not what they would have wished to

---

[1] "Shanxi Lüliang shiye danwei zhaokao yin zhiyi: shijieshi busuan lishixue?" [The examination in Lüliang, Shanxi, provokes controversy: world history is not counted as history?] *Zhongguo qingnian bao* [Chinese youth daily], June 6, 2017, www.chinanews.com/sh/201 7/06–09/8246254.shtml (accessed June 27, 2017).

see. The formation of this antagonistic relationship between world history and national identity, as Liu Ruiling's story exhibits, marks a revival in nationalistic views among the populace.

Yet this book is not just a story of struggles and failures. It is rather a celebration of the past achievements in world-historical studies in China in light of the rising global-historical scholarship in the twenty-first century. Over the course of the last century, world historians in China have been engaged in some central issues in the formation of global historiography, including, but not limited to, how to reconcile the temporal tensions between ancient and modern, how to overcome the spatial gaps between East and West, and how to combat ethnic biases both domestically and internationally. In response to these questions, they have not only developed long-term views in world-historical writing to transcend the confines of modern nation-states but also tested alternative frameworks to challenge the Eurocentrism in Western historiography. In doing so, they have exposed some false assumptions in Western views of the non-Western world. By taking their critique of "classical antiquity" as an example, I conclude the book and reiterate one of its central arguments; that is, the study of world history in twentieth-century China is a valuable legacy for historians across the world to reconstruct a more egalitarian view of history in the twenty-first century.

World history seeks to transcend national boundaries in understanding the common human past. In North America, some scholars define world history as the study of "connections within the global human community."[2] Contemporary historians view their task as seeking connections across national, ethnic, racial, and religious boundaries in their study of history. By the same token, world-historical studies call for a holistic (or, in William McNeill's word, "ecumenical") view in history writing. The latter is particularly useful in the context of current globalization processes that expand people's understanding of their sense of belonging beyond the past, narrowly defined ethnic, national, and cultural boundaries. It has the potential to cultivate a global awareness among future generations.[3]

In China, world history as a historical concept has had a multiplicity of interpretations over the course of the twentieth century, of which the most common include *waiguo shi* (foreign history), *xiyang shi* (Western

---

[2] Manning, *Navigating World History*, 3.

[3] World historians have long pointed to world history as a dominant factor in shaping global identity. See William McNeill, "Mythistory, or Truth, Myth, and History, and Historians," *American Historical Review* 91, no. 1 (1986): 1–10; Jerry Bentley, "Myth, Wagers, and Some Moral Implications of World History," *Journal of World History* 16, no. 1 (2005): 53.

history), and *shijie shi* (world history). In contrast to some research that insists that only *shijie shi* accounts for world history, in this book I adopt a more liberal view, believing that the past works on *waiguo shi* and *xiyang shi* are significant assets in China's world-historical tradition as well.

World history as a concept evolved over time in China. In the late nineteenth and early twentieth centuries, Chinese translators and foreign missionaries introduced world history as a Western historical genre into the country (sometimes via Japan). They loosely translated it as "foreign history" (*waiguo shi*) or "Western history" (*xiyang shi*). Occasionally, they used today's standard translation "*shijie shi*." As seen in *An Outline of Western History*, these early writers might not have directly covered Chinese history but China was almost a constant reference in their world-historical works. The gap between national and world histories was not emphasized. Following this tradition, historians in the Republican period continued to refer to world history as "foreign" or "Western" histories in contrast to the rise of "national history" (*benguo shi*) in the wake of national historical curriculum reforms. Only in the 1950s, under the Soviet influence, did Chinese historians start to commonly refer to world history as *shijie shi*.

The dominant view in China today is that world history is "the history of the integrated world" (*shijie zhengti de lishi*), to which Wu Yujin offered the most authoritative definition in the 1980s.[4] According to him, world history is about synthesis, and the task in world-historical studies should include efforts in both vertical and horizontal dimensions, as world history results from the interaction of these two historical developments.[5] The horizontal dimension is an interaction of diverse modes of production that transforms social formations across space. The vertical refers to the "objective" progression of economic productivity over time. Accordingly, connections gradually emerge from isolated regions, bridging previously dispersed entities with the end result of an integrated world.[6] This view of synthesis emphasizes connections and interactions among human communities. It has gained wide support and influence. At the end of the twentieth century, one scholar confidently concluded that

---

[4] Wu, "Shijie lishi," 1.

[5] For more on Wu Yujin and his contribution to world-historical studies in China, see Xu, "Reconstructing World History in the People's Republic of China since the 1980s," 329–334.

[6] Wu, "Zongxu," in *Shijieshi*, 9–10.

world history, as the history of the integrated world, had reached a consensus among world historians in China.[7]

It is certainly important to study the formation of global society through connections and interactions. Yet such a definition reminds us of the slippery slope of historical teleology. In other words, if we only focus on integration in historical studies, it might lead us to the unintended consequence of overlooking the value of earlier stages of development. For instance, some scholars in China claim that the integration of the world only took place in the sixteenth century, which offers a contested historical question,[8] is the history of the world prior to the sixteenth century part of world history? Such conceptions of world history present serious problems for Chinese historians of the ancient world whose research rarely extends beyond the sixteenth century.[9]

If scholars choose not to question the strong gap between "ancient" and "modern" inherent in this conception, scholars of the ancient world are left to struggle with the significance of their research subjects. For one, they have to come to terms with the conventional view that the study of the ancient world is knowledge "both ancient and foreign." Liu Jiahe, a leading ancient world historian, observes the state of the field, commenting, "People usually assume that the content of ancient world history (especially under the condition that its study does not include ancient Chinese civilization and only includes ancient foreign civilizations) is distantly separated from our present day by space and time and holds almost no relevance between people and events of that time and those of ours."[10] As such, for many historians, true "world history" did not appear before the sixteenth century;[11] the history of the world before the sixteenth century is only "a prehistory" to world history.[12]

Like the temporal divide between ancient and modern, artificial boundaries such as national, regional, and continental continue to set

---

[7] Hu Suping, "Shijie lishi xueke dingwei qianyi" [A preliminary discussion on the position of the world history discipline], *Shijie lishi* [World history], no. 3 (1999): 89.

[8] Wu, "Zongxu," in *Shijieshi*, 22–23.

[9] Scholars have begun to challenge the past assumption that global integration was a European intervention. An increasing number of scholars believe that Europeans, rather than randomly creating networks of communications and connections themselves, actually adopted and adapted the indigenous communication systems that existed prior to the European dominance of world communication. See, for instance, C. A. Bayly, "'Archaic' and 'Modern' Globalization in the Eurasian and African Arena, ca. 1750–1850," in *Globalization in World History*, ed. A. G. Hopkins (New York: W. W. Norton, 2002), 45–72.

[10] Liu and Liao, *Shijie gudai wenmingshi yanjiu daolun*, 22.

[11] Liu Jiahe, "Ruhe lijie zuowei shijieshi de gudaishi" [How to understand ancient history as world history], Supplement, *Shijie lishi* [World history], S1 (2008): S287–S292.

[12] Yu Jinyao, "Shijie lishi yu shijieshi xueke dingwei" [Defining world history and its discipline], *Shixue yuekan* [Historiography monthly], no. 10 (2009):83.

"East" experiences apart from the "West." Chinese world historians, like Lei Haizong, have long questioned spatial constructs like "nation-states" as the framework for historical inquiry. Yet many Chinese scholars today still treat world history as "foreign history," that is to say, the history of the outside world, reserving China as a special case. Taking the extant structures in the discipline within the Chinese higher education system as an example, scholars in the field regard world history by and large as the lump sum of national histories. It is further divided into thirty-three subfields, which include the histories of primitive society, the ancient, medieval, modern, and contemporary worlds, and general history. Other subjects include Japanese, Indian, Egyptian, US, Canadian, Russian, British, French, German, Italian, Spanish, and Australian history, as well as regional histories such as African (North African, Saharan and South African, and South African federal), Asian (Southeast Asian, South Asian, Central Asian, and West Asian), American (ancient American civilization, Latin American), European (West European, East European and North European), and Oceanic histories.[13] Based on this categorization, all foreign national histories have become "world history." Likewise, any scholar studying the history of a foreign country is considered a "world" historian.[14] The majority of articles published in *World History*, the leading academic journal on world-historical studies in China, examine non-Chinese, national histories.[15]

Alongside the temporal gap and the spatial difference is the issue of identity. This is evident in claims made by some world historians in China. They believe that world history in China should be written in a "Chinese" way. The former director of the World History Institute at the Chinese Academy of Social Sciences, for instance, called for Chinese world historians to "speak our own words, write our own books, and create our own academic trend – the China School" of world-historical studies.[16] This sentiment is embodied in a uniquely Chinese practice of world history, as it may well be; but it also reflects the deep tensions between local and global identities that confront many Chinese scholars, as they face the pressure to maintain a nationalistic standpoint, while engaging in a subject whose content is considered to be not "Chinese."

---

[13] Citied in Zhang Jian, "Lun shijie shi xueke nei de sanji xueke huafen" [On the division of third-level disciplines within the field of world history], *Guangzhou shehui zhuyi xueyuan xuebao* [Journal of Socialist college in Guangzhou] 21, no. 2 (2008): 76.

[14] Sachsenmaier, *Global Perspectives on Global History*, 235.

[15] For a short introduction on the role of the journal *Shijie lishi* in world-historical studies in China, see *Zhongguo shijie lishixue 30 nian*, 4.

[16] Wu Yin, "Shijieshi de xueke dingwei yu fazhan fangxiang" [The role and developmental direction of the world history discipline], *Shijie lishi* [World history], no. 1 (2003): 7.

This paradox creates intense psychological tension among world historians, as fully documented in the earlier chapters of this book.

Like anywhere else in the world, these challenges in world-historical studies persist in China. In seeking solutions, we need to return to the historical roots of these problems. As such, in this book I offer a survey of the development of the discipline of world history in China, with a special focus on the contested legacy of ancient world history. Compared to national histories or the history of the modern world, ancient world history in China remains a small and increasingly isolated field. Yet, precisely because it is small, its development offers us a controllable dataset by which to establish an overview of the historiographical development in China over the entire twentieth century; it is isolated, which begs the question of why modern intellectuals are becoming less interested in the study of ancient pasts. Only in the narrow field of ancient world history do the significant debates on temporality, spatiality, and national identity in world history simultaneously and fully unfold.

Owing to the complex nature of these problems, we need to address them from multiple angles. For one, in this book, I have examined the cultural, social, and political contexts that shaped the trajectory of the field's development from an "outside" perspective. A bird's-eye view exposes the patterns of change in twentieth-century Chinese historiography through one central thread, professionalization. This process institutionalized the historical field, implemented state regulations and standardization of history education, reconfigured leadership within the academic community, and fostered the development of individual and group autonomy in the professions. In doing so, it exerted a profound and lasting impact on the discipline of world history. To analyze this influence, I have documented the lived experiences of four generations of world historians in this book. Scholars from each generation, as I observe, adopted a different position regarding the professionalization of modern Chinese historiography.

The first generation is primarily represented by Zhou Weihan, alongside Zhang Heling, Wang Shunan, Kang Youwei, and Liang Qichao. As members of the gentry, they wrote about world history in the late Qing period. Prior to the emergence of professionalized historical practice, these world history writers were amateur historians. Many of them wrote under the influence of the intellectual debates of late imperial China, especially that on the Classical Studies (*jingxue*). Within the framework of neo-Confucianism, they were keen to explore new ideas from the West (sometimes indirectly via Japan) and sought to structure their work between two worlds. Therefore, their writings represent an intriguing intellectual dialogue between the Chinese tradition and

Western modernity. This fluidity spurred the development of an incipient global consciousness, which gave birth to the early Chinese works on ancient world history, illustrated in *An Outline of Western History*.

The second generation, exemplified by Lei Haizong, alongside Wu Mi, Hu Shi, Gu Jiegang, He Bingsong, and Chen Hengzhe, represented a coming-of-age among Chinese professional historians. Educated at the newly reformed Chinese universities or at reputable institutions abroad, they worked in professional and autonomous higher education institutions. In research carried out in the 1920s–1930s, they followed higher professional standards and insisted on keeping an objective view in historical studies. As a pioneer in world-historical studies, Lei adopted a critical view of the Chinese cultural tradition and participated in the development of the discipline of world history. Despite their pursuit of objectivity, influenced by the rising threat of a Japanese invasion, many historians supplanted objective views of history to nurture Chinese identity and citizenship in a context of national crisis. Such betrayal of professional standards in the service of nationalism was an unfortunate development in Chinese intellectual history but it in fact was the social and political setting in which we must understand the development of world history as a subfield of professional historical studies.[17]

As scholars often point out, the modernization project in China had taken place in the Republican period in an intense way but often on a very limited scale. The same was true of the process of historical professionalization, largely conceived of as part of Chinese modernization efforts. Despite rapid development in some urban institutions like Peking and Tsinghua Universities, the social structure of the fledgling field was small. As a result, knowledge production remained in the hands of a small number of established scholars; and a large number of second- and third-tier intellectuals (many of which were young in the 1940s) had little opportunity to flourish – or to effect change – within such a system.

Some of those scholars emerged at the vanguard of the third generation of world historians in the early People's Republic, among them Tong Shuye and Lin Zhichun. Tong was a part-time teacher and Lin was a little-known professor. The new communist government's radical attempts to control historical knowledge production, however, offered a rare opportunity for Tong and Lin, and others of this generation, to recast the Chinese intellectual tradition. No matter how compliant they were as professors at the newly established socialist education centers (Shandong University and Northeast Normal University), Tong and Lin

[17] Fan, "Gu Jiegang and the Creation of Chinese Historical Geography," 193–218.

both endorsed communism and turned against the second generation. They were pioneers in their application of historical materialism to world-historical studies. Ultimately, they played prominent roles in establishing the professional subfield of world history under the *jiaoyanshi* system. Their close relationship to the state, however, bred distrust, leading colleagues to deride them as communist ideologues, while casting aspersions on their scholarship. Such entanglement between history and politics became the "original sin" of world history in China and contributed to its marginalization from the broader field of historical studies.

With the reform and opening up of China to the West, scholars increasingly found opportunities for intellectual discussion and debate. As a result, many contemporaries, including Lin, began to shed their unwavering support for Marxist historiography. Despite abandoning the Marxist paradigm, old theoretical concerns melded with limited intellectual freedom to give birth to interesting, if contradictory, dialogues in world history. These debates adopted the "old" topics from the earlier periods and transformed into a new global consciousness.

Members of the most recent generation were shaped by their post-Maoist education. Taking the Institute for the History of Ancient Civilizations (IHAC) as an example, scholars enjoyed greater freedom to study abroad and acquire advanced skills in ancient languages. While attempting to "embrace the world," they increasingly viewed their research as less relevant to past debates in the field. Becoming highly specialized, their research topics increasingly lost sight of major issues in historical scholarship. Specialization has now created difficulties and challenges for the field of world history, particularly against the backdrop of the emergent Chinese market economy and increasing professionalization. As elsewhere, scholarship of the mostly "foreign and ancient" world is considered of little value in a neoliberal market economy. In a sense, the challenging condition in which world history finds itself in China illustrates a broader issue in the modern conception of national identity within a global context.[18] As such, a further look into the past writings of these world historians in twentieth-century China will provide us with useful insights for the rethinking of these fundamental issues in Chinese and world historiography.

Indeed, in this book I have exhibited the process by which national history has gradually hijacked the dominant mode of historical thinking in Chinese historiography. This started to unfold from the opening of the twentieth century, though not without struggles. As national historians

---

[18] Victor Davis Hanson and Jean Heath, *Who Killed Homer?: The Demise of Classical Education and the Recovery of Greek Wisdom* (New York: Free Press, 1998), xxv.

take the formation of the modern Chinese nation-state as the *telos* of their writing of history for granted, Chinese historians of the ancient world often see the world from very different perspectives. They are less concerned with nation-statism, as their research does not cover the formative era of the modern nation-state. Hence, they have explored alternative models to national history. Lei Haizong in the Republican period, Lin Zhichun in the 1980s and 1990s, and, to an extent, Zhou Weihan at the opening of the twentieth century have tested the concept of civilization/culture as the central focus of history. In the early People's Republic, Marxist historians such as Lin Zhichun and Tong Shuye repressed their own nationalist emotions and tested the modes of economic production as global stages of historical development.

In contrast to the popularly held belief that China offers a unique case study in world history, Chinese ancient world-historical scholarship has consistently demonstrated that all civilizations (or cultures) share certain fundamental characteristics based on the common nature of humanity. This is the consensus on which the field was established. In the early twentieth century, Zhou Weihan claimed, "Peoples of the East and West are alike, for their intellects are the same." By the 1950s, Chinese world historians proclaimed that all human societies had to follow the same universal stages of development. In the 1980s, Lin Zhichun and his contemporaries staunchly defended the notion that East and West had a shared common developmental trajectory during the debate on the nature of "Asiatic societies." In the 1990s, they proposed the idea of classical antiquity as a global stage in ancient history.

Yet this consensus is fragile and vulnerable, especially when it is in conflict with some popular ideas that are embedded within Eurocentrism. For the latter, its most celebrated manifesto is the idea of Oriental Despotism. Deeply rooted in the European intellectual tradition, this is a cultural essentialist view of the East in the West. In spite of its mutiple variations, it positions the East as a backward and stagnant society in contrast to a progressive and dynamic West. World historians in China were keenly aware of this globally circulated concept and chose to respond to it at various stages in the development of the field. At the opening of the twentieth century, Zhou Weihan, for instance, questioned whether or not the religiously based ideological systems in the West could guide the future, praising the humanistic tradition in Chinese Confucianism. In the Republican period, Lei Haizong criticized linear world-historical narratives in the West, suggesting that the Western culture was lacking a self-regenerating capability and its decline was inevitable. In the 1980s, Lin Zhichun questioned whether despotism was the dominant theme for Asian history, arguing that democracy was not a Western monopoly. Seeing history through the longue durée, they exposed the fundamental flaw in this idea of Western historical superiority: the stretching of the temporary ascendency of Europe as the end product of world history.

The polemical nature of world historiography in China is a reflection of the scholarly sensitivity concerning the discourse of cultural difference. In this book, more specifically, I offer further examples of Chinese scholars' critiques of the Eurocentric biases in the Western historiography of world history. Even in the earliest days, Chinese scholars recognized that the mostly Eurocentric works in translation were not suitable for Chinese audiences. In 1898, Liang Qichao, for instance, angrily pointed to the Eurocentrism in Western world history even prior to its formation as a discipline in China, saying, "Westerners are arrogant, believing that only they own the world." Therefore, they often recorded "the ups and downs of one race, the Aryans, after their westward migration, and incorrectly call it the world."[19] In the 1960s, Wu Yujin again vehemently protested, "Western historiography holds as a deep, firm, and unmovable idea that Europe is the center of the world." Seeing modern European historiography as the worst case of Eurocentrism, he claimed, "Modern world historians in the West have inherited all the parochialisms of their ancient predecessors."[20] Although recent scholarship indicates that the study of world history in China has not fully shed this Eurocentric influence, past critiques of Eurocentrism in the Chinese scholarship of ancient world history are still useful, as they raise cultural awareness in the post–Cold War era.[21]

Identifying this regional bias, Chinese historians developed alternative spatial perspectives to the study of world history. For instance, in 1960 Zhou Gucheng, famous for his 1948 world history textbook, stressed the significance of West Asia in world history. He explained the geographical contour of "xiya" (West Asia), which included the entire area west of the Pamir Plateau and the Indus River, east of Asia Minor and the Tigris River, south of the area between the Caspian Sea and the Aral Sea, and north of the Persian Gulf and the Arabian Sea. He then placed this region

---

[19] Liang Qichao, "Dongji yuedan" [Short comments on Japanese books], in *Yinbinshi heji* [Complete collection from the Yinbing Studio] (Beijing: Zhonghua shuju, 1989). The essay was first published in 1896.

[20] Wu Yujin, "Shidai he shijie lishi: shilun butong shidai guanyu shijie lishi zhongxin de butong guandian" [Times and world history: A preliminary treatise on different perspectives centering on world history at different times], *Jiang- Han luntan* [Jiang-Han forum], no. 7 (1964): 45.

[21] Dorothea A. Martin, "China: Finding a Place for Itself in Modern World History," *The History Teacher* 28 (1995): 149. Han Zhihan, "Zhong-Xi zhiwai bie you dongtian" [Beyond China and the West there is another world], *Ershiyi shiji shuangyue kan* [Twenty-first century bimonthly] 65, no. 6 (2001): 120. Spakowski, "National Aspirations on a Global Stage," 475–495.

in the wider Afro-Asian world, in accordance with Chinese party leaders' agenda to situate China in opposition to Euro-America.[22] For Chinese scholars, the "re-Orient," to use Andre Gunder Frank's terminology, was an attempt to establish a comprehensive and systematic view of world history.[23] More importantly, without realizing the historical significance of West Asia, as Zhou contended and I concur, it is impossible to integrate China and Europe within the world-historical system.[24] As such, West Asia could replace Greece and Rome as the new center of world history. As a matter of fact, the recent revival in scholarly interests in the history of central Eurasia can be regarded as a pleasant development leading to a more globalized view in national, regional, and world-historical studies.

Following the shift in the spatial focus, world historians in China also took issue with the temporal dimension in the Eurocentric world history as well. They took antiquity to be a central concern in their research. Eurocentrism is based on the assumption that East and West have followed divergent paths of development since their earliest historical stages. The concept of antiquity, thus, played a critical role in formulating that difference. In Europe, for instance, Jack Goody has criticized Eurocentric scholars' attempts to construct "antiquity" as a period radically different from either its predecessor (the Bronze Age) or successor (the Modern Age). He further has challenged predominant scholarly presentations of Greek and Roman civilization as a unique foundation of modern society, especially regarding the invention of the modern liberal-democratic tradition.[25] Instead, as Goody suggests, the concept of antiquity is the "historical foundation of Euro-Asia dichotomy."[26]

Within the Chinese context, "antiquity" is also a problematic concept in world history. It is a criticism that has long existed in China. In the early twentieth century, for instance, world history writer Zhou Weihan sensed the ambiguity of the term. He argued that European Protestant historians coined this term for religious reasons. Centrally, they established AD 500, or the end of the Roman Empire, as the end of antiquity in order to portray AD 500–1500, when the Catholic Church was the dominant institution in Europe, as the historical "Dark Ages." This partisan conception made little sense to Zhou. Instead, he ended the first part of *The Outline of Western History* at AD 1, simply for the sake of convenience in organizing the book.

---

[22] This was clearly influenced by the Third World polemics of the early 1960s. For more on Chinese historians' view of the Third World, see Martin, *The Making of a Sino-Marxist World View*, 88–104.

[23] Andre Gunder Frank, *ReOrient: Global Economy in the Asian Age* (Berkeley: University of California Press, 1998).

[24] Zhou, "Lun Xiya gushi de zhongyao xing," 152–159.

[25] Jack Goody, *The Theft of History* (Cambridge: Cambridge University Press, 2006), 65.

[26] Goody, *The Theft of History*, 65.

Disbelief at the Eurocentric periodization of world history continued in Chinese historiography. By the 1930s, Lei Haizong offered a more outspoken critique of the term "antiquity." After debunking the mythical link between time, space, and national history, Lei focused on the Western origin of the term. If antiquity only referred to certain characteristics in European history, how could one apply it to Chinese historical development? Lei criticized European scholars like H. G. Wells for stretching this Eurocentric term to the history of the East. For him, this created confusions in world history.

Following the advent of the People's Republic, Chinese historians of the ancient world more readily accepted the term "antiquity," since Marxist historiographical theory applies the concept to the historical period dominated by the mode of slave production. Believing (or being forced to accept the belief) that world history follows a common trajectory, scholars suppressed public hostility to the term. Figures such as Tong Shuye and Lin Zhichun focused on the question of whether ancient societies in Asia had followed a unique path during this period. Scarcely mentioned in Marx's works, the ambiguous term "Asiatic mode of production" (AMP) offered an alternative to the teleological Stalinist five-stages model of universal history. Pairing the AMP with the slave-owning or feudal stage in European history, historians such as Lin Zhichun defended the linear and teleological view of Marxist historiography.

After the loosening of ideological control in China following Mao's death, historians became increasingly critical of the Eurocentrism embedded in Marxist historiography. In the 1980s, debates over the AMP gradually split: from subtle revisions to open challenges, scholars gradually abandoned Marxist frameworks. Lin Zhichun proposed introducing a "global classical age" as a stage in world history, placing Chinese and Western civilizations on an equal footing.

The study of modern Chinese scholarship of world history illustrates a century-long criticism of the concept of "antiquity" as a relic of Eurocentrism. This critique also points to other problems in modern historiography, namely the simplistic and teleological understanding of world-historical development and the dominance of national history over other historiographical genres. Given the increased contemporary, cross-cultural contact, it is both significant and timely to rehabilitate the historiographical value of ancient world history in China from their efforts of placing China within both a global space and a historical time.

In his seminal work on the demise of the Chinese Confucian tradition, Joseph Levenson put forth a hypothesis on Chinese intellectual history. He suggested that liberalism failed as a historical choice in modern China because of its inability to integrate with Chinese national culture. In contrast, Marxism was able to better balance the relationship between Chinese national tradition and foreign knowledge.[27] As a result, it secured a dominant position in guiding the Chinese revolution. Although one has to be aware of Levenson's underlining assumption of the cultural difference between China and the West, his theory focuses on a significant contribution of Marxism – it offered a way, however flawed, of integrating China with the world.[28]

In the 1990s, the Chinese historian Liu Jiahe examined the theoretical foundations of world history, reflecting on the relationship between East and West in world history. Writing from a tradition that is heavily indebted to Marxist historical materialism, he regarded world history as a concept that registers two layers of meaning: of the globalization in the physical world and of the concept formation in historiography. The common nature of humanity made communications and exchanges possible. Thus, globalization took place in the physical world. Subsequently, it is historians' task to record this process at the conceptual level. This started as a process of subtraction in which they turned historical specifics into general concepts. Using Marxist terminology, he called this a process of *Aufhebung* (sublation). The mission of world-historical writing at this stage was to identify common features across the globe. Yet, as the process of abstraction reached its highest level, the content of world history shrank, which necessitated the second stage of world-historical writing. World historians substantiated abstract ideas with specifics. In Liu's words, this process progressed from similarity back to dissimilarity. He thus believed that the development of world historiography was a self-propelling cycle, in which the dynamics of world-historical study was a pendulum swinging between specification and generalization.[29]

This dialectical analysis recognizes the significance of the double process of world-historical writing. World history as a means of knowledge production gained its popularity in China at the opening of the twentieth century. In developing a master narrative for world history, early generations of world historians attempted to establish a consensus on the common nature of humanity between China and the West. From neo-Confucianism to cultural history, they were testing ways in which to prove

[27] Joseph Levenson, *Confucian China and Its Modern Fate: A Trilogy* (Berkeley: University of California Press, 1968), 1: 141.
[28] Prasenjit Duara, "History and Globalization in China's Long Twentieth Century," *Modern China* 34, no. 1 (2008): 157.
[29] Liu Jiahe, "Lishi de bijiao yanjiu yu shijie lishi" [Comparative historical study and world history], in *Shixue, jingxue yu sixiang, zai shijieshi beijing xia duiyu Zhongguo gudai lishi wenhua de sikao* [Historiography, classicism and thought: Reflections on ancient Chinese history and culture in the context of world history] (Beijing: Beijing shifan daxue chu-banshe, 2005), 1–10.

this cross-cultural equality. By the 1950s, it became the special mission of Marxist historiography, seeking to integrate disjunctive histories into a cohesive global narrative. Liu defined this as the first stage in the world-historical study. Naturally the goal of the second stage of the development of world history is to deconstruct the general framework of commonality and to substantiate it with historical variables. Yet one has to wonder to what extent historical continuity plays out in this historiographical transition. Some contemporary Chinese scholars carelessly dismiss the Marxist historiographical legacy and break with this continuous link in the evolution of world-historical studies.[30] The field has thus encountered great difficulty in determining how to integrate China's past within scholarship of the globalized world.

Not surprisingly, given China's political and economic transition, Marxism as a dominant political ideology has become less relevant in the civic discourse in the twentieth-first century. With the rise of China's economic might in the global marketplace, it seems that the Chinese government is asserting a new role in the international society. From the Belt and Road Initiative to the constant references to China as a "mighty country" (daguo), a strong chauvinistic, nationalist view seems to play an upper hand among Chinese policy-makers.[31]

This change calls for world historians to renew their engagement with some fundamental issues in humanities. In the age of globalization, they need to construct a more diverse and egalitarian global community by referencing the shared experiences of humanity's collective past. A new consensus on a common humanity that transcends nationalist sentiments and ethnic centrisms is in order, and this consensus, as documented in this book, has been a far cry from the legacy of the Chinese studies of world history of the twentieth century. Thus, reexamining this legacy offers valuable lessons for historians today.

Over the course of the past century, Chinese world historians engaged in various conversations, discussions, and debates on the theoretical inventions in historical studies. From the neo-Confucian humanism of the late Qing era to the cultural nationalism of the Republican period and the historical materialism of the People's Republic, theories, however flawed, as they appear to be, were critical in shaping the common focus of research for scholars who command various skills in their own areas of expertise. Amid the heated debates, some of the most creative ideas germinated. Taking the discussion on the AMP as an example, from attempts to clarify

[30] Wang Xuedian, "'Lishi yu xianshi' guanxi wenti de zai jiantao" [Rethinking the issue of the relationship between "history and reality"], Shandong shehui kexue [Social science in Shandong], no. 8 (2004): 5–8.
[31] Spakowski, "National Aspirations on a Global Stage," 485–490.

the ambiguities in orthodox Marxist theory in the 1950s, it gradually evolved into collective efforts to transform a Eurocentric concept into a new foundation for global history during the last two decades of the twentieth century. To be sure, one has to be cautious of not losing the historical specificities in theoretically enriched conversations like this. Yet world historians today need to maintain a sharp theoretical awareness, which is a significant legacy of Chinese world-historical studies.

Equally significant, another aspect of world-historical studies in China is Chinese historians' renewed, though admittedly oftentimes frustrated, efforts to include the longue durée in the writing of the history of the world. At the opening of the twenty-first century, a body of rich and exciting literature follows the "spatial turn." From Linda Colley's *The Ordeal of Elizabeth Marsh* to Dominic Sachsenmaier's *Global Entanglement of a Man Who Never Traveled*, global historians have asked innovative questions about how globalization took place as individual lived experiences either through physical travels or conceptual exchanges.[32] Yet, as a field of scholarly inquiries, global history prioritizes the spatial dimension over the temporal one.[33] In other words, while there are many excellent studies on the integration of the world, the surveys of long-term developments over historical time seem to have fallen out of fashion.

It is true that some of the earlier discussions of the longue durée in Chinese studies of world history are flawed, with ethnic biases and even nationalistic chauvinism. For instance, Lei Haizong's adoption of Oswald Spengler's cultural history was charged with strong nationalist emotions and written in a time of national crisis. Lin Zhichun also recycled this concept to replace historical materialism and fell on the same path to academic nationalism.[34] Yet these avid discussions of historical time through concepts such as "ancient," "Asiatic," and "feudal" have helped us to rethink how Eurocentric biases were embedded in the popular temporal regimes in world historiography. Is the rhythm of world history simply about a dynamic, progressive West versus a stagnant, backward

---

[32] I am grateful to Dominic Sachsenmaier who offered me the opportunity to read his book manuscript before its formal release. Sachsenmaier, *Global Entanglements of a Man Who Never Traveled: A Seventeenth-Century Chinese Christian and His Conflicted Worlds* (New York: Columbia University Press, 2018); Linda Colley, *The Ordeal of Elizabeth Marsh: A Woman in World History* (New York: Anchor, 2008). For a discussion of the "spatial turn," see Matthias Middell and Katja Naumann, "Global History and the Spatial Turn: From the Impact of Area Studies to the Study of Critical Junctures of Globalization," *Journal of Global History* 5, no. 1 (2010): 149–170.

[33] For the authoritative account of the "spatial turn" in global historiography, see Middell and Naumann, "Global History and the Spatial Turn."

[34] Arif Dirlik, "Confounding Metaphors, Inventions of the Word: What Is World History For?" in *Writing World History, 1800–2000*, ed. Benedikt Stuchtey and Eckhardt Fuchs (Oxford: Oxford University Press, 2003), 91–133.

East? Do historians have to divide world-historical development into teleological stages such as the tripartite framework of ancient, medieval, and modern or the five stages of economic modes of production from slavery to communism according to European experiences and predictions? Is Western liberal democracy the end point of humankind's ideological evolution in history? These are critical questions that Chinese world historians have been debating intensely. Their works offer us alternative views to transcend the cultural biases both temporally and spatially in the writing of world history for the future.

Back in China, the twenty-first century opened with the state pouring money into world-historical studies. Like nowhere else in the world, world historians in China are constantly finding new opportunities despite the heavy price of state censorship and intervention under the party regime. New research centers and professional journals sprang up overnight. For instance, both *Quanqiushi pinglun* (*The Global Historical Review*) based in Beijing and *Shijie lishi pinglun* (*The World Historical Review*) based in Shanghai offer exciting opportunities for scholars not only in China but also across the world to publish innovative research outcomes and introduce the latest global scholarship. Meanwhile, the Chinese Scholarship Council provided generous scholarships for Chinese graduate students and scholars to study aboard and even obtain foreign degrees insomuch as the Boxer Indemnity Scholarship did in the Republican period. More importantly, the latest editions of the national textbooks for high school history courses indeed follow a more integrated approach to include both Chinese history and world history within a single narrative.

Despite these developments, I conclude this book by reminding the reader that world historians today are still working under the same social and political structures that were implemented in the early People's Republic. The Soviet-influenced system of the teaching and research unit remains in place, along with the national think tank, the Chinese Academy of Social Sciences, and its branch organization, the World History Institute, which are still issuing guidelines for structural changes in the field. The journals *Lishi yanjiu* (*Historical research*) and *Shijie lishi* (*World history*) remain by far the most authoritative platforms in China. The subtle influence of these social and political institutions on the production of world-historical knowledge is thus a significant factor that one cannot overlook. After all, world historians in China remain state-employees working under the government-supervised socialist workplaces, and the tensions between state interventions and intellectual pursuits of autonomy have yet to be reconciled.

As such, in this book I situate modern Chinese approaches to ancient world history within a dynamic relationship between the globalization process and the nation-building project of the twentieth century. I show that the global circulation of historical concepts and the professionalization of the historical discipline together justified undertaking world history in a local context. The appropriation of the knowledge of world history in the local context enabled Chinese world historians to transform their studies in order to better serve China. Therefore, by locating the Chinese past within a global context or finding relevance of the global past in the Chinese context, particularly through discourses differing from Eurocentrism or Orientalism, the past study of world history in China remains an important legacy for historians today to further develop a more nuanced and integrated thesis in global history.

One last note: On completion of this book, I was introduced to the grandson of the first protagonist of this book, Zhou Weihan. In the spring of 2019, the retired music professor lived in New York City. He and his family graciously agreed to meet me despite his deteriorating health. He was ninety-six years old. I missed the opportunity, however, due to a scheduled trip to China. That fall he passed away. This old gentleman, as seen in Figure 6, was Professor Chou Wen-chung (1923–2019), whom Dun Tan called "the only one who could share a very deep knowledge of the traditions of China, but also bring us into a completely new world." Aside from Tan himself, who won an Oscar for his score to *Crouching Tiger, Hidden Dragon*, this "us" also refers to Chou's other students such as Bright Sheng, the recipient of a MacArthur Foundation Fellowship (the so-called genius grant) and Zhou Long, a Pulitzer Prize winner. As Tan said, Chou built "a dream" for them, one of bridging Eastern and Western cultures through music. Looking back, as I neared the completion of this book, I could not help but believe that this dream did not begin with Chou but was formed a century ago by those aspiring Chinese intellectuals of his grandfather's generation. They started the enterprise to write a history that was to transcend cultural chauvinism and embrace a belief in a common humanity.

To end this book, I quote a few lines from Chou's obituary in the *New York Times*:

Chou Wen-chung, a composer, teacher and cultural diplomat who taught a coterie of celebrated and award-winning Chinese composers and who tended to the legacy of Edgard Varèse, the linchpin of American modernism, died on Friday at his home in Manhattan. He was 96.

. . .

For much of Mr. Chou's career, composition took a back seat to other responsibilities. He was an assistant to Varèse and edited his compositions. He also created new channels of cultural diplomacy, chiefly through the Center for U.S.-China

Figure 6 Portrait of Chou Wen-chung. Photo Credit: Kiersten Chou, Spiralis Music Foundation

Arts Exchange, which he founded in 1978 and which helped bring stars of Western classical music like Luciano Pavarotti and Isaac Stern to China.

And Mr. Chou taught composition to a cohort of students at Columbia University, many of whom had grown up in China in the scorched artistic landscape of the Cultural Revolution and would go on to invigorate the new-music scene in both China and America . . .

. . .

Until the end of his life Mr. Chou lived in the West Village townhouse that had belonged to Varèse, with a portrait of the composer scowling down from a wall. The house was filled with antiques, musical instruments from around the world and framed samples of Mr. Chou's own calligraphy.

That art form was the key to his own compositions. The composer Lei Liang, who edited a Chinese edition of Mr. Chou's writings, recalled a question Mr. Chou loved to lob at students: When is a line not a line?

"If you think of a line that is drawn with a pencil or a pen, it is almost an absurd question," Mr. Liang said. "But if the line is drawn with a brush, it's of course not just a line: It's emotion, it's expression, it encompasses dimensions, even counterpoint. And he essentially made himself into a calligrapher with sound."[35]

[35] "Chou Wen-chung, 96, Leading Chinese Composer and Calligrapher in Sound," *New York Times* (October 31, 2009), B 15.

List of Characters

Ai Siqi	艾思奇
Bunmeiron no Gairyaku	文明論之概略
Cai Yuanpei	蔡元培
[Chai] Xiaoying	[柴]曉穎
Changzhou	常州
Chen Boda	陳伯達
Chen Hengzhe	陳衡哲
Chen Mengjia	陳夢家
Chen Minzhi	陳敏之
Chen Shoupeng	陳壽朋
Chen Tongxie	陳同燮
Chen Yinke (also, Yinque)	陳寅恪
Chen Zhihua	陳之驊
Cheng Fangwu	成仿吾
Cheng Hao	程灝
Cheng Yi	程頤
Chiang Kai-shek (Jiang Jieshi)	蔣介石
Chongqing	重慶
Chou, Wen-chung	周文中
Cui Lianzhong	崔連仲
Dagong bao (Ta Kung Pao; also *L'Impartial*)	大公報
Dai Jitao	戴季陶
Dai Naidie (aka Gladys Yang)	戴乃迭
Danwei	單位
Dao	道
Daxia daxue (Daxia University)	大夏大學
Deng Tuo	鄧拓
Deng Xingbo	鄧星伯
Di	狄
Diguo	帝國
Ding Weiliang (aka W. A. P. Martin)	丁韙良
dizhu zhi	地主制
Dongbei shifan daxue (Northeast Normal University)	東北師範大學
Du Zhengsheng	杜正勝
Feng Guangshi (Zhongzi)	馮光適(仲梓)
Feng Xiaopeng (Dansheng)	馮斅彭(聃生)

Feng Yuanjun	馮沅君
fengjian	封建
Fukuzawa Yukichi	福澤 諭吉
Geng Danru	耿淡如
Gong Yingyan	龔纓晏
Gong Yushu	拱玉書
Gong Zizhen	龔自珍
gonghe guo	共和國
Gongli	公理
Gu Jiegang	顧頡剛
Gu Zhun	顧准
Guangming ribao	光明日報
Gudai chengbang shi yanjiu	古代城邦史研究
gudai shi	古代史
Gui-Mao xuezhi	癸卯學制
Guo Moruo	郭沫若
Guo Songtao	郭嵩濤
Gushi bian	古史辨
Han Jing Tao (Jingtao)	韓井濤
Hanyi shijie xueshu mingzhu	漢譯世界學術名著
He Bingdi (Ping-ti Ho)	何炳棣
He Bingsong	何炳松
He Lin	賀麟
He Shanzhou	何善周
He Zhaowu	何兆武
He Ziquan	何茲全
Heshang	河觴
Hongqi	紅旗
Hou Wailu	侯外盧
Hu Feng	胡風
Hu Sheng	胡繩
Hu Shi	胡適
Hua Gang	華崗
Huang Jiade	黃嘉德
Huang Xianfan	黃現璠
Huang Yang	黃洋
Huang Yunmei	黃雲眉
Itō Hirobumi	伊藤博文
jiti beike	集體備課
Jia Lanpo	賈蘭坡
Jian Bozan	翦伯贊
Jiang Mengyin	蔣孟引

Jiang Qing	江青
Jiang Tingfu	蔣廷黻
jiaoyanshi (teaching and research unit)	教研室
Jin Yufu	金毓黼
Jingji yanjiu suo	經濟研究所
Jingshi	經世
Jingshi wenshen	經世文社
Jingshi xueshe	經世學社
Jingxue	經學
jiti beike	集體備課
Juan	卷
Kang Sheng	康生
Kang Youwei	康有為
Katō Hiroyuki	加藤弘之
Kong Fanyu	孔繁霱
Lei Haizong	雷海宗
Li Fengbao	李鳳苞
Li Helin	李何林
Li Zehou	李澤厚
Liang Ji	梁濟
Liang Qichao (Rengong)	梁啟超 (任公)
Liang Shuming	梁漱溟
Liang Sicheng	梁思成
Liang Zongdai	梁宗岱
lin gongsheng	稟貢生
Lin Lezhi (Young John Allen)	林樂知
Lin Tongji	林同濟
Lin Zhichun (aka Rizhi)	林志純 (日知)
lingzhu zhi	領主制
Lishi yanjiu	歷史研究
Liu Chonghong	刘崇鋐
Liu Jiahe	劉家和
Liu Qige	劉啟戈
Liu Ruiling	劉瑞玲
Liu Simu	劉思慕
Liu Wenpeng	劉文鵬
Lu Ding	陸定
Lu Kanru	陸侃如
Lu Maoju	盧茂榘
Lu Qiaonan (Zhenhua)	盧喬南 (振華)
Lü Simian	呂思勉
Lu Xiaoman	陸小曼

Lu Xun	魯迅
Lu Yao	路遙
Lüliang	呂梁
Luo Changpei	羅常培
Ma Peizhi	馬培之
Man	蠻
Mao Zhaoxi	毛昭晰
Mei Yibao	梅貽寶
Menghe	孟河
mixin	迷信
Nankai daxue (Nankai University)	南開大學
Okamoto Kansuke (Gangben Jianfu)	岡本監輔
Pei Wenzhong	裴文中
Qian Xuantong	錢玄同
Qian Zhongshu	錢鐘書
Qianlong	乾隆
Qing shilu	清實錄
Ren Hongjun	任鴻雋
Rizhi (see Lin Zhichun)	日知
Rong	戎
sandai	三代
Shang	商
Shang Yue	尚鉞
shanggu shi	上古史
Shangshu	尚書
Shenbao	申報
Shen Congwen	沈從文
Shen Shiyuan	瀋士遠
Shi Yamin	史亞民
Shiji	史記
Shijie gudai wenming shi zazhi	世界古代文明史雜誌
Shijie lishi	世界歷史
shijie shi	世界史
Shijie shuju	世界書局
shizi	士子
sijian	私見
Siyi biannian	四裔編年
Sun Furu	孫甫儒
Sun Peiliang	孫培良
Suzhou	蘇州
Tan Sitong	譚嗣同
Tang Xiaowen	唐曉文

Tao Xisheng	陶希聖
Tong Shuye	童書業
Tu Ji	屠寄
Uliyanov Andrey Iosifovich	烏里諾·安德烈·約瑟夫維奇
waiguo shi	外國史
wanshi zhi yan	萬世之言
Wang Dunshu	王敦書
Wang Guowei (Jing'an)	王國維 (靜安)
Wang Shunan	王樹枏
Wang Xingyun	王興運
Wang Xun	汪洵
Wang Zhifang	王志方
Wang Zhongluo	王仲犖
Wang Zhongmin	王重民
wanguo	萬國
Wei Yuan	魏源
Wenhui bao	文匯報
Wenshizhe	文史哲
Wu Changshuo	吳昌碩
Wu Dakun	吳大琨
Wu Fuheng	吳富恆
Wu Han	吳晗
Wu Jingchao	吳景超
Wu Jinglian	吳敬璉
Wu Mi	吳宓
Wu Yujin	吳於廑
Xi'nan shifan xueyuan (Southwest Teachers College)	西南師範學院
Xia	夏
Xiang Da	向達
Xiao Difei	蕭滌非
xing	性
Xing Gongwan	邢公畹
Xinhua ribao	新華日報
Xishi gangmu	西史綱目
xiya	西亞
Xu Zhimo	徐志摩
Xue Fucheng	薛福成
Xue Shaohui	薛紹徽
Yan Fu	嚴復
Yan Liangxun	嚴良勛

Zhou Enlai	周恩來
Zhou Gucheng	周谷城
Zhou Weihan (Xueqiao)	周維翰 (雪樵)
Zhou Yiliang	周一良
Zhu Huan	朱寰
Zhu Jiahua	朱家驊
Zhu Xi	朱熹
Zhu Ziqing	朱自清
zhudao	主導
zhujiao	助教
zhuquan zai min	主權在民
Zhushu jinian	竹書紀年
ziyou zhiye zhe	自由職業者
Zongli Yamen	總理衙門
Zou Youheng	鄒有恆
Zuozhuan (The Commentary of Zuo)	左傳

Bibliography

Archival Sources

IHAC News. IHAC Library Collection, Northeast Normal University, Changchun, Jilin, China.

Jianguo yilai zhongyao wenxian xuanbian [Select collection of important sources since the founding of the People's Republic of China]. 20 vols. Beijing: Zhongyang wenxian chubanshe, 1992.

Lin Zhichun Personnel Archives [*Lin Zhichun geren dang'an*]. Northeast Normal University Archives. Changchun, Jilin, China.

Neibu cankao [Internal reference].

Shanghai Municipal Archives. Shanghai, China.

Zhonggong zhongyao lishi wenxian ziliao huibian [The collection of important historical documents of the CPC], Vol. 30. Los Angeles: Zhongwen chubanwu fuwu zhongxin, 2010.

Zhonggong zhongyang wenjian xuanji [The selected documents by the Central Committee of the CCP] (*ZZWX*) (October 1949 to May 1966). 50 vols. Beijing: Renmin chubanshe, 2013.

Zhongguo xiandai zhexueshi ziliao huibian [A collection of documents on the modern history of Chinese philosophy] (*ZXZZH*). ed. Zhong Limeng and Yang Fenglin. 5 series. 47 vols. Shenyang: Liaoning daxue zhexuexi, 1981.

Zhonghua minguo shi dang'an ziliao huibian [A collection of archival documents on the Republic of China] (*ZMSDZH*). 100 vols. Nanjing: Jiangsu guji chubanshe, 1994.

Primary Sources

Ai Siqi. "Nali zhao genju?" [Where to find the basis?]. *Hongqi* [Red flag], no. 4 (July 16, 1958): 13–16.

Anon. "Daoyan" [Preface]. In *Shijie tongshi: Shanggu bufen* [A general history of the world: Part on antiquity], ed. Qi Sihe. Beijing: Renmin chubanshe, 1973.

Anon. "Jinshi shijieshi zhi guannian" [The concept of world history in modern times]. *Dalu bao* [The continent], no. 2 (January 8, 1903): 21–27.

Avdiev, V. I. "Gudai dongfang shi xulun" [Preface to the history of the ancient Orient], trans. Rizhi [pseud., Lin Zhichun]. *Lishi jiaoxue* [History pedagogy], no. 6 (1954): 6–12.

Book of Dates; Or, Treasury of Universal Reference: Comprising a Summary of the Principal Events in All Ages, From the Earliest Records to the Present Time, With Index of Events. London: Charles Griffin and Company, 1866.

Bridgman, Eliza J. Gillett, ed. *The Pioneer of American Missions in China: The Life and Labors of Elijah Coleman Bridgman.* New York: Anson D. F. Randolph, 1864.

Chen Boda. "Zai Mao Zedong tongzhi de qizhi xia" [Under the flag of Comrade Mao Zedong]. *Hongqi* [Red flag], no. 4 (July 16, 1958): 1–12.

Chen Hengzhe. "Chen Hengzhe xiansheng yanshuo ci" [Speech by M. Chen Hengzhe]. *Beijing daxue rikan* [The daily journal of Beijing University], September 18, 1920.

"Lishi jiaoxue yu renlei qiantu" [History education and the future of humanity], *Chenbao qi zhounian jinian zengkan* [Supplement in celebration of *Chenbao*'s seventh anniversary], no. 7 (1925): 197–201.

Chen Hengzhe [Sophia H. Chen], *Xiyang shi* [History of Western countries]. Shanghai: Shangwu yinshuguan, 1926.

Chen Zen, Sophia H. [Chen Hengzhe], ed., *Symposium on Chinese Culture: Prep. for the 4th Biennial Conference of the Institute of Pacific Relations, Hangchow, Oct. 21 to Nov. 4, 1931.* Shanghai: Institute of Pacific Relations, 1931.

Cheng Fangwu. "Zhongguo Renmin daxue de jiaoyanshi gongzuo" [The work of the unit of teaching and research at Renmin University]. *Renmin jiaoyu* [People's education], no. 4 (1951): 11–12.

Chiang Kai-shek, *Zhongguo zhi mingyun* [The fate of China]. Chongqing: Zhongzheng shu ju, 1943.

Fukuzawa Yukichi, *Bunmeiron no gairyaku* [An outline of a theory of civilization]. Tokyo: Meiji 8 [1875].

Gu Jiegang. "1926 nian shikanci" [Dedication to the first issue of 1926], *Beijing daxue yanjiusuo guoxuemen zhoukan* [Division of national studies at the graduate school of Peking University weekly], 1937. Reprint.

"Dao Wang Jing'an xiansheng" [Mourning for Mr. Wang Jing'an], *Wenxue zhoubao* [Literature weekly], 5, no. 1 (1929): 1–11.

"*Fakan ci*" [Foreword]. *Yugong banyue kan* [Yugong biweekly] 1, no. 1 (March 1, 1934): 2.

Gu Jiegang dushu biji [Gu Jiegang's reading notes]. 15 vols. Taipei: Lianjing, 1990.

Gu Jiegang riji [Gu Jiegang's diaries]. 12 vols. Taipei: Lianjing, 2007.

ed. *Gushibian* [Debates on ancient history], Vol. 1. Shanghai: Shanghai guji, 1981.

"Liang Han zhouzhi kao" [Inquiry on the regional system of the two Han dynasties]. In "Cai Yuanpei xiansheng liushiwu sui qingzhu lunwen ji" [A festschrift for Mr. Cai Yuanpei's 65th birthday], special issue, *Guoli zhongyang yanjiuyuan lishi yuyan yanjiusuo jikan* [Bulletin of the Institute of History and Philology of the Academia Sinica] (1934): 855–902.

Guanyu yuanshi Jidujiao dui caichan he nulizhi de jige xin guandian [Several new perspectives on proto-Christian (conceptions of) property and slavery], trans. Yu Ke and Wu Shuping. Tianjin: History Department of Nankai University, 1988. (Unpublished source in IHAC library.)

Guo Songtao. *Guo Songtao riji* [The diaries of Guo Songtao]. Changsha: Hunan renmin chubanshe, 1980.

He Bingsong, "Xiandai xiyang guojia zhuyi yundong shilue" [A concise history of the nationalist movements of modern Western countries], in *He Bingsong wenji*, vol 2: 204–222.

He Bingsong *He Bingsong wenji* [Collected papers by He Bingsong], ed. Liu Yinsheng and Fang Xinliang. 5 vols. Beijing: Shangwu yinshuguan, 1996–1997.

He Gaoji. "Wo dui gudaishi yanjiu zhong jige wenti de kanfa" [My views concerning several questions in the study of ancient history]. *Wenshizhe* [Literature, history and philosophy], no. 9 (1956): 22–26.

Hu Shi, "Shiping suowei 'Zhongguo benwei wenhua de jianshe'" [A preliminary review of the so-called "reconstruction of China-centered culture"], *Dagong bao* [Ta Kung Pao] (Tianjin), March 31, 1935.

"Huadong qu gaoxiao yuanxi tiaozheng gongzuo shengli wancheng" [The victorious completion of the restructuring of the higher education units in East China], *Wenhui bao* [Wenhui Daily] October 30, 1952.

Jianguo yilai zhongyao wenxian xuanbian [Select collection of important sources since the founding of the People's Republic of China]. 20 vols. Beijing: Zhongyang wenxian chubanshe, 1992.

Jian Bozan. "Lishi kexue zhanxian shang liangtiao luxian de douzheng" [The struggle between two lines in the battlefront of historical science]. *Renmin ribao* [People's Daily], July 15, 1958.

Jin Yufu. *Jingwushi riji* [Diaries in the Jingwu Room]. Shenyang: Liaoshen shushe, 1993.

Lei Haizong. "Duandai wenti yu Zhongguo shi de fenqi" [The question of dividing history and the problems of periodization in Chinese history], *Qinghua daxue shehui kexue* (Social sciences at Tshinghua University) 2 (October 1936 to July 1937): 1–33.

"Duiyu daxue lishi kecheng de yidian yijian" [One suggestion on the college history curriculum]. *Duli pinglun* [Independent review], no. 224 (October 25, 1936): 7–12.

"Keluoqi de shixuelun: lishi yu jishi" [Croce on historiography: History and the recording of events]. *Shixue* [Historiography], no. 1 (1930): 221–232.

"Review of *The Outline of History*, by H. G. Wells." *Shixue* [Historiography], no. 1 (1930): 233–247. (Original title and text in English.)

[(Barnabas Hai-Tsung Lei]. "The Political Ideas of Turgot." PhD thesis, University of Chicago, 1927.

Lin Tongji. "Disanqi de Zhongguo xueshu sichao: xin jieduan de zhanwang" [The intellectual trend of the third period: Prospects for a new stage]. *Zhanguo Ce* [Strategies of the Warring States], no. 14 (1940): 2–16.

Lin Zhichun [Lin, C. C.] "China's Peasant Revolutions." *The China Weekly Review* 112, no. 6 (January 8, 1949): 144.

"The Kuo Min Tang and Chinese Dynasties." *The China Weekly Review* 112, no. 13 (February 26, 1949): 315–316.

"Nuli shehui zhi liangge jieduan yu liuge shiqi" [Two stages and six periods of slave society]. *Lishi jiaoxue* [History pedagogy], no. 3 (1953): 13–17.

"Shijing dili yanjiu" [A study of geography in the Book of Poetry]. *Jiaoyu yu wenhua (Fuzhou)* [Education and culture (Fuzhou)] 1, no. 1 (1945): 51–56.

"Women zai yanjiu gudaishi zhong suo cunzai de yixie wenti (ping Tong Shuye zhu 'Cong zudian zhidu yu lishu nongmin de shenfen tantao gu Balilun shehui de xingzhi')'" [A few problems in the study of ancient history (a critique of Tong Shuye's "Discussing the nature of ancient Babylonian society from the [angle of the] tenancy system and the social status of subordinate peasants")]. *Lishi yanjiu* [Historical research], no. 12 (1956): 1–27.

"Wenming zhi yuanshi" [The origins of civilizations]. *Dushu tongxun* [Reading newsletter], no. 148 (1948): 4–9.

"Yu Tong Shuye xiansheng lun Yaxiya shengchan fangfa wenti" [Discussing the Asiatic mode of production with Mr. Tong Shuye]. *Wenshizhe*, no. 2 (1952): 20–22.

Luoma nuli zhanyou zhi bengkui wenti yiwen ji [Collection of translated essays on the issue of the collapse of the Roman slavery system], ed. and trans. the editorial branch of *Lishi yanjiu* [Historical research]. Beijing: Kexue chubanshe, 1958.

Okamoto Kansuke [Gangben Jiangfu], *Wanguo shiji* [The record of world history]. n.p.: Huaguo tang, 1900.

Wanguo zongshuo [Complete survey of myriad countries]. In *Dunhuai tang yangwu congchao* [Various collected works on Western learning in Dunhuai Hall], ed. Zhang Shusheng. Hefei: 1884.

Pei Wenzhong and Jia Lanpo. *Laodong chuangzao le ren* [Labor created man]. Beijing: Zhonghua quanguo kexue jishu puji xiehui, 1953.

Sanshinian quanguo jiaoyu tongji ziliao, 1949–1978 [The statistics of national education during the past thirty years, 1949–1978] (Zhonghua renmin gongheguo jiaoyubu, 1979). In *Zhonggong zhongyao lishi wenxian ziliao huibian* [The collection of important historical documents of the CPC], Vol. 30. Los Angeles: Zhongwen chubanwu fuwu zhongxin, 2010.

Shijie gudaishi shiliao xuanji [Selection of sources in ancient world history], ed. Department of History of Beijing Normal University and the Department of History of Northeast Normal University. 2 vols. Beijing: Beijing shifan daxue, 1959.

Shu Shicheng. "Xinji bu gongping de ying chongxin ping" [Need to re-evaluate the unfair payment scale]. *Huadong shifan daxue xiaokan* [Magazine of East China Normal University], June 21, 1957.

Sun Dingguo. "Jielu Lei Haizong fan Makesi zhuyi de zhongzhong edu shoufa" [Exposing Lei Haizong's various pernicious anti-Marxist methods]. *Lishi yanjiu* [Historical research], no. 11 (1957): 28–30.

Tang Xiaowen. *Laodong chuangzao le ren* [Labor created man]. Beijing: Renmin chubanshe, 1972.

Tong Shuye. "Cong gudai Babilun shehui xingtai renshi gudai 'Dongfang shehui' de texing" [Understanding the special nature of ancient 'Oriental societies' from the social conditions of ancient Babylon]. *Wenshizhe*, no. 1 (1953): 42–49.

"Cong zudian zhidu yu lishu nongmin de shenfen tantao gu Babilun shehui de xingzhi" [Investigating the nature of ancient Babylonian society from the tenancy system and the social status of subordinate peasants]. *Lishi yanjiu* [Historical research] no. 5 (1956): 17–36.

"Guanyu Zhongguo gudai shehui xingzhi de wenti" [Concerning the question of the nature of ancient Chinese society]. *Wenshizhe*, no. 5 (1952): 39–42.

"Lun nuli zai Babilun de diwei he daiyu" [On the social status and treatment of slaves in Babylon]. *Xueshu yuekan* [Academic monthly], no. 5 (1957): 46–54; no. 6 (1957): 69–75.

"Lun Yaxiya shengchan fangfa" [On the Asiatic mode of production]. *Wenshizhe* 1, no. 4 (1951): 14–17.

Wang Shunan, *Taolu laoren suinian lu* [Yearly record of the old man under the Tao Hut]. In *Jindai shiliao biji congkan* [Series on modern historical materials collections: Miscellaneous notes]. Beijing: Zhonghua shuju, 2007.

Xila chunqiu [Annals of Greece]. In *Taolu congke* [Taolu serial] (Series No. 24). Lanzhou, 1905.

Xila xuean [Intellectual History of Greece]. In *Taolun kecong* (Series No. 21). Lanzhou: 1905.

Wu Dakun. "Zenyang cong zhengzhi jingji xue de jiaodu shang lai kaocha gushi fenqi wenti" [How to examine the question of periodization in ancient history from the perspective political economy]. *Lishi yanjiu* [Historical research] no. 10 (1956): 59–62.

Wu Jingchao, Yang Renpian, Lei Haizong et al. *Tudi gaige yu sixiang gaizao* [Land reform and thought transformation]. Beijing: Guangming ribao chubanshe, 1951.

Wu Mi. *Wu Mi riji* [Diaries of Wu Mi]. 10 vols. Beijing: Sanlian, 1998.

Wu Mi riji xubian [The continued collection of Wu Mi's diaries]. 10 vols. Beijing: Sanlian, 2006.

Xiao Ou, ed. "Zhongguo gushi fenqi wenti zuotan jilu" [Minutes of the symposium on the periodization of ancient Chinese history]. *Wenshizhe*, no. 1 (1955): 53–56.

Xie Yinchang, "Yancang nianshi" [Yearly history of Yancang]. In *Jindai renwu nianpu jikan* [Collected series on the nianpu of modern figures], Vol. 17. Beijing: Guojia tushuguan chubanshe, 2012.

Xue Fucheng. *Chushi Ying Fa Yi Bi siguo riji* [Diaries of visiting four countries: England, France, Italy and Belgium], ed. Zhong Shuhe. Changsha: Yuelu chubanshe, 1985.

Yang Renpian. "Yao zhongshi shijie shi" [On the need to pay attention to world history]. *Renmin ribao*, May 10, 1957.

Yang Xiangkui. "Gudaishi yanjiu zhong de jige wenti" [A few questions in the study of ancient history]. *Wenshizhe*, no. 6 (1956): 20–22.

Yun Yuding, *Yun Yuding Chengzhai riji* [Yun Yuding Chenzhai dairies]. 2 vols. Hangzhou: Zhejiang guji chubanshe, 2004.

"Zanxing kecheng biaozhun" [Provisional curriculum standards]. In *Zhongxiaoxue kecheng zanxing biaozhun* [Temporary standards for middle and primary school], ed. Jiaoyubu zhongxiaoxue kecheng biaozhun qicao weiyuan hui [Ministry of education committee on drafting elementary and high school curricula]. 3 vols. Shanghai: Qingyun tushu gongsi, 1930.

Zhao Lisheng. "Wo de chubu jiantao" [My preliminary self-examination]. *Wenshizhe*, no. 4 (1952): 30–33 (or 372–375).

Zhongguo benwei wenhua jianshe taolun ji [The collection on the discussions on the China-centered culture]. Taipei: Pamier shudian, 1980.

Zhongxiaoxue kecheng zanxing biaozhun [Temporary standards for elementary and high school curricula], ed. Jiaoyubu zhongxiaoxue kecheng biaozhun qicao weiyuan hui [Ministry of education committee on drafting elementary and high school curricula]. 2 vols. Shanghai: Qingyun chuban gongsi, 1930.

Zhou Weihan [pseud. *Xueqiao*]. *Xishi gangmu* [An outline of Western history]. Shanghai: Jingshi wenshe, 1901.

"Da wen" [Answers to questions]. *Gezhi xinbao* [Inquiry news], 7 (1898): 12–14.

"Zhou Xueqiao shishi" [Zhou Xueqiao's obituary], *Zhongxi yixue bao* [Journal of Chinese and Western medicine], no. 8 (1910): 4.

Secondary Sources

Alford, William. *To Steal a Book Is an Elegant Offense: Intellectual Property Law in Chinese Civilization*. Stanford: Stanford University Press, 1995.

Alitto, Guy. *The Last Confucian: Liang Shu-ming and the Chinese Dilemma of Modernity*. Berkeley: University of California Press, 1986.

Bailey, Anne and Josep Llobera. *The Asiatic Mode of Production: Science and Politics*. London: Routledge and Kegan Paul, 1981.

Bailey, Paul John. *Reform the People: Changing Attitudes towards Popular Education in Early Twentieth Century China*. Vancouver: University of British Columbia Press, 1990.

Bayly, C. A. "'Archaic' and 'Modern' Globalization in the Eurasian and African Arena, ca. 1750–1850." In *Globalization in World History*, ed. A. G. Hopkins, 45–72. New York: W. W. Norton, 2002.

Bentley, Jerry. "Myth, Wagers, and Some Moral Implications of World History." *Journal of World History* 16, no. 1 (2005): 51–82.

Biographic Dictionary of Chinese Communism, 1921–1965, ed. Donald W. Klein and Anne B. Clark. 2 vols. Cambridge, MA: Harvard University Press, 1971.

Biographic Dictionary of Republican China, ed. Howard L. Boorman and Richard C. Howard. 5 vols. New York: Columbia University Press, 1967.

Bol, Peter. *Neo-Confucianism in History*. Cambridge, MA: Harvard University Press, 2010.

Bourdieu, Pierre. "The Field of Cultural Production, or: The Economic World Reversed." *Poetics* 12, no. 4 (1983): 311–356.

Brashear, William. "China Update 1997." *The Classical Journal* 94, no. 1 (1998): 81–85.

"Classics in China." *The Classical Journal* 86, no. 1 (1990): 73–78.

Bray, David. *Social Space and Governance in Urban China: The Danwei System from Origins to Reform*. Stanford: Stanford University Press, 2005.

Brindley, Erica Fox. *Ancient China and the Yue: Perceptions and Identities on the Southern Frontier, c. 400 BCE–50 CE.* Cambridge: Cambridge University Press, 2015.

Brook, Timothy, ed. *The Asiatic Mode of Production in China.* Armonk, NY: M. E. Sharpe, 1989.

Brown, Jeremy and Paul Pickowicz, eds. *Dilemmas of Victory: The Early Years of the People's Republic of China.* Cambridge, MA: Harvard University Press, 2007.

Cao Juren. *Wo yu wo de shijie* [Me and my world]. Beijing: Renmin wenxue chubanshe, 1983.

Chakrabarty, Dipesh. *Provincializing Europe: Postcolonial Thought and Historical Difference.* Princeton: Princeton University Press, 2007.

Chan, Wai-keung. "Contending Memories of the Nation: History Education in Wartime China, 1937–1945." In *The Politics of Historical Production in Late Qing and Republican China,* ed. Tze-ki Hon and Robert Culp, 169–210. Leiden: Brill, 2007.

Chang, Hao. *Chinese Intellectuals in Crisis: Search for Order and Meaning (1890–1911).* Berkeley: University of California Press, 1987.

Chang, Peter M. *Chou Wen-Chung: The Life and Work of a Contemporary Chinese-Born American Composer.* Lanham, MD: The Scarecrow Press, 2006.

Cheek, Timothy. *Propaganda and Culture in Mao's China: Deng Tuo and the Intelligentsia.* Oxford: Clarendon Press, 1997.

Chen Dezheng. "Wan-Qing waiguo lishi kecheng yu jiaokeshu shulun" [A comprehensive survey of foreign history curricula and textbooks in late Qing]. *Lishi jiaoxue* [History pedagogy], 549, no. 8 (2008): 97–99.

Chen Hengzhe [Chen Nan-hua]. *Chen Hengzhe zaonian zizhuan* [Autobiography of a Chinese young girl], trans. Feng Jin. Hefei: Anhui jiaoyu chubanshe, 2006.

Chen Hengzhe, ed., *Zhongguo wenhua lun ji: 1930 niandai Zhongguo zhishi fenzi dui Zhongguo wenhua de renshi yu xiangxiang* [Symposium on Chinese culture: The understanding and imagination of Chinese culture among Chinese intellectuals in the 1930s], trans. Wang Xianming and Gao Jimei. Fuzhou: Fujian jiaoyu chubanshe, 2009.

Chen Jilong. "Changzhou jindai bufen lishi renwu minglu zhi er" [A partial list of people in the modern history of Changzhou: Part II]. In *Changzhou wenshi ziliao dijiu ji* [Historical and literary sources for Changzhou], Vol. 9. Changzhou: Changzhou wenshi ziliao weiyuanhui, 1989.

Chen Qineng, ed. *Jianguo yilai shijieshi yanjiu gaishu* [A survey of the study of world history after the founding of the PRC]. Beijing: Shehui kexue wenxian chubanshe, 1991.

Chen Zhihua. "Shijieshi yanjiu yu sige xiandaihua" [World-historical studies and the four modernizations]. *Shijie lishi* [World history], no. 5 (1979): 3–8.

Chen Zhongdan. "Beisong zhujiao de jianggao: Wu Mi jiao 'shijie gudaishi'" [Reciting teaching assistants' lecture notes: Wu Mi teaches "Ancient World History"]. *Nanfang zhoumo* [Southern Weekly] (Guangzhou, China), July 15, 2009.

Chiang, Yung-chen, *Social Engineering and the Social Sciences in China, 1919–1949.* Cambridge: Cambridge University Press, 2001.

"Chou Wen-chung, 96, Leading Chinese Composer and Calligrapher in Sound," *New York Times*, October 31, 2009, B 15.

Chow, Tse-tsung, *The May 4th Movement: Intellectual Revolution in Modern China*. Cambridge, MA: Harvard University Press, 1960.

Clinton, Maggie. *Revolutionary Nativism: Fascism and Culture in China, 1925–1937*. Durham, NC: Duke University Press, 2017.

Cohen, Paul. "The Asymmetry in Intellectual Relations between China and the West in the Twentieth Century." In *Ershi shiji de Zhongguo yu shijie lunwen xuanji* [Selected essays on China and the world in the twentieth century], Vol. 1, ed. Zhang Qixiong, 61–93. Taipei: Academia Sinica, 2001.

Discovering History in China: American Historical Writing on the Recent Chinese Past. New York: Columbia University Press, 1984.

Colley, Linda. *The Ordeal of Elizabeth Marsh: A Woman in World History*. New York: Anchor, 2008.

Costello, Paul. *World Historians and Their Goals: Twentieth-Century Answers to Modernism*. DeKalb: Northern Illinois University Press, 1993.

Croce, Benedetto. *Theory and History of Historiography*, trans. Douglas Ainslie, Vol. 4. n.p.: George G. Harrap and Co., 1921.

Cui Zhiyuan. "Bijiao lishi yanjiu de yige changshi: Gu Zhun *Xila chengbang zhidu pingshu*" [An attempt at comparative historical study: A review of Gu Zhun's *Greek City State System*]. *Dushu* [Reading], no. 4 (1984): 33–39.

Culp, Robert J. *Articulating Citizenship: Civic Education and Student Politics in Southeastern China, 1912–1940*. Cambridge, MA: Harvard University Asia Center, 2007.

"'Weak and Small Peoples' in a 'Europeanizing World': World History Textbooks and Chinese Intellectuals' Perspectives on Global Modernity." In *The Politics of Historical Production in Late Qing and Republican China*, ed. Tze-ki Hon and Robert Culp, 211–245. Leiden: Brill, 2007.

Day, Jenny Huangfu. *Qing Travelers to the Far West: Diplomacy and the Information Order*. Cambridge: Cambridge University Press, 2018.

Davies, Gloria. *Worrying about China: The Language of Chinese Critical Inquiry*. Cambridge, MA: Harvard University Press, 2007.

De Ste. Croix, G. E. M. *The Class Struggle in the Ancient Greek World from the Archaic Age to the Arab Conquests*. London: Duckworth, 1981.

Denton, Kirk. "The Hu Feng Group: Genealogy of a Literary School." In *Literary Societies in Republican China*, ed. Kirk Denton and Michel Hockx, 413–73. Lanham, MD: Lexington Books, 2008.

Di Cosmo, Nicola. *The Cambridge History of Ancient China: From the Origins of Civilization to 221 B.C.*, ed. Michael Loewe and Edward Shaughnessy. Cambridge: University of Cambridge Press, 1999.

Diakonoff, I. M., ed. *Early Antiquity*, trans. Alexander Kirjanov. Chicago: University of Chicago Press, 1991.

Dikötter, Frank. *The Age of Openness: China before Mao*. Berkeley: University of California Press, 2008.

The Discourse of Race in Modern China. Hong Kong: Hong Kong University Press, 1992.

Dirlik, Arif. "Confounding Metaphors, Inventions of the World: What Is World History for?" In *Writing World History, 1800–2000*, ed. Benedikt Stuchtey and Eckhardt Fuchs, 91–133. Oxford: Oxford University Press, 2003.

The Revolution and History: Origins of Marxist Historiography in China, 1919–1937. Berkeley: University of California Press, 1978.

Dodson, Michael. *Orientalism, Empire and National Culture: India, 1770–1880*. Cambridge: Cambridge University Press, 2007.

Dong Honggen, Zhai Huaiqiang, and Wang Yanping, "Menghe yipai de xueshu puxi ji yongyao guilü chutan" [A preliminary study of the intellectual genealogy of the Menghe School of Medicine and the common principles of their medical practice], *Guoji Zhongyi Zhongyao zazhi* [International Journal of Chinese Medicine] 34, no. 6 (June 2012): 481–484.

Dongen, Els van. *Realistic Revolution: Contesting Chinese History, Culture, and Politics after 1989*. Cambridge: Cambridge University Press, 2019.

Du, Chunmei. "Gu Hongming as a Cultural Amphibian: A Confucian Universalist Critique of Modern Western Civilization," *Journal of World History* 22, no. 4 (2011): 715–746.

Du Zhengsheng, *Zhoudai chengbang* [City-states in the Zhou dynasty]. Taipei: Lianjing, 1979.

Duara, Prasenjit. "The Discourse of Civilization and Pan-Asianism." *Journal of World History* 12, no. 1 (2001): 99–130.

"History and Globalization in China's Long Twentieth Century." *Modern China* 34, no. 1 (2008): 152–164.

Rescuing History from the Nation: Questioning Narratives of Modern China. Chicago: University of Chicago Press, 1995.

Dutton, Michael. *Policing Chinese Politics: A History*. Durham, NC: Duke University Press, 2005.

Elman, Benjamin. *Classicism, Politics, and Kinship: The Ch'ang-chou School of New Text Confucianism in Late Imperial China*. Berkeley: University of California Press, 1990.

From Philosophy to Philology: Intellectual and Social Aspects of Change in Late Imperial China. Los Angeles: UCLA Asian Pacific Monograph Series, 2001.

Engels, Friedrich. *The Part Played by Labour in the Transition from Ape to Man* [Anteil der Arbeit an die Menschwerdung des Affen]. 1st English ed. Moscow: Progress Publishers, 1934. (Original written in 1876. 1st German ed. In *Die Neue Zeit*, 1895–96.)

Fan, Xin. "The Anger of Ping-Ti Ho: The Chinese Nationalism of a Double Exile." *Storia Della Storiografia* (History of Historiography) 69, no. 1 (2016): 147–160.

"Gu Jiegang and the Creation of Chinese Historical Geography." *The Chinese Historical Review* 17, no. 2 (2010): 193–218.

Feng Chengbai. "Shixue dashi Lei Haizong xiansheng 1957 nian mengnan shimo" [A note on how the great historian Lei Haizong met with disaster in 1957]. *Lishi jiaoxue* [History pedagogy], no. 3 (2003): 11–15.

Fogel, Joshua A. "The Debates over the Asiatic Mode of Production in Soviet Russia, China, and Japan." *American Historical Review* 93, no. 1 (1988): 56–79.

Foucault, Michel. *Power/Knowledge: Selected Interviews and Other Writings 1972–1977*, ed. Colin Gordon, trans. Colin Gordon, Leo Marshall, John Mepham, and Kate Soper. New York: Pantheon Books, 1980.

Frank, Andre Gunder. *ReOrient: Global Economy in the Asian Age.* Berkeley: University of California Press, 1998.

Fung, Edmund S. *In Search of Chinese Democracy: Civil Opposition in Nationalist China, 1929–1949.* Cambridge: Cambridge University Press, 2000.

The Intellectual Foundations of Chinese Modernity: Cultural and Political Thought in the Republican Era. Cambridge: Cambridge University Press, 2010.

"Nationalism and Modernity: The Politics of Cultural Conservatism in Republican China," *Modern Asian Studies* 43, no. 3 (2009): 777–813.

Ge Zhaoguang. "The Evolution of a World Consciousness in Traditional Chinese Historiography," *Global Intellectual History*, 2020. https://doi.org/10.1080/2 3801883.2020.1738651 (accessed June 1, 2020).

Godley, Michael. "Politics from History: Lei Haizong and the Zhanguo Ce Clique," *Papers on Far Eastern History* 40 (September 1989): 95–122.

Gong Yingyan. "Guanyu 'laodong chuangzao ren' de mingti" [On the thesis "labor created man"]. *Shixue lilun yanjiu* [Historiography Quarterly], no. 2 (1994): 19–26.

"Rang women jiaota shidi de maixiang xinshiji: Zhili xingzou ji women de xueshu" ["Walking erectly" and our researches (original English title)]. *Shixue lilun yanjiu*, no. 1 (1996): 62–70.

Gong, Yushu. "Die mittelbabylonischen Namen der Keilschriftzeichen aus Hattusa und Emar." *Zeitschrift für Assyriologie* 85, no. 1 (1995): 47–57.

Goody, Jack. *The Theft of History.* Cambridge: Cambridge University Press, 2006.

Goossaert, Vincent. "1898: The Beginning of the End for Chinese Religion?" *Journal of Asian Studies* 65, no. 2 (2006): 307–336.

Graham, Hugh F. "The Significant Role of the Study of Ancient History in the Soviet Union." *The Classical World* 61, no. 3 (1967): 85–97.

Gray, G. F. S. *Anglicans in China: A History of the Zhonghua Shenggong Hui* (Chung Hua Sheng Kung Huei) (The Episcopal China Mission History Project). http://anglicanhistory.org/asia/china/cpscott/07.html

Grieder, Jerome. *Hu Shih and the Chinese Renaissance: Liberalism in the Chinese Revolution, 1917–1937.* Cambridge, MA: Harvard University Press, 1970.

Gu Chao. *Lijie zhongjiao zhi buhui: wo de fuqin Gu Jiegang* [Through successive disasters his determination was not extinguished: My father Gu Jiegang]. Shanghai: Huadong shifan daxue chubanshe, 1997.

Gu Jiegang and Liu Qiyu. *Shangshu jiaoshi yilun* [Correction, critique, and translation of the *Shangshu*]. Beijing: Zhonghua shuju, 2005.

Gu Zhun, *Xila chengbang zhidu: du Xila shi biji* [Greek city-state system: Notes from reading Greek history]. Beijing: Zhongguo shehui kexue chubanshe, 1982.

Guo Xiaoling. "Lei Haizong xiansheng yu ta de tida jingshen de lishi gangyao" [Mr. Lei Hai-zong and his great and intensive outline of history (original English title)]. *Anhui shixue* [Anhui historiography], no. 1 (2004): 17–21.

Han Minqing. "Shi shengwuxue wenti, haishi lishiguan wenti" [Is it a question of biology or historical view?]. *Zhexue yanjiu* [Philosophical studies], no. 4 (1995): 11–19.

Han Zhihan, "Zhong-Xi zhiwai bie you dongtian" [Beyond China and the West there is another whole world]. *Ershiyi shiji shuangyuekan* [Twenty-first century bimonthly] 65, no. 6 (2001): 119–121.

Hanfu [pseud.]. "'Zhanguo' pai de Faxisi zhuyi shizhi" [The true fascist nature of the "Zhanguo" clique]. In *Zhongguo xiandai zhexue shi ziliao huibian (disan ji disan ce): Zhanguo ce pai Faxisi zhuyi pipan* [Collection of materials for the history of modern Chinese philosophy, Vol. 3, Series 3: Critiques of the fascism of the Zhanguo ce Clique], ed. Zhong Limeng and Yang Fenglin, 1–5. Shenyang: Liaoning daxue zhexuexi, 1981–1983.

Hanson, Victor Davis and Jean Heath. *Who Killed Homer? The Demise of Classical Education and the Recovery of Greek Wisdom*. New York: Free Press, 1998.

He Bingdi [Ping-ti Ho]. *Dushi yueshi bashinian* [Eighty years of studying history and experiencing the world]. Guilin: Guangxi shifan daxue chubanshe, 2005.

He Zhaowu. *Shangxue ji* [School days]. Beijing: Sanlian, 2006.

He Ziquan. *Aiguo yi shusheng: Bashiwu zishu* [A scholar who loves his country: An autobiography at the age of eighty-five]. Shanghai: Huadong shifan daxue chubanshe, 1997.

Hon, Tze-ki. "From a Hierarchy in Time to a Hierarchy in Space: The Meanings of Sino-Babylonianism in Early Twentieth-Century China." *Modern China* 36, no. 2 (2010): 139–169.

Hon, Tze-ki and Robert Culp, eds. *The Politics of Historical Production in Late Qing and Republican China*. Leiden: Brill, 2007.

Hou Jianxin. "Zhongguo shijieshi yanjiu 50 nian" [Chinese world-historical studies of 50 years]. *Lilun yu xiandaihua* [Theory and modernization], no. 2 (2000): 16–17.

Hou Wailu. *Ren de zhuiqiu* [The tenacious pursuit]. Beijing: Shanlian shudian, 1985.

Hu Fengxiang. "Xiandai Zhongguo shixue zhuanye jigou de jianzhi yu yunzuo" [The organizational system and operation of modern Chinese historiography institutions]. *Shilin* [Forest of history], no. 3 (2007): 168–169.

Hu Sheng. "Lun fan lixing zhuyi de niliu" [On the counter-trend of anti-rationalism] and "Shi shengren haishi pianzi: Lun weixinlun zai shiji shenghuo zhong de biaoxian" [Are they saints or swindlers: On the implications of idealism in daily life]. In *Zhongguo xiandai zhexueshi ziliao huibian (disan ji, disan ce): Zhanguo ce pai Faxisi zhuyi pipan*, ed. Zhong Limeng and Yang Fenglin, 21–34. Shenyang: Liaoning daxue zhexuexi, 1981–1983.

Hu Shi. "Hu Shi koushu zizhuan" [An oral autobiography of Hu Shi]. In *Hu Shi wenji* [Hu Shi's collected writings], ed. Ouyang Zhesheng, Vol. 1. Beijing: Beijing daxue chubanshe, 1998.

Hu Shi wanglai shuxin xuan [Selected letters to and from Hu Shi]. 3 vols. Beijing: Zhonghua shuju, 1983.

Hu Suping. "Shijie lishi xueke dingwei qianyi" [A preliminary discussion on the positioning of the world history discipline]. *Shijie lishi* [World history], no. 3 (1999): 89–91.

Huang Kewu [Max K. W. Huang]. "Jiang Jieshi yu He Lin" [Chiang Kai-shek and He Lin], *Zhongyang yanjiuyuan jindaishi yanjiusuo jikan* [Bulletin of the Institute of Modern History, Academia Sinica] 67, no. 3 (2010): 17–58.

Huang Miantang. "Huainian Tong Shuye xiansheng" [Remembering Mr. Tong Shuye]. *Wenshizhe*, no. 6 (1998): 24–27.

Huang Yang and Fritz-Heiner Mutschler, "Rome and the Surrounding World in Historical Narratives from the Late Third Century BC to the Early First Century AD." In *Conceiving the Empire: China and Rome Compared*, ed. Fritz-Heiner Mutschler and Achim Mittag, 88–111. Oxford: Oxford University Press, 2008.

Iggers, Georg and Q. Edward Wang, with Supriya Mukherjee. *A Global History of Modern Historiography*. Harlow: Longman, 2008.

Ji Xianlin. *Liude shinian* [Ten years in Germany]. Beijing: Dongfang chubanshe, 1992.

Jiang Pei. *Zhanguo ce pai sichao yanjiu* [A study of the intellectual thought-tide of the Zhanguo Ce clique]. Tianjin: Tianjin renmin chubanshe, 2001.

Jiang Tingfu. *Jiang Tingfu huiyilu* [Memoir of Jiang Tingfu], trans. Xie Zhonglian. Taipei: Zhuanji wenxue chubanshe, 1979.

"Zhishi jieji yu zhengzhi" [The intellectual class and politics]. *Duli pinglun* 51 (1933): 15–19.

"Lun zhuanzhi bing da Hu Shizhi xiansheng" [On dictatorship and in reply to Mr. Hu Shizhi (Hu Shi)]. *Duli pinglu* 83 (1933): 2–6.

Jin Chongji, *Yi ben shu de lishi: Hu Qiaomu, Hu Sheng tan* Zhongguo Gongchandang de qishinian [The history of a book: Hu Qiaomu and Husheng on *The Seventy Years of the Chinese Communist Party*]. Beijing: Zhongyang wenxian chubanshe, 2014.

Jin Yufu. *Zhongguo shixueshi* [History of Chinese historiography]. Shanghai: Shangwu yinshu guan, 1957.

Jindaishi yanjiusuo Minguo shi yanjiushi and Sichuan shifan daxue lishi wenhua xueyuan [Republican-Period History Seminar of the Institute of Modern History at CASS and the School of Historical and Cultural Studies of Sichuan Normal University], ed. 1930 niandai de Zhongguo [China in the 1930s]. Beijing: Shehui kexue wenxian chubanshe, 2006.

Judge, Joan. *Print and Politics: "Shibao" and the Culture of Reform in Late Qing China*. Stanford: Stanford University Press, 1996.

Karl, Rebecca. *The Magic of Concepts: History and the Economic in Twentieth-Century China*. Durham, NC and London: Duke University Press, 2017.

Staging the World: Chinese Nationalism at the Turn of the Twentieth Century. Durham, NC: Duke University Press, 2002.

Kirby, William. "Engineering China: Birth of the Developmental State, 1928–1937." In *Becoming Chinese: Passages to Modernity and Beyond*, ed. Wen-Hsin Yeh, 137–160. Berkeley and Los Angeles: University of California Press, 2000.

"The Internationalization of China: Foreign Relations at Home and Abroad in the Republican Era," *The China Quarterly*, no. 150 (1997): 433–458.

Kong Lingping. "Shijie gudaishi yanjiu de xin chengguo" [New fruits of ancient world-historical studies]. *Lishi yanjiu* [Historical research], no. 1 (1980): 177–189.

Kramer, S. N. *From the Tablets of Sumer: Twenty-five Firsts in Man's Recorded History*. Indian Hills, CO: Falcon's Wing Press, 1956.

History Begins at Sumer: Thirty-Nine Firsts in Man's Recorded History. Garden City, NY: Doubleday Anchor Books, 1959.

Lazich, Michael. "Placing China in Its 'Proper Rank among the Nations': The Society for the Diffusion of Useful Knowledge in China and the First Systematic Account of the United States in Chinese." *Journal of World History* 22, no. 3 (2011): 527–551.

Leese, Daniel. "Mao the Man and Mao the Icon." In *A Critical Introduction to Mao*, ed. Timothy Cheek, 219–240. Cambridge: Cambridge University Press, 2010.

Legge, James. *The Chinese Classics with a Translation, Critical and Exegetical Notes, Prolegomena, and Copious Indexes: The She-king*, Vol. 2. London: Lane, Crawford & Company, 1871.

Lei Haizong. *Bolun shixue ji* [A collection of Lei Haizong's historiographical works], ed. Wang Dunshu. Beijing: Zhonghua shuju, 2002.

Lei Haizong, *Chinese Culture and the Chinese Military*, trans. George Fleming, intro. Xin Fan. Cambridge: Cambridge University Press, 2020.

Leung, Vincent S. *The Politics of the Past in Early China*. Cambridge: Cambridge University Press, 2019.

Levenson, Joseph Richmond. *Confucian China and Its Modern Fate: A Trilogy*, 3 vols. Berkeley: University of California Press, 1968.

Lewis, Mark Edward. *Writing and Authority in Early China*. Albany: State University of New York Press, 1999.

Lewis, Martin and Kären Wigen. *The Myth of Continents: A Critique of Metageography*. Berkeley: University of California Press, 1997.

Li, Huaiyin. *Reinventing Modern China: Imagination and Authenticity in Chinese Historical Writing*. Honolulu: University of Hawai'i Press, 2013.

Li Xiaoqian. *Xifang shixue zai Zhongguo de chuanbo, 1882–1949* [The spread of Western historiography in China, 1882–1949]. Shanghai: Huadong shifan daxue chubanshe, 2007.

Li Xueqin. "The Xia-Shang-Zhou Chronology Project: Methodology and Results." *Journal of East Asian Archaeology* 4, no. 1 (2002): 321–333.

Li Zehou. *Meixue sijiang* [Four lectures on aesthetics]. Beijing: Sanlian shudian, 1989.

Li Zheng. "Shijieshi yihuo shi daguo shi? Shijie wenming shi yihuo shi daguo wenming shi? – cong jinnian lai wenshi de guonei ban youguan zhuzuo zhong de shijie shanggushi bufen tanqi" ["History of World" or "History of Great Powers"? "History of Civilizations of World" or "History of Civilizations of Great Powers"?: From the Point of View of Ancient World History in Chinese Monographs and Textbooks; original title in English]. *Xi'nan daxue xuebao* [Journal of Southwest University] 37, no. 4 (July 2011): 201–09.

Liang Qichao. "Dongji yuedan" [Short comments on Japanese books], in *Yinbingshi heji* [Complete collection from the Yinbing Studio]. Beijing: Zhonghua shuju, 1989.

Liao Xuesheng. "*Xila chengbang zhidu* duhou" [After reading *System of the Greek City States*], *Shijie lishi* [World history], no. 4 (1984): 87–89.

"Guanyu Dongfang zhuanzhi zhuyi" [On oriental despotism]. *Shijie lishi* [World history], no. 1 (1980): 89–93, and 96.

"Weitefu de 'Dongfang zhuanzhi zhuyi' yu gudai Xila de lishi" [Wittfogel's "Oriental Despotism" and ancient Greek history]. *Shixue lilun yanjiu* [Historiography Quarterly] no. 1 (1992): 29–37.

"Zhongguo shijie gudaishi yanjiuhui juxing diyici daibiao dahui" [The first representative conference of the Chinese Research Association of Ancient World History]. *Shijie lishi* [World history], no. 6 (1979): 92.

Lin Zhichun [Rizhi], "Chengbang yu chengbang lianmeng" [City-states and city-state federations]. In *Gudai chengbang shi yanjiu* [Study of the history of ancient city-states]. Beijing: Renmin chubanshe, 1989.

"'Fengjian zhuyi' wenti (Lun Feudalism bainian lai de wuyi)" [Problems of the term "feudalism (*fengjian*)": An incorrect translation of the past one hundred years]. *Shijie lishi* [World history], no. 6 (1991): 30–41 and 125.

ed. *Gudai chengbang shi yanjiu* [Study of the history of ancient city-states]. Beijing: Renmin chubanshe, 1989.

"Lun Zhong-Xi gudian shi shang de 'heian shidai' wenti" [On the issue of an "Age of Darkness" in Chinese and Western classical history]. *Xushu yuekan*, no. 1 (1999): 68–74.

"Yuanshi qun wenti biannian tigang" [Outline for chronicling the primitive groups issue]. *Jilin shifan daxue xuebao* [Journal of Jilin Normal University], no. 2 (1973): 81–92.

Liu Guangyu. "Hua Gang yu *Wenshizhe*" [Hua Gang and (the journal) *Literature, History and Philosophy*], *Chuban shiliao* [Historical sources on publishing], no. 4 (2006): 4–11.

Liu Jiahe and Liao Xuesheng, eds. *Shijie gudai wenmingshi yanjiu daolun* [An introduction to the study of the history of ancient civilizations]. Beijing: Gaodeng jiaoyu chubanshe, 2001.

Liu Jiahe. "Lishi de bijiao yanjiu yu shijie lishi" [Comparative historical study and world history]. In *Shixue, jingxue yu sixiang, zai shijieshi beijing xia duiyu Zhongguo gudai lishi wenhua de sikao* [Historiography, classicism and thought: Reflections on ancient Chinese history and culture in the context of world history], 1–10. Beijing: Beijing shifan daxue chubanshe, 2005.

"Lun Heilaoshi zhidu" [On the Helot system]. In *Gudai de Zhongguo he shijie* [Ancient China and the world], 78–139. Wuhan: Wuhan chubanshe, 1995.

"*Rizhi wenji* xu" [Preface to the *Collected Works of Zhichun Lin* (original English title)], *Gudai wenming* [Journal of ancient civilizations] 7, no. 1 (January 2013): 2–6.

"Ruhe lijie zuowei shijieshi de gudaishi" [How to understand ancient history as world history]. Supplement. *Shijie lishi* [World history], S1 (2008): S287–S292.

Shixue, jingxue yu sixiang, zai shijieshi beijing xia duiyu Zhongguo gudai lishi wenhua de sikao [Historiography, classicism, and thought: Reflections on ancient Chinese history and culture in the context of world history]. Beijing: Beijing shifan daxue chubanshe, 2005.

"Wei wo xue shijie gudaishi yinlu de laoshi: Huainian Rizhi Lin xiansheng" [Memorial to Professor Lin Zhichun (original English title)]. *Gudai wenming*, no. 2 (April 2008): 2–4.

Liu, Jinyu. "Translating and Rewriting Western Classics in China (1920s–1930s): The Case of the Xueheng Journal." In *Receptions of Greek and Roman Antiquity in East Asia*, eds. Almut-Barbara Renger and Xin Fan, 91–111. Boston: Brill, 2018.

Liu Xincheng and Liu Wenming. "Zhongguo de shijieshi yanjiu liushi nian" [China's world-historical studies in the last sixty years]. *Lishi yanjiu* [Historical research] no. 5 (2009): 15–22.

Lu Caixia. "Qingmo Jing Jin yongyi wenti chutan" [A preliminary study of the problem of the "crooked doctors" in the Beijing and Tianjin areas in the late Qing dynasty]. *Zhongguo shehui lishi pinglun* [The Chinese review of social history] 8, no. 3 (July 2007): 128–148.

Lu Wenzhong. "Guanyu renlei qiyuan de jige wenti" [Several questions regarding the origins of humans]. *Jilin shifan daxue xuebao*, no. 2 (1978): 39–43.

Lu Yao and Hu Xiaozhong. "Tong Shuye zai Shandong daxue" [Tong Shuye at Shandong University]. *Shandong daxue bao* [Shandong University newspaper], February 25, 2009.

Luo Lie. "Nü fanyijia Xue Shaohui yu *Bashi ri huanyou ji* zhong nüxing xingxiang de chonggou" [Woman translator Xue Shaohui and the image of woman in *Around the World in Eighty Days*]. *Waiguo yuyan wenxue (jikan)* [Foreign languages and literature (quarterly)] 98, no. 4 (2008): 262–270.

MacFarquhar, Roderick. *The Origins of the Cultural Revolution*. New York: Columbia University Press, 1974.

MacFarquhar, Roderick and Michael Schoenhals. *Mao's Last Revolution*. Cambridge: Cambridge University Press, 2006.

Manela, Erez. *The Wilsonian Moment: Self-Determination and the International Origins of Anticolonial Nationalism*. Oxford: Oxford University Press, 2007.

Manning, Patrick. *Navigating World History: Historians Create a Global Past*. New York: Palgrave Macmillan, 2003.

Mao Zedong. *Lun renmin minzhu zhuanzheng* [On the people's democratic dictatorship]. Beijing: Renmin chubanshe, 1949.

Martin, Dorothea A. "China: Finding a Place for Itself in Modern World History." *The History Teacher* 28 (1995): 149–159.

The Making of a Sino-Marxist World View: Perceptions and Interpretations of World History in the People's Republic of China. Armonk, NY: M. E. Sharpe, 1990.

Marx, Karl. *A Contribution to the Critique of Political Economy.* Chicago: C. H. Kerr, 1904.

McNeill, William. "Mythistory, or Truth, Myth, and History, and Historians." *American Historical Review* 91, no. 1 (1986): 1–10.

Meisner, Maurice J. *Li Ta-chao and the Origins of Chinese Marxism.* Cambridge, MA: Harvard University Press, 1967.

Meng Zhongjie. "Shijieshi xueke fazhan 30 nian dashi ji (1978–2008) (shang)" [Chronicle of the 30-year development of the world history discipline (Vol. 1)]. *Lishi jiaoxue wenti* [Questions in world history pedagogy], no. 1 (2009): 105–110.

Middell, Matthias and Katja Naumann. "Global history and the spatial turn: From the impact of area studies to the study of critical junctures of globalization." *Journal of Global History* 5, no. 1 (2010): 149–170.

Mittler, Barbara. *A Newspaper for China?: Power, Identity, and Change in Shanghai's News Media, 1872–1912.* Cambridge, MA: Harvard University Press, 2004.

Mosca, Matthew. *From Frontier Policy to Foreign Policy: The Question of India and the Transformation of Geopolitics in Qing China.* Stanford: Stanford University Press, 2013.

Mühlhahn, Klaus. *Criminal Justice in China: A History.* Cambridge, MA: Harvard University Press, 2009.

Nedostrup, Rebecca. *Superstitious Regimes: Religion and Politics of Chinese Modernity.* Cambridge, MA: Harvard University Asia Center, 2009.

Ni Bo, Mu Weiming, and Zhang Zhiqiang, eds. *Jiangsu chuban dashi ji, 77BC to 1948* [Chronicle of major events in Jiangsu publishing, 77 BC to 1948]. Nanjing: Jiangsu renmin chubanshe, 1996.

Novick, Peter. *That Noble Dream: The "Objectivity Question" and the American Historical Profession.* Cambridge: Cambridge University Press, 1988.

Pepper, Suzanne. *Radicalism and Education Reform in Twentieth-Century China: The Search for an Ideal Development Model.* Cambridge: Cambridge University Press, 2000.

Perdue, Peter. *China Marches West: The Qing Conquest of Central Eurasia.* Cambridge, MA: Belknap Press, 2010.

Plumb, J. H. *The Death of the Past.* London: Macmillan, 1969.

Price, Don. "A Foreign Affairs Expert's View of Western History: Wang Shu-Nan 王樹柟." Paper prepared for delivery at the Twentieth-Ninth International Congress of Orientalists. Paris, July 16–22, 1973. (Unpublished paper.)

Qian Zhongshu. *Weicheng* [Fortress besieged]. Beijing: Renmin wenxue chubanshe, 1991.

Ravina, Mark. *To Stand with the Nations of the World: Japan's Meiji Restoration in World History.* Oxford: Oxford University Press, 2017.

Reed, Christopher. *Gutenberg in Shanghai: Chinese Print Capitalism, 1876–1937.* Vancouver: UBC Press, 2004.

Ren Hongjun Chen Hengzhe jiashu [Family correspondences by Ren Hongjun and Chen Hengzhe], ed. Qiangjiu minjian jiashu xiangmu weiyuanhui [Committee on the project to preserve private correspondences]. Beijing: shangwu yinshuguan, 2007.

Reynolds, Douglas. *China, 1898–1912: The Xinzheng Revolution and Japan.* Cambridge, MA: Council on East Asian Studies, Harvard University, 1993.

Rhodes, P. J. *A Commentary on the Aristotelian Athenaion politeia.* New York: Oxford University Press, 1981.

Rizhi. See Lin Zhichun.

Robinson, James Harvey. *The New History: Essays Illustrating the Modern Historical Outlook.* New York: The Macmillan Company, 1918.

Rowe, William. *China's Last Empire: The Great Qing.* Cambridge. MA: Harvard University Press, 2009.

Sachsenmaier, Dominic. *Global Entanglements of a Man Who Never Traveled: A Seventeenth-Century Chinese Christian and His Conflicted Worlds.* New York: Columbia University Press, 2018.

Global Perspectives on Global History: Theories and Approaches in a Connected World. Cambridge: Cambridge University Press, 2011.

Sawer, Marian. *Marxism and the Question of the Asiatic Mode of Production.* The Hague: Springer, 1977.

Schaberg, David. *A Patterned Past: Form and Thought in Early Chinese Historiography.* Cambridge, MA: Harvard University Asia Center, 2001.

Scheid, Volker. *Currents of Tradition in Chinese Medicine, 1626–2006.* Seattle: Eastland Press, 2007.

Schmalzer, Sigrid. *The People's Peking Man: Popular Science and Human Identity in Twentieth-Century China.* Chicago: University of Chicago Press, 2008.

Schurmann, Franz. *Ideology and Organization in Communist China.* Berkeley: University of California Press, 1968.

Schwartz, Benjamin. *The World of Thought in Ancient China.* Cambridge, MA: Harvard University Press, 1989.

Scott, James C. *Seeing Like a State: How Certain Schemes to Improve the Human Condition Have Failed.* New Haven, CT: Yale University Press, 1999.

Sen, Tansen. *India, China and the World: A Connected History.* London: Rowman & Littlefield, 2017.

Shang Xiaoming. "Jindai Zhongguo daxue shixue jiaoshou qunxiang" [The collective image of history professors in modern Chinese universities]. *Jindaishi yanjiu* [Studies on modern history], no. 1 (2011): 74–104.

"Shanxi Lüliang shiye danwei zhaokao yin zhiyi: shijieshi busuan lishixue?" [The examination in Lvliang, Shanxi, provokes controversy: world history is not counted as history?]. *Zhongguo qingnian bao* [Chinese youth daily], June 6, 2017, www.chinanews.com/sh/2017/06–09/8246254.shtml (accessed June 27, 2017).

Shen Zhi. "Jidai zhongshi de shijie gudai shi jiaoxue" [Ancient world history pedagogy: (an issue that) urgently awaits our attention]. *Zhongxue lishi jiaoxue cankao* [Reference for history pedagogy in middle schools], no. 6 (2003): 21.

Shen Zhihua. "Cong Bo-Xiong shijian dao fanyoupai yundong" [From the Poland-Hungary Incident to the Anti-rightist Campaign]. In *Wushinian wuji erji* [To commemorate after no commemoration in fifty years], ed. Zhang Yihe, 15–124. Hong Kong: Thinker, 2007.

Shi Guirong. "1929 nian zhongxue lishi zanxing kecheng biaozhun yanjiu" [A study of the temporary standard for the middle school history curriculum in 1929]. MA thesis, Yangzhou University, 2007.

Shi Zhisheng and Guo Fang, eds. *Gudai minzhu yu gonghe zhidu* [Ancient democracy and Republican institutions]. Beijing: Zhongguo shehui kexue chubanshe, 1998.

Shi Zhisheng and Liu Xinru, eds. *Gudai wangquan yu zhuanzhi zhuyi* [Ancient kingship and autocracy]. Beijing: Zhongguo shehui kexue chubanshe, 1993.

Shiao, Ling. "Printing, Reading, and Revolution: Kaiming Press and the Cultural Transformation of Republican China." PhD thesis, Brown University, 2009.

Shijie shanggu shigang bianxiezu [Editorial unit for *An Outline of Ancient World History*], ed. *Shijie shanggushi gang* [An outline of ancient world history]. Beijing: Renmin chubanshe, 1979.

"Yaxiya shengchan fangshi: bu chengwei wenti de wenti" [The Asiatic mode of production: A problem that does not constitute a problem]. *Lishi yanjiu* [Historical research] no. 2 (1980): 3–24.

Smith, Aminda M. *Thought Reform and China's Dangerous Classes: Reeducation, Resistance, and the People*. Lanham, MD: Rowman & Littlefield, 2012.

Spakowski, Nicola. "National Aspirations on a Global Stage: Concepts of World/Global History in Contemporary China." *Journal of Global History* 4, no. 3 (2009): 475–495.

Spence, Jonathan. *The Gate of Heavenly Peace: The Chinese and Their Revolution, 1895–1980*. New York: Penguin, 1981.

Spengler, Oswald. *The Decline of the West*, trans. Charles Atkinson. New York: Alfred A. Knopf, 1926.

Starr, John. *Continuing the Revolution: The Political Thought of Mao*. Princeton: Princeton University Press, 1979.

Stiffler, Douglas. "Sulian zhuanjia zai Zhongguo Renmin daxue (1950–1957)" [Soviet specialists at People's University, 1950–1957], trans. Yang Jingxia. *Lengzhan guoji shi yanjiu* [Cold War international history studies], no. 2 (2010): 13–25.

Strauss, Julia. "Morality, Coercion and State Building by Campaign in the Early PRC: Regime Consolidation and After, 1949–1956." *The China Quarterly* 188, no. 1 (2006): 891–912.

Stuchtey, Benedikt and Eckhardt Fuchs, eds. *Writing world history 1800–2000*. Oxford: Oxford University Press, 2003.

Su Zhihong and Hao Lidan. "Dui 'Guanyu (Laodong chuangzao ren) de mingti' de zhiyi" [Questioning [the article] "On the thesis that labor created man"]. *Shixue lilun yanjiu* [Historiography Quarterly] no. 2 (1995): 35–40 and 13.

Sun Longji. *Lishi xuejia de jingwei* [Historians' coordinates]. Guilin: Guangxi shifan daxue chubanshe, 2004.

Tan Dong and Hu Zhongbo. "Shijieshi zai zhongxue lishi jiaoxue zhong de diwei tantao" [A discussion on the role of world history in high school history education]. *Zhongxue lishi jiaoxue* [Secondary school history pedagogy], no. 8 (2002): 29–32.

Tang, Xiaobing. *Global Space and the Nationalist Discourse of Modernity: The Historical Thinking of Liang Qichao.* Stanford: Stanford University Press, 1996.

Teggart, Frederick. *Rome and China: A Study of Correlations in Historical Events.* Berkeley: University of California Press, 1939.

Teiwes, Frederick. *Politics and Purges in China: Rectification and the Decline of Party Norms, 1950–1965.* 2nd ed. Armonk, NY: M. E. Sharpe, 1993.

Tong Jiaoying. *Cong lianyu zhong shenghua: Wo de fuqin Tong Shuye* [Rising above purgatory: My father Tong Shuye]. Shanghai: Huadong daxue chubanshe, 2001.

Tong Shuye. *Jingshenbing yu xinli weisheng* [Mental illness and psychological health], ed. Tong Jiaoying. Beijing: Zhonghua shuju, 2007.

Tong Shuye gudai shehui lunji [Collection of Tong Shuye's works on ancient society], ed. Tong Jiaoying. Beijing: Zhonghua shuju, 2006.

U, Eddy. *Disorganizing China: Counter-Bureaucracy and the Decline of Socialism.* Stanford: Stanford University Press, 2007.

Unger, Jonathan, ed. *Using the Past to Serve the Present: Historiography and Politics in Contemporary China.* Armonk, NY: M. E. Sharpe, 1993.

Waley-Cohen, Joanna. "China and Western Technology in the Late 18th Century," *American Historical Review* 98, no. 5 (1993): 1525–1544.

The Sextants of Beijing: Global Currents in Chinese History. New York: W. W. Norton, 1999.

Wang, Ban, ed. *Chinese Visions of World Order: Tianxia, Culture, and World Politics.* Durham, NC and London: Duke University Press, 2017.

Wang Deyi, ed. *Yao Congwu xiansheng nianpu* [Annalistic biography of Master Yao Congwu]. Taipei: Xinwenfeng, 2000.

Wang Dunshu. "Lin Zhichun he Zhongguo shijie gudaishi xueke de jianshe yu fazhan" [Lin Zhichun and the establishment and development of the Chinese discipline of ancient world history]. *Shijie lishi* [World history], no. 2 (2000): 121–126.

"Luelun gudai shijie de zaoqi guojia xingtai: Zhongguo gushi xuejie guanyu gudai chengbang wenti de yanjiu yu tantao" [A brief disquisition on the forms of early states in the ancient world: Research and discussion on the issue of ancient city-states in the field of ancient history in China]. *Shijie lishi* [World history], no. 5 (2010): 116–125.

"Yingguo Makesi zhuyi gushi xuejia De · Sheng · Keluwa fangtan zhuiji" [Recollection of an interview with the British Marxist ancient historian De Ste Croix]. *Shixue lilun yanjiu* [Historiography Quarterly] no. 2 (2007): 138–139.

Yishutang shiji [Historiographical collection from the Yishu Hall]. Beijing: Zhonghua shuju, 2003.

Wang Dunshu and Yu Ke. "Guanyu chengbang yanjiu de jige wenti – jian ping *Shijie shanggu shigang* guanyu chengbang he diguo de guandian" [Several issues regarding the study of city-states – and a critique of the point of view on city-states and empires in *An Outline of Ancient World History*]. *Shijie lishi* [World history], no. 5 (1982): 48–57.

Wang, Fan-sen (Wang Fansen). *Fu Ssu-nien: A Life in Chinese History and Politics.* New York: Cambridge University Press, 2000.

Wang, Fan-sen. *Zhongguo jindai sixiang yu xueshu de xipu* [A genealogy of modern Chinese thought and scholarship]. Taipei: Lianjing, 2003.

"'Zhuyi Chongbai' yu jindai Zhongguo xueshu shehui de mingyun: yi Chen yinke wei li" [The "blind belief in isms" and the fate of modern Chinese academic society: Chen Yinke as an example]. In *Zhongguo jindai sixiang yu xueshu de xipu* [A genealogy of modern Chinese thought and scholarship], 463–488. Taipei: Lianjing, 2003.

Wang, Fei-Hsien. *Pirates and Publishers: A Social History of Copyright in Modern China*. Princeton: Princeton University Press, 2019.

Wang, Jing. "*Heshang* and the Paradoxes of the Chinese Enlightenment." In *High Cultural Fever: Politics, Aesthetics, and Ideology in Deng's China*, 118–136. Berkeley: University of California Press, 2003.

High Culture Fever: Politics, Aesthetics, and Ideology in Deng's China. Berkeley: University of California Press, 2003.

Wang, Ning. *Banished to the Great Northern Wilderness: Political Exile and Re-education in Mao's China*. Vancouver and Toronto: UBC Press, 2017.

Wang Lixin. "Guanzhu xianshi: wo kan shijie Lishi" [Paying attention to reality: My view of *World History*]. *Shijie lishi* [World history], no. 6 (1998): 67.

Wang, Q. Edward. "Between Marxism and Nationalism: Chinese Historiography and the Soviet Influence, 1949–1963." *Journal of Contemporary China* 9 (2000): 95–111.

"Encountering the World: China and Its Other(s) in Historical Narratives, 1949–89." *Journal of World History* 14, no. 3 (2003): 327–358.

Inventing China through History: The May Fourth Approach to Historiography. Albany, NY: State University of New York Press, 2001.

Wang Qingjia. "Shijieshi lilun, fangfa ji waiguo shixueshi de yanjiu gaishu" [A survey of research on the theory and methodology of world history as well as on the history of foreign historiography]. In *Jianguo yilai shijieshi yanjiu gaishu* [An overview of world-historical studies since establishment of the (PRC) state], ed. Chen Qineng, 24–53. Beijing: Shehui kexue wenxian chubanshe, 1991.

Wang Qisheng. *Zhongguo liuxuesheng de lishi guiji, 1872–1949* [The historical pattern of Chinese students who have studied abroad]. Wuhan: Hubei jiaoyu chubanshe, 1992.

Wang Weijiang. "Wushi niandai lishi xuejia de mingyun" [The fate of historians in the fifties]. *Yanhuang chunqiu* [Yan-Huang chronicle], no. 6 (2009): 40–41.

Wang Xingyun. "Wo suo liaojie de Wu Mi jiaoshou" [The Professor Wu Mi that I know]. *Nanfang zhoumo* [Southern Weekly], September 30, 2009.

Wang Xuedian. "'Lishi yu xianshi' guanxi wenti de zai jiantao" [Rethinking the issue of the relationship between "history and reality"]. *Shandong shehui kexue* [Social science in Shandong], no. 8 (2004): 5–8.

Wang Yizhu. "Fanyi shi mafan, feixin dan ting you yiyi de shi" [Translation is a troublesome, mentally taxing, but quite meaningful thing]. *Nanfang dushi bao* [Southern metropolitan daily], May 9, 2007.

Wang Hui, "From Empire to State: Kang Youwei, Confucian Universalism, and Unity." In *Chinese Visions of World Order: Tianxia, Culture, and World Politics*, ed. Ban Wang, 49–64. Durham, NC and London: Duke University Press, 2017.

Wang Yue, "Jindai Zhongguo de zhishi fenzi, weishenme xihuan taolun Xila Luoma" [Why did intellectuals in modern China like discussing ancient Greece and Rome]. *Pengpai xinwen* (The Paper), www.thepaper.cn/baidu .jsp?contid=1313047 (accessed January 7, 2018).

Wells, H. G. *The Outline of History*. Garden City, NY: Garden City Books, 1920.

Wen Rumin and Ding Xiaoping, eds. *Shidai zhi bo: Zhanguo ce pai wenhua lunzhu jiyao* [Tide of the times: A selection of the main cultural works from the Zhanguo ce Clique]. Beijing: Zhonguo guangbo dianshi chubanshe, 1995).

Weston, Timothy. *The Power of Position: Beijing University, Intellectuals, and Chinese Political Culture, 1898–1929*. Berkeley: University of California Press, 2004.

Wittfogel, Karl, *Oriental Despotism: A Comparative Study of Total Power*. New Haven, CT: Yale University Press, 1957.

Wright, Mary Clabaugh. *The Last Stand of Chinese Conservatism: The T'ung-Chih Restoration, 1862–1874*. Stanford: Stanford University Press, 1957.

Wu Yin. "Shijieshi de xueke dingwei yu fazhan fangxiang" [The role and developmental direction of the world history discipline]. *Shijie lishi* [World history], no. 1 (2003): 6–7.

Wu Yuhong. "Laoshi! Zhaoliang wo de zhilu mingdeng, Lin Zhichun xiansheng, Yashuxue he wo" [Teacher! Light my path. Mr. Lin Zhichun, Assyriology and me]. Northeast Normal University, www5.nenu.edu.cn/linzc/z04.htm (accessed April 2, 2012).

"Rabies and Rabid Dogs in Sumerian and Akkadian Literature." *Journal of the American Oriental Society* 121, no. 1 (2001): 32–43.

Wu Yujin. "Shidai he shijie lishi: shilun butong shidai guanyu shijie lishi zhongxin de butong guandian" [Times and world history: A preliminary treatise on different perspectives centering on world history at different times]. *Jiang-Han luntan* [Jiang-Han forum], no. 7 (1964): 43–50 and 20.

"Shijie lishi" [World history]. *Zhongguo dabaike quanshu: Waiguo lishi juan, Part I* [Encyclopedia sinica: Volume on foreign history, Part 1]. Beijing: Zhongguo dabaike quanshu chubanshe, 1990.

"Zongxu" [Preface]. In *Shijie lishi: Gudaishi bian: shang juan* [World history: Vol. 1, ancient world history], ed. Wu Yujin and Qi Shirong. Beijing: Gaodeng jiaoyu chubanshe, 1995.

Xu Guansan. *Xinshixue jiushi nian* [New historiography of the last ninety years]. Hong Kong: Chinese University Press, 1986.

Xu, Guoqi. *China and the Great War: China's Pursuit of a New National Identity and Internationalism*. Cambridge: Cambridge University Press, 2005.

Xu, Luo. "Reconstructing World History in the People's Republic of China since the 1980s." *Journal of World History* 18, no. 3 (2007): 325–350.

Xu, Xiaoqun. *Chinese Professionals and the Republican State: The Rise of Professional Associations in Shanghai, 1912–1937.* Cambridge: Cambridge University Press, 2001.

Yan Xuetong, *Ancient Chinese Thought, Modern Chinese Power*, ed. Daniel A. Bell and Sun Zhe, trans. Edmund Ryden. Princeton: Princeton University Press, 2011.

Yang, Bin, *Between Winds and Clouds: The Making of Yunnan (Second Century BCE to Twentieth Century CE).* New York: Columbia University Press, 2008.

Yang Kuisong. *"Zhongjian didai" de geming: Zhongguo gemin de celue zai guoji Beijing xia de yanbian* [Revolution in the "middle zone": Evolution of the Chinese revolutionary strategy in international context]. Taiyuan: Shanxi renmin chubanshe, 2010.

Yao Yanli. "Qingmo yijia Zhou Xueqiao yishi huodong jiqi Zhong-Xi yi huitong tantao" [An investigation of the late Qing medical specialist Zhou Xueqiao's medical activities and his attempt to integrate Chinese and Western medicine]. *Zhongyi wenxian zazhi* [Journal for documentation of Chinese medicine], no. 2 (2011): 46–48.

Ye Zhou. "Rongzhu zhongwai: Zhou Weihan yu *Yixue bao*" [Bridging China and the West: Zhou Weihan and the *Yixue bao* (Journal of medical sciences)]. *Difang wenhua yanjiu* [Studies on local cultures] 34, no. 4 (2018): 93–101.

Yeh, Wen-hsin. *The Alienated Academy: Culture and Politics in Republican China, 1919–1937.* Cambridge, MA: Harvard University Press, 1990.

Shanghai Splendor: Economic Sentiments and the Making of Modern China, 1843–1949. Berkeley: University of California Press, 2007.

Yu Jinyao. "Shijie lishi yu shijieshi xueke dingwei" [Defining world history and its discipline]. *Shixue yuekan* [Historiography monthly], no. 10 (2009): 81–89.

Yu Ke and Wu Shuping, eds. *Guanyu yuanshi Jidujiao dui caichan he nulizhi de jige xin guandian* [Several new views regarding proto-Christian views of property and slavery]. Tianjin: History Department of Nankai University, 1988. (Manuscript preserved at the IHAC library.)

Yu Pei and Zhou Yaohui, eds. *Zhongguo shijie lishixue 30 nian (1978–2008)* [China's world history of thirty years, 1978–2008]. Beijing: Zhongguo shehui kexue chubanshe, 2008.

Yu Piao and Li Hongcheng. *Cheng Fangwu zhuan* [A biography of Cheng Fangwu]. Beijing: Dangdai Zhongguo chubanshe, 1997.

Zarrow, Peter. *China in War and Revolution, 1895–1949.* London: Routledge, 2005.

Educating China: Knowledge, Society, and Textbooks in a Modernizing World, 1902–1937. Cambridge: Cambridge University Press, 2015.

Zhan Ziqing. "Yizhan changmingdeng: zhuisi Lin Zhichun laoshi" [A light that ever shines: Remembering Professor Lin Zhichun]. Northeast Normal University, www5.nenu.edu.cn/linzc/z05.htm (accessed March 20, 2012).

Zhang Aohui and Song Binyu. "Cheng Fangwu nianpu" [Annalistic biography of Cheng Fangwu]. *Dongbei shifan daxue xuebao (zhexue shehui kexue ban)* [Journal of Northeast Normal University (edition on philosophy and social sciences)], no. 3–5 (1985); no. 1, 3 (1986).

Zhang Chuanxi. *Jian Bozan zhuan* [Biography of Jian Bozan]. Beijing: Beijing daxue chubanshe, 1998.

Zhang Guangzhi. *Zhongguo gushi fenqi taolun de huigu yu fansi* [Reflection on past debates over the periodization of ancient Chinese history]. Xi'an: Shaanxi shifan daxue chubanshe, 2003.

Zhang Jian. "Lun shijie shi xueke nei de sanji xueke huafen" [On the division of third-level disciplines within the field of world history], *Guangzhou shehui zhuyi xueyuan xuebao* [Journal of Socialist college in Guangzhou] 21, no. 2 (2008): 76.

Zhang Jianping. *Xin Zhongguo shixue wushinian* [New China's historiography (of the past) fifty years]. Beijing: Xueyuan chubanshe, 2003.

Zhang Jingfu. "Wo de huiyi" [My memories]. In *Zhongguo de bing* [China's military]. Beijing: Zhonghua shuju, 2005.

Zhang Qing. "Hu Shi pai xuerenqun yu xiandai Zhongguo ziyouzhuyi de quxiang" [The Hu Shi group of intellectuals and the trend of liberalism in modern China]. *Shilin* [Historical review], no. 1 (1998): 36–49.

Zhang Tianming and Zhou Shengming. "20 shiji shangbanqi woguo zhongxue shijieshi jiaoyu de zongti tedian ji xianshi qishi" [The general features and real inspiration of our country's world-historical education in middle schools in the early half of the twentieth century]. *Nei menggu shifan daxue xuebao* [Journal of Inner Mongolia Normal University (Education science edition)] 32, no. 2 (2010): 96–98.

Zhang Zige. *Xinxiang leijiu ji Wu Mi* [Commemorating Wu Mi with the heart as incense and tears as wine]. Guangzhou: Guangzhou chubanshe, 1997.

Zhao, Dingxin. *The Confucian-Legalist State: A New Theory of Chinese History*. Oxford: Oxford University Press, 2015.

Zhao Lisheng. *Lijintang zixu* [Self-account in the Lijin Hall]. Shanghai: Shanghai guji chubanshe, 1999.

Zhao Tingyang, *Tianxia tixi: Shijie zhidu zhexue daolun* [The Tianxia system: An introduction to the Philosophy of World Institution]. Beijing: Renmin daxue chubanshe, 2011.

Zhao Yuanren, *Zhao Yuanren zaonian zizhuan* [Yuen Ren Chao's autobiography: First 30 years, 1892–1921]. Tapei, Zhuanji wenxue chubanshe, 1984.

Zhongguo dabaike quanshu: waiguo lishi [Encyclopedia Sinica: Foreign history]. Beijing: Zhongguo dabaike quanshu chubanshe, 1990.

Zhou Gucheng. *Shijie tongshi* [A general history of the world], new ed., Shijiazhuang: Hebei jiaoyu chubanshe, 2000.

Zhou Gucheng shixue lunwen xuanji [A selective collection of Zhou Gucheng's essays on historiography]. Beijing: Renmin chubanshe, 1982.

Zhou Gucheng, Wu Yujin, and Lin Zhichun. "Gudian wenming yanjiu zai woguo de kongbai bixu tianbu" [The void in the study of ancient civilizations in our country must be filled]. *Shijie lishi* [World history] (1985): 1–3; reprinted in *Journal of Ancient Civilizations* 1 (1986), 3–11.

Zhou Mingsheng. "Minguo shiqi zhongxue de shijieshi jiaoyu de tedian ji qishi" [The special characteristics and inspiration of secondary-school world-history pedagogy in the Republican period]. *Zhongguo jiaoyu xuekan*

[Journal of the Chinese Society of Education], no. 9 (September 2009): 61–62.

Zhou Rongjia and Ding Jie, *Tianxia mingshi you buluo: Changzhou renwu yu wenhua qunti* [The prestigious have their own community: Changzhou people and their cultural community]. Hong Kong: Sanlian shudian, 2013.

Zhou, Yiqun, "Greek Antiquity, Chinese Modernity, and the Changing World Order." In *Chinese Visions of World Order: Tianxia, Culture, and World Politics*, ed. Ban Wang, 106–128. Durham, NC and London: Duke University Press, 2017.

Zhu Huan. "Chentong daonian Lin Zhichun xiansheng" [Mourning Mr. Lin Zhichun with deep pain]. Northeast Normal University, www5 .nenu.edu.cn/linzc/z01.htm (accessed March 20, 2012).

Zhu, Lee. "Communist Cadres on the Higher Education Front, 1955–1962." *Twentieth-Century China* 34, no. 1 (2008): 73–95.

Zhu Yujin. "'Jiuquan wenxun yi xinran!' Huainian Hua Gang tongzhi" ["Pleased to hear news from the afterworld!" Remembering Comrade Hua Gang]. *Dushu*, no. 11 (1980): 110–113.

Zong Liang. "1949 nian qianhou de Lei Haizong" [Lei Haizong before and after 1949]. *Zhonghua dushu bao* [Chinese Reader's Weekly (Beijing)], July 10, 2013.

Zou Zhenhuan. *Xifang chuanjiaoshi yu wan-Qing Xishi dongjian: yi 1815 zhi 1900 Xifang lishi yizhu de chuanbo yu yingxiang wei zhongxin* [Western missionaries and the eastward spread of Western histories: Focusing on the spread and influence of translated Western histories from 1815 to 1900]. Shanghai: Shanghai guji chubanshe, 2007.

Zuo Wenhua. "Guanyu nuli shehuishi de jige wenti" [Several issues concerning the social history of slavery]. *Jilin daxue xuebao*, no. 2 (1980): 98–103.

Index